Lysander Spooner

The Unconstitutionality of Slavery

Lysander Spooner

The Unconstitutionality of Slavery

ISBN/EAN: 9783744733137

Printed in Europe, USA, Canada, Australia, Japan

Cover: Foto ©ninafisch / pixelio.de

More available books at **www.hansebooks.com**

ENLARGED EDITION. 75 CENTS.

THE

UNCONSTITUTIONALITY

OF

SLAVERY.

BY LYSANDER SPOONER.

SEVENTH THOUSAND.

BOSTON:
PUBLISHED BY BELA MARSH.
No. 14 BROMFIELD ST.

THE

UNCONSTITUTIONALITY OF SLAVERY

ENLARGED EDITION.

BY LYSANDER SPOONER.

———

PUBLISHED AND FOR SALE BY

BELA MARSH,

14 BROMFIELD STREET, BOSTON.

———

PRICE:

In paper covers, ... $0.75.
In cloth, ... 1.00.

Postage on the work, in paper, 15 cents ; in cloth, 20 cents.

A liberal discount will be made to Booksellers and Agents who buy to sell again.

———

NOTICES.

HON. WILLIAM H. SEWARD writes to Gerrit Smith concerning it as follows:

"AUBURN, November 9th, 1855.

MY DEAR SIR: I thank you for sending me a copy of Mr. Spooner's treatise. I had bought a copy of the first edition. It is a very able work, and I wish that it might be universally studied. The writing and publishing of such books is the most effective way of working out the great reformation which this nation is required to make by the spirit of humanity.

Very sincerely your friend and obedient servant,

WILLIAM H. SEWARD.

The HONORABLE GERRIT SMITH."

HON. ALBERT G. BROWN, *Senator in Congress from Mississippi*, in the Senate, Dec.

21.1856, (as reported in the Congressional Globe) after describing the book, as "making an argument in favor of the Constitutional power of Congress, not only to interfere with, but to abolish, slavery in the southern States of the Union," said:

"The Senator [Wilson] did not say, — what I am willing to say myself — that the book is ingeniously written. No mere simpleton could ever have drawn such an argument. If his premises were admitted, I should say at once that it would be a herculean task to overturn his argument."

[Although Mr. Brown thus leaves it to be inferred that he thought there might be some error in the premises, he made no attempt to point out any. It would seem to be incumbent on him to do so.]

GERRIT SMITH says: "The more I read that admirable, invincible, and matchless argument, which Lysander Spooner has made to show the unconstitutionality of slavery, the more I am pleased with it. He yields nothing but what the legal rules of interpretation compel him to yield. And why should he make unnecessary concessions in an argument undertaken in behalf of all that is sacred and vital in the rights of man? Were I studious of fame or usefulness, I had rather be the author of this manly, brave, and independent argument against the constitutionality of slavery, than of any other law argument ever written, either in this age, or in any former age—either on this side, or on the other side, of the Atlantic. Why will not all lawyers read it? Who of them could read it without being convinced that slavery is unconstitutional?"

WENDELL PHILLIPS, without confessing his conviction of its truth, says: "This claim (of the anti-slavery character of the constitution) has received the fullest investigation from Mr. Lysander Spooner, who has urged it with all his unrivalled ingenuity, laborious research, and coment gic."

ELIZUR WRIGHT calls it "One of the most magnificent constitutional arguments ever produced in any country. It needs such a work as Mr. Spooner's on constitutional law, to make the constitution of the least value to us as a shield of rights."

WILLIAM LLOYD GARRISON, speaking of Part First, and disagreeing to its conclusions on the ground that the words of the constitution do not fully express the intentions of the authors, yet says: "He legacy may be faultless, as a mere legal effort. We admit Mr. Spooner's reasoning to be ingenious, perhaps, as an effort of logic, unanswerable. It impresses us as the production of a mind equally honest and acute. Its ability, and the importance of the subject on which it treats, will doubtless secure for it a wide circulation and a careful perusal."

JOSHUA LEAVITT says, of Part First: "It is unanswerable. There will never be an honest attempt to answer it. Neither priest nor politician, lawyer nor judge, will ever dare undertake to sunder that iron linked chain of argument, which runs straight through this book from beginning to end."

NATHANIEL P. ROGERS, speaking of Part First, and agreeing with some of its positions and disagreeing with others, says: "It is a splendid essay. If the talent laid out in it were laid out in the law, it would make the author distinguished and rich." "This essay we fear the author a name at the Boston bar. It will at the bar of posterity."

SAMUEL E. SEWALL, Esq., says of Part First: — "It merits general attention, not merely from the importance of the subject, but from the masterly manner in which it is executed. It everywhere overflows with thought. We regard it as a great arsenal of legal weapons to be used in the great contest between liberty and slavery. I hope it will receive the widest circulation."

J. FULTON Jr. says of Part First: "Now that I have read it, I feel bound to say that it is the most clear and luminous production that I have ever read on the subject. It begins without a line of preface, and ends without a word of apology. It is a solid mass of the most brilliant argument, unbroken, as it seems to me, by a single flaw, and treads down as dust everything which has preceded it upon that subject. Let every friend of the slave read the work without delay. I believe it is destined to give a new phase to our struggle."

RICHARD HILDRETH says of Part First: " No one can deny to the present work the merit of great ability and great learning. If anybody wishes to see this argument handled in a masterly manner, with great clearness and plainness, and an array of constitutional learning, which, in the hands of most lawyers, would have expanded into at least three royal octavos, we commend them to Mr. Spooner's modest pamphlet of one hundred and fifty pages."

ELIHU BURRITT says: " It evinces a depth of legal erudition, which would do honor to the first jurist of the age."

The *True American*, (Cortland County, N. Y.,) says: " It is an imperishable and triumphant work. A law argument that would add to the fame of the most famed jurist, living or dead."

The *Bangor Gazette* says: " It is indeed a masterly argument. No one, unprejudiced, who has supposed that that instrument (the constitution) contained guarantees of slavery, or who has had doubts upon the point, can rise from the perusal without feeling relieved from the supposition that our great national charter is one of slavery and not of freedom. And no lawyer can read it without admiring, besides its other great excellences, the clearness of its style, and its logical precision."

The *Hampshire Herald*, (Northampton) says: " It is worthy the most gifted intellect in the country."

WILLIAM L. CHAPLIN says: " This effort of Mr. Spooner is a remarkable one in many respects. It is unrivalled in the simplicity, clearness, and force of style with which it is executed. The argument is original, steel-ribbed and triumphant. It bears down all opposition. Pettifogging, black-letter dullness, and pedantry, special pleading and demagogism, all retire before it. If every lawyer in the country could have it put into his hands, and be induced to study it, as he does his brief, it would alone overthrow slavery. There is moral force enough in it for that purpose."

The *Liberty Press*, (Utica,) says: " The author labors to show, and does show, that slavery in this country is unconstitutional, and unsustained by law, either state or federal."

The *Granite Freeman* says: " We wish every voter in the Union could have the opportunity to read this magnificent argument. We should hear no more, after that, of the ' compromises of the Constitution ' as an argument to close the lips and palsy the hands of those who abhor slavery, and labor for its removal."

The *Charter Oak* says: " Of its rare merit as a controversial argument, it is superfluous to speak. It may, in fact, be regarded as unanswerable, and we are persuaded that its general circulation would give a new aspect to the Anti Slavery cause, by exploding the popular, but mistaken notion, that slavery is somehow entrenched behind the Constitution."

The *Liberty Gazette* (Burlington, Vt.,) says : " This work cannot be too highly praised, or too extensively circulated. Its reasoning is conclusive, and no one can read it without being convinced that the constitution, instead of being the friend and protector of slavery, is a purely Anti-Slavery document."

The *Indiana Freeman* says: " Every Abolitionist should have this admirable work, and keep it in constant circulation among his neighbors."

SYNOPSIS.

CHAP I. *What is Law?* (p. 5.) Nothing inconsistent with justice can be law. [Speaks of the definition, that " Law is a rule of civil conduct, prescribed by the supreme power of a State

Where [no] genuine trial by jury prevails, this principle can be carried out in practice.]

CHAP II. *Written Constitutions.* (p. 15.) Admits, for the sake of the argument, that [written and] unwritten statutes, inconsistent with justice, may be made law ; and insists only [that there] be split [rules] us shall be interpreted by the established rules, by which all other legal [instruments] are interpreted: one of which rules is, that all words, that are susceptible of [two meanings], one favorable to justice, and the other to injustice, shall be taken in the [sense favorable] to justice.

CHAP III. *The Colonial Charters.* (p. 21.) That these charters were the constitu-[tional law] of the Colonies up to the time of the Revolution; that the provisions in them to [the effect] that [their] legislation should be " consonant to reason, and not repugnant or [con]trary, but as far as conveniently may be, agreeable to the laws, statutes, customs, and [rights of the] our kingdom of England," made it impossible that slavery could have any [legal existence] in the Colonies up to the time of the Revolution; and that the decision of [Lord Mans]field, in Somersett's case, was as much applicable to the Colonies as to Eng-[land]. Notice [is] taken [of] Bancroft's statement, that England ever legalized the slave trade.

CHAP IV. *Colonial Statutes.* (p. 32.) Shows that the Colonial legislation, on the [subject] of slavery, failed to identify, with legal accuracy. the persons to be made slaves; [and therefore], even if such legislation had been constitutional, would have failed to legal-[ize slavery]. That, consequently, there was no legal slavery in the country, up to the time [of the Revolution].

CHAP V. *The Declaration of Independence.* (p. 36.) By this the nation declares it [to be a "self-evi]dent truth," that all men are created free and equal. All " self-evident [truths]" are necessarily a part of the law of the land, unless expressly denied. The na-[tion, as a nation], has never denied this self-evident truth, which it once asserted. This [truth is therefore] a part of the law of the land, and makes slavery illegal.

CHAP VI. *The State Constitutions of 1789.* (p. 39.) None of the State constitutions [existing in 1789], established or authorized slavery. All of them. on their face, are free. [Argues] shows that the word "*free*," and "*freeman*," used in these constitutions, [are used in the] English or political sense, to designate native or naturalized persons, as [contradistin]guished [from] aliens, or persons of foreign birth not naturalized; and that they were. [never used to designate] a free person, as distinguished from a slave. That the use of [these words in the] sense, in the State constitutions of 1789, as they had been previously used [in the colonial] charters, and colonial legislation, furnish an authoritative precedent, by [which to fix the meaning] of the words, "*free persons*," in the Constitution of the United [States], in the clause relative to representation and direct taxation.

CHAP VII. *The Articles of Confederation,* (p. 51). contain no recognition of slavery; [and use the word "free"] in the English or political sense, to signify the native and natural-[ized, as contradistin]guished from aliens, and thus furnishes a precedent. authorized by [which to determine] the meaning to the word "*free*" in the constitution.

CHAP VIII. *The Constitution of the United States.* (p. 54.) This chapter, *in the* [argument, takes it] for granted to have been shown that slavery had no legal existence up [to the time of the adop]tion of the United States Constitution. It then says that that coustitution certainly did not create or establish slavery as a new institution; that the most that can be claimed, is that it recognized the legality of slavery so far as it then legally existed under the State governments; but that, as slavery then had no legal existence, under the State governments, any intended recognition of it, by the Constitution of the United States, must necessarily have failed of effect. That consequently *all* " the people of the United States " were made " citizens of the United States " by the constitution; and therefore could never afterwards be made slaves by the State governments.

Secondly. (p 56.) Shows, from its provisions, that the Constitution of the United States does not recognize slavery as a legal institution, but presumes all men to be free; denies the right of property in man; and, of itself, makes it impossible for slavery to have a legal existence in any of the United States. Shows, (p. 67,) that the clause relative to persons held to service or labor, has no reference to slaves; that (p. 73) the term, "*free persons*," in the clause relative to representation, is used in the political sense, to designate native and naturalized persons, as distinguished from persons of foreign birth, not naturalized; that (p. 81) the clause relative to " migration and importation of persons," does not imply that the persons imported are slaves; that it makes no discrimination as to the persons, whether African or European, to be imported: that it as much authorizes the importation of Englishmen, or Frenchmen, as slaves, as it does Africans; that it would, therefore, be a piratical constitution if the importation of persons implied that the persons to be imported were slaves; that (p. 87) the clause relative to the protection of " the States against domestic violence," does not imply the existence or legality of slavery, or protection against slave insurrections; that (p. 90) " We, the people of the United States," means *all* the people of the United States ; the constitution, therefore, made citizens of *all* the then people of the United States; that (p. 95) the " power to regulate commerce," is a power to regulate commerce among *all* the people of the United States, and implies that all are free to carry on commerce; that (p. 96) the power to establish post offices, is a power to carry letters for all the people, and implies that all the people are free to send letters; that (p. 96) the power to secure to authors and inventors their exclusive right to their writings and discoveries, implies that all capable of writings and discoveries, are capable of being the owners thereof ; that (p. 96) the power to raise armies, implies that Congress have power to accept volunteers, or hire soldiers by contract with themselves, and that all are free to make such contracts; that (p. 97) the power to arm and discipline the militia, implies that all are liable to be armed and disciplined; that the right to keep and bear arms, is a right of the whole people; that (p. 98) the prohibition upon any State law impairing the obligation of contracts, implies that all men have the right to enter into all contracts naturally obligatory; that (p. 99) all natural born citizens are eligible to the Presidency, to the Senate, and to the House of Representatives; that (p. 102) the trial by jury implies that all persons are free; that (p. 102) the *Habeas Corpus* denies the right of property in man; that (p. 105) the guaranty to every State of a republican form of government, is a guaranty against slavery.

CHAP. IX. *The Intentions of the Convention.* (p. 114.) Personal intentions of the framers of no legal consequence to fix the legal meaning of the constitution. The instrument must be interpreted as being the instrument of the whole people.

CHAP. X. *The Practice of the Government.* (p. 123.) The practice of the government, under the constitution, has not altered the meaning of the constitution itself. The instrument means the same now, that it did before it was ratified, when it was first offered to the people for their adoption or rejection.

CHAP. XI. *The Understanding of the People.* (p. 124.) No legal proof, and not even a matter of history, that the people, before they adopted the constitution, understood that it was to support slavery. Could never have been adopted, had they so understood it.

CHAP. XII. *The State Constitutions of* 1845. (p. 126.) Do not authorize slavery ; do not designate, nor authorize the State legislatures to designate, the persons to be made slaves. Have provisions repugnant to slavery. The treaties for the purchase of Louisi-

1*

ans and Florida, imply that *all* the " inhabitants ", were free, possessing the rights of liberty, property, and religion, and were to become citizens of the United States.

Chap. XIII. *The Children of Slaves are born Free.* (p. 129.) Shows that, even if the persons held as slaves at the adoption of the Constitution, were to continue to be held as slaves, their children, born in the country, were nevertheless all to be free by virtue of natural birth in the country

PART SECOND.

Chap. XIV. *The Definition of Law.* (p. 137.) The definition of law, given in chapter first insisted on and defended. Additional authorities cited in note.

Chap. XV. *Ought Judges to resign their seats?* (p. 147.) No; but to continue to hold them, and do justice.

Chap. XVI. *The Supreme power of a State.* (p. 153.) Absurd results from the theory that the legislature represents " the supreme power of the State."

Chap. XVII. *Rules of Interpretation.* (p. 155.) Examines the established rules of legal interpretation, and shows that they required the word " FREE," or the term " FREE PERSONS," in the clause relative to representation, to be interpreted to mean, native and naturalized persons, as distinguished from immigrants not naturalized; and not to mean persons enjoying their personal liberty, as distinguished from slaves.

Chap. XVIII. *Servants counted as Units.* (p. 237.) The provision that " those bound to service for a term of years," should be included among the " FREE PERSONS," implies that there were to be no slaves.

Chap. XIX. *Slave Representation.* (p. 238.) Absurdity and injustice of it, a conclusive reason against any interpretation authorizing it.

Chap. XX. *Why aliens are counted as three-fifths.* (p. 242.) Not BEING full citizens, ought not to be counted as such. Inequality produced among the States by doing so.

Chap. XXI. *Why the words "Free Persons" were used.* The word " FREE," had always been the technical word, both in this country and in England, for describing native and naturalized persons, as distinguished from aliens. The indefiniteness of the word " CITIZEN " made it an improper word to be used, where precision of meaning was required.

Chap. XXII. *"All other Persons."* (p. 257.) These words used to avoid the use of the unfriendly and inappropriate word "aliens," and also to include " Indians not taxed."

Chap. XXIII. *Additional Arguments on the word* FREE. (p. 265.) Showing that this word must be taken in the political sense, before mentioned, and not as distinguished from slaves.

Chap. XXIV. *Power of the General Government over Slavery.* (p. 270.) Origin and necessity of the power to abolish slavery in the States.

APPENDIX A. FUGITIVE SLAVES. (p. 279.) Extended legal and historical argument on this subject

APPENDIX B. SUGGESTIONS TO ABOLITIONISTS. (p. 299.) Abolitionists can abolish slavery legally, only by taking the ground that the United States Constitution authorizes the general government to abolish it

AN ESSAY

ON THE

TRIAL BY JURY.

BY LYSANDER SPOONER.

———

PUBLISHED AND FOR SALE BY

BELA MARSH,

14 BROMFIELD STREET, BOSTON.

———

PRICE:

In pamphlet, ... $1.00.

In cloth,... 1.25.

In law sheep,... 1.50.

Postage on pamphlet, 13 cts.; on cloth, 18 cts.; on law sheep, 13 cts.

Books will be sent by mail on receipt of the price, *and the postage.* Postage stamps may be sent for all change over $1.00, or if $2.00 be sent, the change will be returned in postage stamps.

CONTENTS.

Page.

CHAP. I. THE RIGHT OF JURIES TO JUDGE OF THE JUSTICE OF
LAWS, - - - - - - - - 5
 Section 1, - - - - - - - 5
 Section 2, - - - - - - - - 11

CHAP. II. THE TRIAL BY JURY, AS DEFINED BY MAGNA CARTA, 20
 Section 1. The History of Magna Carta, - - - 20
 Section 2. The Language of Magna Carta, - - 25

CHAP. III. ADDITIONAL PROOFS OF THE RIGHTS AND DUTIES OF
JURORS, - - - - - - - 51
 Section 1. Weakness of the Regal Authority, - - 51
 Section 2. The Ancient Common Law Juries were mere
 Courts of Conscience, - - - - 63
 Section 3. The Oaths of Jurors, - - - - 85
 Section 4. The Right of Jurors to fix the Sentence, - 91
 Section 5. The Oaths of Judges, - - - 98
 Section 6. The Coronation Oath, - - - 102

CHAP. IV. THE RIGHTS AND DUTIES OF JURIES IN CIVIL SUITS, 110

CHAP. V. OBJECTIONS ANSWERED, - - - - 123

CHAP. VI. JURIES OF THE PRESENT DAY ILLEGAL, - - 142

CHAP. VII. ILLEGAL JUDGES, - - - - - 157

CHAP. VIII. THE FREE ADMINISTRATION OF JUSTICE, - 172

CHAP. IX. THE CRIMINAL INTENT, - - - - 178

CHAP. X. MORAL CONSIDERATIONS FOR JURORS, - - 192

CHAP. XI. AUTHORITY OF MAGNA CARTA, - - 192

CHAP. XII. LIMITATIONS IMPOSED UPON THE MAJORITY BY THE
TRIAL BY JURY, - - - - - 206

APPENDIX—TAXATION, - - - - - 222

THE theory of this book is that the ancient and common-law juries, such as we are now constitutionally entitled to, were mere courts of conscience, who tried, and whose oaths required them to try, all causes, both civil and criminal, according to their own notions of justice, regardless of all legislative enactments, and all judicial opinions, which did not correspond with their own sense of right.

And inasmuch as it was necessary that the jurors should be drawn by lot, or otherwise taken at random, from the whole body of male adults, without any choice, dictation, or interference, by the government, it was reasonably presumed that substantially all opinions, prevailing among the people, would be represented in the jury; that, in other words, a jury would be, in fact, a fair epitome of " the country," or whole community, which it was designed to represent.

And since the twelve, thus selected, could render no judgment, unless by an unanimous assent, it follows that no laws were intended to be enforced, except such as substantially the whole people were agreed in, as being just.

From this statement, it will be seen that our modern idea, that the majority have the right arbitrarily to govern the minority, and to establish any thing they may please as law, without regard to justice, is wholly incompatible with the principles of the Trial by Jury.

NOTICES.

The following is from the pen of RICHARD HILDRETH, ESQ., the historian.

" ESSAY ON THE TRIAL BY JURY."

MESSRS. EDITORS :— This remarkable book, by Lysander Spooner, will richly repay perusal on the part of all who feel the least interest in the theory of government, that is to say, all the thinking men of the United States, and indeed of all the world over. The charming ease and lucidity of Mr. Spooner's style, — in which, among all the writers of the English language, he has very few competitors, — the close coherence of his ideas, and the sharp dexterity of his logic, give to his book, what we seldom find now-a-days, the interest of a well-compacted drama, with all the Aristotelian unities complete, and a regular beginning, middle, and end. Having begun to read it, we found it impossible to lay it down till we got to the end of it, though obliged to sit up long past midnight, and though we were already informed of the general tenor of the argument, from having seen the greater part of the proof-sheets. The book indeed has this further resemblance to a poem of the first class, that it will not only bear re-perusal, but gain by it — which we take to be the great distinction between the true poem, whether in verse or prose, and the mere novel or romance. There are, however, some citations and notes, which may be skipped on the second perusal, and indeed on the first, by those inveterately given to that practice, as not essential to the argument, only corroborative of it. But if any reader intends to take issue — as the lawyers say — with Mr. Spooner, he had better read the whole at least twice over.

The trial by jury has enjoyed and enjoys a most lofty traditional reputation as "the palladium of English liberty." Looking at jury trial as it now actually exists, the judges dictating not only the conclusion in law, that is, the decision to which the jury is bound to come upon any such state of facts as they may consider to be proved, but having also the exclusive decision as to what evidence shall be admitted to prove these facts, and the instructing of the jury what weight they ought to allow to this or that piece of evidence, and what conclusions they ought to draw from it; with all these assumptions of authority on the part of the judges, the jury seems to have become very much what the late Mr. Justice Story was accustomed, in private conversation, to describe it as being — a mere stalking-horse, from behind which the judge may shoot quietly and safely, deciding everything, at the same time that he escapes the responsibility, and in some cases. the odium, of doing so.

Such being the practical character of our modern juries, mere cloaks and shields of judicial dictation, it has come, among thinking men. to be a great puzzle how they ever got their immense reputation as a "palladium of liberty;" and some writers have not scrupled to denounce the whole idea as a mere humbug.

Mr. Spooner, however, has shown very conclusively, and by a skilful array of authorities that cannot be got over, that in its original institution, and during the whole time in which it got this reputation as the "palladium of liberty," the jury was a totally different thing from what it has become in these later times under the plastic hands of the judges, the juries having been originally sole judges of both law and fact, indeed possessing substantially a veto on the execution of any such laws as they did not consider conformable to justice and the public good.

All readers may not agree with Mr. Spooner's somewhat enthusiastic admiration of this jury veto power; but that it did exist, and that it was this which made the jury the "palladium of English liberty," he has proved beyond the shadow of a doubt; and in so doing has shed a great deal of new light upon the gradual formation of what is known as the British constitution, the source from which so large a part of our American constitutions are derived.

Nothing is more certain than that the great, indeed the sole value of the trial by jury is political. As a mere contrivance for deciding matters of fact — according to the common representation made of it by modern lawyers — it is clumsy, inconvenient, and liable to a variety of objections. In those countries on the continent of Europe, in which it has been introduced of late years, for the trial of criminal cases, it has greatly disappointed the expectations formed by those who had been accustomed to read of it in books as the "palladium of liberty," and is generally esteemed a total failure.

We are not entirely prepared to go with Mr. Spooner, for the complete re-establishment of the jury veto on the ancient model. But that it is absolutely essential to the liberties of the people to preserve to juries the right of deciding law as well as fact, in all criminal cases, we do not entertain the slightest doubt. And considering the recent and alarming strides, as well of legislative as judicial usurpation, — especially the fact recently announced from the bench of the Federal Court of the United States for this circuit, that ALL the judges of the Supreme Court of the United States scout the idea of any right in a jury to judge of the law in any case whatsoever, — we think Mr. Spooner has done excellent service in calling attention, as he has so ably, to the ancient conservative jury veto.

Mr. Spooner is a thorough-going Democrat, — as zealous for the rights of the people, and as fierce against judicial usurpation, as Jefferson himself. Indeed some of the lunges which he makes at their honors on the bench — as in the note on page 164 — have a hearty frankness about them highly refreshing to one who has been sickened and disgusted — as what hater of falsehood and cant has not been? — by the systematic routine flattery and servility of the bar towards the judges. But more consistent, more comprehensive, and truer to liberty than Jefferson ever was. Mr. Spooner is equally hostile to the usurpations and tyranny of a domineering majority under the forms of legislation. And, indeed, in our

American States, judicial usurpation is seldom very boldly ventured upon, except in the service of a tyrant majority, eager to trample under foot the constitutional and natural rights of the minority. The Conservatives, therefore, no less than the Democrats, owe a debt of gratitude to Mr. Spooner. It is truth and justice in whose cause he is enlisted, not that of party.

R. H.

HON. STEPHEN ROYCE, formerly Chief Justice, and afterwards Governor, of Vermont, says:

EAST BERKSHIRE, VERMONT,
September 21, 1857.

G. W. SEARLE, ESQ.: Sir,—You will please accept my thanks for the favor of Mr. Spooner's book upon "The Trial by Jury." I have derived much pleasure from a hasty perusal of it, and hope the author will persevere and produce the other works, of which he has given indications in this. Although I do not look to see his theories extensively carried out in practice, yet I think his labors must have effect for good. Investigations so decidedly able and searching, can scarcely fail to excite reflection and serious enquiry,—as well with honest legislators and statesmen, as among enlightened jurists. And the result may be, at least, a step taken towards restoring to suitors some of those common-law rights, of which, in the lapse of centuries, they have been gradually deprived.

With high respect, your ob't serv't,

STEPHEN ROYCE.

GEORGE W. SEARLE, ESQ., says: The general proposition assumed and aimed to be sustained is, that "for more than six hundred years—that is, since Magna Carta in 1215—there has been no clearer principle of English or American constitutional law, than that, in criminal cases, it is not only the right and duty of juries to judge what are the facts, what is the law, and what was the moral intent of the accused; but that it is also their right, and their primary and paramount duty, to judge of the justice of the law, and to hold all laws invalid, that are, in their opinion, unjust or oppressive, and all persons guiltless in violating, or resisting the execution of, such laws." It will be seen that this is a bold proposition, and at first glance it may appear untenable; but it is certainly a position not to be entirely appreciated by a glance. It must be confessed that it elevates the tribunal of the Jury to the highest pinnacle of power, making them the judge of the judges, and giving them authority to sit in judgment upon the legislature itself. This position the author seeks to maintain in a very learned and ingenious argument of 224 pages, in the first instance from the general nature of the jury as the palladium of liberty, and a bulwark against the tyranny of authority—by the history, spirit, and language of Magna Carta—and by a variety of reasoning in detail. This head is followed by a general refutation of objections.

It is not our purpose to enter at length upon any discussion, either in support or refutation of the doctrines laid down by the author; for the former task we feel our incompetency, and for the discharge of the latter, that much more time would be requisite than we have at our command, if indeed any time would justify the undertaking. Whatever doubts there may be as to the author's opinions upon many subjects, we may say of his writings what Charles James Fox once said of a speech he was about to reply to in the House of Commons, to one who noticed his serious perturbation, " it is not so easy a matter to answer such an argument as that." * * * That the positions assumed are novel and heretical, judged in the light of prevailing adjudications, is quite true, but that for that reason they are any the less worthy of regard, is quite wide of the truth. To the thinking man we recommend it as food upon which he may feed and grow strong; and to the professional man, in an age of progressive jurisprudence, when the science of law, too long bound with an iron grasp to antiquated decisions and principles having nothing but their antiquity and their folly for their authority, is beginning to take its march by the side of modern science, we recommend its candid and impartial examination, assuring him that in it he will find the bold expression of manly truths, without fear or favor.

WENDELL PHILLIPS, Esq., says of it: "Though I dissent from Mr. Spooner's main conclusion, I must confess this effort is marked with all his pre eminent ingenuity and ability. He has laid all history under contribution for light as to the origin and functions of juries; and I am debtor to his diligence and research for much that was new to me. The original province of a jury has never before been fully investigated in any work accessible and intelligible to common readers. I am not aware that there has been any able and extended argument about it since Erskine's.

The fullness, therefore, of historical illustration, which Mr. Spooner has given to those points, even, on which many of the profession would agree with him, makes the volume a valuable contribution to legal literature.

Though he has not converted me to his views, yet I always read him with pleasure, and admire him for an opponent on one account — he states his questions so fairly, and faces the difficulties like a man.

I quite agree that juries have the right, in both civil and criminal cases, to judge *what the law is*, i. e. what the Legislature have constitutionally enacted — but I cannot allow them the right to set aside statutes because they think them unjust."

ROBERT E. APTHORP, Esq., says of it: If it cannot be answered, it must make a deep impression on the conscience, and thus on the jurisprudence, of the age in which we live. That it *can* be answered I greatly doubt; or rather I should say, I have no doubt about it. One thing is certain, — no *tyro* will venture to flesh his sword upon such a structure of logic and fact; and should any *worthy* antagonist present himself in the lists, our generation and all future ones would owe Mr. Spooner a debt of gratitude for having *forced* attention, in high places, to a subject than which, I may safely say, none more intimately and vitally concerns this Republic.

REV. EDWARD BEECHER, D. D., says of it: Thus stated, it is plain that no point of history can exceed in dignity and importance that which Mr. Spooner has undertaken to discuss.

The mode of his discussion is worthy of the gravity of the point at issue. It does not at all consist of rhetorical declamation, but is a sober, earnest, learned, and powerful argument, based on copious citations from numerous and weighty legal and historical authorities, ancient and modern.

ELIZUR WRIGHT says of it: "To me it seems not only very remarkable as a book, but as a discovery; one which may be more useful to the world than new gold regions."

HON. SAMUEL E. SEWALL says of it: "This is a work of deep research and powerful argument. It ought to be in the hands not merely of every judge and every lawyer, but of every man who values liberty, and wishes to examine its sacred foundations."

HON. JOSHUA R. GIDDINGS says of it: "It should be placed in the library of every lawyer, and of every reader of general literature."

THE

UNCONSTITUTIONALITY

OF

SLAVERY.

BY LYSANDER SPOONER.

BOSTON:
PUBLISHED BY BELA MARSH,
No. 14 Bromfield St.
1860.

CONTENTS OF PART FIRST.

———

	PAGE
CHAPTER I.—WHAT IS LAW?	5
" II.—WRITTEN CONSTITUTIONS,	15
" III.—THE COLONIAL CHARTERS,	21
" IV.—COLONIAL STATUTES,	32
" V.—THE DECLARATION OF INDEPENDENCE,	36
" VI.—THE STATE CONSTITUTIONS OF 1789. MEANING OF THE WORD "FREE,"	39
" VII.—THE ARTICLES OF CONFEDERATION,	51
" VIII.—THE CONSTITUTION OF THE UNITED STATES,	54
" IX.—THE INTENTIONS OF THE CONVENTION,	114
" X.—THE PRACTICE OF THE GOVERNMENT,	123
" XI.—THE UNDERSTANDING OF THE PEOPLE,	124
" XII.—THE STATE CONSTITUTIONS OF 1845,	126
" XIII.—THE CHILDREN OF SLAVES ARE BORN FREE,	129

☞ APPENDIX A. has been added to the former edition of this work; also the second note on page 264.

UNCONSTITUTIONALITY OF SLAVERY.

CHAPTER I.

WHAT IS LAW?

BEFORE examining the language of the Constitution, in regard to Slavery, let us obtain a view of the principles, by virtue of which *law* arises out of those constitutions and compacts, by which people agree to establish government.

To do this it is necessary to define the term *law.* Popular opinions are very loose and indefinite, both as to the true definition of law, and also as to the principle, by virtue of which law results from the compacts or contracts of mankind with each other.

What then is LAW? That law, I mean, which, and which only, judicial tribunals are morally bound, under all circumstances, to declare and sustain?

In answering this question, I shall attempt to show that law is an intelligible principle of right, necessarily resulting from the nature of man; and not an arbitrary rule, that can be established by mere will, numbers or power.

To determine whether this proposition be correct, we must look at the *general* signification of the term *law.*

The true and general meaning of it, is that *natural*, permanent, unalterable principle, which governs any particular thing or class of things. The principle is strictly a *natural* one; and the term applies to every *natural* principle, whether mental, moral or physical. Thus we speak of the laws of mind; meaning thereby those *natural*, universal and necessary principles, according to which mind acts, or by which it is governed. We speak too of the moral law; which is merely an universal principle of moral obligation, that arises out of the nature of men, and their relations to each

1*

other, and to other things—and is consequently as unalterable as
the nature of men. And it is solely because it is unalterable in
its nature, and universal in its application, that it is denominated
law. If it were changeable, partial or arbitrary, it would be no
law. Thus we speak of physical laws ; of the laws, for instance,
that govern the solar system ; of the laws of motion, the laws of
gravitation, the laws of light, &c., &c.—Also the laws that govern
the vegetable and animal kingdoms, in all their various departments : among which laws may be named, for example, the one
that like produces like. Unless the operation of this principle
were uniform, universal and necessary, it would be no law.

Law, then, applied to any object or thing whatever, signifies a
natural, unalterable, universal principle, governing such object or
thing. Any rule, not existing in the nature of things, or that is
not permanent, universal and inflexible in its application, is no
law, according to any correct definition of the term law.

What, then, is that *natural*, universal, impartial and inflexible
principle, which, under all circumstances, *necessarily* fixes, determines, defines and governs the civil rights of men ? Those rights
of person, property, &c., which one human being has, as against
other human beings ?

I shall define it to be simply *the rule, principle, obligation or
requirement of natural justice.*

This rule, principle, obligation or requirement of natural justice,
has its origin in the natural rights of individuals, results necessarily from them, keeps them ever in view as its end and purpose,
secures their enjoyment, and forbids their violation. It also
secures all those acquisitions of property, privilege and claim,
which men have a *natural* right to make by labor and contract.

Such is the true meaning of the term law, as applied to the
civil rights of men. And I doubt if any other definition of law
can be given, that will prove correct in every, or necessarily in
any possible case. The very idea of law originates in men's
natural rights. There is no other standard, than natural rights,
by which civil law can be measured. Law has always been the
name of that rule or principle of justice, which protects those rights.
Thus we speak of *natural law.* Natural law, in fact, constitutes
the great body of the law that is *professedly* administered by
judicial tribunals : and it always necessarily must be—for it is
impossible to anticipate a thousandth part of the cases that arise,
so as to enact a special law for them. Wherever the cases have

not been thus anticipated, the natural law prevails. We thus politically and judicially *recognize* the principle of law as originating in the nature and rights of men. By recognizing it as originating in the nature of men, we recognize it as a principle, that is necessarily as immutable, and as indestructible as the nature of man. We also, in the same way, recognize the impartiality and universality of its application.

If, then, law be a natural principle—one necessarily resulting from the very nature of man, and capable of being destroyed or changed only by destroying or changing the nature of man—it necessarily follows that it must be of higher and more inflexible obligation than any other rule of conduct, which the arbitrary will of any man, or combination of men, may attempt to establish. Certainly no rule can be of such high, universal and inflexible obligation, as that, which, if observed, secures the rights, the safety and liberty of all.

Natural law, then, is the paramount law. And, being the paramount law, it is necessarily the only law: for, being applicable to every possible case that can arise touching the rights of men, any other principle or rule, that should arbitrarily be applied to those rights, would necessarily conflict with it. And, as a merely arbitrary, partial and temporary rule must, of necessity, be of less obligation than a natural, permanent, equal and universal one, the arbitrary one becomes, in reality, of no obligation at all, when the two come in collision. Consequently there is, and can be, correctly speaking, *no law but natural law.* There is no other principle or rule, applicable to the rights of men, that is obligatory in comparison with this, in any case whatever. And this natural law is no other than that rule of natural justice, which results either directly from men's natural rights, or from such acquisitions as they have a *natural* right to make, or from such contracts as they have a *natural* right to enter into.

Natural law recognizes the validity of all contracts which men have a *natural* right to make, and which justice requires to be fulfilled: such, for example, as contracts that render equivalent for equivalent, and are at the same time consistent with morality, the natural rights of men, and those rights of property, privilege, &c., which men have a natural right to acquire by labor and contract.

Natural law, therefore, inasmuch as it recognizes the natural right of men to enter into obligatory contracts, permits the formation of government, founded on contract, as all our governments

profess to be. But in order that the contract of government may
be valid and lawful, it must purport to authorize nothing inconsistent with natural justice, and men's natural rights. It cannot
lawfully authorize government to destroy or take from men their
natural rights : for natural rights are inalienable, and can no more
be surrendered to government—which is but an association of
individuals—than to a single individual. They are a necessary
attribute of man's nature; and he can no more part with them—
to government or anybody else—than with his nature itself.
But the contract of government may lawfully authorize the adoption of means—not inconsistent with natural justice—for the
better protection of men's natural rights. And this is the legitimate and true object of government. And rules and statutes, not
inconsistent with natural justice and men's natural rights, if
enacted by such government, are binding, on the ground of contract, upon those who are parties to the contract, which creates the
government, and authorizes it to pass rules and statutes to carry
out its objects.*

But natural law tries the contract of government, and declares it
lawful or unlawful, obligatory or invalid, by the same rules by
which it tries all other contracts between man and man. A contract for the establishment of government, being nothing but a
voluntary contract between individuals for their mutual benefit,
differs, in nothing that is essential to its validity from any other
contract between man and man, or between nation and nation.
If two individuals enter into a contract to commit trespass, theft,
robbery or murder upon a third, the contract is unlawful and void,
simply because it is a contract to violate natural justice, or men's
natural rights. If two nations enter into a treaty, that they will
unite in plundering, enslaving or destroying a third, the treaty is
unlawful, void and of no obligation, simply because it is contrary

* It is obvious that legislation can have, in this country, no higher or other authority, than that which results from natural law, and the obligation of contracts ; for
our constitutions are but contracts, and the legislation they authorize can of course
have no other or higher authority than the constitutions themselves. The stream
cannot rise higher than the fountain. The idea, therefore, of any *inherent* authority or sovereignty in our governments, *as governments*, or of any inherent right
in the majority to restrain individuals, by arbitrary enactments, from the exercise
of any of their natural rights, is as sheer an imposture as the idea of the divine
right of kings to reign, or any other of the doctrines on which arbitrary governments
have been founded. And the idea of any necessary or inherent authority in legislation, *as such*, is, of course, equally an imposture. If legislation be consistent
with natural justice, and the natural or intrinsic obligation of the contract of government, it is obligatory : if not, not.

to justice and men's natural rights. On the same principle, if the majority, however large, of the people of a country, enter into a contract of government, called a constitution, by which they agree to aid, abet or accomplish any kind of injustice, or to destroy or invade the natural rights of any person or persons whatsoever, whether such persons be parties to the compact or not, this contract of government is unlawful and void—and for the same reason that a treaty between two nations for a similar purpose, or a contract of the same nature between two individuals, is unlawful and void. Such a contract of government has no moral sanction. It confers no rightful authority upon those appointed to administer it. It confers no legal or moral rights, and imposes no legal or moral obligation upon the people who are parties to it. The only duties, which any one can owe to it, or to the government established under color of its authority, are disobedience, resistance, destruction.

Judicial tribunals, sitting under the authority of this unlawful contract or constitution, are bound, equally with other men, to declare it, and all unjust enactments passed by the government in pursuance of it, unlawful and void. These judicial tribunals cannot, by accepting office under a government, rid themselves of that paramount obligation, that all men are under, to declare, if they declare anything, that justice is law; that government can have no lawful powers, except those with which it has been invested by lawful contract; and that an unlawful contract for the establishment of government, is as unlawful and void as any other contract to do injustice.

No oaths, which judicial or other officers may take, to carry out and support an unlawful contract or constitution of government, are of any moral obligation. It is immoral to take such oaths, and it is criminal to fulfil them. They are, both in morals and law, like the oaths which individual pirates, thieves and bandits give to their confederates, as an assurance of their fidelity to the purposes for which they are associated. No man has any moral right to assume such oaths; they impose no obligation upon those who do assume them; they afford no moral justification for official acts, in themselves unjust, done in pursuance of them.

If these doctrines are correct, then those contracts of government, state and national, which we call constitutions, are void, and unlawful, so far as they purport to authorize, (if any of them do authorize,) anything in violation of natural justice, or the natural rights of any man or class of men whatsoever. And all judicial tribunals are bound, by the highest obligations that can rest upon them, to declare that these contracts, in all such particulars, (if any such there be,) are void, and not law. And all agents, legislative, executive, judicial and popular, who voluntarily lend their aid to the execution of any of the unlawful purposes of the government, are as much personally guilty, according to all the moral and legal principles, by which crime, in its essential character, is measured, as though they performed the same acts independently, and of their own volition.

Such is the true character and definition of law. Yet, instead of being allowed to signify, as it in reality does, that natural, universal and inflexible principle, which has its origin in the nature of man, keeps pace everywhere with the rights of man, as their shield and protector, binds alike governments and men, weighs by the same standard the acts of communities and individuals, and is paramount in its obligation to any other requirement which can be imposed upon men — instead, I say, of the term law being allowed to signify, as it really does, this immutable and overruling principle of natural justice, it has come to be applied to mere arbitrary rules of conduct, prescribed by individuals, or combinations of individuals, self-styled governments, who have no other title to the prerogative of establishing such rules, than is given them by the possession or command of sufficient physical power to coerce submission to them.

The injustice of these rules, however palpable and atrocious it may be, has not deterred their authors from dignifying them with the name of *law*. And, what is much more to be deplored, such has been the superstition of the people, and such their blind veneration for physical power, that this injustice has not opened their eyes to the distinction between law and force, between the sacred requirements of natural justice, and the criminal exactions of unrestrained selfishness and power. They have thus not only suffered the name of law to be stolen, and applied to crime as a cloak to conceal its true nature, but they have rendered homage and obedience to crime, under the name of law, until the very name of law, instead of signifying, in their minds, an immutable principle of right, has come to signify little more than an arbitrary command of power, without reference to its justice or its injustice, its innocence or its criminality. And now, commands the most criminal, if christened with the name of law, obtain nearly as ready an

obedience, oftentimes a more ready obedience, than law and justice itself. This superstition, on the part of the people, which has
thus allowed force and crime to usurp the name and occupy the
throne of justice and law, is hardly paralleled in its grossness,
even by that superstition, which, in darker ages of the world, has
allowed falsehood, absurdity and cruelty to usurp the name and
the throne of religion.

But I am aware that other definitions of law, widely different
from that I have given, have been attempted—definitions too,
which practically obtain, to a great extent, in our judicial tribunals,
and in all the departments of government. But these other definitions are nevertheless, all, in themselves, uncertain, indefinite,
mutable ; and therefore incapable of being standards, by a reference to which the question of law, or no law, can be determined.
Law, as defined by them, is capricious, arbitrary, unstable ; is
based upon no fixed principle ; results from no established fact ; is
susceptible of only a limited, partial and arbitrary application ;
possesses no intrinsic authority ; does not, in itself, recognize any
moral principle ; does not necessarily confer upon, or even
acknowledge in individuals, any moral or civil rights ; or impose
upon them any moral obligation.

For example. One of these definitions—one that probably embraces the essence of all the rest—is this :

That " law is a rule of civil conduct, prescribed by the supreme
power of a state, commanding what its subjects are to do, and
prohibiting what they are to forbear."—*Noah Webster.*

In this definition, hardly anything, that is essential to the idea
of law, is made certain. Let us see. It says that,

" Law is a rule of civil conduct, prescribed by the *supreme
power* of a state."

What is the " supreme power," that is here spoken of, as the
fountain of law ? Is it the supreme physical power ? Or the
largest concentration of physical power, whether it exist in one man
or in a combination of men ? Such is undoubtedly its meaning.
And if such be its meaning, then the law is uncertain ; for it is
oftentimes uncertain where, or in what man, or body of men, in a
state, the greatest amount of physical power is concentrated.
Whenever a state should be divided into factions, no one having
the supremacy of all the rest, law would not merely be inefficient,
but the very principle of law itself would be actually extinguished.
And men would have no " rule of civil conduct." This result
alone is sufficient to condemn this definition.

Again. If physical power be the fountain of law, then law and force are synonymous terms. Or, perhaps, rather, law would be the result of a combination of will and force ; of will, united with a physical power sufficient to compel obedience to it, but not necessarily having any moral character whatever.

Are we prepared to admit the principle, that there is no real distinction between law and force? If not, we must reject this definition.

It is true that law may, in many cases, depend upon force as the means of its practical efficiency. But are law and force therefore identical in their essence ?

According to this definition, too, a command to do injustice, is as much law, as a command to do justice. All that is necessary, according to this definition, to make the command a law, is that it issue from a will that is supported by physical force sufficient to coerce obedience.

Again. If mere will and power are sufficient, of themselves, to establish law — legitimate law — such law as judicial tribunals are morally bound, or even have a moral right to enforce — then it follows that wherever will and power are united, and continue united until they are successful in the accomplishment of any particular object, to which they are directed, they constitute the only legitimate law of that case, and judicial tribunals can take cognizance of no other.

And it makes no difference, on this principle, whether this combination of will and power be found in a single individual, or in a community of an hundred millions of individuals. — The numbers concerned do not alter the rule — otherwise law would be the result of numbers, instead of " supreme power." It is therefore sufficient to comply with this definition, that the power be equal to the accomplishment of the object. And the will and power of one man are therefore as competent to make the law relative to any acts which he is able to execute, as the will and power of millions of men are to make the law relative to any acts which they are able to accomplish.

On this principle, then — that mere will and power are competent to establish the law that is to govern an act, without reference to the justice or injustice of the act itself, the will and power of any single individual to commit theft, would be sufficient to make theft lawful, as lawful as is any other act of· injustice, which the will and power of communities, or large bodies of men, may be united to accomplish And judicial tribunals are as much bound to recognize, as lawful, any act of injustice or crime, which the will and power of a single individual may have succeeded in accomplishing, as they are to recognize as lawful any act of injustice, which large and organized bodies of men, self-styled governments, may accomplish.

But, perhaps it will be said that the soundness of this definition depends upon the use of the word " state "— and that it therefore makes a distinction between " the supreme power of *a state*," over a particular act, and the power of an individual over the same act.

But this addition of the word " state," in reality leaves the definition just where it would have been without it. For what is " a state ? " It is just what, and only what, the will and power of individuals may arbitrarily establish.

There is nothing *fixed* in the nature, character or boundaries of " a state." Will and power may alter them at pleasure. The will and power of Nicholas, and that will and power which he has concentrated around, or rather within himself, establishes all Russia, both in Europe and Asia, as " a state." By the same rule, the will and power of the owner of an acre of ground, may establish that acre as a state, and make his will and power, for the time being, supreme and lawful within it.

The will and power, also, that established " a state " yesterday, may be overcome to-day by an adverse will and power, that shall abolish that state, and incorporate it into another, over which this latter will and power shall to-day be " supreme." And this latter will and power may also to-morrow be overcome by still another will and power mightier than they.

" A state," then, is nothing fixed, permanent or certain in its nature. It is simply the boundaries, within which any single combination or concentration of will and power are efficient, or irresistible, *for the time being*.

This is the only true definition that can be given of " a state." It is merely an arbitrary name given to the territorial limits of power. And if such be its true character, then it would follow, that the boundaries, though but two feet square, within which the will and power of a single individual are, *for the time being,* supreme, or irresistible, are, for all *legal* purposes, " a state "— and his will and power constitute, for the time being, the law within those limits ; and his acts are, therefore, for the time being,

2

as necessarily lawful, without respect to their intrinsic justice or injustice, as are the acts of larger bodies of men, within those limits where their will and power are supreme and irresistible.

If, then, law really be what this definition would make it, merely "a rule of civil conduct prescribed by the supreme power of a state "—it would follow, as a necessary consequence, that law is synonymous merely with will and force, wherever they are com bined and in successful operation, for the present moment.

Under this definition, law offers no permanent guaranty for the safety, liberty, rights or happiness of any one. It licenses all possible crime, violence and wrong, both by governments and individuals. The definition was obviously invented by, and is suited merely to gloss over the purposes of, arbitrary power. We are therefore compelled to reject it, and to seek another, that shall make law less capricious, less uncertain, less arbitrary, more just, more safe to the rights of all, more permanent. And if we seek another, where shall we find it, unless we adopt the one first given, viz., that *law is the rule, principle, obligation or requirement of natural justice?*

Adopt this definition, and law becomes simple, intelligible, scientific; always consistent with itself; always harmonizing with morals, reason and truth. Reject this definition, and law is no longer a science : but a chaos of crude, conflicting and arbitrary edicts, unknown perchance to either morals, justice, reason or truth, and fleeting and capricious as the impulses of will, interest and power.

If, then, law really be nothing other than the rule, principle obligation or requirement of natural justice, it follows that government can have no powers except such as individuals may *rightfully* delegate to it : that no law, inconsistent with men's natural rights, can arise out of any contract or compact of government : *that constitutional law, under any form of government, consists only of those principles of the written constitution, that are consistent with natural law, and man's natural rights;* and that any other principles, that may be expressed by the letter of any constitution, are void and not law, and all judicial tribunals are bound to declare them so.

Though this doctrine may make sad havoc with constitutions and statute books, it is nevertheless law. It fixes and determines the real rights of all men; and its demands are as imperious as any that can exist under the name of law.

It is possible, perhaps, that this doctrine would spare enough of our existing constitutions, to save our governments from the necessity of a new organization. But whatever else it might spare, one thing it would not spare. It would spare no vestige of that system of human slavery, which now claims to exist by authority of law.*

CHAPTER II.

WRITTEN CONSTITUTIONS.

TAKING it for granted that it has now been shown that no rule of civil conduct, that is inconsistent with the natural rights of men, can be rightfully established by government, or consequently be made obligatory as law, either upon the people, or upon judicial tribunals—let us now proceed to test the legality of slavery by those written constitutions of government, which judicial tribunals actually recognize as authoritative.

In making this examination, however, I shall not insist upon the principle of the preceding chapter, that there can be no law

---

* The mass of men are so much accustomed to regard law as an arbitrary command of those who administer political power, that the idea of its being a *natural*, fixed, and immutable principle, may perhaps want some other support than that of the reasoning already given, to commend it to their adoption. I therefore give them the following corroborations from sources of the highest authority.

"Jurisprudence is the science of what is just and unjust." — *Justinian*.

"The primary and principal objects of the law are rights and wrongs." — *Blackstone.*

"Justice is the constant and perpetual disposition to render to every man his due." — *Justinian.*

"The precepts of the law are to live honestly; to hurt no one; to give to every one his due." — *Justinian & Blackstone.*

"LAW. The rule and bond of men's actions; or it is a rule for the well governing of civil society, to give to every man that which doth belong to him." — *Jacob's Law Dictionary.*

"Laws are arbitrary or positive, and natural; the last of which are essentially just and good, and bind everywhere, and in all places where they are observed. * * * * Those which are natural laws, are from God; but those which are arbitrary, are properly human and positive institutions." — *Selden on Fortescue,* C. 17, *also Jacob's Law Dictionary.*

"The law of nature is that which God, at man's creation, infused into him, for his preservation and direction; and this is an eternal law, and may not be changed."—2 *Shep. Abr.* 356, *also Jac. Law Dict.*

contrary to natural right; but shall admit, for the sake of the argument, that there may be such laws.   I shall only claim that in the interpretation of all statutes and constitutions, the ordinary legal

---

" All laws derive their force from the law of nature ; and those which do not, are accounted as no laws."— *Fortescue, Jac. Law Dict.*

" No law will make a construction to do wrong ; and there are some things which the law favors, and some it dislikes ; it favoreth those things that come from the order of nature."—1 *Inst.* 183, 197.— *Jac. Law Dict.*

" Of law no less can be acknowledged, than that her seat is the bosom of God, her voice the harmony of the world.   All things in heaven and earth do her homage ; the least as feeling her care, and the greatest as not exempted from her power."— *Hooker.*

Blackstone speaks of law as " A science, which distinguishes the criterions of right and wrong ; which teaches to establish the one, and prevent, punish or redress the other ; which employs in its theory the noblest faculties of the soul, and exerts in its practice the cardinal virtues of the heart ; a science, which is universal in its use and extent, accommodated to each individual, yet comprehending the whole community."— *Blackstone's Lecture on the Study of the Law.*

" This law of nature being coeval with mankind, and dictated by God himself, is of course superior in obligation to any other.   It is binding over all the globe, in all countries, and at all times : no human laws are of any validity, if contrary to this ; and such of them as are valid, derive all their force, and all their authority mediately or immediately, from this original."— *Blackstone, Vol.* 1, *p.* 41.

Mr. Christian, one of Blackstone's editors, in a note to the above passage, says :

" Lord Chief Justice Hobart has also advanced, that even an act of Parliament made against natural justice, as to make a man judge in his own cause, is void in itself, for *jura naturæ sunt immutabilia,* and they are *leges legum*"—(the laws of nature are immutable— they are the laws of laws.) — *Hob.* 87.

Mr. Christian then adds :

" With deference to these high authorities, (Blackstone and Hobart,) I should conceive that in no case whatever can a judge oppose his own opinion and authority to the clear will and declaration of the legislature.   His province is to interpret and obey the mandates of the supreme power of the state.   And if an act of Parliament, if we could suppose such a case, should, like the edict of Herod, command all the children under a certain age to be slain, the judge ought to resign his office rather than be auxiliary to its execution ; but it could only be declared void by the same legislative power by which it was ordained.   If the judicial power were competent to decide that an act of parliament was void because it was contrary to natural justice, upon an appeal to the House of Lords this inconsistency would be the consequence, that as judges they must declare void, what as legislators they had enacted should be valid.

" The learned judge himself (Blackstone) declares in p. 91, if the Parliament will positively enact a thing to be done which is unreasonable, I know of no power in the ordinary forms of the constitution, that is vested with authority to control it."

It will be seen from this note of Mr. Christian, that he concurs in the opinion that an enactment contrary to natural justice is *intrinsically* void, and not law ; and that the principal, if not the only difficulty, which he sees in carrying out that doctrine, is one that is peculiar to the British constitution, and does not exist in the United States.   That difficulty is, the " inconsistency" there would be, if the House of Lords, (which is the highest law court in England, and at the same time one branch of the legislature,) were to declare, in their capacity as judges, that an act was void, which, as legislators, they had declared should be valid.   And this is probably the

rules of interpretation be observed. The most important of these rules, and the one to which it will be necessary constantly to refer, is the one that all language must be construed "*strictly*" in favor

---

reason why Blackstone admitted that he knew of no power in the ordinary forms of the (British) constitution, that was vested with authority to control an act of Parliament that was unreasonable, (against natural justice.) But in the United States, where the judicial and legislative powers are vested in different bodies, and where they are so vested for the very purpose of having the former act as a check upon the latter, no such inconsistency would occur.

The constitutions that have been established in the United States, and the discussions had on the formation of them, all attest the importance which our ancestors attached to a separation of the judicial, from the executive and legislative departments of the government. And yet the benefits, which they had promised to liberty and justice from this separation, have in slight only, if any degree, been realized.—Although the legislation of the country generally has exhibited little less than an entire recklessness both of natural justice and constitutional authority, the records of the judiciary nevertheless furnish hardly an instance where an act of a legislature has, for either of these reasons, been declared void by its co-ordinate judicial department. There have been cases, few and far between, in which the United States courts have declared acts of state legislatures unconstitutional. But the history of the co-ordinate departments of the same governments has been, that the judicial sanction followed the legislative act with nearly the same unerring certainty, that the shadow follows the substance. Judicial decisions have consequently had the same effects in restraining the actions of legislatures, that shadows have in restraining the motions of bodies.

Why this uniform concurrence of the judiciary with the legislature? It is because the separation between them is nominal, not real. The judiciary receive their offices and salaries at the hands of the executive and the legislature, and are amenable only to the legislature for their official character. They are made entirely independent of the people at large, (whose highest interests are liberty and justice,) and entirely dependent upon those who have too many interests inconsistent with liberty and justice. Could a real and entire separation of the judiciary from the other departments take place, we might then hope that their decisions would, in some measure, restrain the usurpations of the legislature, and promote progress in the science of law and of government.

Whether any of our present judges would, (as Mr. Christian suggests they ought,) "resign their offices" rather than be auxiliary to the execution of an act of legislation, that, like the edict of Herod, should require all the children under a certain age to be slain, we cannot certainly know. But this we do know — that our judges have hitherto manifested no intention of resigning their offices to avoid declaring it to be law, that "children of two years old and under," may be wrested forever from that parental protection which is their birthright, and subjected for life to outrages which all civilized men must regard as worse than death.

To proceed with our authorities : —

"Those human laws that annex a punishment to murder, do not at all increase its moral guilt, or superadd any fresh obligation in the forum of conscience to abstain from its perpetration. Nay, if any human law should allow or enjoin us to commit it, we are bound to transgress that human law, or else we must offend both the natural and the divine." — *Blackstone, Vol.* 1, *p.* 42, 43.

"The law of nations depends entirely upon the rules of *natural law*, or upon mutual compacts, treaties, leagues and agreements between these several communities ; in the construction also of which compacts, we have no other rule to resort to

of natural right. The rule is laid down by the Supreme Court of
the United States in these words, to wit :

"Where rights are infringed, where fundamental principles are

but the law of nature : (that) being the only one to which all the communities are
equally subject." — *Blackstone, Vol.* 1, *p.* 43.

"Those rights then which God and nature have established, and are therefore
called natural rights, such as are life and liberty, need not the aid of human laws to
be more effectually invested in every man than they are ; neither do they receive
any additional strength when declared by the municipal laws to be inviolable. On
the contrary, no human legislature has power to abridge or destroy them, unless the
owner shall himself commit some act that amounts to a forfeiture." — *Blackstone,*
Vol. 1, *p.* 54.

"By the absolute rights of individuals, we mean those which are so in their
primary and strictest sense ; such as would belong to their persons merely in a state
of nature, and which every man is entitled to enjoy, whether out of society, or in
it." — *Blackstone, Vol.* 1, *p.* 123.

"The principal aim of society (government) is to protect individuals in the enjoyment of those absolute rights, which were vested in them by the immutable laws of
nature ; but which could not be preserved in peace without that mutual assistance
and intercourse, which is gained by the institution of friendly and social communities. Hence it follows, that the first and primary end of human laws is to maintain
and regulate these absolute rights of individuals. Such rights as are social and
relative result from, and are posterior to, the formation of states and societies ; so
that to maintain and regulate these, is clearly a subsequent consideration. And
therefore the principal view of human law is, or ought always to be, to explain,
protect, and enforce such rights as are absolute ; which, in themselves, are few and
simple : and then such rights as are relative, which, arising from a variety of connexions, will be far more numerous and more complicated. These will take up a greater
space in any code of laws, and hence may appear to be more attended to, though in
reality they are not, than the rights of the former kind." — *Blackstone, Vol.* 1, *p.* 124.

"The absolute rights of man, considered as a free agent, endowed with discern
ment to know good from evil, and with power of choosing those measures which
appear to him most desirable, are usually summed up in one general appellation, and
denominated the natural liberty of mankind. This natural liberty consists properly
in a power of acting as one thinks fit, without any restraint or control, unless by the
law of nature, being a right inherent in us by birth, and one of the gifts of God to
man at his creation, when he endowed him with the faculty of free will." — *Black-*
stone, Vol. 1, *p.* 125.

"Moral or natural liberty, (in the words of Burlamaqui, ch. 3, s. 15,) is the right,
which nature gives to all mankind of disposing of their persons and property after
the manner they judge most consonant to their happiness, on condition of their
acting within the limits of the law of nature, and that they do not any way abuse it
to the prejudice of any other men." — *Christian's note, Blackstone, Vol.* 1, *p.* 126.

"The law of Nature is antecedent and paramount to all human governments.
* * * Every individual of the human race comes into the world with rights, which,
if the whole aggregate of human power were concentrated in one arm, it could not
take away. * * * The Declaration of Independence recognizes no despotism,
monarchical, aristocratic, or democratic. It declares that individual man is possessed of rights of which no government can deprive him." — *John Quincy Adams.*

All the foregoing definitions of law, rights and natural liberty, although some of
them are expressed in somewhat vague and indefinite terms, nevertheless recognize
he primary idea, that law is a fixed principle, resulting from men's natural rights :

overthrown, where the general system of the laws is departed from, the legislative intention must be expressed with *irresistible clearness*, to induce a court of justice to suppose a design to effect such objects." *

and that therefore the acknowledgment and security of the natural rights of individuals constitute the whole basis of law as a science, and a *sine qua non* of government as a legitimate institution.

And yet writers generally, who acknowledge the true theory of government and law, will nevertheless, when discussing matters of legislation, violate continually the fundamental principles with which they set out. On some pretext of promoting a great public good, the violation of individual rights will be justified in particular cases ; and the guardian principle being once broken down, nothing can then stay the irruption of the whole horde of pretexts for doing injustice ; and government and legislation thenceforth become contests between factions for power and plunder, instead of instruments for the preservation of liberty and justice equally to all.

The current doctrine that private rights must yield to the public good, amounts, in reality, to nothing more nor less than this, that an individual or the minority must consent to have less than their rights, in order that other individuals, or the majority, may have more than their rights. On this principle no honest government could ever be formed by voluntary contract, (as our governments purport to be ;) because no man of common sense would consent to be one of the plundered minority, and no honest man could wish to be one of the plundering majority.

The apology, that is constantly put forth for the injustice of government, viz., that a man must consent to give up some of his rights, in order to have his other rights protected — involves a palpable absurdity, both legally and politically. It is an absurdity in law, because it says that the law must be violated in some cases, in order that it may be maintained in others. It is an absurdity politically, because a man's giving up one of his rights has no tendency whatever to promote the protec-.ion of others. On the contrary, it only renders him less capable of defending himself, and consequently makes the task of his protection more burdensome to the government. At the same time it places him in the situation of one who has conceded a part of his rights, and thus cheapened the character of all his rights in the eyes of those of whom he asks assistance. There would be as much reason in saying that a man must consent to have one of his hands tied behind him, in order that his friends might protect the rest of his body against an enemy, as there is in saying that a man must give up some of his rights in order that government may protect the remainder. Let a man have the use of both of his hands, and the enjoyment of all his rights, and he will then be more competent to his own defence ; his rights will be more respected by those who might otherwise be disposed to invade them ; he will want less the assistance and protection of others ; and we shall need much less government than we now have.

If individuals choose to form an association or government, for the mutual protection of each other's rights, why bargain for the protection of an *indefinite* portion of them, at the price of giving to the association itself liberty to violate the equally indefinite remainder ? By such a contract, a man really surrenders everything, and secures nothing. Such a contract of government would be a burlesque on the wisdom of asses. Such a contract never was, nor ever will be *voluntarily* formed. Yet all our governments act on that principle ; and so far as they act upon it, they are as essentially usurping and tyrannical as any governments can be. If a man pay his proportion of the aggregate cost of protecting all the rights of each of the

* United States *vs.* Fisher, 2 Cranch, 390.

It will probably appear from this examination of the written constitutions, that slavery neither has, *nor ever had* any constitutional
existence in this country; that it has always been a mere abuse,
sustained, in the first instance, merely by the common consent of
the strongest party, without any law on the subject, and, in the
second place, by a few unconstitutional enactments, made in defiance of the plainest provisions of their fundamental law.

For the more convenient consideration of this point, we will
divide the constitutional history of the country into three periods;
the first embracing the time from the first settlement of the country
up to the Declaration of Independence; the second embracing the
time from the Declaration of Independence to the adoption of the
Constitution of the United States in 1789; and the third embracing all the time since the adoption of the Constitution of the United
States.

Let us now consider the first period; that is, from the settlement
of the country, to the Declaration of Independence.

---

members of the association, he thereby acquires a claim upon the association to
have his own rights protected without diminution.

The ultimate truth on this subject is, that man has an inalienable right to so
much personal liberty as he will use without invading the rights of others. This
liberty is an inherent right of his nature and his faculties. It is an inherent right
of his nature and his faculties to develope themselves freely, and without restraint
from other natures and faculties, that have no superior prerogatives to his own.
And this right has only this limit, viz., that he do not carry the exercise of his own
liberty so far as to restrain or infringe the equally free development of the natures
and faculties of others. The dividing line between the equal liberties of each must
never be transgressed by either. This principle is the foundation and essence of
law and of civil right. And legitimate government is formed by the voluntary
association of individuals, for the mutual protection of each of them in the enjoyment of this natural liberty, against those who may be disposed to invade it. Each
individual being secured in the enjoyment of this liberty, must then take the responsibility of his own happiness and well-being. If his necessities require more
than his faculties will supply, he must depend upon the voluntary kindness of his
fellow-men; unless he be reduced to that extremity where the necessity of self-
preservation over-rides all abstract rules of conduct, and makes a law for the occasion — an extremity, that would probably never occur but for some antecedent injustice.

CHAPTER III.

THE COLONIAL CHARTERS.

WHEN our ancestors came to this country, they brought with them the common law of England, including the writ of *habeas corpus*, (the essential principle of which, as will hereafter be shown, is to deny the right of property in man,) the trial by jury, and the other great principles of liberty, which prevail in England, and which have made it impossible that her soil should be trod by the foot of a slave.

These principles were incorporated into all the charters, granted to the colonies, (if all those charters were like those I have examined, and I have examined nearly all of them.) — The general provisions of those charters, as will be seen from the extracts given in the note, were, that the laws of the colonies should " not be repugnant or contrary, but, as nearly as circumstances would allow, conformable to the laws, statutes and rights of our kingdom of England." *

---

* The second charter to Virginia (1609) grants the power of making " orders, ordinances, constitutions, directions and instructions," " so always as the said statutes, ordinances and proceedings, as near as conveniently may be, be agreeable to the laws, statutes, government and policy of this our realm of England."

The third charter (1611 — 12) gave to the " General Court" " power and authority" to " make laws and ordinances" " so always as the same be not contrary to the laws and statutes of our realm of England."

The first charter to Carolina, (including both North and South Carolina,) dated 1663, authorized the making of laws under this proviso — " Provided nevertheless, that the said laws be consonant to reason, and as near as may be conveniently, agreeable to the laws and customs of this our kingdom of England."

The second charter (1665) has this proviso. " Provided nevertheless, that the said laws be consonant to reason, and as near as may be conveniently, agreeable to the laws and customs of this our realm of England."

The charter to Georgia, (1732,) an hundred years after slavery had actually existed in Virginia, makes no mention of slavery, but requires the laws to be " reasonable and not repugnant to the laws of this our realm." " The said corporation shall and may form and prepare laws, statutes and ordinances fit and necessary for and concerning the government of the said colony, and not repugnant to the laws and statutes of England."

The charter to Maryland gave the power of making laws, " So, nevertheless, that the laws aforesaid be consonant to reason, and be not repugnant or contrary, but (so far as conveniently may be,) agreeable to the laws, statutes, customs, and rights of this our kingdom of England."

Those charters were the fundamental constitutions of the
colonies, with some immaterial exceptions, up to the time of the
revolution ; as much so as our national and state constitutions are
now the fundamental laws of our governments.

The authority of these charters, during their continuance, and
the general authority of the common law, prior to the revolution,
have been recognized by the Supreme Court of the United States.*

The charter granted to Sir Edward Plowden had this proviso. " So, nevertheless,
that the laws aforesaid be consonant to reason, and not repugnant and contrary,
(but as convenient as may be to the matter in question,) to the laws, statutes, customs
and rights of our kingdoms of England and Ireland."

In the charter to Pennsylvania, power was granted to make laws, and the people
were required to obey them, " Provided nevertheless that the said laws be consonant to reason, and be not repugnant or contrary, but, as near as conveniently may
be, agreeable to the laws, statutes, and rights of this our kingdom of England."

I have not been able to find a copy of the charter granted to the Duke of York,
of the territory comprising New York, New Jersey, &c. But Gordon, in his history
of the American Revolution, (vol. 1, p. 43,) says, " The King's grant to the Duke
of York, is plainly restrictive to the laws and government of England."

The charter to Connecticut gave power " Also from time to time, to make, ordain
and establish all manner of wholesome and reasonable laws, statutes, ordinances,
directions and instructions, not contrary to the laws of this realm of England."

The charter to the Massachusetts Bay Colony, (granted by William and Mary,)
gave " full power and authority, from time to time, to make, ordain and establish
all manner of wholesome and reasonable orders, laws, statutes and ordinances,
directions and instructions, either with penalties or without, so as the same be not
repugnant or contrary to the laws of this our realm of England."

The charter to Rhode Island granted the power of making laws, " So as such
laws, ordinances, constitutions, so made, be not contrary and repugnant unto, but
(as near as may be) agreeable to the laws of this our realm of England, considering
the nature and constitution of the place and people there."

Several other charters, patents, &c., that had a temporary existence, might be
named, that contained substantially the same provision.

* In the case of the town of Pawlet v. Clarke and others, the court say—

" Let us now see how far these principles were applicable to New Hampshire, at
the time of issuing the charter to Pawlet.

" New Hampshire was originally erected into a royal province in the thirty-first
year of Charles II., and from thence until the revolution continued a royal province,
under the immediate control and direction of the crown. By the first royal commis-
sion granted in 31 Charles II., among other things, judicial powers, in all actions,
were granted to the provincial governor and council, ' So always that the form of
proceeding in such cases, and the judgment thereupon to be given, be as consonant
and agreeable to the laws and statutes of this our realm of England, as the present
state and condition of our subjects inhabiting within the limits aforesaid (i. e. of
the province) and the circumstances of the place will admit.' *Independent, however, of such a provision, we take it to be a clear principle that the common law in
force at the emigration of our ancestors, is deemed the birthright of the colonies,
unless so far as it is inapplicable to their situation, or repugnant to their other rights
and privileges. A fortiori the principle applies to a royal province.*"—(9 Cranch's
U. States' Reports, 332 - 3.)

No one of all these charters that I have examined—and I have examined nearly all of them— contained the least intimation that slavery had, or could have any legal existence under them. Slavery was therefore as much unconstitutional in the colonies, as it was in England.

It was decided by the Court of King's Bench in England— Lord Mansfield being Chief Justice—before our revolution, and while the English Charters were the fundamental law of the colonies—that the principles of English liberty were so plainly incompatible with slavery, that even if a slaveholder, from another part of the world, brought his slave into England—though only for a temporary purpose, and with no intention of remaining—he nevertheless thereby gave the slave his liberty.

Previous to this decision, the privilege of bringing slaves into England, for temporary purposes, and of carrying them away, had long been tolerated.

This decision was given in the year 1772.* And for aught I see, it was equally obligatory in this country as in England, and must have freed every slave in this country, if the question had then been raised here. But the slave knew not his rights, and had no one to raise the question for him.

The fact, that slavery was *toleiated* in the colonies, is no evidence of its legality; for slavery was tolerated, to a certain extent, in England, (as we have already seen,) for many years previous to the decision just cited—that is, the holders of slaves from abroad were allowed to bring their slaves into England, hold them during their stay there, and carry them away when they went. But the toleration of this practice did not make it lawful, notwithstanding all customs, not palpably and grossly contrary to the principles of English liberty, have great weight, in England, in establishing law.

The fact, that England *tolerated*, (i. e. did not punish criminally,) the African *slave-trade* at that time, could not legally establish slavery in the colonies, *any more than it did in England*— especially in defiance of the positive requirements of the charters, that the colonial legislation should be consonant to reason, and not repugnant to the laws of England.

Besides, the mere toleration of the slave *trade* could not make slavery itself— *the right of property in man*— lawful anywhere;

---

* Somerset *v.* Stewart.—Lofft's Reports, p. 1 to 19, of Easter Term, 1772. In he Dub.in edition the case is not entered in the Index.

not even on board the slave ship. Toleration of a wrong is not
law. And especially the toleration of a wrong, (i. e. the bare
omission to punish it criminally,) does not legalize one's claim to
property obtained by such wrong. Even if a wrong can be legalized at all, so as to enable one to acquire rights of property by
such wrong, it can be done only by an explicit and positive provision.

The English statutes, on the subject of the slave trade, (so far
as I have seen,) never attempted to legalize the right of property
in man, *in any of the thirteen North American colonies.* It is
doubtful whether they ever attempted to do it anywhere else. It
is also doubtful whether Parliament had the power — or perhaps
rather it is certain that they had not the power — to legalize it
anywhere, if they had attempted to do so.* And the cautious
and curious phraseology of their statutes on the subject, indicates
plainly that they themselves either doubted their power to legalize
it, or feared to exercise it. They have therefore chosen to con-
nive at slavery, to insinuate, intimate, and imply their approbation
of it, rather than risk an affirmative enactment declaring that one
man may be the property of another. But Lord Mansfield said,
in Somerset's case, that slavery was *"so odious that nothing can
be suffered to support it, but positive law."* No such positive law
(I presume) was ever passed by Parliament — certainly not with
reference to any of these thirteen colonies.

The statute of 1788, (which I have not seen,) in regard to the
slave *trade*, may perhaps have relieved those engaged in it, in
certain cases, from their liability to be punished criminally for the
act. But there is a great difference between a statute, that should
merely screen a person from punishment for a crime, and one that
should legalize his right to property acquired by the crime.
Besides, this act was passed after the separation between America
and England, and therefore could have done nothing towards
legalizing slavery in the United States, even if it had legalized it
in the English dominions.

The statutes of 1750, (23, George 2d, Ch. 31,) may have
possibly authorized, by implication, (so far as Parliament could
thus authorize,) the colonial governments, (if governments they
could be called,) *on the coast of Africa*, to allow slavery under

---

* Have Parliament the constitutional prerogative of abolishing the writ of *habeas
corpus?* the trial by jury? or the freedom of speech and the press? If not, have
they the prerogative of abolishing a man's right of property in his own person ?

certain circumstances, *and within the " settlements " on that coast.*
But, if it did, it was at most a grant of a merely local authority.
It gave no authority to carry slaves from the African coast. But
even if it had purported distinctly to authorize the slave trade from
Africa to America, and to legalize the right of property in the
particular slaves thereafter brought from Africa to America, it
would nevertheless have done nothing towards legalizing the
right of property in the slaves that had been brought to, and born
in, the colonies for an hundred and thirty years previous to the
statute. Neither the statute, nor any right of property acquired
under it, (in the individual slaves thereafterwards brought from
Africa,) would therefore avail anything for the legality of slavery
in this country now ; because the descendants of those brought
from Africa under the act, cannot now be distinguished from the
descendants of those who had, for the hundred and thirty years
previous, been held in bondage without law.

But the presumption is, that, even after this statute was passed
in **1750,** if the slave trader's *right of property* in the slave he was
bringing to America, could have been brought before an English
court for adjudication, the same principles would have been held to
apply to it, as would have applied to a case arising within the
island of Great Britain. And it must therefore always have been
held by English courts, (in consistency with the decisions in
Somerset's case,) that the slave trader had no legal ownership of
his slave. And if the slave trader had no legal right of property
in his slave, he could transfer no legal right of property to a pur-
chaser in the colonies. Consequently the slavery of those that
were brought into the colonies after the statute of 1750, was equally illegal with that of those who had been brought in before.*

---

* Mr. Bancroft, in the third volume of his history, (pp. 413–14,) says :

" And the statute book of England soon declared the opinion of its king and its
Parliament, that ‘ the trade,’ " (by which he means the *slave* trade, of which he is
writing,) " ‘ is highly beneficial and advantageous to the kingdom and the colonies.’ "
To prove this he refers to statute of " 1695, 8 and 10 Wm. 3, ch. 26." (Should be
1697, 8—9 and 10 Wm. 3, ch. 26.)

Now the truth is that, although this statute may have been, and very probably
was designed to *insinuate* to the slave traders the personal approbation of Parliament to the slave trade, yet the statute itself says not a word of slaves, slavery, or
the slave trade, except to forbid, under penalty of five hundred pounds, any governor,
deputy-governor or judge, in the colonies or plantations in America, or any other
person or persons, for the use or on the behalf of such governor, deputy-governor or
judges, to be " a factor or factor's agent or agents" " for the sale or disposal of any
negroes."

The statute does not declare, as Mr. Bancroft asserts, that " the (slave) trade is

The conclusion of the whole matter is, that until some reason
appears against them, we are bound by the decision of the King's

highly beneficial and advantageous to the kingdom and the colonies ;" but that
" *the trade to Africa* is highly beneficial and advantageous," &c. It is an *inference*
of Mr. Bancroft's that " the trade to Africa" was the *slave* trade. Even this inference is not justified by the words of the statute, considering them in that legal
view, in which Mr. Bancroft's remarks purport to consider them.

It is true that the statute assumes that " *negroes*" will be " imported" from
Africa into " England," (where of course they were not slaves,) and into the
" plantations and colonies in America."   But it nowhere calls these " negroes"
slaves, nor assumes that they are slaves. For aught that appears from the statute,
they were free men and passengers, voluntary emigrants, going to " England" and
" the plantations and colonies" as laborers, as such persons are now going to the
British West Indies.

The statute, although it apparently desires to insinuate or faintly imply that they
are property, or slaves, nevertheless studiously avoids to acknowledge them as such
distinctly, or even by any necessary implication ; for it exempts them from duties
as merchandize, and from forfeiture for violation of revenue laws, and it also re-
lieves the masters of vessels from any obligation to render any account of them at
the custom houses.

When it is considered that slavery, property in man, can be legalized, according
to the decision of Lord Mansfield, by nothing less than positive law ; that the rights
of property and person are the same on board an English ship, as in the island of
Great Britain ; and that this statute implies that these " negroes" were to be " imported" into " England," as well as into the " plantations and colonies in America,"
and that it therefore no more implies that they were to be *slaves* in " the plantations and colonies" than in " England," where we know they could not be slaves ;
when these things are considered, it is perfectly clear, as a *legal* proposition, that
the statute legalized neither slavery in the plantations and colonies, nor the slave
trade from Africa to America — however we may suppose it to have been designed
to hint a personal approbation, on the part of Parliament, of the actual traffic.

But lest I may be suspected of having either misrepresented the words of the
statute, or placed upon them an erroneous legal construction, I give *all* the words
of the statute, that make any mention of " negroes," or their importation, with so
much of the context as will enable the reader to judge for himself of the legal import of the whole.

The act is entitled, " *An Act to settle the Trade to Africa.*" Sec. 1, recites as
follows : —

" Whereas, the Trade to Africa is highly beneficial and advantageous to this
kingdom and to the Plantations and Colonies thereunto belonging."

The act contains *twenty-one* sections, regulating trade, duties, &c., like any other
navigation act. " Negroes" are mentioned only in the following instances and
connexions, to wit :

Sec. 7. " And be it enacted by the authority aforesaid, That from and after the
four-and-twentieth day of June, one thousand six hundred ninety-and-eight, it shall
and may be lawful to and for any of the subjects of his majesty's realms of England,
as well as the said Company,* to trade from England or any of his majesty's plantations or colonies in America to the coast of Africa, between Blanco and Cape
Mount, answering and paying a duty of ten pounds per centum ad valorem for the
goods and merchandises to be exported from England or any of his majesty's plan-

* The Royal African Company.

Bench in 1772, and the colonial charters. That decision declared that there was, at that time, in England, no right of property in

tations or colonies in America to and for the coast of Africa, between Cape Blanco and Cape Mount, and in proportion for a greater or lesser value, and answering and paying a further sum and duty of ten pounds per centum ad valorem, red wood only excepted, which is to pay five pounds per centum ad valorem, at the place of importation upon all goods and merchandize (negroes excepted) imported in (into) England or any of his majesty's plantations or colonies in America, from the coast of Africa, between Cape Blanco and Cape Mount aforesaid. * * * And that all goods and merchandize, (negroes excepted,) that shall be laded or put on board any ship or vessel on the coast of Africa, between Cape Blanco and Cape Mount, and shall be imported into England or into any of his majesty's plantations or colonies aforesaid, shall answer and pay the duties aforesaid, and that the master or chief officer of every such ship or vessel that shall lade or receive any goods or merchandize (negroes excepted) on board of his or their ship or vessel between Cape Blanco and Cape Mount, shall upon making entry at any of his majesty's custom houses aforesaid of the said ship or vessel, or before any goods or merchandize be landed or taken out of the said ship or vessel (negroes excepted) shall deliver in a manifest or particular of his cargo, and take the following oath, viz.

"I, A. B., do swear that the manifest or particular now by me given in and signed, to the best of my knowledge and belief doth contain, signify and express all the goods, wares and merchandizes, (negroes excepted,) which were laden or put on board the ship called the ——————————, during her stay and continuing on the coast of Africa between Cape Blanco and Cape Mount, whereof I, A. B., am master."

Sec. 8. "And that the owner or importer of all goods and merchandize (negroes excepted) which shall be brought to England or any of his majesty's plantations from any port of Africa between Cape Blanco and Cape Mount aforesaid shall make entry of all such goods and merchandize at one of his majesty's chief custom houses in England, or in such of his majesty's plantations where the same shall be imported," &c.

Sec. 9. * * * * "that all goods or merchandizes (negroes excepted) which shall be brought from any part of Africa, between Cape Blanco and Cape Mount aforesaid, which shall be unladed or landed before entry made and signed and oath of the true and real value thereof made and the duty paid as aforesaid, shall be forfeited, or the value thereof."

Sec. 20. "And be it further enacted by the authority aforesaid, that no governor, or deputy-governor of any of his majesty's colonies or plantations in America, or his majesty's judges in any courts there for the time being, nor any other person or persons for the use or on behalf of such governor or deputy-governor or judges, from and after the nine-and-twentieth day of September, one thousand six hundred and ninety-eight, shall be a factor or factor's agent or agents for the said Company,* or any other person or persons for the sale or disposal of any negroes, and that every person offending herein shall forfeit five hundred pounds to the uses aforesaid, to be recovered in any of his majesty's courts of record at Westminster, by action of debt, bill, plaint or information, wherein no essoign, protection, privilege or wager of law shall be allowed, nor any more than one imparlance."

Sec. 21. "Provided that this act shall continue and be in force *thirteen years*, and from thence to the end of the next sessions of Parliament, and no longer."

Even if this act had legalized (as in reality it did not legalize) the slave trade during those thirteen years, it would be impossible now to distinguish the descend-

* The Royal African Company.

man, (notwithstanding the English government had for a long
time connived at the slave trade.) — The colonial charters required

---

ants of those who were imported under it, from the descendants of those who had
been previously, and were subsequently imported and sold into slavery without law.
The act would therefore avail nothing towards making the existing slavery in this
country legal.

The next statute, of which I find any trace, passed by Parliament, with any apparent view to countenance the slave trade, was the statute of 23d George II., ch.
31, (1749 — 50.)

Mr. Bancroft has committed another still more serious error in his statement of
the *words* (for he professes to quote precise words) of this statute. He says, (vol.
3, p. 414,)

" At last, in 1749, to give the highest activity to the trade, (meaning the slave
trade,) every obstruction to private enterprise was removed, and the ports of Africa
were laid open to English competition, for ' the *slave* trade,' — such" (says Mr.
Bancroft,) " are the words of the statute — ' the *slave* trade is very advantageous
to Great Britain.' "

As words are, in this case, things — and things of the highest *legal* consequence
— and as this history is so extensively read and received as authority — it becomes
important, in a legal, if not historical, point of view, to correct so important an
error as that of the word *slave* in this statement. " The *words* of the statute" are
not that " the *slave* trade," but that " *the trade to and from Africa* is very advantageous to Great Britain." " The trade to and from Africa" no more means, *in law,*
" the *slave* trade," than does the trade to and from China. From aught that appears, then, from *so much* of the preamble, " the trade to and from Africa" may
have been entirely in other things than slaves. And it actually appears from another
part of the statute, that trade was carried on in " gold, elephant's teeth, wax, gums
and drugs."

From the words immediately *succeeding* those quoted by Mr. Bancroft from the
preamble to this statute, it might much more plausibly, (although even from them
it could not be legally) inferred that the statute legalized the slave trade, than from
those pretended to be quoted by him. That the succeeding words may be seen, the
title and preamble to the act are given, as follows :

" *An act for extending and improving the trade to Africa.*"

" Whereas, the trade to and from Africa is very advantageous to Great Britain,
*and necessary for supplying the plantations and colonies thereunto belonging, with
a sufficient number of* NEGROES *at reasonable rates ;* and for that purpose the said
trade" (i. e. " the trade to and from Africa") " ought to be free and open to all his
majesty's subjects. Therefore be it enacted," &c.

" Negroes" were not slaves by the English law, and therefore the word " negroes,"
in this preamble, does not *legally* mean slaves. For aught that appears from the
words of the preamble, *or even from any part of the statute itself,* these " negroes,"
with whom it is declared to be necessary that the plantations and colonies should
be supplied, were free persons, voluntary emigrants, that were to be induced to go
to the plantations as hired laborers, as are those who, at this day, are induced, in
large numbers, and by the special agency of the English government, to go to the
British West Indies. In order to facilitate this emigration, it was necessary that
" the trade to and from Africa" should be encouraged. And the form of the preamble is such as it properly might have been, if such had been the real object of
Parliament. Such is undoubtedly the true *legal* meaning of this preamble, for this
meaning being consistent with natural right, public policy, and with the fundamental principles of English law, legal rules of construction imperatively require

the legislation of the colonies to be " consonant to reason, and not repugnant or contrary, but conformable, or agreeable, as nearly as

that this meaning should be ascribed to it, rather than it should be held to authorize anything contrary to natural right, or contrary to the fundamental principles of British law.

We are obliged to put this construction upon this preamble, for the further reason that it corresponds with the enacting clauses of the statute — not one of which mentions such a thing *as the transportation of slaves to, or the sale of slaves in* " the plantations and colonies." The first section of the act is in these words, to wit:

"That it shall and may be lawful for all his majesty's subjects to trade and traffic to and from any port or place in Africa, between the port of Sallee in South Barbary, and the Cape of Good Hope, when, at such times, and in such manner, and in or with such quantity of *goods, wares and merchandizes,* as he or they shall think fit, without any restraint whatsoever, save as is herein after expressed."

Here plainly is no authority given " to trade and traffic " in anything except what is known either to the English law, or the law of nature, as " goods, wares, or merchandizes " — among which *men* were *not* known, either to the English law, or the law of nature.

The second section of the act is in these words:

" That all his majesty's subjects, who shall trade to or from any of the ports or places of Africa, between Cape Blanco and the Cape of Good Hope, shall forever hereafter be a body corporate and politic, in name and in deed, by the name of the Company of Merchants Trading to Africa, and by the same name shall have perpetual succession, and shall have a common seal, and by that name shall and may sue, and be sued, and do any other act, matter and thing, which any other body corporate or politic, as such, may lawfully do."

Neither this nor any other section of the act purports to give this "Company," in its corporate capacity, any authority to buy or sell slaves, or to transport slaves to the plantations and colonies.

The twenty-ninth section of the act is in these words:

"And be it further enacted, by the authority aforesaid, that no commander or master of any ship trading to Africa, shall by *fraud, force or violence,* or by any other indirect practice whatsoever, take on board, or carry away from the coast of Africa, any negro or native of the said country, or commit, or suffer to be committed, any violence on the natives, to the prejudice of the said trade; and that every person so offending shall, for every such offence, forfeit the sum of one hundred pounds of lawful money of Great Britain ; one moiety thereof to the use of the said Company hereby established, and their successors, for and towards the maintaining of said forts and settlements, and the other moiety to and for the use of him or them who shall inform or sue for the same."

Now, although there is perhaps no good reason to doubt that the *secret* intention of Parliament in the passage of this act, was to stimulate the slave trade, and that there was a tacit understanding between the government and the slave dealers, that the slave trade should go on unharmed (in practice) by the government, and although it was undoubtedly understood that this penalty of one hundred pounds would either not be sued for at all, or would be sued for so seldom as *practically* to interpose no obstacle to the general success of the trade, still, as no part of the whole statute gives any authority to this "Company of Merchants trading to Africa " to transport men from Africa against their will, and as this twenty-ninth section contains a special prohibition to individuals, under penalty, to do so, no one can pretend that the trade was legalized. If the penalty had been but one pound, instead of one hundred pounds, it would have been sufficient, *in law* to have

3*

circumstances would allow, to the laws, statutes and rights of the realm of England." That decision, then, if correct, settled the

---

rebutted the pretence that the trade was legalized. The act, on its face and in its legal meaning, is much more an act to prohibit, than to authorize the slave trade.

The only possible *legal* inference from the statute, *so far as concerns the "supplying the plantations and colonies with negroes at reasonable rates,"* is, that these negroes were free laborers, voluntary emigrants, that were to be induced to go to the plantations and colonies; and that "the trade to and from Africa" was thrown open in order that the facilities for the transportation of these emigrants might be increased.

But although there is, in this statute, no authority given for — but, on the contrary, a special prohibition upon — the transportation of the natives from Africa against their will, yet I freely admit that the statute contains one or two strong, perhaps decisive implications in favor of the fact that slavery was allowed in the English settlements on *the coast of Africa,* apparently in conformity with the customs of the country, and with the approbation of Parliament. But that is the most that can be said of it. Slavery, wherever it exists, is a local institution; and its toleration, or even its legality, *on the coast of Africa,* would do nothing towards making it legal in any other part of the English dominions. Nothing but positive and explicit legislation could transplant it into any other part of the empire.

The implications, furnished by the act, in favor of the toleration of slavery, in the English settlements, on the coast of Africa, are the following:

The third section of the act refers to another act of Parliament "divesting the Royal African Company of their *charter,* forts, castles and military stores, canoe men and *castle-slaves;"* and section thirty-first requires that such "officers of his majesty's navy," as shall be appointed for the purpose, "shall inspect and examine the state and condition of the forts and settlements on the coast of Africa, in the possession of the Royal African Company, and of the number of the soldiers therein, and also the state and condition of the military stores, castles, *slaves,* canoes and other vessels and things, belonging to the said company, *and necessary for the use and defence of the said forts and settlements,* and shall with all possible despatch report how they find the same."

Here the fact is stated that the "Royal African Company," (a company that had been in existence long previous to the passing of this act,) had held "castle slaves" "for the use and defence of the said forts and settlements." The act does not say directly whether this practice was legal or illegal; although it seems to imply that, whether legal or illegal, it was tolerated with the knowledge and approbation of Parliament. '

But the most distinct approbation given to slavery by the act, is implied in the twenty-eighth section, in these words:

"That it shall and may be lawful for any of his majesty's subjects trading to Africa, for the security of their goods and *slaves,* to erect houses and warehouses, under the protection of the said forts," &c.

Although even this language would not be strong enough to overturn previously established principles of English law, and give the slave holders a legal right of property in their slaves, in any place where English law had previously been expressly established, (as it had been in the North American colonies,) yet it sufficiently evinces that Parliament approved of Englishmen holding slaves in the settlements *on the coast of Africa,* in conformity with the customs of that country. But it implies no authority for transporting their slaves to America; it does nothing towards legalizing slavery in America; it implies no *toleration* even of slavery anywhere, except upon the coast of Africa. Had slavery been positively and *law* both for England and the colonies. And if so, there was no *constitutional* slavery in the colonies up to the time of the revolution.

---

explicitly legalized on the coast of Africa, it would still have been a local institution.

This reasoning may appear to some like quibbling ; and it would perhaps be so, were not the rule well settled that nothing but explicit and irresistible language can be legally held to authorize anything inconsistent with natural right, and with the fundamental principles of a government.

That this statute did not legalize the right of property in man, (unless as a local principle on the coast of Africa,) we have the decision of Lord Mansfield, who held that it did not legalize it in England ; and if it did not legalize it in England, it did not legalize it in any of the colonies where the principles of the common law prevailed. Of course it did not legalize it in the North American colonies.

But even if it were admitted that this statute legalized the right of property, on the part of the slave trader, in his slaves taken in Africa after the passage of the act, and legalized the sale of such slaves in America, still the statute would be ineffectual to sustain the legality of slavery, *in general,* in the colonies. It would only legalize the slavery of those particular individuals, who should be transported from Africa to America, subsequently to the passage of this act, and in strict conformity with the law of this act — (a thing, by the way, that could now be proved in no case whatever.) This act was passed in 1749 — 50, and could therefore do nothing towards legalizing the slavery of all those who had, for an hundred and thirty years previous, been held in bondage in Virginia and elsewhere. And as no distinction can now be traced between the descendants of those who were imported under this act, and those who had illegally been held in bondage prior to its passage, it would be of no practical avail to slavery now, to prove, (if it could be proved,) that those introduced into the country subsequent to 1750, were legally the property of those who introduced them.

CHAPTER IV.

COLONIAL STATUTES.

But the colonial legislation on the subject of slavery, was not only void as being forbidden by the colonial charters, but in many of the colonies it was void for another reason, viz., *that it did not sufficiently define the persons who might be made slaves.*

Slavery, if it can be legalized at all, can be legalized only by positive legislation. Natural law gives it no aid. Custom imparts to it no legal sanction. This was the doctrine of the King's Bench in Somerset's case, as it is the doctrine of common sense. Lord Mansfield said, " So high an act of dominion must be recognized by the law of the country where it is used. ＊ ＊ ＊ The state of slavery is of such a nature, that it is incapable of being introduced on any reasons, moral or political — but only positive law, which preserves its force long after the reasons, occasion, and time itself from whence it was created, is erased from the memory. It is so odious that nothing can be suffered to support it but positive law."

Slavery, then, being the creature of positive legislation alone, can be created only by legislation that shall so particularly describe the persons to be made slaves, that they may be distinguished from all others. If there be any doubt left by the *letter* of the law, as to the persons to be made slaves, the efficacy of all other slave legislation is defeated simply by that uncertainty.

In several of the colonies, including some of those where slaves were most numerous, there were either no laws at all defining the persons who might be made slaves, or the laws, which attempted to define them, were so loosely framed that it cannot now be known who are the descendants of those designated as slaves, and who of those held in slavery without any color of law. As the presumption must — *under the United States constitution* — and indeed under the state constitutions also — be always in favor of liberty, it would probably now be impossible for a slaveholder to prove, in one case in an hundred, that his slave was descended, (through the maternal line, according to the slave code,) from any one who was originally a slave within the description given by the statutes.

When slavery was first introduced into the country, there were no laws at all on the subject. Men bought slaves of the slave traders, as they would have bought horses; and held them, and compelled them to labor, as they would have done horses, that is, by brute force. By common consent among the white race, this practice was tolerated without any law. At length slaves had in this way become so numerous, that some regulations became necessary, and the colonial governments began to pass statutes, which *assumed* the existence of slaves, although no laws defining the persons who might be made slaves, had ever been enacted. For instance, they passed statutes for the summary trial and punishment of slaves; statutes permitting the masters to chastise and baptize their slaves,* and providing that baptism should not be considered, in law, an emancipation of them. Yet all the while no act had been passed declaring who might be slaves. Possession was apparently all the evidence that public sentiment

* *"Chastise."* An act passed in South Carolina in 1740, authorized slaves to sue for their liberty, by a guardian appointed for the purpose. The act then provides that if judgment be for the slave, he shall be set free, and recover damages; "but in case judgment shall be given for the defendant, (the master,) the said court is hereby fully empowered to inflict such corporeal punishment, not extending to life or limb, on the ward of the plaintiff, (the slave,) as they in their discretion shall see fit."— *Brevard's Digest, vol. 2, p.* 130.

"*Baptize.*" In 1712 South Carolina passed this act:

" Since charity and the Christian religion which we profess, obliges us to wish well to the souls of all men, and that religion may not be made a pretence to alter any man's property and right, and that no persons may neglect to baptize their negroes or slaves, or suffer them to be baptized, for fear that thereby they should be manumitted and set free: *Be it therefore enacted,* That it shall be, and is hereby declared lawful for any negro or Indian slave, or any other slave or slaves whatsoever, to receive and profess the Christian faith, and be thereunto baptized. But that notwithstanding such slave or slaves shall receive and profess the Christian religion, and be baptized, he or they shall not thereby be manumitted or set free, or his or their owner, master or mistress lose his or their civil right, property and authority over such slave or slaves, but that the slave or slaves, with respect to his or their servitude, shall remain and continue in the same state and condition, that he or they was in before the making of this act."— *Grimke, p.* 18. *Brevard, vol. 2, p.* 229.

In 1667, the following statute was passed in Virginia:

" Whereas, some doubts have arisen whether children that are slaves by birth, and by the charity and piety of their owners made partakers of the blessed sacrament of baptism, should by virtue of their baptism be made free; *It is enacted and declared by this grand assembly, and the authority thereof,* that the conferring of baptism doth not alter the condition of the person as to his bondage or freedom; that divers masters, freed from this doubt, may more carefully endeavour the propagation of Christianity by permitting children, though slaves, or those of greater growth, if capable to be admitted to that sacrament."— *Hening's Statutes, vol 2. p.* 260.

demanded, of a master's property in his slave.   Under such a code, multitudes, who had either never been purchased as slaves, or who had once been emancipated, were doubtless seized and reduced to servitude by individual rapacity, without any more public cognizance of the act, than if the person so seized had been a stray sheep.

Virginia.   Incredible as it may seem, slavery had existed in Virginia fifty years before even a statute was passed for the purpose of declaring who might be slaves ; and then the persons were so described as to make the designation of no legal effect, at least as against Africans generally.   And it was not until seventy-eight years more, (an hundred and twenty-eight years in all,) that any act was passed that would cover the case of the Africans generally, and make them slaves.   Slavery was introduced in 1620, but no act was passed even purporting to declare who might be slaves, until 1670.   In that year a statute was passed in these words : " That all *servants*, not being Christians, imported into this country by shipping, shall be slaves for their lives."[*]

This word " servants " of course legally describes individuals known as such to the laws, and distinguished as such from other persons generally.   But no class of Africans " imported," were known as " servants," as distinguished from Africans generally, or in any manner to bring them within the legal description of " servants," as here used.   In 1682 and in 1705 acts were again passed declaring " that all servants," &c., imported, should be slaves.   And it was not until 1748, *after slavery had existed an hundred and twenty-eight years*, that this description was changed for the following :

" That all *persons*, who have been or shall be imported into this colony," &c., &c., shall be slaves.[†]

In 1776, the only statute in Virginia, under which the slaveholders could make any claim at all to their slaves, was passed as late as 1753, (one hundred and thirty-three years after slavery had been introduced;) all prior acts having been then repealed, without saving the rights acquired under them.[‡]

---

[*] Hening, vol. 2, p. 283.

[†] Hening, vol. 5, p. 547–8.

[‡] In 1753 Virginia passed a statute, occupying some twelve or fifteen pages of the statute book, and intended to cover the whole general subject of slavery.   One of the sections of this act is as follows :

" That all and every other act and acts, clause and clauses, heretofore made, for

Even if the colonial charters had contained no express prohibition upon slave laws, it would nevertheless be absurd to pretend that the colonial legislature had power, in 1753, to look back an hundred and thirty-three years, and arbitrarily reduce to slavery all colored persons that had been imported into, or born in the colony within that time. If they could not do this, then it follows that all the colored persons in Virginia, up to 1753, (only twenty-three years before the revolution,) and all their descendants to the present time, were and are free; and they cannot now be distinguished from the descendants of those subsequently imported. Under the presumption — furnished by the constitution of the United States — that all are free, few or no exceptions could now be proved.

In North Carolina no general law at all was passed, prior to the revolution, declaring who might be slaves —(See Iredell's statutes, revised by Martin.)

In South Carolina, the only statutes, prior to the revolution, tha' attempted to designate the slaves, was passed in 1740 —after slavery had for a long time existed. And even this statute, in reality, defined nothing; for the whole purport of it was, to declare that all negroes, Indians, mulattoes and mestizoes, *except those who were then free,* should be slaves. Inasmuch as no prior statute had ever been passed, declaring who should be slaves, *all were legally free;* and therefore all came within the exception in favor of free persons.*

---

or concerning any matter or thing within the provision of this act, shall be and are hereby repealed."— *Hening's Statutes, vol. 6, p. 369.*

No reservation being made, by this section, of rights acquired under former statutes, and slave property being a matter dependent entirely upon statute, all title to slave property, acquired under former acts, was by this act annihilated; and all the slaves in the State were made freemen, *as against all prior legislation.* And the slaves of the State were thenceforward held in bondage only by virtue of another section of the same act, which was in these words:

"That all persons *who have been,* or shall be imported into this colony, by sea or land, and were not Christians in their native country, except Turks and Moors in amity with his majesty, and such who can prove their being free in England, or any other Christian country, before they were shipped for transportation hither, shall be accounted slaves, and as such be here bought and sold, notwithstanding a conversion to Christianity after their importation." —*Hening, vol. 6, p. 356–7.*

The act also provided, "That all children shall be bond or free, according to the condition of their mothers and the particular directions of this act."

* The following is the preamble and the important enacting clause of this statute of 1740:

"Whereas, in his majesty's plantations in America, slavery has been introduced

The same law, in nearly the same words, was passed in Georgia, in 1770.

These were the only general statutes, under which slaves were held in those four States, (Virginia, North Carolina, South Carolina and Georgia,) at the time of the revolution. They would all, for the reasons given, have amounted to nothing, as a foundation for the slavery now existing in those states, even if they had not been specially prohibited by their charters.

CHAPTER V.

THE DECLARATION OF INDEPENDENCE.

ADMITTING, for the sake of the argument, that prior to the revolution, slavery had a constitutional existence, (so far as it is possible that crime can have such an existence,) was it not abolished by the declaration of independence ?

The declaration was certainly the constitutional law of this country for certain purposes. For example, it absolved the people from their allegiance to the English crown. It would have been so declared by the judicial tribunals of this country, if an American, during the revolutionary war, or since, had been tried for treason to the crown. If, then, the declaration were the constitutional law of the country for that purpose, was it not also constitutional law for the purpose of recognizing and establishing, as law, the natural and inalienable right of individuals to life, liberty, and the pursuit of happiness ? The lawfulness of the act of absolving

---

and allowed ; and the people commonly called negroes, Indians, mulattos and mestizoes have (been) deemed absolute slaves, and the subjects of property in the hands of particular persons ; the extent of whose power over such slaves ought to be settled and limited by positive laws, so that the slaves may be kept in due subjection and obedience, and the owners and other persons having the care and government of slaves, may be restrained from exercising too great rigor and cruelty over them ; and that the public peace and order of this province may be preserved : *Be it enacted,* That all negroes, Indians, (*free* Indians in amity with this government, and negroes, mulattos and mestizoes, *who are now free, excepted,*) mulattos and mestizoes, who now are or shall hereafter be in this province, and all their issue and offspring born or to be born, shall be and they are hereby declared to be and remain forever hereafter absolute slaves, and shall follow the condition of the mother," &c. — *(Grimke, p.* 163 – 4. *Brevard, vol.* 2, *p.* 229.

themselves from their allegiance to the crown, was avowed by the people of the country—and that too in the same instrument that declared the absolution—to rest entirely upon, and to be only a consequence of the natural right of all men to life, liberty, and the pursuit of happiness. If, then, the act of absolution was lawful, does it not necessarily follow that the principles that legalized the act, were also law? And if the country ratified the act of absolution, did they not also necessarily ratify and acknowledge the principles which they declared legalized the act?

It is sufficient for our purpose, if it be admitted that this principle was the law of the country at that particular time, (1776)—even though it had continued to be the law for only a year, or even a day. For if it were the law of the country even for a day, it freed every slave in the country — (if there were, as we say there were not, any legal slaves then in the country.) And the burden would then be upon the slaveholder to show that slavery had *since* been *constitutionally* established. And to show this, he must show an express *constitutional* designation of the particular individuals, who have since been made slaves. Without such particular designation of the individuals to be made slaves, (and not even the present constitutions of the slave States make any such designation,) all constitutional provisions, purporting to authorize slavery, are indefinite, and uncertain in their application, and for that reason void.

But again. The people of this country—in the very instrument by which they first announced their independent political existence, and first asserted their right to establish governments of their own—declared that the natural and inalienable right of all men to life, liberty, and the pursuit of happiness, was a "*self-evident truth*."

Now, all "*self-evident truths*," except such as may be explicitly, or by necessary implication, denied, (and no government has a right to deny any of them,) enter into, are taken for granted by, and constitute an essential part of all constitutions, compacts, and systems of government whatsoever. Otherwise it would be impossible for any systematic government to be established; for it must obviously be impossible to make an actual enumeration of all the "self-evident truths," that are to be taken into account in the administration of such a government. This is more especially true of governments founded, like ours, upon contract. It is clearly impossible, in a contract of government, to enumerate all

4

the "self-evident truths" which must be acted upon in the
administration of law.   And therefore they are *all* taken for
granted unless particular ones be plainly denied.

This principle, that all "self-evident truths," though not enume-
rated, make a part of all laws and contracts, unless clearly denied,
is not only indispensable to the very existence of civil society, but
it is even indispensable to the administration of justice in every
individual case or suit, that may arise, out of contract or otherwise,
between individuals.   It would be impossible for individuals to
make contracts at all, if it were necessary for them to enumerate
all the "self-evident truths," that might have a bearing upon their
construction before a judicial tribunal.   All such truths are therefore taken for granted.   And it is the same in all compacts of
government, unless particular truths are plainly denied.   And
governments, no more than individuals, have a right to deny them
in any case.   To deny, in any case, that "self-evident truths" are
a part of the law, is equivalent to asserting that "self-evident
falsehood" is law.

If, then, it be a "self-evident truth," that all men have a natural
and inalienable right to life, liberty, and the pursuit of happiness,
that truth constitutes a part of all our laws and all our constitutions, unless it have been unequivocally and authoritatively denied.

It will hereafter be shown that this "self-evident truth" has
never been denied by the people of this country, in their fundamental constitution, or in any other explicit or authoritative manner.   On the contrary, it has been reiterated, by them, annually,
daily and hourly, for the last sixty-nine years, in almost every
possible way, and in the most solemn possible manner.   On the
4th of July, '76, they collectively asserted it, as their justification
and authority for an act the most momentous and responsible of
any in the history of the country.   And this assertion has never
been retracted by us as a people.   We have virtually reässerted
the same truth in nearly every state constitution since adopted.
We have virtually reässerted it in the national constitution.   It
is a truth that lives on the tongues and in the hearts of all.   It is
true we have, in our practice, been so unjust as to withhold the
benefits of this truth from a certain class of our fellow-men.   But
even in this respect, this truth has but shared the common fate of
other truths.   They are generally allowed but a partial application.   Still, this truth itself, *as a truth*, has never been denied by
us, *as a people*, in any authentic form, or otherwise than impliedly

by our practice in particular cases. If it have, say when and where If it have not, it is still law; and courts are bound to adminiter it, as law, impartially to all.

Our courts would want no other authority than this truth, thus acknowledged, for setting at liberty any individual, other than one having negro blood, whom our governments, state or national, should assume to authorize another individual to enslave. Why then, do they not apply the same law in behalf of the African? Certainly not because it is not as much the law of his case, as of others. *But it is simply because they will not.* It is because the courts are parties to an understanding, prevailing among the white race, but expressed in no authentic constitutional form, that the negro may be deprived of his rights at the pleasure of avarice and power. And they carry out this unexpressed understanding in defiance of, and suffer it to prevail over, all our constitutional principles of government — all our authentic, avowed, open and fundamental law.

CHAPTER VI.

THE STATE CONSTITUTIONS OF 1789.

Of all the state constitutions, that were in force at the adoption of the constitution of the United States, in 1789, *not one of them established, or recognized slavery.*

All those parts of the state constitutions, (i. e. of the old thirteen states,) that recognize and attempt to sanction slavery, *have been inserted, by amendments, since the adoption of the constitution of the United States.*

All the states, except Rhode Island and Connecticut, formed constitutions prior to 1789. Those two states went on, beyond this period, under their old charters.*

---

* The State Constitutions of 1789 were adopted as follows: Georgia, 1777 · South Carolina, 1778; North Carolina, 1776; Virginia, 1776; Maryland, 1776; Delaware, 1776; Pennsylvania, 1776; New Jersey, 1776; New York, 1777; Massachusetts, 1780; New Hampshire, 1783.

These early Constitutions ought to be collected and published with appropriate notes.

The eleven constitutions formed, were all democratic in their general character. The most of them eminently so. They generally recognized, in some form or other, the natural rights of men, as one of the fundamental principles of the government. Several of them asserted these rights in the most emphatic and authoritative manner. Most or all of them had also specific provisions incompatible with slavery. Not one of them had any specific recognition of the existence of slavery. Not one of them granted any specific authority for its continuance.

The only provisions or words in any of them, that could be claimed by anybody as recognitions of slavery, are the following, viz. :

1. The use of the words " our negroes " in the preamble to the constitution of Virginia.

2. The mention of " slaves " in the preamble to the constitution of Pennsylvania.

3. The provisions, in some of the constitutions, for continuing in force the laws that had previously been " in force " in the colonies, except when altered by, or incompatible with the new constitution.

4. The use, in several of the constitutions, of the words " free " and " freemen."

As each of these terms and clauses may be claimed by some persons as recognitions of slavery, they are worthy of particular notice.

1. The preamble to the frame of government of the constitution of Virginia speaks of negroes in this connexion, to wit : It charges George the Third, among other things, with " prompting *our negroes* to rise in arms among us, those very negroes, whom. by an inhuman use of his negative, he hath refused us permission to exclude by law."

Here is no assertion that these " negroes " were slaves ; but only that they were a class of people whom the Virginians did not wish to have in the state, *in any capacity* — whom they wished " to exclude by law." The language, considered as legal language, no more implies that they were slaves, than the charge of having prompted " our women, children, farmers, mechanics, or our people with red hair, or our people with blue eyes, or our Dutchmen, or our Irishmen to rise in arms among us," would have implied that those portions of the people of Virginia were slaves. And especially when it is considered that slavery had had no prior *legal* existence, this reference to "negroes" authorizes no legal inference whatever in regard to slavery.

The rest of the Virginia constitution is eminently democratic. The bill of rights declares "that all men are by nature equally free and independent, and have certain inherent rights," * * "namely, the enjoyment of life and liberty, with the means of acquiring and possessing property, and pursuing and obtaining happiness and safety."

2. The preamble to the Pennsylvania constitution used the word "slaves" in this connexion. It recited that the king of Great Britain had employed against the inhabitants of that commonwealth, "foreign mercenaries, savages and slaves."

This is no acknowledgment that they themselves had any slaves of their own; much less that they were going to continue their slavery; for the constitution contained provisions plainly incompatible with that. Such, for instance, is the following, which constitutes the first article of the "Declaration of Rights of the Inhabitants," (i. e. of *all* the inhabitants) "of the state of Pennsylvania."

"1. That all men are born equally free and independent, and have certain natural, inherent and inalienable rights, among which are, the enjoying and defending life and liberty, acquiring, possessing and protecting property, and pursuing and obtaining happiness and safety."

The 46th section of the frame of government is in these words.

"The Declaration of Rights is hereby declared to be a part of the constitution of this commonwealth, and ought never to be violated on any pretence whatever."

Slavery was clearly impossible under these two constitutional provisions, to say nothing of others.

3. Several of the constitutions provide that all the laws of the colonies, previously " *in force* " should continue in force until repealed, *unless repugnant to some of the principles of the constitutions themselves.*

Maryland, New York, New Jersey, South Carolina, and perhaps one or two others had provisions of this character. *North Carolina had none, Georgia none, Virginia none.* The slave laws of these three latter states, then, necessarily fell to the ground on this change of government.

Maryland, New York, New Jersey and South Carolina had acts upon their statute books, *assuming* the existence of slavery, and

4*

pretending to legislate in regard to it; and it may perhaps be argued that those laws were continued in force under the provision referred to. But those acts do not come within the above description of " laws in force "— and for this reason, viz., the acts were originally unconstitutional and void, as being against the charters, under which they were passed; and therefore never had been *legally* " in force," however they might have been actually carried into execution as a matter of might, or of pretended law, by the white race.

This objection applies to the slave acts of all the colonies None of them could be continued under this provision.— None of them, legally speaking, were " laws in force."

But in particular states there were still other reasons against the colonial slave acts being valid under the new constitutions. For instance: South Carolina had no statute (as has before been mentioned) that designated her slaves with such particularity as to distinguish them from free persons ; and for that reason none of her slave statutes were *legally* " in force."

New Jersey also was in the same situation. She had slave statutes ; but none designating the slaves so as to distinguish them from the rest of her population. She had also one or more specific provisions in her constitution incompatible with slavery, to wit: " That the common law of England * * * * * *shall remain in force,* until altered by a future law of the legislature; such parts only as are repugnant to the rights and privileges contained in this charter." (Sec. 22.)

Maryland had also, in her new constitution, a specific provision incompatible with the acts on her colonial statute book in regard to slavery, to wit :

" Sec. 3. That the *inhabitants*"— mark the word, for it includes *all* the inhabitants —" that the *inhabitants* of Maryland are entitled to the common law of England, and the trial by jury, according to the course of that law," &c.

This guaranty, of " the common law of England " to *all* " the inhabitants of Maryland," without discrimination, is incompatible with any slave acts that existed on the statute book ; and the latter would therefore have become void under the constitution, even if they had not been previously void under the colonial charter.

4. Several of these state constitutions have used the words " free " and " freemen."

For instance: That of South Carolina provided, (Sec. 13,)

THE STATE CONSTITUTIONS OF 1789.

that the electors of that state should be "*free* white men." That of Georgia (Art. 11,) and that of North Carolina (Art. 40,) use the term " free citizen." That of Pennsylvania (Sec. 42,) has the term " free denizen."

These four instances are the only ones I have found in all the eleven constitutions, where any class of persons are designated by the term " free." And it will be seen hereafter, from the connexion and manner in which the word is used, in these four cases, that it implies no recognition of slavery.

Several of the constitutions, to wit, those of Georgia, South Carolina, North Carolina, Maryland, Delaware, Pennsylvania, New York—but not Virginia, New Jersey, Massachusetts or New Hampshire — repeatedly use the word " freeman" or " freemen," when describing the electors, or other members of the state.

The only questions that can arise from the use of these words " free " and " freeman," are these, viz. : Are they used as the correlatives, or opposites of slaves? Or are they used in that political sense, in which they are used in the common law of England, and in which they had been used in the colonial charters, viz., to describe those persons possessed of the privilege of citizenship, or some corporate franchise, as distinguished from aliens, and those not enjoying franchises, although free from personal slavery ?

If it be answered, that they are used in the sense first mentioned, to wit, as the correlatives or opposites of slavery — then it would be argued that they involved a recognition, at least, of the existence of slavery.

But this argument — whatever it might be worth to support an implied admission of the *actual* existence of slavery — would be entirely insufficient to support an implied admission either of its *legal*, or its *continued* existence. Slavery is so entirely contrary to natural right; so entirely destitute of authority from natural law; so palpably inconsistent with all the legitimate objects of government, that nothing but express and explicit provision can be recognized, in law, as giving it any sanction. No hints, insinuations, or unnecessary implications can give any ground for so glaring a ·parture from, and violation of all the other, the general and the le itimate principles of the government. If, then, it were admitted that the words " free " and " freemen " were used as the correlatives of slaves, still, of themselves, the words would give no direct or sufficient authority for laws establishing or continuing slavery. To call one man free, gives no legal authority for mak

ing another man a slave.   And if, as in the case of these constitutions, no express authority for slavery were given, slavery would
be as much unconstitutional as though these words had not been
used.   The use of these words in that sense, in a constitution,
under which all persons are presumed to be free, would involve no
absurdity, although it might be gratuitous and unnecessary.

It is a rule of law, in the construction of all statutes, contracts
and legal instruments whatsoever — *that is, those which courts
design, not to invalidate, but to enforce* — that where words are
susceptible of two meanings, one consistent, and the other inconsistent, with liberty, justice and right, that sense is always to be
adopted, which is consistent with right, unless there be something
in other parts of the instrument sufficient to prove that the other
is the true meaning.   In the case of no one of all these early state
constitutions, is there anything in the other parts of them, to show
that these words " free " and " freemen " are used as the correlatives of slavery.   The rule of law, therefore, is imperative, that
they must be regarded in the sense consistent with liberty and
right.

If this rule, that requires courts to give an innocent construction
to all words that are susceptible of it, were not imperative, courts
might, at their own pleasure, pervert the honest meaning of the
most honest statutes and contracts, into something dishonest, for
there are almost always words used in the most honest legislation,
and in the most honest contracts, that, by implication or otherwise,
are capable of conveying more than one meaning, and even a dishonest meaning.   If courts *could* lawfully depart from the rule,
that requires them to attribute an honest meaning to all language
that is susceptible of such a meaning, it would be nearly impossible
to frame either a statute or a contract, which the judiciary might
not *lawfully* pervert to some purpose of injustice.   There would
obviously be no security for the honest administration of any
honest law or contract whatsoever.

This rule applies as well to constitutions as to contracts and
statutes; for constitutions are but contracts between the people,
whereby they grant authority to, and establish law for the government.

What other meaning, then, than as correlatives of slavery, are
the words " free " and " freemen " susceptible of, as they are used
in the early state constitutions ?

Among the definitions given by Noah Webster are these :

" *Freeman.* One who enjoys, or is entitled to a franchise **or** peculiar privilege ; as the freemen of a city or state."

"*Free.* Invested with franchises ; enjoying certain immunities : with *of*— as a man *free of* the city of London."

" Possessing without vassalage, or slavish conditions ; as a man *free of* his farm."

In England, and in the English law throughout, as it existed before and since the emigration of our ancestors to this country, the words " free " and " freemen " were political terms in the most common use ; and employed to designate persons enjoying some franchise or privilege, from the most important one of general citizenship in the nation, to the most insignificant one in any incorporated city, town or company. For instance : A man was said to be a " free British subject "— meaning thereby that he was a naturalized or native born citizen of the British government, as distinguished from an alien, or person neither naturalized nor native born.

Again. A man was said to be " free of a particular trade in the city of London "— meaning thereby, that by the bye-laws of the city of London, he was permitted to follow that trade — a privilege which others could not have without having served an apprenticeship in the city, or having purchased the privilege of the city government.

The terms " free " and " freemen " were used with reference to a great variety of privileges, which, in England, were granted to one man, and not to another. Thus members of incorporated companies were called "*freemen* of the company," or "*free* members of the company ;" and were said to be "*free* of the said company." The citizens of an incorporated city were called " the freemen of the city," as " freemen of the city of London."

In Jacobs' Law Dictionary the following definitions, among others, are given of the word " freeman."

" *Freeman* — *liber homo.*" * * " In the distinction of a freeman from a vassal under the feudal policy, *liber homo* was commonly opposed to *vassus,* or *vassalus ;* the former denoting an *allodial* proprietor ; the latter one who held of a superior."

" The title of a *freeman* is also given to any one admitted to the freedom of a corporate town, or of any other corporate body, consisting, among other members, of those called *freemen.*"

" There are three ways to be a *freeman* of London ; by servitude of an apprenticeship ; by birthright, as being the son of a *freeman;* and by redemption, i. e. by purchase, under an order of the court of aldermen."

" The customs of the city of London shall be tried by the certificate of the Mayor and Aldermen, * * * as the custom of distributing the effects of freemen deceased: of enrolling apprentices, or that he who is *free of one trade* may use another."

" Elections of aldermen and common-councilmen are to be by *freemen* householders."

" An agreement on marriage, that the husband shall take up the freedom of London, binds the distribution of the effects."

The foregoing and other illustrations of the use of the words " free " and " freemen," may be found in Jacob's Law Dictionary, under the head of Freeman, London, &c.

And this use of these words has been common in the English laws for centuries. The term " freeman " is used in Magna Charta, (1215). The English statutes abound with the terms, in reference to almost every franchise or peculiar privilege, from the highest to the lowest, known to the English laws. It would be perfectly proper, and in consonance with the legal meaning and common understanding of the term, to say of Victoria, that " she is free of the throne of England," and of a cobbler, that he " is free of his trade in the city of London."

But the more common and important signification of the words is to designate the *citizens,* native or naturalized, and those specially entitled, as a matter of political and acknowledged right, to participate in, or be protected by the government, as distinguished from aliens, or persons attainted, or deprived of their political privileges as members of the state. Thus they use the term " free British subject " — " freeman of the realm," &c. In short, the terms, when used in political papers, have a meaning very nearly, if not entirely synonymous, with that which we, in this country, now give to the word *citizen.*

But throughout the English law, and among all the variety of ways, in which the words " free " and " freemen " are used, as *legal* terms, they are *never used as the correlatives, or opposites of slaves or slavery* — and for the reason that they have in England no such persons or institutions, known to their laws, as slaves or slavery. The use of the words " free " and " freemen," therefore, do not in England at all imply the existence of slaves or slavery.

This use of the words " free " and " freemen," which is common to the English law, was introduced into this country at its first settlement, in all, or very nearly all the colonial charters, patents, &c., and continued in use, in this sense, until the time of the revolution ; and, of course, until the adoption of the first state constitutions. *

The persons and companies, to whom the colonial charters were granted, and those who were afterwards to be admitted as their associates, were described as " freemen of said colony," " freemen of said province," " freemen of said company," " freemen of the said company and body politick," &c. (See charter of Rhode Island.)

Many, if not all the charters had a provision similar in substance to the following in the charter to Rhode Island, viz. :

" That all and every the subjects of us, our heirs and successors," (i. e. of the king of England granting the charter,) " which are already planted and settled within our said colony of Providence Plantations, or which shall hereafter go to inhabit within the said colony, and all and every of their children which have been born there, or which shall happen hereafter to be born there, or on the sea going thither, or returning from thence, shall have and enjoy all liberties and immunities of *free* and natural subjects, within any of the dominions of us, our heirs and successors, to all intents, constructions and purposes whatsoever, as if they and every of them were born within the realm of England."

The following enactment of William Penn, as proprietary and Governor of the Province of Pennsylvania and its territories, illustrates one of the common uses of the word " freeman," as known to the English law, and as used in this country prior to the revolution — that is, as distinguishing a native born citizen, and one capable of holding real estate, &c., from a foreigner, *not naturalized*, and on that account subject to certain disabilities, such as being incompetent to hold real estate.

" And forasmuch as it is apparent that the just encouragement of the inhabitants of the province, and territories thereunto belonging, is likely to be an effectual way for the improvement thereof; and since some of the people that live therein and are likely to come thereunto, *are foreigners, and so not freemen, according to the acceptation of the laws of England, the consequences of which may prove very detrimental to them in their estates and traffic,*

---

* Since that time the words " free" and " freemen" have been gradually falling into disuse, and the word citizen been substituted — doubtless for the reason that it is not pleasant to our pride or our humanity to use words, one of whose significations serves to suggest a contrast between ourselves and slaves.

and so injurious to the prosperity of this province and territories thereof. *Be it enacted,* by the proprietary and governor of the province and counties aforesaid, by and with the advice and consent of the deputies of the *freemen* thereof, in assembly met, *That all persons who are strangers and foreigners,* that do now inhabit this province and counties aforesaid, *that hold land in fee in the same, according to the law of a freeman,* and who shall solemnly promise, within three months after the publication thereof, in their respective county courts where they live, upon record, faith and allegiance to the king of England and his heirs and successors, and fidelity and lawful obedience to the said William Penn, proprietary and governor of the said province and territories, and his u. rs and assigns, according to the king's letters patents and deed aforesaid, *shall be held and reputed freemen of the province and counties aforesaid, in as ample and full a manner as any person residing therein.* And it is hereby further enacted, by the authority aforesaid, That when at any time any person, that is a stranger will make his request to the proprietary and governor this province and territories thereof, *for the aforesaid freedom,* then shall 'be admitted on the conditions herein ex-

l   at his admission twenty shillings sterling, and no
no   in this law, or any other law, act, or thing in this
pr   contrary in any wise notwithstanding."

"Given   hester," &c., "under the hand and broad seal of
W   Pe   proprietary and governor of this province and
ter   into belonging, in the second year of his govern-
me   g's authority.   W. PENN."*

The use of our revolution, the *only* meaning which the wor "free" and "freemen" had, in the English law, in the charters granted to the colonies, and in the important documents of a political character, when used to designate one person as distinguished from another, was to designate a person enjoying some immunity or privilege, as distinguished from aliens or persons not enjoying a similar franchise. They were never used to denote a free person as distinguished from a slave — for the very sufficient reason that all these *fundamental* laws presumed that there were no slaves.

Such is the meaning of the words "free" and "freemen," as used in the constitutions adopted prior to 1789, in the States of Georgia, North and South Carolina, Maryland, Delaware and New York.

The legal rule of interpretation before mentioned, viz., that an innocent meaning must be given to all words that are susceptible

---

* Dallas' edition of the Laws of Pennsylvania, vol. 1, Appendix, page 25.

of it — would compel us to give the words this meaning, instead
of a meaning merely correlative with slavery, even if we had no
other ground than the rule alone, for so doing. But we have
other grounds. For instance : — Several of these constitutions
have themselves explicitly given to the words this meaning.
While not one of them has given them a meaning correlative
with slaves, inasmuch as none of them purport either to establish,
authorize, or even to know of the existence of slavery.

The constitution of Georgia (adopted in 1777) evidently uses
the word " free " in this sense, in the following article :

" Art. 11. No person shall be entitled to more than one vote,
which shall be given in the county where such person resides.
except as before excepted ; *nor shall any person who holds any title
of nobility, be entitled to a vote, or be capable of serving as a
representative, or hold any post of honor, profit or trust, in this
State, while such person claims his title of nobility ; but if the person shall give up such distinction,* in the manner as may be directed
by any future legislature, *then, and in such case,* he shall be
entitled to a *vote, and represent,* as before directed, and enjoy all
the other benefits of a FREE citizen."

The constitution of North Carolina, (adopted in 1776,) used the
word in a similar sense, as follows :

" 40. That every *foreigner,* who comes to settle in this State,
having first taken an oath of allegiance to the same, may purchase,
or by other just means acquire, hold, and transfer land, or other
real estate, *and after one year's residence* be deemed a FREE
citizen."

This constitution also repeatedly uses the word " freeman ;"
meaning thereby " a free citizen," as thus defined.

The constitution of Pennsylvania, (adopted in 1776,) uses the
word in the same sense :

" Sec. 42. Every *foreigner,* of good character, who comes to
settle in this State, having first taken an oath or affirmation of
allegiance to the same, may purchase, or by other just means
acquire, hold and transfer land or other real estate ; *and after one
year's residence, shall be deemed a* FREE *denizen thereof,* and
entitled to all the rights of a natural born subject of this state,
except that he shall not be capable of being elected a representative
until after two years' residence."

The constitution of New York, (adopted in 1777,) uses the word
in the same manner :

5

" Sec. 6. That every male inhabitant of full age, who has personally resided in one of the counties of this State for six months, immediately preceding the day of election, shall at such election be entitled to vote for representatives of the said county in assembly, if during the time aforesaid he shall have been a free-holder, possessing a freehold of the value of twenty pounds, within the said county, or have rented a tenement therein of the yearly value of forty shillings, and been rated and actually paid taxes to the State. *Provided always,* That every person who now is a *freeman of the city of Albany, or who was made a freeman of the city of New York,* on or before the fourteenth day of October, in the year of our Lord one thousand seven hundred and seventy-five, and shall be actually and usually resident in the said cities respectively, shall be entitled to vote for representatives in assembly within his place of residence."

The constitution of South Carolina, (formed in 1778,) uses the word "free" in a sense which may, at first thought, be supposed to be different from that in which it is used in the preceding cases:

Sec. 13. The qualification of electors shall be that "every *free white man,* and no other person," &c., "shall be deemed a person qualified to vote for, and shall be capable of being elected a representative."

It may be supposed that here the word "free" is used as the correlative of slavery; that it presumes the "whites" to be "free;" and that it therefore implies that other persons than "white" may be slaves. Not so. No other parts of the constitution authorize such an inference; and the implication from the words themselves clearly is, that *some* "white" persons might not be "free." The distinction implied is between those "white" persons that were "free," and those that were not "free." If this were not the distinction intended, and if *all* "white" persons were "free," it would have been sufficient to have designated the electors simply as "white" persons, instead of designating them as both "free" and "white." If, therefore, it were admitted that the word "free," in this instance, were used as the correlative of slaves, the implication would be that *some* "white" persons were, or might be slaves. There is, therefore, no alternative but to give the word "free," in this instance, the same meaning that it has in the constitutions of Georgia, North Carolina and Pennsylvania.

In 1704 South Carolina passed an act entitled, "*An act for making aliens* FREE *of this part of the Province.*" This statute remained in force until 1784, when it was repealed by an act entitled "*An act to confer the right of citizenship on aliens.*" *

One more example of this use of the word "*freeman.*" The constitution of Connecticut, adopted as late as 1818, has this provision :

"Art. 6, Sec. 1.   All persons who have been, *or shall hereafter*, previous to the ratification of this constitution, *be admitted freemen*, according to the existing laws of this State, shall be electors."

Surely no other proof can be necessary of the meaning of the words "free" and "freeman," as used in the constitutions existing in 1789; or that the use of those words furnish no implication in support of either the existence, or the constitutionality of slavery, prior to the adoption of the constitution of the United States in that year.

I have found, in *none* of the State constitutions before mentioned, (existing in 1789,) any other evidence or intimation of the existence of slavery, than that already commented upon and refuted. And if there be no other, then it is clear that slavery had no legal existence under them.   And there was consequently no *constitutional* slavery in the country up to the adoption of the constitution of the United States.

CHAPTER VII.

THE ARTICLES OF CONFEDERATION.

THE Articles of Confederation, (formed in 1778,) contained no recognition of slavery.   The only words in them, that could be claimed by anybody as recognizing slavery, are the following, in Art. 4, Sec. 1.

"The better to secure and perpetuate mutual friendship and intercourse among the people of the different States in this Union, *the free inhabitants* of each of these States, paupers, vagabonds and fugitives from justice excepted, shall be entitled to all the privileges and immunities of *free citizens* in the several States ; and *the people* of each State shall have free ingress and regress to and from any other State, and shall enjoy therein all the privileges of

---

* Cooper's edition of the Laws of South Carolina, vols. 2 and 4.   " Aliens."

trade and commerce, subject to the same duties, impositions and restrictions, as the inhabitants thereof respectively."

There are several reasons why this provision contains no legal recognition of slavery.

1. The true meaning of the word "free," as used in the English law, in the colonial charters, and in the State constitutions up to this time, when applied to persons, was to describe citizens, or persons possessed of franchises, as distinguished from aliens or persons not possessed of the same franchises. Usage, then, would give this meaning to the word "free" in this section.

2. The rules of law require that an innocent meaning should be given to all words that will bear an innocent meaning.

3. The Confederation was a league between States in their corporate capacity; and not, like the constitution, a government established by the people in their individual character. The Confederation, then, being a league between states or corporations, as such, of course recognized nothing in the character of the State governments except what their corporate charters or State constitutions uthorized. And as none of the State constitutions of the day ecognized slavery, the confederation of the State governments could not of course recognize it. Certainly none of its language can, consistently with legal rules, have such a meaning given to it, when it is susceptible of another that perfectly accords with the sense in which it is used in the constitutions of the States, that were parties to the league.

4. No other meaning can be given to the word "free" in this case, without making the sentence an absurd, or, at least, a foolish and inconsistent one. For instance, — The word "free" is joined to the word "citizen." What reason could there be in applying the term "free" to the word "citizen," if the word "free" were used as the correlative of slavery? Such an use of the word would imply that *some* of the "citizens" were, or might be slaves — which would be an absurdity. But used in the other sense, it implies only that some citizens had franchises not enjoyed by others; such, perhaps, as the right of suffrage, and the right of being elected to office; which franchises were only enjoyed by a part of the "citizens." All who were born of English parents, for instance, were "citizens," and entitled to the protection of the government, and freedom of trade and occupation, &c., &c., and in these respects were distinguished from aliens. Yet a property qualification was necessary, in some, if not all the States, to en-

,itle even such to the franchises of suffrage, and of eligibility to office.

The terms " free inhabitants" and " people" were probably used as synonymous either with " free citizens," or with " citizens" not " free"—that is, not possessing the franchises of suffrage and eligibility to office.

Mr. Madison, in the 42d No. of the Federalist, in commenting upon the power given to the general government by the new constitution, of naturalizing aliens, refers to this clause in the Articles of Confederation; and takes it for granted that the word " free" was used in that political sense, in which I have supposed it to be used—that is, as distinguishing " citizens" and the " inhabitants" or " people" proper, from aliens and persons not allowed the franchises enjoyed by the " inhabitants" and " people" of the States. Even the privilege of residence he assumes to be a franchise entitling one to the denomination of " free."

He says: " The dissimilarity in the rules of naturalization," (i. e. in the rules established by the separate States, for under the confederation each State established its own rules of naturalization,) " has long been remarked as a fault in our system, and as laying a foundation for intricate and delicate questions. In the fourth article of confederation, it is declared, ' that the *free inhabitants* of each of these States, paupers, vagabonds, and fugitives from justice excepted, shall be entitled to all the privileges and immunities of *free citizens* in the several States; and *the people* of each State shall, in every other, enjoy all the privileges of trade and commerce,' &c. There is a confusion of language here, which is remarkable. Why the terms *free inhabitants* are used in one part of the article, *free citizens* in another, and *people* in another; or what was meant by superadding to ' all privileges and immunities of free citizens,' ' all the privileges of trade and commerce,' cannot easily be determined. It seems to be a construction scarcely avoidable, however, that those who come under the denomination of *free inhabitants* of a State, although not citizens of such State, are entitled, in every other State, to all the privileges of *free citizens* of the latter; that is to greater privileges than they may be entitled to in their own State; so that it may be in the power of a particular State, or rather every State is laid under the necessity, not only to confer the rights of citizenship in other States upon any whom it may admit to such rights within itself, but upon any whom it may allow to become inhabitants within its jurisdiction. But were an exposition of the term ' inhabitant' to be admitted, which would confine the stipulated privileges to citizens alone, the difficulty is diminished only, not removed. The very improper power would still be retained by each State, of naturalizing aliens in every

other State. In one State, residence for a short time confers all the
rights of citizenship ; in another, qualifications of greater importance are required. An alien, therefore, legally incapacitated for
certain rights in the latter, may, by previous residence only in the
former, elude his incapacity, and thus the law of one State be pre-
posterously rendered paramount to the laws of another, within the
jurisdiction of the other.

"We owe it to mere casualty, that very serious embarrassments
on this subject have been hitherto escaped. By the laws of several
States, certain descriptions of aliens, who had rendered themselves
obnoxious, were laid under interdicts inconsistent, not only with
the rights of citizenship, but with the privileges of residence. What
would have been the consequence, if such persons, by residence,
or otherwise, had acquired the character of citizens under the laws
of another State, and then asserted their rights as such, both to residence and citizenship, within the State proscribing them ? Whatever the legal consequences might have been, other consequences
would probably have resulted of too serious a nature, not to be
provided against. The new constitution has, accordingly, with
great propriety, made provision against them, and all others proceeding from the defect of the confederation on this head, by
authorizing the general government to establish an uniform rule
of naturalization throughout the United States."

Throughout this whole quotation Mr. Madison obviously takes
it for granted that the word " free" is used in the articles of confederation, as the correlative of aliens. And in this respect he no
doubt correctly represents the meaning then given to the word by
the people of the United States. And in the closing sentence of
the quotation, he virtually asserts that such is the meaning of the
word " free" in " the new constitution."

CHAPTER VIII.

THE CONSTITUTION OF THE UNITED STATES.

WE come now to the period commencing with the adoption of
the constitution of the United States.

We have already seen that slavery had not been authorized or
established by any of the fundamental constitutions or charters
that had existed previous to this time ; that it had always been a
mere abuse sustained by the common consent of the strongest
party, in defiance of the avowed constitutional principles of their

governments. And the question now is, whether it was constitutionally established, authorized or sanctioned by the constitution of the United States?

It is perfectly clear, in the first place, that the constitution of the United States did not, *of itself, create or establish* slavery as a *new* institution; or even give any authority to the state governments to establish it as a new institution. — The greatest sticklers for slavery do not claim this. The most they claim is, that it recognized it as an institution already legally existing, under the authority of the State governments; and that it virtually guarantied to the States the right of continuing it in existence during their pleasure. And this is really the only question arising out of the constitution of the United States on this subject, viz., whether it *did* thus recognize and sanction slavery as an *existing* institution?

This question is, in reality, answered in the negative by what has already been shown; for if slavery had no constitutional existence, under the State constitutions, prior to the adoption of the constitution of the United States, then it is absolutely certain that the constitution of the United States did *not* recognize it as a constitutional institution; for it cannot, of course, be pretended that the United States constitution recognized, as constitutional, any State institution that did not constitutionally exist.

Even if the constitution of the United States had *intended* to recognize slavery, as a constitutional *State* institution, such intended recognition would have failed of effect, and been legally void, because slavery then had no constitutional existence to be recognized.

Suppose, for an illustration of this principle, that the constitution of the United States had, by implication, plainly taken it for granted that the State legislatures had power — derived from the *State* constitutions — to order arbitrarily that infant children, or that men without the charge of crime, should be maimed — deprived, for instance, of a hand, a foot, or an eye. This intended recognition, on the part of the constitution of the United States, of the legality of such a practice, would obviously have failed of all legal effect — would have been mere surplusage — if it should appear, from an examination of the State constitutions themselves, that they had really conferred no such power upon the legislatures. And this principle applies with the same force to laws that would arbitrarily make men or children slaves, as to laws that should arbitrarily order them to be maimed or murdered.

We might here safely rest the whole question—for no one, as
has already been said, pretends that the constitution of the United
States, by its own authority, created or authorized slavery as a
new institution; but only that it intended to recognize it as one
already established by authority of the State constitutions. This
intended recognition—if there were any such—being founded on
an error as to what the State constitutions really did authorize,
necessarily falls to the ground, a defunct intention.

We make a stand, then, at this point, and insist that the main
question—the only material question—is already decided against
slavery; and that it is of no consequence what recognition or
sanction the constitution of the United States may have intended
to extend to it.

The constitution of the United States, at its adoption, certainly
took effect upon, and made citizens of *all* "the people of the
United States," who were *not slaves* under the State constitutions.
No one can deny a proposition so self-evident as that. If, then,
the *State* constitutions, then existing, authorized no slavery at all,
the constitution of the United States took effect upon, and made
citizens of *all* "the people of the United States," without discrimination. And if *all* "the people of the United States" were made
citizens of the United States, by the United States constitution, at
its adoption, it was then forever too late for the *State* governments
to reduce any of them to slavery. They were thenceforth citizens of a higher government, under a constitution that was "the
supreme law of the land," "anything in the constitution or laws
of the States to the contrary notwithstanding." If the State governments could enslave citizens of the United States, the State
constitutions, and not the constitution of the United States, would
be the "supreme law of the land"—for no higher act of
supremacy could be exercised by one government over another,
than that of taking the citizens of the latter out of the protection
of their government, and reducing them to slavery.

SECONDLY.

Although we might stop—we yet do not choose to stop—at
the point last suggested. We will now go further, and attempt to
show, specifically from its provisions, that the constitution of the
United States, not only does not recognize or sanction slavery, as
a legal institution, but that, on the contrary, it presumes all men

to be free; that it positively denies the right of property in man; and that it, *of itself*, makes it impossible for slavery to have a legal existence in *any* of the United States.

In the first place — although the assertion is constantly made, and rarely denied, yet it is palpably a mere begging of the whole question in favor of slavery, to say that the constitution *intended* to sanction it; for if it *intended* to sanction it, it *did* thereby necessarily sanction it, (that is, if slavery then had any constitutional existence to be sanctioned.) The *intentions* of the constitution are the only means whereby it sanctions anything. And its intentions necessarily sanction everything to which they apply, and which, in the nature of things, they are competent to sanction. To say, therefore, that the constitution *intended* to sanction slavery, is the same as to say that it *did* sanction it; which is begging the whole question, and substituting mere assertion for proof.

Why, then, do not men say distinctly, that the constitution *did* sanction slavery, instead of saying that it *intended* to sanction it? We are not accustomed to use the word "*intention*," when speaking of the other grants and sanctions of the constitution. We do not say, for example, that the constitution *intended* to authorize congress "to coin money," but that it *did* authorize them to coin it. Nor do we say that it intended to authorize them "to declare war;" but that it did authorize them to declare it. It would be silly and childish to say merely that it *intended* to authorize them "to coin money," and "to declare war," when the language authorizing them to do so, is full, explicit and positive. Why, then, in the case of slavery, do men say merely that the constitution *intended* to sanction it, instead of saying distinctly, as we do in the other cases, that it *did* sanction it? The reason is obvious. If they were to say unequivocally that it *did* sanction it, they would lay themselves under the necessity of pointing to the *words* that sanction it; and they are aware that the *words alone* of the constitution do not come up to that point. They, therefore, assert simply that the constitution *intended* to sanction it; and they then attempt to support the assertion by quoting certain words and phrases, which they say are *capable* of covering, or rather of concealing such an intention; and then by the aid of exterior, circumstantial and historical evidence, they attempt to enforce upon the mind the conclusion that, as matter of fact, such was the intention

of those who *drafted* the constitution ; and thence they finally
infer that such was the intention of the constitution itself.

The error and fraud of this whole procedure — and it is one
purely of error and fraud — consists in this — that it artfully sub-
stitutes the supposed intentions of those who drafted the constitution, for the intentions of the constitution itself; and, secondly, it
personifies the constitution as a crafty individual ; capable of both
open and secret intentions ; capable of legally participating in, and
giving effect to all the subtleties and double dealings of knavish
men ; and as actually intending to secure slavery, while openly
professing to " secure and establish liberty and justice." It personifies the constitution as an individual capable of having private
and criminal intentions, which it dare not distinctly avow, but only
darkly hint at, by the use of words of an indefinite, uncertain and
double meaning, whose application is to be gathered from external
circumstances.

The falsehood of all these imaginings is apparent, the moment
it 's considered that the constitution is not a *person*, of whom an
" intention," not legally expressed, can be asserted ; that it has
none of the various and selfish passions and motives of action,
which sometimes prompt *men* to the practice of duplicity and dis-
guise ; that it is merely a written legal instrument ; that, as such,
it must have a fixed, and not a double meaning; that it is made up
entirely of intelligible words ; and that it has, and *can* have, no
soul, no " *intentions*," no motives, no being, no personality, except
what those words alone express or imply. Its " intentions" are
nothing more nor less than the legal meaning of its words. Its
intentions are no guide to its legal meaning — as the advocates of
slavery all assume ; but its legal meaning is the sole guide to its
intentions. This distinction is all important to be observed ; for if
we can gratuitously assume the intentions of a legal instrument to
be what we may wish them to be, and can then strain or pervert
the ordinary meaning of its words, in order to make them utter
those intentions, we can make anything we choose of any legal
instrument whatever. The legal meaning of the words of an instrument is, therefore, necessarily our only guide to its intentions.

In ascertaining the legal meaning of the words of the constitution, these rules of law, (the reasons of which will be more fully
explained hereafter,) are vital to be borne constantly in mind, viz. :
1st, that no intention, in violation of natural justice and natural
right, (like that to sanction slavery,) can be ascribed to the consti-

tution, unless that intention be expressed in terms that are *legally competent* to express such an intention; and, 2d, that no terms, except those that are plenary, express, explicit, distinct, unequivocal, *and to which no other meaning can be given,* are legally competent to authorize or sanction anything contrary to natural right. The rule of law is materially different as to the terms necessary to legalize and sanction anything contrary to natural right, and those necessary to legalize things that are consistent with natural right. The latter may be sanctioned by natural implication and inference ; the former only by inevitable implication, or by language that is full, definite, express, explicit, unequivocal, and whose *unavoidable* import is to sanction the *specific wrong* intended.

To assert, therefore, that the constitution *intended* to sanction slavery, is, in reality, equivalent to asserting that the *necessary* meaning, the *unavoidable* import of the *words alone* of the constitution, come fully up to the point of a clear, definite, distinct, express, explicit, unequivocal, necessary and peremptory sanction of the specific thing, *human slavery, property in man.* If the *necessary* import of its *words alone* do but fall an iota short of this point, the instrument gives, and, legally speaking, intended to give, no legal sanction to slavery. Now, who can, in good faith, say that the *words alone* of the constitution come up to this point? No one, who knows anything of law, and the meaning of words. Not even the name of the thing, alleged to be sanctioned, is given. The constitution itself contains no designation, description, or necessary admission of the existence of such a thing as slavery, servitude, or the right of property in man. We are obliged to go out of the instrument, and grope among the records of oppression lawlessness and crime — records unmentioned, and of course unsanctioned by the constitution — to *find* the thing, to which it is said that the words of the constitution apply. And when we have found this thing, which the constitution dare not name, we find that the constitution has sanctioned it (if at all) only by enigmatical words, by unnecessary implication and inference, by innuendo and double entendre, and under a name that entirely fails of describing the thing. Everybody must admit that the constitution itself contains no language, from which *alone* any court, that were either strangers to the prior existence of slavery, or that did not assume its prior existence to be legal, could legally decide that the constitution sanctioned it. And this is the true test for determining whether the constitution does, or does not, sanction slavery, **viz.**, whether a court of law, strangers to the prior existence of slavery or not assuming its prior existence to be legal — looking only at the naked language of the instrument — could, consistently with legal rules, judicially determine that it sanctioned slavery. Every lawyer, who at all deserves that name, knows that the claim for slavery could stand no such test. The fact is palpable, that the constitution contains no such legal sanction ; that it is only by unnecessary implication and inference, by innuendo and double-entendre, by the aid of exterior evidence, the assumption of the prior legality of slavery, and the gratuitous imputation of criminal intentions that are not avowed in legal terms, that any sanction of slavery, (as a legal institution,) can be extorted from it.

But legal rules of interpretation entirely forbid and disallow all such implications, inferences, innuendos and double-entendre, all aid of exterior evidence, all assumptions of the prior legality of slavery, and all gratuitous imputations of criminal unexpressed intentions ; and consequently compel us to come back to the *letter* of the instrument, and find *there* a distinct, clear, necessary, peremptory sanction for slavery, or to surrender the point.

To the unprofessional reader these rules of interpretation will appear stringent, and perhaps unreasonable and unsound. For his benefit, therefore, the reasons on which they are founded, will be given. And he is requested to fix both the reasons and the rules fully in his mind, inasmuch as the whole legal meaning of the constitution, in regard to slavery, may perhaps be found to turn upon the construction which these rules fix upon its language.

But before giving the reasons of this rule, let us offer a few remarks in regard to *legal* rules of interpretation in general. Many persons appear to have the idea that these rules have no foundation in reason, justice or necessity ; that they are little else than whimsical and absurd conceits, arbitrarily adopted by the courts. No idea can be more erroneous than this. The rules are absolutely indispensable to the administration of the justice arising out of any class of legal instruments whatever — whether the instruments be simple contracts between man and man, or statutes enacted by legislatures, or fundamental compacts or constitutions of government agreed upon by the people at large. In regard to all these instruments, the *law* fixes, and necessarily must fix their meaning ; and for the obvious reason, that otherwise their meaning could not be fixed at all. The parties to the simplest contract may disagree, or pretend to disagree, as to its meaning, and of course as to their respective rights under it. The different members of a legislative body, who vote for a particular statute, may have different intentions in voting 'or it, and may therefore differ, or pretend to differ, as to its meaning. The people of a nation may establish a compact of government. The motives of one portion may be to establish liberty, equality and justice; and they may think, or pretend to think, that the words used in the instrument convey that idea. The motives of another portion may be to establish the slavery or subordination of one part of the people, and the superiority or arbitrary power of the other part; and they may think, or pretend to think, that the language agreed upon by the whole authorizes such a government. In all these cases, unless there were some rules of law, applicable alike to all instruments, and competent to settle their meaning, their meaning could not be settled; and individuals would of necessity lose their rights under them. *The law, therefore, fixes their meaning;* and the rules by which it does so, are founded in the same justice, reason, necessity and truth, as are other legal principles, and are for that reason as inflexible as any other legal principles whatever. They are also simple, intelligible, natural, obvious. Everybody are presumed to know them, as they are presumed to know any other legal principles. No one is allowed to plead ignorance of them, any more than of any other principle of law. All persons and people are presumed to have framed their contracts, statutes and constitutions with reference to them. And if they have not done so — if they have said black when they meant white, and one thing when they meant another, they must abide the consequences. The law will presume that they meant what they said. No one, in a court of justice, can claim any rights founded on a construction different from that which these rules would give to the contract, statute, or constitution, under which he claims. The judiciary cannot depart from these rules, for two reasons. First, because the rules embody in themselves principles of justice, reason and truth; and are therefore as necessarily law as any other principles of justice, reason and truth; and, secondly, because if they could lawfully depart from them in one case, they might in another, at their own caprice. Courts could thus at pleasure become despotic; all certainty as to the legal meaning of instruments would be destroyed; and the administration of justice, according to the true meaning of contracts, statutes and constitutions, would be rendered impossible.

What, then, are some of these rules of interpretation?

6

One of them, (as has been before stated,) is, that where words are susceptible of two meanings, one consistent, and the other inconsistent, with justice and natural right, that meaning, and *only that* meaning, which is consistent with right, shall be attributed to them — unless other parts of the instrument overrule that interpretation.

Another rule, (if indeed it be not the same,) is, that no language except that which is peremptory, and no implication, except one that is inevitable, shall be held to authorize or sanction anything contrary to natural right.

Another rule is, that no *extraneous or historical evidence* shall be admitted to fix upon a statute an unjust or immoral meaning, when the words themselves of the act are susceptible of an innocent one.

One of the reasons of these stringent and inflexible rules, doubtless is, that judges have always known, that, in point of fact, natural justice was itself law, and that nothing inconsistent with it could be made law, even by the most explicit and peremptory language that legislatures could employ. But judges have always, in this country and in England, been dependent upon the executive and the legislature for their appointments and salaries, and been amenable to the legislature by impeachment. And as the executive and legislature have always enacted more or less statutes, and had more or less purposes to accomplish, that were inconsistent with natural right, judges have seen that it would be impossible for them to retain their offices, and at the same time maintain the integrity of the law against the will of those in whose power they were. It is natural also that the executive should appoint, and that the legislature should approve the appointment of no one for the office of judge, whose integrity they should suppose would stand in the way of their purposes. The consequence has been that all judges, (probably without exception,) though they have not dared deny, have yet in practice yielded the vital principle of law; and have succumbed to the arbitrary mandates of the other departments of the government, so far as to carry out their enactments, though inconsistent with natural right. But, as if sensible of the degradation and criminality of so doing, they have made a stand at the first point at which they could make it, without bringing themselves in direct collision with those on whom they were dependent. And that point is, that they will administer, as law, no statute, that is contrary to natural right, unless its language be so explicit and peremptory, that there is no way of evading its authority, but by flatly denying the authority of those who enacted it. They (the court) will themselves add nothing to the language of the statute, to help out its supposed meaning. They will imply nothing, infer nothing, and assume nothing, except what is inevitable; they will not go out of the letter of the statute in search of any *historical* evidence as to the meaning of the legislature, to enable them to effectuate any *unjust* intentions not fully expressed by the statute itself. Wherever a statute is supposed to have in view the accomplishment of any unjust end, they will apply the most stringent principles of construction to prevent that object being effected. They will not go a hair's breadth beyond the literal or inevitable import *of the words* of the statute, even though they should be conscious, all the while, that the real intentions of the makers of it would be entirely defeated by their refusal. The rule (as has been already stated) is laid down by the Supreme Court of the United States in these words:

" Where rights are infringed, where fundamental principles are overthrown, where the general system of the laws is departed from, the legislative intention must be expressed with *irresistible clearness*, to induce a court of justice to suppose a design to effect such objects."—(*United States* vs. *Fisher et al.*, 2 *Cranch*, 390.)*

Such has become the settled doctrine of courts. And although it does not come up to the true standard of law, yet it is good in itself, so far as it goes, and ought to be unflinchingly adhered to, not merely for its own sake, but also as a scaffolding, from which to erect that higher standard of law, to wit, that no language or authority whatever can legalize anything inconsistent with natural justice.†

---

* This language of the Supreme Court contains an admission of the truth of the charge just made against judges, viz., that rather than lose their offices, they will violate what they know to be law, in subserviency to the legislatures on whom they depend; for it admits, 1st, that the preservation of men's *rights* is the vital principle of law, and, 2d, that courts (and the Supreme Court of the United States in particular) will trample upon that principle at the bidding of the legislature, when the mandate comes in the shape of a statute of such " *irresistible clearness*," that its meaning cannot be evaded.

† " Laws are construed strictly to save a right." — *Whitney et al.* vs. *Emmett et al.*, 1 *Baldwin, C. C. R.* 316.

" No law will make a construction to do wrong; and there are some things which the law favors, and some it dislikes; it favoreth those things that come from the order of nature.' — *Jacob's Law Dictionary, title Law.*

Another reason for the rules before given, against all construc
tions, implications and inferences — except inevitable ones — in
favor of injustice, is, that but for them we should have no guaranty
that our honest contracts, or honest laws would be honestly
administered by the judiciary.   It would be nearly or quite
impossible for men, in framing their contracts or laws, to use language so as to exclude every possible implication in favor of
wrong, if courts were allowed to resort to such implications.   *The
law therefore excludes them;* that is, the ends of justice — the
security of men's rights under their honest contracts, and under
honest legislative enactments — make it imperative upon courts of
justice to ascribe an innocent and honest meaning to all language
that will possibly bear an innocent and honest meaning.   If courts
of justice could depart from this rule for the purpose of upholding
what was contrary to natural right, and should employ their ingenuity in spying out some implied or inferred authority, for
sanctioning what was in itself dishonest or unjust, when such was
not the *necessary* meaning of the language used, there could be
no security whatever for the honest administration of honest laws,
or the honest fulfilment of men's honest contracts.   Nearly all
language, on the meaning of which courts adjudicate, would
be liable, at the caprice of the court, to be perverted from
the furtherance of honest, to the support of dishonest purposes.
Judges could construe statutes and contracts in favor of justice or
injustice, as their own pleasure might dictate.

Another reason of the rules, is, that as governments have, and can
have no legitimate objects or powers opposed to justice and natural
right, it would be treason to all the legitimate purposes of government, for the judiciary to give any other than an honest and innocent meaning to any language, that would bear such a construction.

The same reasons that forbid the allowance of any unnecessary
implication or inference in favor of a wrong, in the construction of
a statute, forbids also the introduction of any *extraneous or historical* evidence to prove that the intentions of the legislature were to
sanction or authorize a wrong.

The same rules of construction, that apply to statutes, apply
also to all those private contracts between man and man, *which
courts actually enforce.*   But as it is both the right and the duty
of courts to invalidate altogether such private contracts as are
inconsistent with justice, they will admit evidence exterior to their
words, *if offered by a defendant for the purpose of invalidating*

them. At the same time, a plaintiff, or party that wishes to set up a contract, or that claims its fulfilment, will not be allowed to offer any evidence exterior to its words, to prove that the contract is contrary to justice — because, if his evidence were admitted, it would not make his unjust claim a legal one; but only invalidate it altogether. But as courts do not claim the right of invalidating statutes and constitutions, they will not admit evidence, exterior to their language, to give them such a meaning, that they ought to be invalidated.

I think no one — no lawyer, certainly — will now deny that it is a legal rule of interpretation — that must be applied to all statutes, and also to all private contracts *that are to be enforced* — that an innocent meaning, *and nothing beyond an innocent meaning*, must be given to all language that will possibly bear such a meaning. All will probably admit that the rule, as laid down by the Supreme Court of the United States, is correct, to wit, that "where rights are infringed, where fundamental principles are overthrown, where the general system of the law is departed from, the legislative intention must be expressed with *irresistible clearness*, to induce a court of justice to suppose a design to effect such objects."

But perhaps it will be said that these rules, which apply to all statutes, and to all private contracts that are to be enforced, do not apply to the constitution. And why do they not? No reason whatever can be given. A constitution is nothing but a contract, entered into by the mass of the people, instead of a few individuals. This contract of the people at large becomes a law unto the judiciary that administer it, just as private contracts, (so far as they are consistent with natural right,) are laws unto the tribunals that adjudicate upon them. All the essential principles that enter into the question of obligation, in the case of a private contract, or a legislative enactment, enter equally into the question of the obligation of a contract agreed to by the whole mass of the people. This is too self-evident to need illustration.

Besides, is it not as important to the safety and rights of all interested, that a constitution or compact of government, established by a whole people, should be so construed as to promote the ends of justice, as it is that a private contract or a legislative enactment should be thus construed? Is it not as necessary that some check should be imposed upon the judiciary to prevent them from perverting, at pleasure, the whole purpose and character of

the government, as it is that they should be restrained from perverting the meaning of a private contract, or a legislative enactment? Obviously written compacts of government could not be
upheld for a day, if it were understood by the mass of the people
that the judiciary were at liberty to interpret them according to
their own pleasure, instead of their being restrained by such rules
as have now been laid down.

Let us now look at some of the provisions of the constitution,
and see what crimes might be held to be authorized by them, if
their meaning were not to be ascertained and restricted by such
rules of interpretation as apply to all other legal instruments.

The second amendment to the constitution declares that "the
right of the people to keep and bear arms shall not be infringed."

This right "to keep and bear arms," implies the right to use
them — as much as a provision securing to the people the right to
buy and keep food, would imply their right also to eat it. But this
implied right to use arms, is only a right to use them in a manner
consistent with natural rights — as, for example, in defence of life,
liberty, chastity, &c. Here is an innocent and just meaning, of
which the words are susceptible; and such is therefore the *extent*
of their legal meaning. If the courts could go beyond the innocent and necessary meaning of the words, and imply or infer from
them an authority for anything contrary to natural right, they
could imply a constitutional authority in the people to use arms,
not merely for the just and innocent purposes of defence, but also
for the criminal purposes of aggression — for purposes of murder,
robbery, or any other acts of wrong to which arms are capable of
being applied. The mere *verbal* implication would as much
authorize the people to use arms for unjust, as for just, purposes.
But the *legal* implication gives only an authority for their innocent use. And why? Simply because justice is the end of all
law — the legitimate end of all compacts of government. It is
itself law; and there is no right or power among men to destroy
its obligation.

Take another case. The constitution declares that "Congress
shall have power to *regulate commerce* with foreign nations, and
among the several States, and with the Indian tribes."

This power has been held by the Supreme Court to be an exclusive one in the general government — and one that cannot be
controlled by the States. Yet it gives Congress no constitutional
authority to legalize any commerce inconsistent with natural

justice between man and man ; although the *mere* verbal import of the words, if stretched to their utmost tension in favor of the wrong, would authorize Congress to legalize a commerce in poisons and deadly weapons, for the express purpose of having them used in a manner inconsistent with natural right — as for the purposes of murder.

At natural law, and on principles of natural right, a person, who should *sell* to another a weapon or a poison, knowing that it would, or intending that it should be used for the purpose of murder, would be legally an accessary to the murder that should be committed with it. And if the grant to Congress of a "power to regulate commerce," can be stretched beyond the *innocent* meaning of the words — beyond the power of regulating and authorizing a commerce that is consistent with natural justice — and be made to cover everything, intrinsically criminal, that can be perpetrated under the name of commerce — then Congress have the authority of the constitution for granting to individuals the liberty of bringing weapons and poisons from " foreign nations " into this, and from one State into another, and selling them openly for the express purposes of murder, without any liability to legal restraint or punishment.

Can any stronger cases than these be required to prove the necessity, the soundness, and the inflexibility of that rule of law, which requires the judiciary to ascribe an innocent meaning to all language that will possibly bear an innocent meaning? and to ascribe *only* an innocent meaning to language whose mere verbal import might be susceptible of both an innocent *and* criminal meaning? If this rule of interpretation could be departed from, there is hardly a power granted to Congress, that might not *lawfully* be perverted into an authority for legalizing crimes of the highest grade.

In the light of these principles, then, let us examine those clauses of the constitution, that are relied on as recognizing and sanctioning slavery. They are but three in number.

The one most frequently quoted is the third clause of Art. 4, Sec. 2, in these words :

"No person, held to service or labor in one State, under the laws thereof, escaping into another, shall, in consequence of any law or regulation therein, be discharged from such service or labor; but shall be delivered up on claim of the party to whom such service or labor may be due."

There are several reasons why this clause renders no sanction to slavery.

1. It must be construed, if possible, as sanctioning nothing contrary to natural right.

If there be any "service or labor" whatever, to which any "persons" whatever may be "held," *consistently with natural right*, and which any person may, consistently with natural right, "*claim*" as his "*due*" of another, such "service or labor," and *only* such, is recognized and sanctioned by this provision.

It needs no argument to determine whether the "service or labor," that is exacted of a slave, is such as can be "*claimed*," *consistently with natural right*, as being "*due*" from him to his master. And if it cannot be, some other "service or labor" must, if possible, be found for this clause to apply to.

The proper definition of the word "service," in this case, obviously is, the labor of a *servant*. And we find, that at and before the adoption of the constitution, the persons recognized by the State laws as "servants," constituted a numerous class. The statute books of the States abounded with statutes in regard to "servants." Many seem to have been indented as servants by the public authorities, on account of their being supposed incompetent, by reason of youth and poverty, to provide for themselves. Many were doubtless indented as apprentices by their parents and guardians, as now. The English laws recognized a class of servants — and many persons were brought here from England, in that character, and retained that character afterward. Many indented or contracted themselves as servants for the payment of their passage money to this country. In these various ways, the class of persons, recognized by the statute books of the States as "servants," was very numerous; and formed a prominent subject of legislation. Indeed, no other evidence of their number is necessary than the single fact, that "persons bound to service for a term of years," were specially noticed by the constitution of the United States, (Art. 1, Sec. 2,) which requires that they be counted as units in making up the basis of representation. There is, therefore, not the slightest apology for pretending that there was not a sufficient class for the words "service or labor" to refer to, without supposing the existence of slaves. *

---

* In the convention that framed the constitution, when this clause was under discussion, "servants" were spoken of as a distinct class from "slaves." For instance, "Mr. Butler and Mr. Pickney moved to require 'fugitive slaves *and ser*

2. "*Held to service or labor*," is no legal description of slavery Slavery is property in man. It is not necessarily attended with either "service or labor." A very considerable portion of the slaves are either too young, too old, too sick, or too refractory to render "service or labor." As a matter of fact, slaves, who are able to labor, may, in general, be compelled by their masters to do so. Yet labor is not an essential or necessary condition of slavery. The essence of slavery consists in a person's being owned as property — without any reference to the circumstances of his being compelled to labor, or of his being permitted to live in idleness, or of his being too young, or too old, or too sick to labor.

If "service or labor" were either a test, or a necessary attendant of slavery, that test would of itself abolish slavery ; because all slaves, before they can render "service or labor," must have passed through the period of infancy, when they could render neither service nor labor, and when, therefore, according to this test, they were free. And if they were free in infancy, they could not be subsequently enslaved.

3. "Held to service or labor in one State, *under the laws thereof*."

The "*laws*" take no note of the fact whether a slave "labors," or not. They recognize no obligation, on his part, to labor. They will enforce no "*claim*" of a master, upon his slave, for "service or labor." If the slave refuse to labor, the law will not interfere to compel him. The law simply recognizes the master's *right of property* in the slave — just as it recognizes his right of property in a horse. Having done that, it leaves the master to compel the slave, if he please, and if he can — as he would compel a horse — to labor. If the master do not please, or be not able, to compel the slave to labor, the law takes no more cognizance of the case than it does of the conduct of a refractory horse.

<hr>

rants to be delivered up like criminals.' " Mr. Sherman objected to delivering up either *slaves* or *servants*. He said he " saw no more propriety in the public seizing and surrendering a slave or *servant*, than a horse." — *Madison Papers, p.* 1447 – 8

The language finally adopted shows that they at last agreed to deliver up "*servants*," but *not* "*slaves*" — for as the word "servant" does not mean "slave," the word "service" does not mean slavery.

These remarks in the convention are quoted, not because the intentions of the convention are of the least legal consequence whatever ; but to rebut the silly arguments of those who pretend that the convention, and not the people, adopted the constitution — and that the convention did not understand the legal difference between the word "servant" and "slave," and therefore used the word "service," in this clause, as meaning slavery.

In short, it recognizes no obligation, on the part of the slave, to labor, if he can avoid doing so. It recognizes no "*claim*," on the part of the master, upon his slave, for "services or labor," as "*due*" from the latter to the former.

4. Neither "service" nor "labor" is necessarily slavery; and not being necessarily slavery, the words cannot, in this case, be strained beyond their necessary meaning, to make them sanction a wrong. The law will not allow words to be strained a hair's breadth beyond their *necessary* meaning, to make them authorize a wrong. *The stretching, if there be any, must always be towards the right.* The words "service or labor" do not necessarily, nor in their common acceptation, so much as suggest the idea of slavery — that is, they do not suggest the idea of the laborer or servant being the property of the person for whom he labors. An indented apprentice serves and labors for another. He is "*held*" to do so, under a contract, and for a consideration, that are recognized, by the laws, as legitimate, and consistent with natural right. Yet he is not owned as property. A condemned criminal is "held to labor" — yet he is not owned as property. The law allows no such straining of the meaning of words towards the wrong, as that which would convert the words "service or labor" (of men) into *property in man* — and thus make a man, who serves or labors for another, the property of that other.

5. "No person held to service or labor, in one State, under the *laws* thereof."

The "*laws*," here mentioned, and impliedly sanctioned, are, of course, only *constitutional* laws — laws, that are consistent, both with the constitution of the State, and the constitution of the United States. None others are "*laws*," correctly speaking, however they may attempt to "hold persons to service or labor," or however they may have the forms of laws on the statute books.

This word "laws," therefore, being a material word. leaves the whole question just where it found it — for it certainly does not, *of itself* — nor indeed does any other part of the clause — say that an act of a legislature, declaring one man to be the property of another, is a "*law*" within the meaning of the constitution. As far as the word "*laws*" says anything on the subject, it says that such acts are *not* laws — for such acts are clearly inconsistent with natural law — and it yet remains to be shown that they are consistent with any constitution whatever, state or national.

The burden of proof, then, still rests upon the advocates of slavery, to show that an act of a State legislature, declaring one man to be the property of another, is a "law," within the meaning of this clause. To assert simply that it is, without proving it to be so, is a mere begging of the question — for that is the very point in dispute.

The question, therefore, of the *constitutionality* of the slave acts must first be determined, before it can be decided that they are "laws" within the meaning of the constitution. That is, they must be shown to be consistent with the constitution, before they can be said to be sanctioned as "laws" by the constitution. Can any proposition be plainer than this? And yet the reverse must be assumed, in this case, by the advocates of slavery.

The simple fact, that an act purports to "hold persons to service or labor," clearly cannot, *of itself*, make the act constitutional. If it could, any act, purporting to hold "persons to service or labor," would necessarily be constitutional, without any regard to the "persons" so held, or the conditions on which they were held. It would be constitutional, *solely because it purported to hold persons to service or labor*. If this were the true doctrine, any of us, without respect of persons, might be held to service or labor, at the pleasure of the legislature. And then, if "service or labor" mean slavery, it would follow that any of us, without discrimination, might be made slaves. And thus the result would be, that the acts of a legislature would be constitutional, *solely because they made slaves of the people*. Certainly this would be a new test of the constitutionality of laws.

All the arguments in favor of slavery, that have heretofore been drawn from this clause of the constitution, have been founded on the assumption, that if an act of a legislature did but purport to "hold persons to service or labor" — no matter how, on what conditions, or for what cause — that fact alone was sufficient to make the act constitutional. The entire sum of the argument, in favor of slavery, is but this, viz., the constitution recognizes the constitutionality of "laws" that "hold persons to service or labor," — slave acts "hold persons to service or labor," — therefore slave acts must be constitutional. This profound syllogism is the great pillar of slavery in this country. It has, (if we are to judge by results,) withstood the scrutiny of all the legal acumen of this nation for fifty years and more. If it should continue to withstand it for as many years as it has already done, it will then be time to propound the following, to wit: The State constitutions recognize the right of men to acquire property; theft, robbery, and murder are among the modes in which property may be acquired; therefore theft, robbery, and murder are recognized by these constitutions as lawful.

No doubt the clause contemplates that there may be constitutional " laws," under which persons may be " held to service or labor." But it does not follow, therefore, that every act, that purports to hold " persons to service or labor," is constitutional.

We are obliged, then, to determine whether a statute be constitutional, before we can determine whether the " service or labor" required by it, is sanctioned by the constitution as being lawfully required. The simple fact, that the statute would " hold persons to service or labor," is, *of itself*, no evidence, either for or against its constitutionality. Whether it be or be not constitutional, may depend upon a variety of contingencies — such as the kind of service or labor required, and the conditions on which it requires it. Any service or labor, that is inconsistent with the duties which the constitution requires of the people, is of course not sanctioned by this clause of the constitution as being lawfully required. Neither, of course, is the requirement of service or labor, *on any conditions, that are inconsistent with any rights that are secured to the people by the constitution*, sanctioned by the constitution as lawful. Slave laws, then, can obviously be held to be sanctioned by this clause of the constitution, only by gratuitously assuming, 1st, that the constitution neither confers any rights, nor imposes any duties upon the people of the United States, inconsistent with their being made slaves; and, 2d, that it sanctions the general principle of holding " persons to service or labor" arbitrarily, without contract, without compensation, and without the charge of crime. If this be really the kind of constitution that has been in force since 1789, it is somewhat wonderful that there are so few slaves in the country. On the other hand, if the constitution be not of this kind, it is equally wonderful that we have any slaves at all — for the instrument offers no ground for saying that a colored man may be made a slave, and a white man not.

Again. Slave acts were not " laws" according to any State constitution that was in existence at the time the constitution of the United States was adopted. And if they were not " laws " at that time, they have not been made so since.

6. The constitution itself, (Art. 1, Sec. 2,) in fixing the basis of representation, has plainly *denied* that those described in Art 4

as ' persons held to service or labor," are slaves, — for it declares
that " persons bound to service for a term of years" shall be
" included " in the " number of *free* persons." There is no *legal*
difference between being " bound to service," and being " held to
service or labor." The addition, in the one instance, of the words
" for a term of years," does not alter the case, for it does not appear
that, in the other, they are " held to service or labor" beyond a
fixed term — and, in the absence of evidence from the constitution
itself, the presumption must be that they are not — because such
a presumption saves the necessity of going out of the constitution
to find the persons intended, and it is also more consistent with the
prevalent municipal, and with natural law.

And it makes no difference to this result, whether the word
" free," in the first article, be used in the political sense common
at that day, or as the correlative of slavery. In either case, the
persons described as " free," could not be made slaves.

7. The words " service or labor" cannot be made to include
slavery, unless by reversing the legal principle, that the greater
includes the less, and holding that the less includes the greater;
that the innocent includes the criminal; that a sanction of what is
right, includes a sanction of what is wrong.

Another clause relied on as a recognition of the constitutionality
of slavery, is the following, (Art. 1, Sec. 2:)

" Representatives and direct taxes shall be apportioned among
the several States, which may be included within this Union,
according to their respective numbers, which shall be determined
by adding to the whole number of *free* persons, including those
bound to service for a term of years, and excluding Indians not
taxed, three fifths of all other persons."

The argument claimed from this clause, in support of slavery,
rests entirely upon the word " free," and the words " all other
persons." Or rather, it rests entirely upon the meaning of the
word " free," for the application of the words " all other persons "
depends upon the meaning given to the word " free." The slave
argument *assumes, gratuitously,* that the word " free " is used as the
correlative of slavery, and thence it infers that the words " al.
other persons," mean slaves.

It is obvious that the word " free " affords no argument for
slavery, unless a meaning correlative with slavery be *arbitrarily*
given to it, for the very purpose of *making* the constitution sanction or recognize slavery. Now it is very clear that no such

7

meaning can be given to the word, *for such a purpose.* The
ordinary meaning of a word cannot be thus arbitrarily changed,
for the sake of sanctioning a wrong. A choice of meaning would
be perfectly allowable, and even obligatory, if made for the purpose of *avoiding* any such sanction; but it is entirely inadmissible
for the purpose of giving it. The legal rules of interpretation,
heretofore laid down, imperatively require this preference of the
right, over the wrong, in all cases where a word is susceptible of
different meanings.

The English law had for centuries used the word "free" as
describing persons possessing citizenship, or some other franchise
or peculiar privilege — as distinguished from aliens, and persons
not possessed of such franchise or privilege. This law, and this
use of the word "free," as has already been shown, (Ch. 6,) had
been adopted in this country from its first settlement. The
colonial charters all (probably without an exception) recognized it.
The colonial legislation generally, if not universally, recognized it.
The State constitutions, in existence at the time the constitution of
the United States was formed and adopted, used the word in this
sense, *and no other.* The Articles of Confederation — the then
existing national compact of union — used the word in this sense
and no other. The sense is an appropriate one in itself; the most
appropriate to, and consistent with, the whole character of the constitution, of any of which the word is susceptible. In fact, it is
the only one that is either appropriate to, or consistent with, the
other parts of the instrument. Why, then, is it not the legal
meaning? Manifestly it *is* the legal meaning. No reason whatever can be given against it, except that, if such be its meaning,
the constitution will not sanction slavery! A very good reason —
a perfectly unanswerable reason, in fact — in favor of this meaning; but a very futile one against it.

It is evident that the word "free" is not used as the correlative
of slavery, because "Indians not taxed" are "excluded" from its
application — yet they are not therefore slaves.

Again. The word "free" cannot be presumed to be used as
the correlative of slavery — because slavery then had no *legal*
existence. The word must obviously be presumed to be used as
the correlative of something that did *legally* exist, rather than of
something that did not legally exist. If it were used as the correlative of something that did not legally exist, the words "all
other persons" would have no legal application. Until, then, it

be shown that slavery had a legal existence, authorized either by the United States constitution, or by the then existing State constitutions — a thing that cannot be shown — the word " free" certainly cannot be claimed to have been used as its correlative.

But even if slavery had been authorized by the *State* constitutions, the word " free," in the United States constitution, could not have been claimed to have been used as its correlative, unless it had appeared that the United States constitution had itself provided or suggested no correlative of the word " free ;" for it would obviously be absurd and inadmissible to go out of an instrument to find the intended correlative of one of its own words, when it had itself suggested one. This the constitution of the United States has done, in the persons of aliens. The power of naturalization is, by the constitution, taken from the States, and given exclusively to the United States. The constitution of the United States, therefore, necessarily supposes the existence of aliens — and thus furnishes the correlative sought for. It furnishes a class both for the word " free," and the words " all other persons," to apply to. And yet the slave argument contends that we must overlook these distinctions, necessarily growing out of the laws of the United States, and go out of the constitution of the United States to *find* the persons whom it describes as the " free," and " all other persons." And what makes the argument the more absurd is, that by going out of the instrument to the *then existing State constitutions* — the only instruments to which we can go — we can find there *no other* persons for the words to apply to — no other classes answering to the description of the " free persons" and " all other persons," — than the very classes suggested by the United States constitution itself, to wit, citizens and aliens; (for it has previously been shown that the then existing State constitutions recognized no such persons as slaves.)

If we are obliged (as the slave argument claims we are) to go out of the constitution of the United States to find the class whom it describes as " all other persons " than " the free," we shall, for aught I see, be equally obliged to go out of it to find those whom it describes as the " free" — for " the free," and " all other persons" than " the free," must be presumed to be found described somewhere in the same instrument. If, then, we are obliged to go out of the constitution to find the persons described in it as ' the free" and " all other persons," we are obliged to go out of it to ascertain who are the persons on whom it declares that the representation of the government shall be based, and on whom, of course, the government is founded. And thus we should have the absurdity of a constitution that purports to authorize a government, yet leaves us to go in search of the people who are to be represented in it. Besides, if we are obliged to go out of the constitution, to find the persons on whom the government rests, and those persons are arbitrarily prescribed by some other instrument, independent of the constitution, this contradiction would follow, viz., that the United States government would be a subordinate government—a mere appendage to something else—a tail to some other kite—or rather a tail to a large number of kites at once—instead of being, as it declares itself to be, the supreme government—its constitution and laws being the supreme law of the land.

Again. It certainly cannot be admitted that we must go out of the United States constitution to find the classes whom it describes as " the free," and " all other persons " than " the free," until it be shown that the constitution has told us where to go to find them. *In all other cases,* (without an exception, I think,) where the constitution makes any of its provisions dependent upon the State constitutions or State legislatures, it has particularly described them as depending upon them. But it gives no intimation that it has left it with the State constitutions, or the State legislatures, to prescribe whom *it* means by the terms " free persons " and " all other persons," on whom it requires its own representation to be based. We have, therefore, no more authority from the constitution of the United States, for going to the State constitutions, to find the classes described in the former as the " free persons " and " all other persons," than we have for going to Turkey or Japan. We are compelled, therefore, to find them in the constitution of the United States itself, if any answering to the description can possibly be found there.

Again. If we were permitted to go to the State constitutions, or to the State statute books, to find who were the persons intended by the constitution of the United States ; and if, as the slave argument assumes, it was left to the States respectively to prescribe who should, and who should not, be " free " within the meaning of the constitution of the United States, it would follow that the terms " free " and " all other persons," might be applied in as many different ways, and to as many different classes of persons, as there were different States in the Union. Not only so, but the application might also be varied at pleasure in the same State. One inevitable consequence of this state of things would be, that there could be neither a permanent, nor a uniform basis of representation throughout the country. Another possible, and even probable consequence would be, such inextricable confusion, as to the persons described by the same terms in the different States, that Congress could not apportion the national representation at all, in the manner required by the constitution. The questions of law, arising out of the different uses of the word " free," by the different States, might be made so endless and inexplicable, that the State governments might entirely defeat all the power of the general government to make an apportionment.

If the slave construction be put upon this clause, still another difficulty, in the way of making an apportionment, would follow, viz., that Congress could have no *legal* knowledge of the persons composing each of the two different classes, on which its representation must be based ; for there is no legal record — known to the laws of the United States, or even to the laws of the States — of those who are slaves, or those who are not. The information obtained by the census takers, (who have no legal records to go to,) must, in the nature of things, be of the most loose and uncertain character, on such points as these. Any accurate or *legal* knowledge on the subject is, therefore, obviously impossible. But if the other construction be adopted, this difficulty is avoided — for Congress then have the control of the whole matter, and may adopt such means as may be necessary for ascertaining accurately the persons who belong to each of these different classes. And by their naturalization laws they actually do provide for a *legal* record of all who are made " free " by naturalization.

And this consideration of certainty, as to the individuals and numbers belonging to each of these two classes, " free " and " all other persons," acquires an increased and irresistible force, when it is considered that these different classes of persons constitute also different bases for taxation, as well as representation. The requirement of the constitution is, that " representatives and *direct taxes* shall be apportioned," &c., according to the number of " free persons " and " all other persons." In reference to so important a subject as taxation, *accurate* and *legal* knowledge of the persons and numbers belonging to the different classes, becomes indispensable. Yet under the slave construction this legal knowledge becomes impossible. Under the other construction it is as perfectly

7 *

and entirely within the power of Congress, as, in the nature of things, such a subject can be—for naturalization is a legal process; and legal records, prescribed by Congress, may be, and actually are, preserved of all the persons naturalized or made " free" by their laws.

If we adopt that meaning of the word " free," which is consistent with freedom—that meaning which is consistent with natural right—the meaning given to it by the Articles of Confederation, by the then existing State constitutions, by the colonial charters, and by the English law ever since our ancestors enjoyed the name of freemen, all these difficulties, inconsistencies, contradictions and absurdities, that must otherwise arise, vanish. The word " free" then describes the native and naturalized citizens of the United States, and the words " all other persons" describe resident aliens, " Indians not taxed," and possibly some others. The representation is then placed upon the best, most just, and most rational basis that the words used can be made to describe. The representation also becomes equal and uniform throughout the country. The principle of distinction between the two bases, becomes also a stable, rational and intelligible one—one too necessarily growing out of the exercise of one of the powers granted to Congress; —one, too, whose operation could have been foreseen and judged of by the people who adopted the constitution—instead of one fluctuating with the ever-changing and arbitrary legislation of the various States, whose mode and motives of action could not have been anticipated. Adopt this definition of the word " free," and the same legislature (that is, the national one) that is required by the constitution to apportion the representation according to certain principles, becomes invested—as it evidently ought to be, and as it necessarily must be, to be efficient—with the power of determining, by their own (naturalization) laws, who are the persons composing the different bases on which its apportionment is to be made ; instead of being, as they otherwise would be, obliged to seek for these persons through all the statute books of all the different States of the Union, and through all the evidences of private property, under which one of these classes might be held. Adopt this definition of the word " free," and the United States government becomes, so far at least as its popular representation ·—which is its most important feature—is concerned, an independent government, subsisting by its own vigor, and pervaded throughout by one uniform principle. Reject this definition, and the popular national representation loses at once its nationality, and becomes a mere dependency on the will of local corporations — a mere shuttlecock to be driven hither and thither by the arbitrary and conflicting legislation of an indefinite number of separate States. Adopt this meaning of the word " free," and the national government becomes capable of knowing its own bases of representation and power, and its own subjects of taxation. Reject this definition, and the government knows not whom it represents, or on whom to levy taxes for its support. Adopt this meaning of the word " free," and some three millions of native born, but now crushed human beings, become, with their posterity, men and citizens. Adopt this meaning — this *legal* meaning — this *only* meaning that can, in this clause, be *legally* given to the word " free," and our constitution becomes, instead of a nefarious compact of conspirators against the rights of man, a consistent and impartial contract of government between *all* " the people of the United States," for securing " to themselves and their posterity the blessings of liberty" and " justice."

Again. We cannot unnecessarily place upon the constitution a meaning directly destructive of the government it was designed to establish. By giving to the word "free" the meaning universally given to it by our political papers of a similar character up to the time the constitution was adopted, we give to the government three millions of citizens, ready to fight and be taxed for its support. By giving to the word "free" a meaning correlative with slavery, we locate in our midst three millions of enemies ; thus making a difference of six millions, (one third of our whole number,) in the physical strength of the nation. Certainly a meaning so suicidal towards the government, cannot be given to any part of the constitution, except the language be irresistibly explicit ; much less can it be done, (as in this case it would be,) wantonly, unnecessarily, gratuitously, wickedly, and in violation of all previous usage.

Again. If we look into the constitution itself for the meaning of the word " free," we find it to result from the distinction there recognized between citizens and aliens. If we look into the contemporary State constitutions, we still find the word " free" to express the political relation of the individual to the State, and not any property relation of one individual to another. If we look into the law of nature for the meaning of the word " free," we find that by that law all mankind are free. Whether, therefore, we look to the constitution itself, to the contemporary State constitutions, or to the law of nature, for the meaning of this word "free," the only meaning we shall find is one consistent with the personal liberty of all. On the other hand, if we are resolved to give the word a meaning correlative with slavery, we must go to the lawless code of the kidnapper to find such a meaning. Does it need any argument to prove to which of these different codes our judicial tribunals are bound to go, to find the meaning of the words used in a constitution, that is established professedly to secure liberty and justice ?

Once more. It is altogether a false, absurd, violent, unnatural and preposterous proceeding, in construing a political paper, which purports to establish men's relations to the State, and especially in construing the clause in which it fixes the basis of representation and taxation, to give to the words, which describe the persons to be represented and taxed, and which appropriately indicate those relations of men to the State which make them proper subjects of taxation and representation — to give to such words a meaning, which, instead of describing men's relations to the State, would describe merely a personal or property relation of one individual to another, which the State has nowhere else recognized, and which, if admitted to exist, would absolve the persons described from all allegiance to the State, would deny them all right to be represented, and discharge them from all liability to be taxed.*

---

* It is a well settled rule of interpretation, that each single word of an instrument must be taken to have some appropriate reference or relation to the matters treated of in the rest of the instrument, where it is capable of such a meaning. By this rule the words " free " and " freeman," when used in charters of incorporation, universally apply to persons who are members of the corporation — or are (as it is termed) " free of the company " or corporation, created by the charter — that is, free to enjoy, us a matter of right, the privileges of the corporation. It is not probable that, at the adoption of the constitution, any other use of these words, " free " and " freeman," could have been found in a single charter of incorporation in the English language, whether the charter were one of a trading corporation, of a city, a colony, or a State. Now, the constitution of the United States is but the charter of a corporation. Its object is to form " the people of the United States " into a corporation, or body politic, for the purpose of maintaining government, and for dispensing the benefits of government to the members of the corporation. If the word " free," in such a charter, is to be construed to have any reference to the general subject matter of the charter, it of course refers to those who are members of the corporation ; to the citizens ; those who are " free of the corporation," as distinguished from aliens, or persons not members of the corporation.

But the advocates of slavery are compelled to adopt the absurdity of denying that the meaning of the word " free " has any relation to the rest of the instrument ; or

But it is unnecessary to follow out this slave argument into all its ramifications. It sets out with nothing but assumptions, that are gratuitous, absurd, improbable, irrelevant, contrary to all previous usage, contrary to natural right, and therefore inadmissible. It conducts to nothing but contradictions, absurdities, impossibilities, indiscriminate slavery, anarchy, and the destruction of the very government which the constitution was designed to establish.

The other clause relied on as a recognition and sanction, both of slavery and the slave trade, is the following :

" The migration or importation of such persons as any of the States now existing shall think proper to admit, shall not be prohibited by the Congress prior to the year one thousand eight hundred and eight, but a tax or duty may be imposed on such importation, not exceeding ten dollars for each person."—(Art. 1, Sec. 9.)

The slave argument, drawn from this clause, is, that the word " importation " applies only to property, and that it therefore implies, in this clause, that the persons to be imported are necessarily to be imported as property—that is, as slaves.

But the idea that the word " importation " applies only to property, is erroneous. It applies correctly both to persons and things. The definition of the verb " import " is simply " to bring from a foreign country, or jurisdiction, or from another State, into one's own country, jurisdiction or State." When we speak of " importing" things, it is true that we mentally associate with them the idea of property. But that is simply because *things* are property, and not because the word " import " has any control, in that particular, over the character of the things imported. When we speak of importing " persons," we do not associate with them the idea of property, simply because " persons" are not property.

We speak daily of the " importation of foreigners into the country ;" but no one infers therefrom that they are brought in as slaves, but as passengers. A vessel imports, or brings in, five hundred passengers. Every vessel, or master of a vessel, that

---

any reference to the persons who are really "free of the corporation," which the instrument creates. They are obliged to maintain that it is used only to describe those who are free from some individual tyranny, which the instrument nowhere else recognizes as existing, and which really had no legal existence to be recognized.

All this is a palpable violation of a perfectly well settled rule of interpretation — of a rule, which is obviously indispensable for maintaining any kind of coherence between the different parts of an instrument.

" brings in " passengers, " imports " them. But such passengers are not therefore slaves. A man imports his wife and children — but they are not therefore his slaves, or capable of being owned or sold as his property. A man imports a gang of laborers, to clear lands, cut canals, or construct railroads; but not therefore to be held as slaves. An innocent meaning must be given to the word, if it will bear one. Such is the legal rule.

Even the popular understanding of the word " import," when applied to " persons," does not convey the idea of property. It is only when it is applied distinctly to " slaves," that any such idea is conveyed; and then it is the word " slaves," and not the word " import," that suggests the idea of property. Even slave traders and slave holders attach no such meaning to the word " import," when it is connected with the word " persons;" but only when it is connected with the word " slaves."

In the case of Ogden *vs.* Saunders, (12 Wheaton, 332,) Chief Justice Marshall said, that in construing the constitution, " the intention of the instrument must prevail; that this intention must be collected from its words; that its words are to be understood in that sense in which they are *generally used* by those for whom the instrument was intended." On this principle of construction, there is not the least authority for saying that this provision for ' the importation of persons," authorized the importation of them as slaves. To give it this meaning, requires the same stretching of words *towards the wrong*, that is applied, by the advocates of slavery, to the words " service or labor," and the words " free " and " all other persons."

Another reason, which makes it necessary that this construction should be placed upon the word " *importation*," is, that the clause contains no other word that describes the immigration of foreigners. Yet that the clause related to the immigration of foreigners *generally*, and that it restrained Congress, (up to the year 1808,) from prohibiting the immigration of foreigners generally, there can be no doubt.

The object, and the only *legal* object, of the clause was to restrain Congress from so exercising their " power of regulating commerce with foreign nations, and among the several States, and with the Indian tribes " — (which power has been decided by the Supreme Court of the United States, to include a power over navigation and the transportation of passengers in boats and vessels*)

---

* Gibbons *vs.* Ogden. — (9 Wheaton, 1.)

— as to obstruct the introduction of new population into such of the States as were desirous of increasing their population in that manner. The clause does not imply at all, that the population, which the States were thus to "admit," was to be a slave population.

The word "importation," (I repeat,) is the only word in the clause, that applies to persons that were to *come into* the country from foreign nations. The word "*migration*" applies only to those who were to *go out from* one of our own States or Territories into another. "*Migration*" is the act of *going out* from a state or country; and differs from immigration in this, that immigration is the act of *coming into* a state or country. It is obvious, therefore, that the "*migration*," which Congress are here forbidden to prohibit, is simply the *going out* of persons from one of our own States or Territories into another — (for that is the only "*migration*" that could come within the jurisdiction of Congress) — and that it has no reference to persons *coming in* from foreign countries to our own.

If, then, "migration," as here used, has reference only to persons *going out* from one State into another, the word "*importation*" is the only one in the clause that is applicable to foreigners coming into our country. This word "importation," then, being the only word that can apply to persons coming into the country, it must be considered as substantially synonymous with immigration, and must apply equally to *all* "persons," that are "imported," or brought into the country as passengers. And if it applies equally to all persons, that are brought in as passengers, it does not *imply* that any of those persons are slaves; for no one will pretend that this clause ever authorized the State governments to treat as slaves *all* persons that were brought into the country as passengers. And if it did not authorize them to treat all such passengers as slaves, it did not authorize them to treat any of them as such; for it makes no discrimination between the different "persons" that should be thus imported.

Again. The argument, that the allowance of the "importation" of "persons," implies the allowance of property in such persons, would imply a recognition of the validity of the slave laws of other countries; for unless slaves were obtained by valid purchase abroad — which purchase implies the existence and validity of foreign slave laws — the importer certainly could not claim to import his slaves as property; but he would appear at the custom-house as a mere pirate, claiming to have his captures legalized. So that, *according to the slave argument*, the simple use of the word "importation," in the constitution, as applied to "persons," bound our government, not only to the sanction and toleration of slavery in our own country, but to the recognition of the validity of the slave laws of other countries.

But further. The allowance of the "importation" of slaves, as such, under this clause of the constitution, would imply that Congress must take actual, and even the most critical cognizance of the slave laws of other countries; and that they should allow neither the mere word of the person calling himself the owner, nor anything short of the fullest and clearest legal proof, according to the laws of those countries, to be sufficient to enable him to enter his slaves, as property, at the custom-house; otherwise any masters of vessels, from England or France, as well as from Africa, might, on their arrival here, claim their passengers as slaves. Did the constitution, in this clause, by simply using the word "importation," instead of immigration, intend to throw upon the national government — at the hazard of making it a party to the illegal enslavement of human beings — the responsibility of investigating and deciding upon the legality and credibility of all the evidence that might be offered by the piratical masters of slave ships, to prove their valid purchase of, and their right of property in, their human cargoes, according to the slave laws of the countries from which they should bring them? Such must have been the intention of the constitution, if it intended (as it must, if it intended anything of this kind) that the fact of "importation" under the commercial regulations of Congress, should be thereafter a sufficient authority for holding in slavery the persons imported.

But perhaps it will be said that it was not the intention of the constitution, that Congress should take any responsibility at all in the matter; that it was merely intended that whoever came into the country with a cargo of men, whom he called his slaves, should be permitted to bring them in on his own responsibility, and sell them as slaves for life to our people; and that Congress were prohibited only from interfering, or asking any questions as to how he obtained them, or how they became his slaves. Suppose such were the intention of the constitution — what follows? Why, that the national government, the only government that was 'o be known to foreign nations, the only government that was to be permitted to regulate our commerce or make treaties with foreign nations, the government on whom alone was to rest the responsibility of war with foreign nations, was bound to permit (until 1808) all masters, both of our own ships and of the ships of other nations, to turn pirates, and make slaves of their passengers, whether Englishmen, Frenchmen, or any other civilized people, (for the constitution makes no distinction of "persons" on this point,) bring them into this country, sell them as slaves for life to our people, and thus make our country a rendezvous and harbor for pirates, involve us inevitably in war with every civilized nation in the world, cause ourselves to be outlawed as a people, and bring certain and swift destruction upon the whole nation ; and yet this government, that had the sole responsibility of all our foreign relations, was constitutionally prohibited from interfering in the matter, or from doing anything but lifting its hands in prayer to God and these pirates, that the former would so far depart, and the latter so far desist from their usual courses, as might be necessary to save us until 1808, (after which time we would take the matter into our own hands, and, by prohibiting the cause of the danger, save ourselves,) from the just vengeance, which the rest of mankind were taking upon us.

This is the kind of constitution, under which (according to the slave argument) we lived until 1808.

But is such the real character of the constitution ? By it, did we thus really avow to the world that we were a nation of pirates ? that our territory should be a harbor for pirates ? that our people were constitutionally licensed to enslave the people of all other nations, without discrimination, (for the instrument makes no discrimination,) whom they could either kidnap in their own countries, or capture on the high seas ? and that we had even prohibited our only government that could make treaties with foreign nations, from making any treaty, until 1808, with any particular nation, to exempt the people of that nation from their liability to be enslaved by the people of our own ? The slave argument says that we did avow all this. If we really did, perhaps all that can be said of it now is, that it is very fortunate for us that other nations did not take us at our word. For if they had taken us at our word, we should, before 1808, have been among the nations that were.

Suppose that, on the organization of our government, we had been charged by foreign nations with having established a piratical government — how could we have rebutted the charge otherwise

than by denying that the words "importation of persons" legally
implied that the persons imported were slaves? Suppose that
European ambassadors had represented to President Washington
that their governments considered our constitution as licensing our
people to kidnap the people of other nations, without discrimination, and bring them to the United States as slaves. Would he
not have denied that the legal meaning of the clause did anything
more than secure the free introduction of foreigners as passengers
and freemen? Or would he—*he*, the world-renowned champion
of human rights—have indeed stooped to the acknowledgment
that in truth he was the head of a nation of pirates, whose constitution did guaranty the freedom of kidnapping men abroad, and
importing them as slaves? And would he, in the event of this
acknowledgment, have sought to avert the destruction, which such
an avowal would be likely to bring upon the nation, by pleading
that, although such was the legal meaning of the words of our
constitution, we yet had an understanding, (an honorable understanding!) among ourselves, that we would not take advantage of
the license to kidnap or make slaves of any of the citizens of those
civilized and powerful nations of Europe, that kept ships of war,
and knew the use of gunpowder and cannon; but only the people
of poor, weak, barbarous and ignorant nations, who were incapable
of resistance and retaliation?

Again. Even the allowance of the simple "*importation*" of
slaves—(and that is the most that is *literally* provided for—and
the word "importation" must be construed to the letter,) would
not, of itself, give any authority for the continuance of slavery
after "importation." If a man bring either property or persons
into this country, he brings them in to abide the constitutional
laws of the country; and not to be held according to the customs
of the country from which they were brought. Were it not so,
the Turk might import a harem of Georgian slaves, and, at his
option, either hold them as his own property, or sell them as
slaves to our own people, in defiance of any principles of freedom
that should prevail amongst us. To allow this kind of "importation," would be to allow not merely the importation of foreign
"persons," but also foreign laws to take precedence of our own.

Finally. The conclusion, that Congress were restrained, by
this clause, only from prohibiting the immigration of a foreign
population, and not from prohibiting the importation of slaves, to
be held as slaves after their importation—is the more inevitable

from the fact that the power given to Congress of naturalizing foreigners, is entirely unlimited — except that their laws must be uniform throughout the United States. They have perfect power to pass laws that shall naturalize every foreigner without distinction, the moment he sets foot on our soil. And they had this power as perfectly prior to 1808, as since. And it is a power entirely inconsistent with the idea that they were bound to admit, and forever after to acknowledge as slaves, all or any who might be attempted to be brought into the country as such.*

One other provision of the constitution, viz., the one that " the United States shall protect each of the States against domestic violence " — has sometimes been claimed as a special pledge of impunity and succor to that kind of " violence," which consists in one portion of the people's standing constantly upon the necks of another portion, and robbing them of all civil privileges, and trampling upon all their personal rights. The argument seems to take it for granted, that the only proper way of protecting a " *republican*" State (for the States are all to be " republican ") against " domestic violence," is to plant men firmly upon one another's necks, (about in the proportion of two upon one,) arm the two with whip and spur, and then keep an armed force standing by to cut down those that are ridden, if they dare attempt to throw the riders. When the ridden portion shall, by this process, have been so far subdued as to bear the burdens, lashings and spurrings of the other portion without resistance, then the state will have been secured against " domestic violence," and the " republican form of government" will be completely successful.

This version of this provision of the constitution presents a fair illustration of those new ideas of law and language, that have been invented for the special purpose of bringing slavery within the pale of the constitution.

If it have been shown that none of the other clauses of the constitution refer to slavery, this one, of course, cannot be said to

* Since the publication of the first edition, it has been asked whether the " tax or duty " authorized by the clause, does not imply that the persons imported are property? The answer is this. " A tax or duty " on persons is a poll tax; and a poll tax is a tax or duty on persons — nothing more — nothing less. A poll tax conveys no implication that the persons, on whom the tax is levied, are property — otherwise all of us, on whom a poll tax has ever been levied, were deemed by the law to be property — and if property, slaves. A poll tax on immigrants no more implies that they are slaves, than a poll tax on natives implies that the latter are slaves.

refer to slave insurrections; because if the constitution presumes
everybody to be free, it of course does not suppose that there can
be such a thing as an insurrection of slaves.

But further. The *legal* meaning, and the only legal meaning
of the word "violence," in this clause, is *unlawful force.* The
guaranty, therefore, is one of protection only against *unlawful*
force. Let us apply this doctrine to the case of the slaves and
their masters, and see which party is entitled to be protected
against the other. Slaveholding is not an act of law; it is an act
of pure "violence," or unlawful force. It is a mere trespass, or
assault, committed by one person upon another. For example
— one person beats another, until the latter will obey him, work
for him without wages, or, in case of a woman, submit to be violated. Such was the character (as has been already shown) of all
the slaveholding practised in this country at the adoption of the
constitution. Resistance to such slaveholding is not "violence,"
nor resistance to law; it is nothing more nor less than self-defence
against a trespass. It is a perfectly lawful resistance to an assault
and battery. It can no more be called "violence," (unlawful
force,) than resistance to a burglar, an assassin, a highwayman,
or a ravisher, can be called "violence." All the "violence"
(unlawful force) there is in the case, consists in the aggression, not
in the resistance. This clause, then, so far as it relates to slavery,
is a guaranty against the "violence" of slaveholding, not against
any necessary act of self-defence on the part of the slave.

We have thus examined all those clauses of the constitution,
that have been relied on to prove that the instrument recognizes
and sanctions slavery. No one would have ever dreamed that
either of these clauses alone, or that all of them together, contained so much as an allusion to slavery, had it not been for
circumstances extraneous to the constitution itself. And what are
these extraneous circumstances? They are the existence and
toleration, in one portion of the country, of a crime that embodies
within itself nearly all the other crimes, which it is the principal
object of all our governments to punish and suppress; a crime
which we have therefore no more right to presume that the constitution of the United States intended to sanction, than we have
to presume that it intended to sanction all the separate crimes
which slavery embodies, and our governments prohibit. Yet we
have *gratuitously* presumed that the constitution intended to
sanction all these separate crimes, as they are comprehended in

the general crime of slavery. And acting upon this gratuitous presumption, we have sought, in the words of the constitution, for some hidden meaning, which we could imagine to have been understood, by the initiated, as referring to slavery; or rather we have presumed its words to have been used as a kind of cipher, which, among confederates in crime, (as we presume its authors to have been,) was meant to stand for slavery. In this way, and in this way only, we pretend to have discovered, in the clauses that have been examined, a hidden, yet legal sanction of slavery. In the name of all that is legal, who of us are safe, if our governments, instead of searching our constitutions to find authorities for maintaining justice, are to continue to busy themselves in such prying and microscopic investigations, after such disguised and enigmatical authorities for such wrongs as that of slavery, and their pretended discoveries are to be adopted as law, which they are sworn to carry into execution?

The clauses mentioned, taken either separately or collectively, neither assert, imply, sanction, recognize nor acknowledge any such thing as slavery. They do not even speak of it. They make no allusion to it whatever. They do not suggest, and, of themselves, never would have suggested the idea of slavery. There is, in the whole instrument, no such word as slave or slavery; nor any language that can legally be made to assert or imply the existence of slavery. There is in it nothing about color; nothing from which a liability to slavery can be predicated of one person more than another; or from which such a liability can be predicated of any person whatever. The clauses, that have been claimed for slavery, are all, in themselves, honest in their language, honest in their legal meaning; and they can be made otherwise only by such gratuitous assumptions against natural right, and such straining of words in favor of the wrong, as, if applied to other clauses, would utterly destroy every principle of liberty and justice, and allow the whole instrument to be perverted to every conceivable purpose of tyranny and crime.

Yet these perversions of the constitution are made by the advocates of slavery, not merely in defiance of those legal rules of interpretation, which apply to all instruments of the kind, but also in defiance of the express language of the preamble, which declares that the object of the instrument is to "establish justice" and "secure liberty"—which declaration alone would furnish an imperative rule of interpretation, independently of all other rules.

8*

Let us now look at the *positive* provisions of the constitution, *in favor of liberty*, and see whether they are not only inconsistent with any legal sanction of slavery, but also whether they must not, of themselves, have necessarily extinguished slavery, if it had had any constitutional existence to be extinguished.

And, first, the constitution made all "the people of the United States" *citizens* under the government to be established by it; for all of those, by whose authority the constitution declares itself to be established, must of course be presumed to have been made citizens under it. And whether they were entitled or not to the right of suffrage, they were at least entitled to all the personal liberty and protection, which the constitution professes to secure to "the people" generally.

Who, then, established the constitution?

The preamble to the constitution has told us in the plainest possible terms, to wit, that "We, *the people* of the United States," "do ordain and establish this constitution," &c.

By "the people of the United States," here mentioned, the constitution intends *all* "the people" then permanently inhabiting the United States. If it does not intend all, who were intended by "the people of the United States?" — The constitution itself gives no answer to such a question. — It does not declare that "we, the *white* people," or "we, the *free* people," or "we, a *part* of the people" — but that "we, *the* people" — that is, we the *whole* people — of the United States, "do ordain and establish this constitution."

If the *whole* people of the United States were not recognized as citizens by the constitution, then the constitution gives no information as to what portion of the people were to be citizens under it. And the consequence would then follow that the constitution established a government that could not know its own citizens.

We cannot go out of the constitution for evidence to prove who were to be citizens under it. We cannot go out of a written instrument for evidence to prove the parties to it, nor to explain its meaning, except the language of the instrument on that point be ambiguous. In this case there is no ambiguity. The language of the instrument is perfectly explicit and intelligible.

Because the whole people of the country were not allowed to vote on the ratification of the constitution. it does not follow that they were not made citizens under it; for women and children did not vote on its adoption; yet they are made citizens by it, and are entitled as citizens to its protection; and the State governments cannot enslave them. The national constitution does not limit the right of citizenship and protection by the right of suffrage, any more than do the State constitutions. Under the most, probably under all, the State constitutions, there are persons who are denied the right of suffrage — but they are not therefore liable to be enslaved.

Those who did take part in the actual ratification of the constitution, acted in behalf of, and, *in theory*, represented the authority of the whole people. Such is the theory in this country wherever suffrage is confined to a few; and such is the virtual declaration of the constitution itself. The declaration that "we *the people* of the United States do ordain and establish this constitution," is equivalent to a declaration that those who actually participated in its adoption, acted in behalf of all others, as well as for themselves.

Any private intentions or understandings, on the part of one portion of the people, as to who should be citizens, cannot be admitted to prove that such portion only were intended by the constitution, to be citizens; for the intentions of the other portion would be equally admissible to exclude the exclusives. The mass of the people of that day could claim citizenship under the constitution, on no other ground than as being a part of "the people of the United States;" and such claim necessarily admits that all other "people of the United States" were equally citizens.

That the designation, "We, the people of the United States," included the whole people that properly belonged to the United States, is also proved by the fact that no exception is made in any other part of the instrument.

If the constitution had intended that any portion of "the people of the United States" should be excepted from its benefits, disfranchised, outlawed, enslaved, it would of course have designated these exceptions with such particularity as to make it sure that none but the true persons intended would be liable to be subjected to such wrongs. Yet, instead of such particular designation of the exceptions, we find no designation whatever of the kind. But on the contrary, we *do* find, in the preamble itself, a sweeping declaration to the effect that there are no such exceptions; that the whole people of the United States are citizens, and entitled to liberty, protection, and the dispensation of justice under the constitution.

If it be admitted that the constitution designated its own citizens, then there is no escape from the conclusion that it designated the whole people of the United States as such. On the other hand, if it be denied that the constitution designated its own citizens, one of these two conclusions must follow, viz., 1st, that it has no citizens; or, 2d, that it has left an unrestrained power in the *State* governments to determine who may, and who may not be citizens of the *United States* government. If the first of these conclusions be adopted, viz., that the constitution has no citizens, then it follows that there is really no United States government, except on paper — for there would be as much reason in talking of an army without men, as of a government without citizens. If the second conclusion be adopted, viz., that the State governments have the right of determining who may, and who may not be citizens of the United States government, then it follows that the state governments may at pleasure destroy the government of the United States, by enacting that none of their respective inhabitants shall be citizens of the United States.

This latter is really the doctrine of some of the slave States — the "state-rights" doctrine, so called. That doctrine holds that the general government is merely a confederacy or league of the several States, *as States;* not a government established by the people, *as individuals.* This "state-rights" doctrine has been declared unconstitutional by reiterated opinions of the Supreme Court of the United States;* and, what is of more consequence, it is denied also by the preamble to the constitution itself, which declares that it is "the people" (and not the State governments) that ordain and establish it. It is true also that the constitution was ratified by conventions of the people, and not by the legislatures of the States. Yet because the constitution was ratified by conventions of the States *separately*, (as it naturally would be for convenience, and as it necessarily must have been for the reason that none but

---

* " The government (of the U. S.) proceeds directly from the people; is ' ordained and established' in the name of the people." — *M'Culloch* vs. *Maryland*, 4 *Wheaton*, 403.

" The government of the Union is emphatically and truly, a government of the people; and in form and in substance it emanates from them. Its powers are granted by them, and are to be exercised directly on them, and for their benefit." — *Same*, pages 404, 405.

" The constitution of the United States was ordained and established, *not* by the United States in their sovereign capacities, but emphatically, as the preamble of the constitution declares, by ' the people of the United States.' " — *Martin* vs. *Hunter's lessee*, 1 *Wheaton*, 324.

the people of the respective States could recall any portion of the authority they had delegated to their State governments, so as to grant it to the United States government,) — yet because it was thus ratified, I say, some of the slave States have claimed that the general government was a league of States, instead of a government formed by "the people." The true reason why the slave States have held this theory, probably is, because it would give, or appear to give, to the States the right of determining who should, and who should not, be citizens of the United States. They probably saw that if it were admitted that the constitution of the United States had designated its own citizens, it had undeniably designated the whole people of the then United States as such; and that, as a State could not enslave a citizen of the United States, (on account of the supremacy of the constitution of the United States,) it would follow that there could be no constitutional slavery in the United States.

Again. If the constitution was established by authority of all "the people of the United States," they were all legally parties to it, and citizens under it. And if they were parties to it, and citizens under it, it follows that neither they, *nor their posterity,* nor any nor either of them, can ever be legally enslaved within the territory of the United States; for the constitution declares its object to be, among other things, "to secure the blessings of liberty to *ourselves, and our posterity.*" This purpose of the national constitution is a law paramount to all State constitutions; for it is declared that "this constitution, and the laws of the United States that shall be made in pursuance thereof, and all treaties made, or which shall be made under the authority of the United States, shall be the supreme law of the land; and the judges *in every State* shall be bound thereby, anything in the constitution or laws of any State to the contrary notwithstanding."

No one, I suppose, doubts that if the State governments were to abolish slavery, the slaves would then, without further legislation, become citizens of the United States. Yet, in reality, if they would become citizens then, they are equally citizens now — else it would follow that the State governments had an arbitrary power of making citizens of the United States; or — what is equally absurd — it would follow that disabilities, arbitrarily imposed by the State governments, upon native inhabitants of the country, were, of themselves, sufficient to deprive such inhabitants of the citizenship, which would otherwise have been conferred upon them by the constitution of the United States. To suppose that the State governments are thus able, arbitrarily, to keep in abeyance, or arbitrarily to withhold from any of the inhabitants of the country, any of the benefits or rights which the national constitution intended to confer upon them, would be to suppose that the State constitutions were paramount to the national one. The conclusion, therefore, is inevitable, that the State governments have no power to withhold the rights of citizenship from any who are otherwise competent to become citizens. And as all the native born inhabitants of the country are at least competent to become citizens of the United States, (if they are not already such,) the State governments have no power, by slave laws or any other, to withhold the rights of citizenship from them.

But however clear it may be, that the constitution, in reality, made citizens of all " the people of the United States," yet it is not necessary to maintain that point, in order to prove that the constitution gave no guaranty or sanction to slavery — for if it had not already given citizenship to all, it nevertheless gave to the government of the United States unlimited power of offering citizenship to all. The power given to the government of passing naturalization laws, is entirely unrestricted, except that the laws must be uniform throughout the country. And the government have undoubted power to offer naturalization and citizenship to every person in the country, whether foreigner or native, who is not already a citizen. To suppose that we have in the country three millions of native born inhabitants, not citizens, and whom the national government has no power to make citizens, when its power of naturalization is entirely unrestricted, is a palpable contradiction.

But further. The constitution of the United States must be made consistent with itself throughout ; and if any of its parts are irreconcilable with each other, those parts that are inconsistent with liberty, justice and right, must be thrown out for inconsistency. Besides the provisions already mentioned, there are numerous others, in the constitution of the United States, that are entirely and irreconcilably inconsistent with the idea that there either was, or could be, any constitutional slavery in this country.

Among these provisions are the following :

First. Congress have power to lay a capitation or poll tax upon the people of the country. Upon whom shall this tax be levied ? and who must be held responsible for its payment ? Suppose a poll tax were laid upon a man, whom the State laws should pretend to call a slave. Are the United States under the necessity of investigating, or taking any notice of the fact of slavery, either for the purpose of excusing the man himself from the tax, or of throwing it upon the person claiming to be his owner? Must the government of the United States find a man's pretended owner, or only the man himself, before they can tax him? Clearly the United States are not bound to tax any one but the individual himself, or to hold any other person responsible for the tax. Any other principle would enable the State governments to defeat any tax of this kind levied by the United States. Yet a man's liability to be held personally responsible for the payment of a tax, levied upon himself by the government of the United States, is inconsistent with the idea that the government is bound to recognize him as not having the ownership of his own person.

Second. "The Congress shall have power to regulate commerce with foreign nations, and among the several States, and with the Indian tribes."

This power is held, by the Supreme Court of the United States, to be an exclusive one in the general government; and it obviously must be so, to be effectual — for if the States could also interfere to regulate it, the States could at pleasure defeat the regulations of Congress.

Congress, then, having the exclusive power of regulating this commerce, they only (if anybody) can say who may, and who may not, carry it on; and probably even they have no power to discriminate arbitrarily between individuals. But, in no event, have the *State* governments any right to say who may, or who may not, carry on "commerce with foreign nations," or "among the several States," or "with the Indian tribes." Every individual — naturally competent to make contracts — whom the State laws declare to be a slave, probably has, and certainly may have, under the regulations of Congress, as perfect a right to carry on "commerce with foreign nations, and among the several States, and with the Indian tribes," as any other citizen of the United States can have — "anything in the constitution or laws of any State to the contrary notwithstanding." Yet this right of carrying on commerce is a right entirely inconsistent with the idea of a man's being a slave.

Again. It is a principle of law that the right of traffic is a natural right, and that all commerce (that is intrinsically innocent) is therefore lawful, except what is prohibited by positive legislation. Traffic with the slaves, either by people of foreign nations, or by people belonging to other States than the slaves, has never (so far as I know) been prohibited by Congress, which is the only government (if any) that has power to prohibit it. Traffic with the slaves is therefore as lawful at this moment, under the constitution of the United States, as is traffic with their masters ; and this fact is entirely inconsistent with the idea that their bondage is constitutional.

Third. " The Congress shall have power to establish post offices and post roads."

Who, but Congress, have any right to say who may send, or receive letters by the United States posts ? Certainly no one. They have undoubted authority to permit any one to send and receive letters by their posts —" anything in the constitutions or laws of the States to the contrary notwithstanding." Yet the right to send and receive letters by post, is a right inconsistent with the idea of a man's being a slave.

Fourth. " The Congress shall have power to promote the progress of science and useful arts, by securing for limited times to authors and inventors the exclusive right to their respective writings and discoveries."

Suppose a man, whom a State may pretend to call a slave, should make an invention or discovery — Congress have undoubted power to secure to such individual himself, by patent, the " *exclusive* "—(mark the word) — the " exclusive right " to his invention or discovery. But does not this " *exclusive right* " in the inventor himself, exclude the right of any man, who, under a State law, may claim to be the owner of the inventor ? Certainly it does. Yet the slave code says that whatever is a slave's is his owner's. This power, then, on the part of Congress, to secure to an individual the exclusive right to his inventions and discoveries, is a power inconsistent with the idea that that individual himself, and all he may possess, are the property of another.

Fifth. " The Congress shall have power to declare war, grant letters of marque and reprisal, and make rules concerning captures on land and water;" also " to raise and support armies;" and " to provide and maintain a navy."

Have not Congress authority, under these powers, to enlist soldiers and sailors, *by contract with themselves,* and to pay them

tneir wages, grant them pensions, and secure their wages and
pensions to their own use, without asking the permission either of
the State governments, or of any individuals whom the State
governments may see fit to recognize as the owners of such soldiers and sailors? Certainly they have, in defiance of all State
laws and constitutions whatsoever; and they have already asserted that principle by enacting that pensions, paid by the United
States to their soldiers, shall not be liable to be taken for debt,
under the laws of the States. Have they not authority also to
grant letters of marque and reprisal, and to secure the prizes, to a
ship's crew of blacks, as well as of whites? To those whom the
State governments call slaves, as well as to those whom the State
governments call free? Have not Congress authority to make
contracts, for the defence of the nation, with any and all the inhabitants of the nation, who may be willing to perform the service?
Or are they obliged first to ask and obtain the consent of those
private individuals who may pretend to own the inhabitants of
this nation? Undoubtedly Congress have the power to contract
with whom they please, and to secure wages and pensions to such
individuals, in contempt of all State authority. Yet this power is
inconsistent with the idea that the constitution recognizes or sanctions the legality of slavery.

Sixth. "The Congress shall have power to provide for the
organizing, *arming* and disciplining the *militia*, and for governing such part of them as may be employed in the service of the
United States, reserving to the States respectively the appointment of the officers, and the authority of training the militia,
according to the discipline prescribed by Congress." Also " to
provide for calling forth the militia to execute the laws of the
Union, suppress insurrections, and repel invasions."

Have not Congress, under these powers, as undoubted authority
to enroll in the militia, and " *arm* " those whom the States call
slaves, and authorize them always to keep their arms by them,
even when not on duty, (that they may at all times be *ready* to
be " called forth " " to execute the laws of the Union, suppress
insurrections, and repel invasions,") as they have thus to enroll
and arm those whom the States call free? Can the State governments determine who may, and who may not, compose the militia
of the " United States ?"

Look, too, at this power, in connection with the second amend
ment to the constitution; which is in these words:

" A well regulated militia being necessary to the security of a free State, the right of *the people* to keep and bear arms shall not be infringed."

These provisions obviously recognize the natural right of all men " to keep and bear arms " for their personal defence ; and prohibit both Congress and the State governments from infringing the right of " the people "—that is, of *any* of the people—to do so ; and more especially of any whom Congress have power to include in their militia.   This right of a man " to keep and bear arms," is a right palpably inconsistent with the idea of his being a slave.   Yet the right is secured as effectually to those whom the States presume to call slaves, as to any whom the States condescend to acknowledge free.

Under this provision any man has a right either to give or sell arms to those persons whom the States call slaves ; and there is no *constitutional* power, in either the national or State governments, that can punish him for so doing ; or that can take those arms from the slaves ; or that can make it criminal for the slaves to use them, if, from the inefficiency of the laws, it should become necessary for them to do so, in defence of their own lives or liberties ; for this constitutional right to keep arms implies the constitutional right to use them, if need be, for the defence of one's liberty or life.

Seventh.   The constitution of the United States declares that " no State shall pass *any* law impairing the obligation of contracts."

" The obligation of contracts," here spoken of, is, of necessity, the *natural obligation ;* for that is the only real or true obligation that any contracts can have.   It is also the only obligation, which courts recognize in any case, except where legislatures arbitrarily interfere to impair it.   But the prohibition of the constitution is upon the States passing any law whatever that shall impair the natural obligation of men's contracts.   Yet, if slave laws were constitutional, they would effectually impair the obligation of all contracts entered into by those who are made slaves ; for the slave laws must necessarily hold that all a slave's contracts are void.

This prohibition upon the States to pass *any* law impairing the natural obligation of men's contracts, implies that all men have a constitutional right to enter into all contracts that have a natural obligation.   It therefore *secures* the constitutional right of all men to enter into such contracts, and to have them respected by the State governments.   Yet this constitutional right of all men to enter into all contracts that have a natural obligation, and to have those contracts recognized by law as valid, is a right plainly inconsistent with the idea that men can constitutionally be made slaves.

This provision, therefore, absolutely prohibits the passage of slave laws, because laws that make men slaves must necessarily impair the obligation of all their contracts.

Eighth. Persons, whom some of the State governments recognize as slaves, are made eligible, by the constitution of the United States, to the office of President of the United States. The constitutional provision on this subject is this :

" No person, except a natural born citizen, or a citizen of the United States at the time of the adoption of this constitution, shall be eligible to the office of President ; neither shall any person be eligible to that office, who shall not have attained the age of thirty-five years, and been fourteen years a resident of the United States."

According to this provision, *all* "persons," * who have resided

---

* That is, male persons. The constitution, whenever it uses the pronoun, in speaking of the President, uniformly uses the masculine gender — from which it may be inferred that male persons only were intended to be made eligible to the office.

Perhaps this inference might not be allowable, if either the office, or eligibility to the office, were anything that any one could naturally claim as a right. But neither can be claimed as a right. The office is not given to any one because he has a right to it, nor because it may be even a benefit to him. It is conferred upon him, or rather confided to him, as a trust, and solely as a trust, for the sole benefit of the people of the United States. The President, as President, is not supposed to have any rights in the office on his own account ; or any rights except what the people, for their own benefit, and not for his, have voluntarily chosen to grant to him. And the people have a right to confide this trust to whomsoever they please, or to whomsoever they think it will be most for *their* interest to confide it. And no one can say that his rights are either violated or withheld, merely because he is not selected for the trust, even though his real fitness for the trust should be altogether superior to that of the one selected. He can only say that his merits or qualifications are not properly appreciated. The people have naturally the same free, unqualified, irresponsible right to select their agents or servants, according to their pleasure or discretion, that a private individual has to select his, without giving any one, who is not selected, any reason to say that his rights are violated. The most fit person has no more claim, in the nature of a *right*, to the office, than a person the least fit ; he has only qualifications ; no one has rights.

The people, then, who establish this office, and for whose benefit alone it is to be filled, and whose servant he President is, have naturally an unqualified right to exercise their free pleasure or discretion in the selection of the person to fill it, without giving any one, who is not selected, any ground for saying that his rights are withheld, or for saying anything other than that his merits or abilities are not

within the United States fourteen years, have attained the age of thirty-five years, and are either *natural born citizens, or were citizens of the United States at the time of the adoption of the con stitution,* are eligible to the office of President.   No other qualifi- cations than these being required by the constitution, no others can be legally demanded.   The only question, then, that can arise, is as to the word "citizen."   Who are the persons that come within this definition, as here used?   The clause itself divides them into two classes, to wit, the "natural born," and those who were "citizens of the United States at the time of the adoption of the constitution."   In regard to this latter class, it has before been shown, from the preamble to the constitution, that all who were "people of the United States" (that is, permanent inhabitants) at the time the constitution was adopted, were made citizens by it. And this clause, describing those eligible to the office of President, implies the same thing.   This is evident; for it speaks of those who were "citizens of the *United States* at the time of the adop- tion of the constitution."   Now there clearly could have been no "citizens of the United States, at the time of the adoption of the constitution," unless they were made so by the constitution itself; for there were *no* "citizens of the *United States*" *before* the adop- tion of the constitution.   The confederation had no citizens.   It

---

properly estimated.   The people, for example, have a right to say, as in their con- stitution they have said, that they will confide this trust to no one who is not thirty-five years old ; and they do not thereby infringe or withhold any of the *rights* of those who are under thirty-five years old ; although it is possible that they do not properly estimate their fitness for the office.   So they have a perfect right to say that they will not confide this trust to women ; and women cannot say that their *rights* are thereby withheld ; although they are at liberty to think and say that their qualifications for the office are not appreciated.

Inasmuch, then, as no *rights* are withheld or violated by making male persons only eligible to the office, we are at perfect liberty to construe the language of the constitution according to its grammatical meaning, without seeking to go beyond it.   According to this meaning, male persons only are eligible — for the constitu- tion speaks of "the President" *as a single individual;* and very properly too — for although different individuals may fill the office, yet only one can fill it at a time, and the office is presumed never to be vacant.   It is therefore of *the officer, as a single and perpetual one,* and not of the different individuals, (as individuals,) who may at different times fill the office, that the constitution speaks, when it speaks of "the President."   And in speaking of this perpetual officer as a single individual, it uniformly uses the masculine pronoun.   Inasmuch as it would be a plain violation of grammatical rules to speak of a single and particular individual as a male person, if the individual were a female, it may (and probably must) be inferred that the constitution did not intend that the office should ever be filled by any other than a male person.

was a mere league between the State governments. The separate States belonging to the confederacy had each their own citizens respectively. But the confederation itself, as such, had no citizens. There were, therefore, no "citizens of the United States," (but only citizens of the respective States,) before the adoption of the constitution. Yet this clause asserts that immediately on the adoption, or "at the time of the adoption of this constitution," there *were* "citizens of the United States." Those, then, who were "citizens of the United States at the time of the adoption of the constitution," were necessarily those, and only those, who had been made so by the adoption of the constitution; because they could have become citizens at that precise "time" in no other way. If, then, any persons were made citizens by the adoption of the constitution, who were the *individuals* that were thus made citizens? They were "the people of the United States," of course —as the preamble to the constitution virtually asserts. And if "the people of the United States" were made citizens by the adoption of the constitution, then *all* "the people of the United States" were necessarily made citizens by it—for no discrimination is made by the constitution between different individuals. "people of the United States"—and there is therefore no means of determining who were made citizens by the adoption of the constitution, unless *all* "the people of the United States" were so made. Any "person," then, who was one of "the people of the United States" "at the time of the adoption of this constitution," and who is thirty-five years old, and has resided fourteen years within the United States, is eligible to the office of President of the United States. And if every such person be eligible, under the constitution, to the office of President of the United States, the constitution certainly does not recognize them as slaves.

The other class of citizens, mentioned as being eligible to the office of President, consists of the "natural born citizens." Here is an implied assertion that *natural birth* in the country gives the right of citizenship. And if it gives it to one, it necessarily gives it to all—for no discrimination is made; and if all persons born in the country are not entitled to citizenship, the constitution has given us no test by which to determine who of them are entitled to it.

Every person, then, born in the country, and that shall have attained the age of thirty-five years, and been fourteen years a resident within the United States, is eligible to the office of Presi-

9*

dent. And if eligible to that office, the constitution certainly does not recognize him as a slave.

Persons, who are "citizens" of the United States, according to the foregoing definitions, are also eligible to the offices of representative and senator of the United States; and therefore cannot be slaves.

Ninth. The constitution declares that "the trial of all crimes, except in cases of impeachment, shall be *by jury.*" Also that "Treason against the United States shall consist only in levying war against them, or in adhering to their enemies, giving them aid and comfort."

It is obvious that slaves, if we have any, might "levy war against the United States," and might also "adhere to their enemies, giving them aid and comfort." It may, however, be doubted whether they could commit the crime of treason — for treason implies a breach of fidelity, trust or allegiance, where fidelity, trust or allegiance is due. And it is very clear that slaves could owe allegiance, trust or fidelity, neither to the United States, nor to the State governments; for allegiance is due to a government only from those who are protected by it. Slaves could owe to our governments nothing but resistance and destruction. If, therefore, they were to levy war against the United States, they might not perhaps be liable to the technical charge of treason; although there would, in reality, be as much treason in their act, as there would of any other crime — for there would, in truth, be neither legal nor moral crime of any kind in it. Still, the government would be compelled, in order to protect itself against them, to charge them with some crime or other — treason, murder, or something else. And this charge, whatever it might be, would have to be tried by a jury. And what (in criminal cases) is the "trial by jury?" It is a trial, both of the law and the fact, by the "peers" or equals, of the person tried. Who are the "peers" of a slave? None, evidently, but slaves. If, then, the constitution recognizes any such class of persons, in this country, as slaves, it would follow that for any crime committed by them against the United States, they must be tried, both on the law and the facts, by a jury of slaves. The result of such trials we can readily imagine.

Does this look as if the constitution guarantied, or even recognized the legality of slavery?

Tenth. The constitution declares that "The privilege of the writ of *habeas corpus* shall not be suspended, unless when, in cases of rebellion or invasion, the public safety may require it.'

The privilege of this writ, wherever it is allowed, is of itself sufficient to make slavery impossible and illegal. The object and prerogative of this writ are to secure to all persons their natural right to personal liberty, against all restraint except from the government; and even against restraints by the government itself, unless they are imposed in conformity with established general laws, and upon the charge of some legal offence or liability. It accordingly liberates all who are held in custody against their will, (whether by individuals or the government,) unless they are held *on some formal writ or process, authorized by law, issued by the government, according to established principles, and charging the person held by it with some legal offence or liability.* The principle of the writ seems to be, that no one shall be restrained of his natural liberty, unless these three things conspire ; 1st, that the restraint be imposed by *special command of the government ;* 2d, that there be a general law authorizing restraints for specific causes ; and, 3d, that the government, previously to issuing process for restraining any particular individual, shall itself, by its proper authorities, take express cognizance of, and inquire cautiously into the facts of each case, and ascertain, by reasonable evidence, that the individual has brought himself within the liabilities of the general law. All these things the writ of *habeas corpus* secures to be done, before it will suffer a man to be restrained of his liberty ; for the writ is a mandate to the person holding another in custody, commanding him to bring his prisoner before the court, and show the authority by which he holds him. Unless he then exhibit a legal precept, warrant or writ, issued by, and bearing the seal of the government, specifying a legal ground for restraining the prisoner, and authorizing or requiring him to hold him in custody, he will be ordered to let him go free. Hence all keepers of prisons, in order to hold their prisoners against the authority of this writ, are required, in the case of each prisoner, to have a written precept or order, bearing the seal of the government, and issued by the proper authority, particularly describing the prisoner by name or otherwise, and setting forth the legal grounds of his imprisonment, and requiring the keeper of the prison to hold him in his custody.

Now the master does not hold his slave in custody by virtue of any formal or legal writ or process, either authorized by law, or

issued by the government, or that charges the slave with any
legal offence or liability. A slave is incapable of incurring any
legal liability, or obligation to his master. And the government
could, with no more consistency, grant a writ or process to the
master, to enable him to hold his slave, than it could to enable
him to hold his horse. It simply recognizes his right of property
in his slave, and then leaves him at liberty to hold him by brute
force, if he can, as he holds his ox, or his horse—and not otherwise. If the slave escape, or refuse to labor, the slave code no
more authorizes the government to issue legal process against the
slave, to authorize the master to catch him, or compel him to
labor, than it does against a horse for the same purpose.—The
slave is held simply as property, by individual force, without legal
process. But the writ of *habeas corpus* acknowledges no such
principle as the right of property in man. If it did, it would be
perfectly impotent in all cases whatsoever; because it is a principle of law, in regard to property, that simple possession is *prima
facie* evidence of ownership; and therefore any man, who was
holding another in custody, could defeat the writ by pleading that
he owned his prisoner, and by giving, as proof of ownership, the
simple fact that he was in possession of him. If, therefore, the
writ of *habeas corpus* did not, of itself, involve a denial of the
right of property in man, the fact stated in it, that one man was
holding another in custody, would be *prima facie* evidence that
he owned him, and had a right to hold him ; and the writ would
therefore carry an absurdity on its face.

The writ of *habeas corpus*, then, *necessarily* denies the right of
property in man. And the constitution, by declaring, without any
discrimination of persons, that "the privilege of this writ shall not
be suspended,"—that is, shall not be denied to any human being
—has declared that, under the constitution, there can be no right
of property in man.

This writ was unquestionably intended as a great constitutional
guaranty of personal liberty. But unless it denies the right of
property in man, it in reality affords no protection to any of us
against being made slaves. If it does deny the right of property
in man, the slave is entitled to the privilege of the writ ; for he is
held in custody by his master, simply on the ground of property.

Mr. Christian, one of Blackstone's editors, says that it is this
writ that makes slavery impossible in England. It was on this
writ, that Somerset was liberated. The writ, in fact, asserts, as a

great constitutional principle, the natural right of personal liberty. And the privilege of the writ is not confined to citizens, but extends to all human beings.* And it is probably the only absolute guaranty, that our national constitution gives to foreigners and aliens, that they shall not, on their arrival here, be enslaved by those of our State governments that exhibit such propensities for enslaving their fellow-men. For this purpose, it is a perfect guaranty to people who come here from any part of the world. And if it be such a guaranty to foreigners and aliens, is it no guaranty to those born under the constitution? Especially when the constitution makes no discrimination of persons?

Eleventh. "The United States shall guaranty to every State in this Union a republican form of government, and shall protect each of them against invasion; and, on application of the legislature, or of the executive, (when the legislature cannot be convened,) against domestic violence."

Mark the strength and explicitness of the first clause of this section, to wit, "The United States *shall guaranty* to every State in this Union a republican form of government." Mark also especially that this guaranty is one of liberty, and not of slavery.

We have all of us heretofore been compelled to hear, from individuals of slaveholding principles, many arrogant and bombastic assertions, touching the constitutional "*guaranties*" given to *slavery;* and persons, who are in the habit of taking their constitutional law from other men's mouths, instead of looking at the constitution for themselves, have probably been led to imagine that the constitution had really given such guaranties in some explicit and tangible form. We have, nevertheless, seen that all those pretended guaranties are at most nothing but certain vague hints, insinuations, ciphers and innuendoes, that are imagined to be covered up under language which legally means nothing of the kind. But, in the clause now cited, we do have an explicit and peremptory "guaranty," depending upon no implications, inferences or conjectures, and couched in no uncertain or ambiguous terms. And what is this guaranty? Is it a guaranty of slavery? No. It is a guaranty of something flatly incompatible with

---

* Somerset was not a citizen of England, or entitled, as such, to the protection of the English law. The privilege of the writ of *habeas corpus* was granted to him on the ground simply of his being a man.

slavery : a guaranty of "a republican form of government to every State in this Union."

And what is "a republican form of government?" It is where the government is a commonwealth—the property of the public, of the mass of the people, or of the entire people. It is where the government is made up of, and controlled by the combined will and power of the public, or mass of the people—and where, of natural consequence, it will have, for its object, the protection of the rights of all. It is indispensable to a republican form of government, that the public, the mass of the people, if not the entire people, participate in the grant of powers to the government, and in the protection afforded by the government. It is impossible, therefore, that a government, under which any considerable number of the people (if indeed any number of the people, are disfranchised and enslaved, can be a republic. A slave government is an oligarchy; and one too of the most arbitrary and criminal character.

Strange that men, who have eyes capable of discovering in the constitution so many covert, implied and insinuated guaranties of crime and slavery, should be blind to the legal import of so open, explicit and peremptory a guaranty of freedom, equality and right.

Even if there had really been, in the constitution, two such contradictory guaranties, as one of liberty or republicanism in every State of the Union, and another of slavery in every State where one portion of the people might succeed in enslaving the rest, one of these guaranties must have given way to the other—for, being plainly inconsistent with each other, they could not have stood together. And it might safely have been left either to legal or to moral rules to determine which of the two should prevail—whether a provision to perpetuate slavery should triumph over a guaranty of freedom.

But it is constantly asserted, in substance, that there is "*no propriety*" in the general government's interfering in the local governments of the States. Those who make this assertion appear to regard a State as a single individual, capable of managing his own affairs, and of course unwilling to tolerate the intermeddling of others. But a State is not an individual. It is made up of large numbers of individuals, each and all of whom, amid the intestine mutations and strifes to which States are subject, are liable, at some time or other, to be trampled upon by the strongest party, and may therefore reasonably choose to secure, in advance, some external protection against such emergencies, by making reciprocal contracts with other people similarly exposed in the neighboring States. Such contracts for mutual succor and protection, are perfectly fit and proper for any people who are so situated as to be able to contribute to each other's security. They are as fit and proper as any other political contracts whatever; and are founded on precisely the same principle of combination for mutual defence—for what are any of our political contracts and forms of government, but contracts between man and man for mutual protection against those who may conspire to injure either or all of them? But these contracts, fit and proper between all men, are peculiarly appropriate to those, who, while they are members of various local and subordinate associations, are, at the same time, united for specific purposes under one general government. Such a mutual contract, between the people of all the States, is contained in this clause of the constitution. And it gives to them all an additional guaranty for their liberties.

Those who object to this guaranty, however, choose to overlook all these considerations, and then appear to imagine that their notions of "propriety" on this point, can effectually expunge the guaranty itself from the constitution. In indulging this fancy, however, they undoubtedly overrate the legal, and perhaps also the moral effect of such superlative fastidiousness; for even if there were "*no propriety*" in the interference of the general government to maintain a republican form of government in the States, still, the unequivocal pledge to that effect, given in the constitution, would nevertheless remain an irresistible rebutter to the allegation that the constitution intended to guaranty its opposite, slavery, an oligarchy, or a despotism. It would, therefore, entirely forbid all those inferences and implications, drawn by slaveholders, from those other phrases, which they quote as guaranties of slavery.*

---

* From whom come these objections to the " propriety " of the general government's interfering to maintain republicanism in the states ? Do they not come from those who have ever hitherto claimed that the general government was bound to interfere to *put down republicanism?* And that those who were *republicans* at the north, might with perfect "propriety" and consistency, pledge their assistance to the despots of the south, to sustain the worst, the meanest and most atrocious of tyrannies ? Yes, from the very same. To interfere to assist one half of the people of a state in the cowardly, cruel and fiendish work of crushing the other half into the earth, corresponds precisely with their chivalrous notions of " propriety ;" but it is insufferable officiousness for them to form any political compacts that will require them to interfere to protect the weak against the tyranny of the strong, or to maintain justice, liberty, peace and freedom.

But the "propriety," and not only the propriety, but the necesity of this guaranty, may be maintained on still other grounds.

One of these grounds is, that it would be impossible, consistently with the other provisions of the constitution, that the general government itself could be republican, unless the State governments were republican also. For example. The constitution provides, in regard to the choice of congressional representatives, that "the electors in each State shall have the qualifications requisite for electors of the most numerous branch of the State legislature." It was indispensable to the internal quiet of each State, that the same body of electors, who should participate in the suffrage of the State governments, should participate also in the suffrage of the national one—and *vice versa*, that those who should participate in the national suffrage, should also participate in that of the State. If the general and State constitutions had each a different body of electors within each State, it would obviously give rise at once to implacable and irreconcilable feuds, that would result in the overthrow of one or the other of the governments within the State. Harmony or inveterate conflict was the only alternative. As conflict would necessarily result in the destruction of one of the governments, harmony was the only mode by which both could be preserved. And this harmony could be secured only by giving to the same body of electors, suffrage in both the governments.

If, then, it was indispensable to the existence and authority of both governments, within the territory of each State, that the same body, and only the same body of electors, that were represented in one of the governments, should be represented in the other, it was clearly indispensable, in order that the national one should be republican, that the State governments should be republican also. Hence the interest which the nation at large have in the republicanism of each of the State governments.

It being necessary that the suffrage under the national government, within each State, should be the same as for the State government, it is apparent that unless the several State governments were all formed on one general plan, or unless the electors of all the States were united in the acknowledgment of some general controlling principle, applicable to both governments, it would be impossible that they could unite in the maintenance of a general government that should act in harmony with the State governments ; because the same body of electors, that should support a despotic government in the State, could not consistently or cordially unite, or even unite at all, in the support of a republican government for the nation. If one portion of the State governments should be republican, like Vermont, where suffrage is open to all—and another portion should be oligarchies, like South Carolina, and the other slave States—another portion limited monarchies, like England—another portion ecclesiastical, like that of the Pope of Rome, or that of the ancient Jews—and another portion absolute despotisms, like that of Nicholas, in Russia, or that of Francia, in Paraguay,—and the same body, and only the same body, of electors, that sustained each of these governments at home, should be represented in the national government, each State would send into the national legislature the representatives of its own peculiar system of government; and the national legislature, instead of being composed of the representatives of any one theory, or principle of government, would be made up of the representatives of all the various theories of government that prevailed in the different States—from the extreme of democracy to the extreme of despotism. And each of these various representatives would be obliged to carry his local principles into the national legislature, else he could not retain the confidence of his peculiar constituents. The consequence would be, that the national legislature would present the spectacle of a perfect Babel of discordant tongues, elements, passions, interests and purposes, instead of an assembly, united for the accomplishment of any agreed or distinct object.

Without some distinct and agreed object as a bond of union, it would obviously be impracticable for any general union of the whole people to subsist; and that bond of union, whatever it be, must also harmonize with the principles of each of the State governments, else there would be a collision between the general and state governments.

Now the great bond of union, agreed upon in the general government, was " the rights of man"—expressed in the national constitution by the terms " liberty and justice." What other bond could have been agreed upon? On what other principle of government could they all have united? Could they have united to sustain the divine right of kings? The feudal privileges of nobles? Or the supremacy of the Christian, Mahometan, or any other church? No. They all denied the divine right of kings, and the feudal rights of nobles; and they were of all creeds in religion. But they were agreed that all men had certain natural, inherent, essential and inalienable rights, among which were life, liberty, and the pursuit of happiness ; and that the preservation of these rights was the legitimate purpose of governments among men. They had avowed this principle before the world, had fought for it, and successfully defended it, against the mightiest power in the world. They had filled the world with its glory ; and it, in turn, had filled the world with theirs. It had also gathered, and was then gathering, choice spirits, and large numbers of the oppressed from other nations unto them. And this principle—in which were involved the safety, interests and rights of each and every one of " the people," who were to unite for the formation of the government—now furnished a bond of union, that was at once sufficient, legitimate, consistent, honorable, of universal application, and having more general power over the hearts and heads of all of them, than any other that could be found to hold them together. It comported with their theory of the true objects of government. This principle, therefore, they adopted as the corner-stone of their national government; and, as a matter of necessity, all other things, on which this new government was in any degree to depend, or which was to depend in any degree upon this government, were then made to conform to this principle. Hence the propriety of the power given to the general government, of " guarantying to every State in the Union a republican form of government." Had not this power been given to the general government, the majorities in each State might have converted the State governments into oligarchies, aristocracies, monarchies or despotisms, that should not only have trampled upon the minorities, and defeated their enjoyment of the national constitution, but also introduced such factions and feuds into the national government as would have distracted its councils, and prostrated its power.

But there were also motives of a pecuniary and social, as well as political nature, that made it proper that the nation should guaranty to the States a republican form of government.

Commerce was to be established between the people of the different States. The commerce of a free people is many times more valuable than that of slaves. Freemen produce and consume vastly more than slaves. They have therefore more to buy and more to sell. Hence the free States have a direct pecuniary interest in the civil freedom of all the other States. Commerce between free and slave states is not reciprocal or equal. Who can measure the increase that would have been made to the industry and prosperity of the free States, if all the slaves in the country had been freemen, with all the wants and energies of freemen? And their masters had had all the thrift, industry and enterprise of men who depend upon their own labor, instead of the labor of slaves, for their prosperity? Great Britain thought it policy to carry on a seven years' war against us principally to secure to herself the control and benefits of the commerce of three millions of people and their posterity. But we now have nearly or quite the same number of slaves within our borders, and yet we think that commerce with them and their posterity is a matter with which we have no concern; that there is "*no propriety*" in that provision of the national constitution, which requires that the general government—which we have invested with the exclusive control of all commerce among the several States—should secure to these three millions the right of traffic with their fellow-men, and to their fellow-men the right of traffic with them, against the impertinent usurpations and tyranny of subordinate governments, that have no constitutional right to interfere in the matter.

Again. The slave States, in proportion to their population, contribute nothing like an equal or equitable share to the aggregate of national wealth. It would probably be within the truth to say that, in proportion to numbers, the people of the free States have contributed ten times as much to the national wealth as the people of the slave States. Even for such wealth as the culture of their great staple, cotton, has added to the nation, the south are indebted principally, if not entirely, to the inventive genius of a single northern man.* The agriculture of the slave States is carried on with rude and clumsy implements; by listless, spiritless and thriftless laborers; and in a manner speedily to wear out the natural fertility of the soil, which fertility slave cultivation seldom or never replaces. The mechanic arts are comparatively dead among them. Invention is utterly dormant. It is doubtful whether either a slave or a slave holder has ever invented a single important article of labor-saving machinery since the foundation of the government. And they have hardly had the skill or enterprise to apply any of those invented by others. Who can estimate the loss of wealth to the nation from these causes alone? Yet we

---

* Eli Whitney.

of the free States give to the south a share in the incalculable
wealth produced by our inventions and labor-saving machinery,
our steam engines, and cotton gins, and manufacturing machinery
of all sorts, and yet say at the same time that we have no interest,
and that there is " no propriety" in the constitutional guaranty of
that personal freedom to the people of the south, which would
enable them to return us some equivalent in kind.

For the want, too, of an enforcement of this guaranty of a
republican form of government to each of the States, the population of the country, by the immigration of foreigners, has no doubt
been greatly hindered. Multitudes almost innumerable, who
would have come here, either from a love of liberty, or to better
their conditions, and given the country the benefit of their talents,
industry and wealth, have no doubt been dissuaded or deterred
by the hideous tyranny that rides triumphant in one half of the
nation, and extends its pestiferous and detested influence over the
other half.

Socially, also, we have an interest in the freedom of all the
States. We have an interest in free personal intercourse with all
the people living under a common government with ourselves.
We wish to be free to discuss, with any and all of them, all the
principles of liberty and all the interests of humanity. We wish,
when we meet a fellow-man, to be at liberty to speak freely with
him of his and our condition ; to be at liberty to do him a service ;
to advise with him as to the means of improving his condition ;
and, if need be, to ask a kindness at his hands. But all these
things are incompatible with slavery. Is this such a union as we
bargained for ? Was it " nominated in the bond," that we should
be cut off from these the common rights of human nature ? If so,
point to the line and letter, where it is so written. Neither of
them are to be found. But the contrary *is* expressly guarantied
against the power of both the governments, state and national; for
the national government is prohibited from passing any law
abridging the freedom of speech and the press, and the state
governments are prohibited from maintaining any other than a
republican form of government, which of course implies the same
freedom.

The nation at large have still another interest in the republicanism of each of the States ; an interest, too, that is indicated in the
same section n which this republicanism is guarantied. This
interest results from the fact that the nation are pledged to " pro-

ect" each of the States "against domestic violence." Was there no account taken—in reference either to the cost or the principle of this undertaking—as to what might be the character of the State governments, which we are thus pledged to defend against the risings of the people? Did we covenant, in this clause, to wage war against the rights of man? Did we pledge ourselves that those, however few, who might ever succeed in getting the government of a State into their hands, should thenceforth be recognized as the legitimate power of the State, and be entitled to the whole force of the general government to aid them in subjecting the remainder of the people to the degradation and injustice of slavery? Or did the nation undertake only to guaranty the preservation of "a republican form of government" against the violence of those who might prove its enemies? The reason of the thing, and the connexion, in which the two provisions stand in the constitution, give the answer.

We have yet another interest still, and that no trivial one, in the republicanism of the State governments; an interest indicated, too, like the one last mentioned, in the very section in which this republicanism is assured. It relates to the defence against invasion. The general government is pledged to defend each of the States against invasion. Is it a thing of no moment, whether we have given such a pledge to free or to slave States? Is there no difference in the cost and hazard of defending one or the other? Is it of no consequence to the expense of life and money, involved in this undertaking, whether the people of the State invaded shall be united, as freemen naturally will be, as one man against the enemy? Or whether, as in slave States, half of them shall be burning to join the enemy, with the purpose of satisfying with blood the long account of wrong that shall have accrued against their oppressors? Did Massachusetts—who during the war of the revolution furnished more men for the common defence, than all the six southern States together—did she, immediately on the close of that war, pledge herself, as the slave holders would have it, that she would lavish her life in like manner again, for the defence of those whose wickedness and tyranny in peace should necessarily multiply their enemies and make them defenceless in war? If so, on what principle, or for what equivalent, did she do it? Did she not rather take care that the guaranty for a republican government should be inserted in the same paragraph with that for protection against invasion, in order that both the principle

10*

and the extent of the liability she incurred, might distinctly appear.

The nation at large, then, as a political community under the constitution, have both interests and rights, and both of the most vital character, in the republicanism of each of the State governments. The guaranty given by the national constitution, securing such a government to each of the States, is therefore neither officious nor impertinent. On the contrary, this guaranty was a *sine qua non* to any rational contract of union; and the enforcement of it is equally indispensable, if not to the continuance of the union at all, certainly to its continuance on any terms that are either safe, honorable or equitable for the north.

This guaranty, then, is not idle verbiage. It is full of meaning. And that meaning is not only fatal to slavery itself, but it is fatal also to all those pretences, constructions, surmises and implications, by which it is claimed that the national constitution sanctions, legalizes, or even tolerates slavery.

CHAPTER IX.

THE INTENTIONS OF THE CONVENTION.

THE intentions of the framers of the constitution, (if we could have, as we cannot, any *legal* knowledge of them, except from the words of the constitution,) have nothing to do with fixing the legal meaning of the constitution. That convention were not delegated to adopt or establish a constitution; but only to consult, devise and recommend. The instrument, when it came from their hands, was a mere proposal, having no legal force or authority. It finally derived all its validity and obligation, as a frame of government, from its adoption by the people at large.* Of course the intentions of the people at large are the only ones, that are of any importance to be regarded in determining the legal meaning of the instrument. And their intentions are to be gathered entirely from the words, which they adopted to express them. And their intentions must be presumed to be just what, and only what the words of the instrument *legally* express. In adopting the consti-

---

* The Supreme Court say, "The instrument, when it came from their hands, (that is, the hands of the convention,) was a mere proposal, without obligation or pretension to it." "The people were at perfect liberty to accept or reject it; and their act was final." — *M'Cullock* vs. *Maryland,* — 4 *Wheaton* 403 — 4.

tution, the people acted as legislators, in the highest sense in
which that word can be applied to human lawgivers. They were
establishing a law that was to govern both themselves and their
government. And their intentions, like those of other legislators,
are to be gathered from the words of their enactments. Such is
the dictate of both law and common sense.* The instrument had

---

* The Supreme Court of the United States say :
" The intention of the instrument must prevail : *this intention must be collected
from its words.*" — *Ogden* vs. *Saunders,* — 12 *Wheaton,* 332.
" The intention of the legislature is to be searched for in the words which the
legislature has employed to convey it." — *Schr. Paulina's Cargo* vs. *United States,*
— 7 *Cranch,* 60.
Judge Story, in giving an opinion upon the bankrupt act, replies as follows to an
argument analogous to that, which is often drawn from the debates of the convention, in opposition to the language of the constitution itself. He says :
" At the threshold of the argument, we are met with the suggestion, that when
the (Bankrupt) act was before Congress, the opposite doctrine was then maintained
in the House of Representatives, and it was confidently stated, that no such jurisdiction was conferred by the act, as is now insisted on. What passes in Congress
upon the discussion of a bill can hardly become a matter of strict judicial inquiry ;
and if it were, it could scarcely be affirmed, that the opinions of a few members,
expressed either way, are to be considered as the judgment of the whole House, or
even of a minority. But, in truth, little reliance can or ought to be placed upon
such sources of interpretation of a statute. The questions can be, and rarely are,
there debated upon strictly legal grounds, with a full mastery of the subject and of
the just rules of interpretation. The arguments are generally of a mixed character,
addressed by way of objection or of support, rather with a view to carry or defeat
a bill, than with the strictness of a judicial decision. But if the House entertained
one construction of the language of the bill, *non constat,* that the same opinion was
entertained either by the Senate or by the President ; and their opinions are certainly, in a matter of the sanction of laws, entitled to as great weight as the other
branch. *But in truth, courts of justice are not at liberty to look at considerations
of this sort. We are bound to interpret the act as we find it, and to make such an
interpretation as its language and its apparent objects require. We must take it
to be true, that the legislature intend precisely what they say,* and to the extent
which the provisions of the act require, for the purpose of securing their just operation and effect. *Any other course would deliver over the court to interminable
doubts and difficulties ; and we should be compelled to guess what was the law, from
the loose commentaries of different debates, instead of the precise enactments of the
statute.* Nor have there been wanting illustrious instances of great minds, which,
after they had, as legislators, or commentators, reposed upon a short and hasty
opinion, have deliberately withdrawn from their first impressions, when they came
upon the judgment seat to re-examine the statute or law in its full bearings." —
Mitchell vs. *Great Works Milling and Manufacturing Company. Story's Circuit
Court Reports, Vol. 2, page* 653.
If the intentions of legislatures, who are invested with the actual authority of
prescribing laws, are of no consequence otherwise than as they are expressed in the
language of their statutes, of how much less consequence are any unexpressed
intentions of the framers of the constitution, who had no authority to establish a
constitution, but only to draft one to be offered to the people for their voluntar~
~~~~on or rejection.

been reported by their committee, the convention. But the peopl ·
did not ask this committee what was the legal meaning of the
instrument reported. They adopted it, judging for themselves of
its legal meaning, as any other legislative body would have done.
The people at large had not even an opportunity of consultation
with the members of the convention, to ascertain their opinions.
And even if they had consulted them, they would not have been
bound at all by their opinions. But being unable to consult them,
they were compelled to adopt or reject the instrument, on their
own judgment of its meaning, without any reference to the
opinions of the convention. The instrument, therefore, is now to
be regarded as expressing the intentions of the people at large ;
and not the intentions of the convention, if the convention had
any intentions differing from the meaning which the law gives to
the words of the instrument.

But why do the partisans of slavery resort to the debates of the
convention for evidence that the constitution sanctions slavery?
Plainly for no other reason than because the words of the instrument do not sanction it. But can the intentions of that convention, attested only by a mere skeleton of its debates, and not by
any impress upon the instrument itself, add anything to the words,
or to the legal meaning of the words of the constitution ? Plainly
not. Their intentions are of no more consequence, in a legal
point of view, than the intentions of any other equal number of
the then voters of the country. Besides, as members of the convention, they were not even parties to the instrument ; and no
evidence of their intentions, at *that* time, is applicable to the case.
They became parties to it only by joining with the rest of the
people in its subsequent adoption ; and they themselves, equally
with the rest of the people, must then be presumed to have
adopted its legal meaning, and that alone—notwithstanding anything they may have previously said. What absurdity then is it
to set up the opinions expressed in the convention, and by a few
only of its members, in opposition to the opinions expressed by
the whole people of the country, in the constitution itself.

But notwithstanding the opinions expressed in the convention
by some of the members, we are bound, as a matter of law, to
presume that the convention itself, in the aggregate, had no intention of sanctioning slavery—and why ? Because, after all their
debates, they agreed upon an instrument that did not sanction it.
This was confessedly the result in which all their debates termi-

nated.   This instrument is also the *only* authentic evidence of
their intentions. It is subsequent in its date to all the other evidence.
It comes to us, also, as none of the other evidence does, *signed
with their own hands.*   And is this to be set aside, and the constitution itself to be impeached and destroyed, and free government overturned, on the authority of a few meagre snatches of
argument, intent or opinion, uttered by a few only of the members; jotted down by one of them, (Mr. Madison,) merely for his
own convenience, or from the suggestions of his own mind; and
only reported to us fifty years afterwards by a posthumous publication of his papers?   If anything could excite the utter contempt
of the people of this nation for the miserable subterfuges, to which
the advocates of slavery resort, it would seem that their offering
.such evidence as this in support of their cause, must do it.   And
yet these, and such as these mere fragments of evidence, all
utterly inadmissible and worthless in their kind, for any legal
purpose, constitute the warp and the woof, the very *sine qua non*
of the whole argument for slavery.

   Did Mr. Madison, when he took his oath of office, as President
of the United States, swear to support these scraps of debate,
which he had filed away among his private papers?—Or did he
swear to support that written instrument, which the people of the
country had agreed to, and which was known to them, and to all
the world, as the constitution of the United States?*

---

* "Elliot's Debates," so often referred to, are, if possible, a more miserable
authority than Mr. Madison's notes.   He seems to have picked up the most of them
from the newspapers of the day, in which they were reported by nobody now probably knows whom.   In his preface to his first volume, containing the debates in
the Massachusetts and New York conventions, he says:

   "In the compilation of this volume, care has been taken to search into contemporary publications, in order to make the work as perfect as possible; still, however,
the editor is sensible, from the daily experience of newspaper reports of the present time, that the sentiments they contain may, in some instances, have been in-
accurately taken down, and in others, probably too faintly sketched, fully to gratify
the inquisitive politician."   He also speaks of them as "rescued from the ephemeral
prints of that day, and now, for the first time, presented in a uniform and durable
form."

   In the preface to his second volume, which is devoted to the Virginia convention,
he says the debates were reported by an able stenographer, David Robertson; and
then quotes the following from Mr. Wirt, in a note to the Life of Patrick Henry:

   "From the skill and ability of the reporter, there can be no doubt that the substance of the debates, as well as their general course, are accurately preserved."

   In his preface to the third volume, embracing the North Carolina and Pennsylvania conventions, he says:

   "The *first* of the two North Carolina conventions is contained in this volume;

But even if the unexpressed intentions, which these notes of debate ascribed to certain members, had been participated in by the whole convention, we should have had no right to hold the people of the country at large responsible for them. *This convention sat with closed doors*, and it was not until near fifty years after the people had adopted the constitution itself, that these private intentions of the framers authentically transpired. And even now all the evidence disclosed implicates, *directly and absolutely*, but few of the members—not even all from the slaveholding states. The intentions of all the rest, we have a right to presume, concurred with their votes and the words of the instrument; and they had therefore no occasion to express contrary ones in debate.

But suppose that *all* the members of the convention had participated in these intentions—what then? Any forty or fifty men, like those who framed the constitution, may now secretly concoct another, that is honest in its terms, and yet in secret conclave confess to each other the criminal objects they intended to accomplish by it, if its honest character should enable them to secure for it the adoption of the people.—But if the people should adopt such constitution, would they thereby adopt any of the criminal and secret purposes of its authors? Or if the guilty confessions of these conspirators should be revealed fifty years afterwards, would judicial tribunals look to them as giving the government any authority for violating the legal meaning of the words of such constitution, and for so construing them as to subserve the criminal and shameless purpose of its originators?

The members of the convention, as such, were the mere scriveners of the constitution; and their individual purposes, opin-

---

the *second* convention, it is believed, *was neither systematically reported nor printed.*" The debates in the Pennsylvania convention, that have been preserved, it appears, *are on one side only;* a search into the contemporary publications of the day, has been unsuccessful to furnish us with the other side of the question."

In his preface to the fourth volume, he says:

" In compiling the opinions, on constitutional questions, delivered in Congress, by some of the most enlightened senators and representatives, the files of the New York and Philadelphia newspapers, from 1789 to 1800, had to be relied on ; from the latter period to the present, the National Intelligencer is the authority consulted for the desired information."

It is from such stuff as this, collected and published thirty-five and forty years after the constitution was adopted — stuff very suitable for constitutional dreams to be made of—that our courts and people now make their constitutional law, in preference to adopting the law of the constitution itself. In this way they manufacture law strong enough to bind three millions of men in slavery.

ions or expressions, then uttered in secret cabal, though now revealed, can no more be evidence of the intentions of the people who adopted the constitution, than the secret opinions or expressions of the scriveners of any other contract can be offered to prove the intentions of the true parties to such contract.   As framers of the constitution, the members of the convention gave to it no validity, meaning, or legal force.   They simply drafted it, and offered it, such as it legally might be, to the people for their adoption or rejection.   The people, therefore, in adopting it, had no reference whatever to the opinions of the convention.   They had no authentic evidence of what those opinions were.   They looked simply at the instrument.   And they adopted even its legal meaning by a bare majority.   If the instrument had contained any tangible sanction of slavery, the people, in some parts of the country certainly, would sooner have had it burned by the hands of the common hangman, than they would have adopted it, and thus sold themselves as pimps to slavery, covered as they were with the scars they had received in fighting the battles of freedom.   And the members of the convention knew that such was the feeling of a large portion of the people; and for that reason, if for no other, they dared insert in the instrument no legal sanction of slavery. They chose rather to trust to their craft and influence to corrupt the government, (of which they themselves expected to be important members,) after the constitution should have been adopted, rather than ask the necessary authority directly from the people. And the success they have had in corrupting the government, proves that they judged rightly in presuming that the government would be more flexible than the people.

For other reasons, too, the people should not be charged with designing to sanction any of the secret intentions of the convention.   When the States sent delegates to the convention, no avowal was made of any intention to give any national sanction to slavery.   The articles of confederation had given none; the then existing State constitutions gave none; and it could not have been reasonably anticipated by the people that any would have been either asked for or granted in the new constitution.   If such a purpose had been avowed by those who were at the bottom of the movement, the convention would doubtless never have been held. The avowed objects of the convention were of a totally different character.   Commercial, industrial and defensive motives were the prominent ones avowed.   When, then, the constitution came from the hands of such a convention, unstained with any legal or tangible sanction of slavery, were the people — who, from the nature of the case, could not assemble to draft one for themselves — bound either to discard it, or hold themselves responsible for all the secret intentions of those who had drafted it? Had they no power to adopt its legal meaning, and that alone? Unquestionably they had the power; and, as a matter of law, as well as fact, it is equally unquestionable that they exercised it. Nothing else than the constitution, as a legal instrument, was offered to them for their adoption. Nothing else was legally before them that they could adopt. Nothing else, therefore, did they adopt.

This alleged design, on the part of the convention, to sanction slavery, is obviously of no consequence whatever, unless it can be transferred to the people who adopted the constitution. Has any such transfer ever been shown? Nothing of the kind. It may have been known among politicians, and may have found its way into some of the State conventions. But there probably is not a tittle of evidence in existence, that it was generally known among the mass of the people. And, in the nature of things, it was nearly impossible that it should have been known by them. The national convention had sat with closed doors. Nothing was known of their discussions, except what was personally reported by the members. Even the discussions in the *State* conventions could not have been known to the people at large; certainly not until after the constitution had been ratified by those conventions. The ratification of the instrument, by those conventions, followed close on the heels of their discussions. — The population meanwhile was thinly scattered over the country. The public papers were few, and small, and far between. They could not even make such reports of the discussions of public bodies, as newspapers now do. The consequence must have been that the people at large knew nothing of the intentions of the framers of the constitution, but from its words, until after it was adopted. Nevertheless, it is to be constantly borne in mind, that even if the people had been fully cognizant of those intentions, they would not therefore have adopted them, or become at all responsible for them, so long as the intentions themselves were not incorporated in the instrument. Many selfish, ambitious and criminal purposes, not expressed in the constitution, were undoubtedly intended to be accomplished by one and another of the thousands of unprincipled politicians, that would naturally swarm around the birth-place and assist at the nativity of a new and splendid government. But the people are not therefore responsible for those purposes; nor are those purposes, therefore, a part of the constitution ; nor is its language to be construed with any view to aid their accomplishment.

But even if the people intended to sanction slavery by adopting the intentions of the convention, it is obvious that they, like the convention, intended to use no language that should legally convey that meaning, or that should necessarily convict them of that intention in the eyes of the world.—They, at least, had enough of virtuous shame to induce them to conceal this intention under the cover of language, whose legal meaning would enable them always to aver,

"Thou canst not say I did it."

The intention, therefore, that the judiciary should construe certain language into an authority for slavery, when such is not the legal meaning of the language itself, cannot be ascribed to the people, except upon the supposition that the people presumed their judicial tribunals would have so much less of shame than they themselves, as to *volunteer* to carry out these their secret wishes, by going beyond the words of the constitution they should be sworn to support, and violating all legal rules of construction, and all the free principles of the instrument. It is true that the judiciary, (whether the people intended it or not,) have proved themselves to be thus much, at least, more shameless than the people, or the convention. Yet that is not what ought to have been expected of judicial tribunals. And whether such were really the intention of the convention, or the people, is, at best, a matter of conjecture and history, and not of law, nor of any evidence cognizable by any judicial tribunal.

Why should we search at all for the intentions, either of the convention, or of the people, beyond the words which both the convention and the people have agreed upon to express them ? What is the object of written constitutions, and written statutes, and written contracts ? Is it not that the meaning of those who make them may be known with the most absolute precision of which language is capable ? Is it not to get rid of all the fraud, and uncertainty, and disagreements of oral testimony ? Where would be our constitution, if, instead of its being a written instrument, it had been merely agreed upon orally by the members of the convention ? And by them only orally reported to the people ? **And**

11

only this oral report of it had been adopted by the people? And all our evidence of what it really was, had rested upon reports of what Mr. A. and B., members of the convention, had been heard to say? Or upon Mr. Madison's notes of the debates of the convention? Or upon the oral reports made by the several members to their respective constituents, or to the respective State conventions? Or upon flying reports of the opinions which a few individuals, out of the whole body of the people, had formed of it when they adopted it? No two of the members of the convention would probably have agreed in their representations of what the constitution really was. No two of the people would have agreed in their understanding of the constitution when they adopted it. And the consequence would have been that we should really have had no constitution at all. Yet there is as much ground, both in reason and in law, for thus throwing aside the *whole* of the written instrument, and trusting entirely to these other sources for evidence of what any part of the constitution really is, as there is for throwing aside those particular portions of the written instrument, which bear on slavery, and attempting to supply their place from such evidence as these other sources may chance to furnish. And yet, to throw aside the written instrument, so far as its provisions are prohibitory of slavery, and make a new constitution on that point, out of other testimony, is the only means, confessedly the only means, by which slavery can be made constitutional.

And what is the object of resorting to these flying reports for evidence, on which to change the meaning of the constitution? Is it to change the instrument from a dishonest to an honest one? from an unjust to a just one? No. But directly the reverse—and solely that dishonesty and injustice may be carried into effect. A purpose, for which no evidence of any kind whatever could be admitted in a court of justice.

Again. If the principle be admitted, that the meaning of the constitution can be changed, on proof being made that the scriveners or framers of it had secret and knavish intentions, which do not appear on the face of the instrument, then perfect license is given to the scriveners of constitutions to contrive any secret scheme of villany they may please, and impose it upon the people as a system of government, under cover of a written instrument that is so plainly honest and just in its terms, that the people readily agree to it. Is such a principle to be admitted in a

country where the people claim the prerogative of establishing
their own government, and deny the right of anybody to impose
a government upon them, either by force, or fraud, or against their
will ?

Finally.   The constitution is a contract; a written contract,
consisting of a certain number of precise words, to which, and to
which only, all the parties to it have, in theory, agreed.   Manifestly neither this contract, nor the meaning of its words, can be
changed, without the consent of all the parties to it.   Nor can it
be changed on a representation, to be made by any number of
them less than the whole, that they intended anything different
from what they have said.   To change it, on the representation
of a part, without the consent of the rest, would be a breach of
contract as to all the rest.   And to change its *legal meaning*,
without their consent, would be as much a breach of the contract,
as to change its words.   If there were a single honest man in the
nation, who assented, in good faith, to the honest and legal meaning
of the constitution, it would be unjust and unlawful towards him
to change the meaning of the instrument so as to sanction slavery,
even though every other man in the nation should testify that, in
agreeing to the constitution, he intended that slavery should be
sanctioned.   If there were *not* a single honest man in the nation,
who adopted the constitution in good faith, and with the intent
that its legal meaning should be carried into effect, its legal meaning would nevertheless remain the same ; for no judicial tribunal
could lawfully allow the parties to it to come into court and allege
their dishonest intentions, and claim that they be substituted for
the legal meaning of the words of the instrument.

CHAPTER X.

THE PRACTICE OF THE GOVERNMENT.

THE practice of the government, under the constitution, has not
altered the legal meaning of the instrument.   It means now what
it did before it was ratified, when it was first offered to the people
for their adoption or rejection.   One of the advantages of a written
constitution is, that it enables the people to see what its character
is before they adopt it ; and another is, that it enables them to see

after they have adopted it, whether the government adheres to it, or departs from it. Both these advantages, each of which is indispensable to liberty, would be entirely forfeited, if the legal meaning of a written constitution were one thing when the instrument was offered to the people for their adoption, and could then be made another thing by the government after the people had adopted it.

It is of no consequence, therefore, what meaning the government *have* placed upon the instrument; but only what meaning they were *bound to place upon it* from the beginning.

The only question, then, to be decided, is, what was the meaning of the constitution, *as a legal instrument*, when it was first drawn up, and presented to the people, and before it was adopted by them?

To this question there certainly can be but one answer. There is not room for a doubt or an argument, on that point, in favor of slavery. The instrument itself is palpably a free one throughout, in its language, its principles, and all its provisions. As a legal instrument, there is no trace of slavery in it. It not only does not sanction slavery, but it does not even recognize its existence. More than this, it is palpably and wholly incompatible with slavery. It is also the supreme law of the land, in contempt of any State constitution or law that should attempt to establish slavery.

Such was the character of the constitution when it was offered to the people, and before it was adopted. And if such was its character then, such is its character still. It cannot have been changed by all the errors and perversions, intentional or unintentional, of which the government may have since been guilty.

CHAPTER XI.

THE UNDERSTANDING OF THE PEOPLE.

ALTHOUGH the inquiry may be of no legal importance, it may nevertheless be one pertinent to the subject, whether it be matter of *history* even — to say nothing of legal proof — that the *people* of the country did really understand or believe that the constitution sanctioned slavery? Those who make the assertion are bound to prove it. The presumption is against them. Where is their contrary history ?

They will say that a part of the people were actually slaveholders, and that it is unreasonable to suppose they would have agreed to the constitution, if they had understood it to be a free one.

The answer to this argument is, that the actual slaveholders were few in number compared with the whole people; comprising probably not more than one eighth or one sixth of the voters, and one fortieth or one thirtieth of the whole population. They were so few as to be manifestly incapable of maintaining any separate political organization; or even of holding their slave property, except under the sufferance, toleration and protection of the non-slaveholders. They were compelled, therefore, to agree to any political organization, which the non-slaveholders should determine on. This was at that time the case even in the strongest of the slaveholding States themselves. In all of them, without exception, the slaveholders were either obliged to live, or from choice did live, under free constitutions. They, of course, held their slave property in defiance of their constitutions. They were enabled to do this through the corrupting influence of their wealth and union. Controlling a large proportion of the wealth of their States, their social and political influence was entirely disproportionate to their numbers. They could act in concert. They could purchase talent by honors, offices and money. Being always united, while the non-slaveholders were divided, they could turn the scale in elections, and fill most of the offices with slaveholders. Many of the non-slaveholders doubtless were poor, dependent and subservient, (as large portions of the non-slaveholders are now in the slaveholding States,) and lent themselves to the support of slavery almost from necessity. By these, and probably by many other influences that we cannot now understand, they were enabled to maintain their hold upon their slave property in defiance of their constitutions. It is even possible that the slaveholders themselves did not choose to have the subject of slavery mentioned in their constitutions ; that they were so fully conscious of their power to corrupt and control their governments, that they did not regard any constitutional provision necessary for their security ; and that out of mere shame at the criminality of the thing, and its inconsistency with all the principles the country had been fighting for and proclaiming, they did not wish it to be named.

11*

But whatever may have been the cause of the fact, the fact itself is conspicuous, that from some cause or other, either with the consent of the slaveholders, or in defiance of their power, the constitutions of every one of the thirteen States were at that time free ones.

Now is it not idle and useless to pretend, when even the strongest slaveholding States had free constitutions — when not one of the separate States, acting for itself, would have any but a free constitution — that the whole thirteen, when acting in unison, should concur in establishing a slaveholding one ? The idea is preposterous. The single fact that all the State constitutions were at that time free ones, scatters forever the pretence that the majority of the people of all the States either intended to establish, *or could have been induced to establish*, any other than a free one for the nation. Of course it scatters also the pretence that they believed or understood that they were establishing any but a free one.

There very probably may have been a general belief among the people, that slavery would for a while live on, on sufferance ; that the government, until the nation should have become attached to the constitution, and cemented and consolidated by the habit of union, would be too weak, and too easily corrupted by the innumerable and powerful appliances of slaveholders, to wrestle with and strangle slavery. But to suppose that the nation at large did not look upon the constitution as destined to destroy slavery, whenever its principles should be carried into full effect, is obviously to suppose an intellectual impossibility ; for the instrument was plain, and the people had common sense ; and those two facts cannot stand together consistently with the idea that there was any general, or even any considerable misunderstanding of its meaning.

CHAPTER XII.

THE STATE CONSTITUTIONS OF 1845.

Of all the State constitutions existing at this time, 1845, (excepting that of Florida, which I have not seen,) not one of them contains provisions that are sufficient, (or that would be sufficient

if not restrained by the constitution of the United States,) to authorize the slavery that exists in the States. The material deficiency
in all of them is, that they neither designate, nor give the legislatures any authority to designate the persons, who may be made
slaves. Without such a provision, all their other provisions in
regard to slaves are nugatory, simply because their application is
legally unknown. They would apply as well to whites as to
blacks, and would as much authorize the enslavement of whites as
of blacks.

We have before seen that none of the State constitutions, that
were in existence in 1789, recognized slavery at all. Since that
time, four of the old thirteen States, viz., Maryland, North Carolina, South Carolina and Georgia, have altered their constitutions
so as to make them recognize slavery; yet not so as to provide
for any legal designation of the persons to be made slaves.

The constitution of South Carolina has a provision that implies
that *some* of the slaves, at least, are "negroes;" but not that all
slaves are negroes, nor that all negroes are slaves. The provision, therefore, amounts to nothing for the purposes of a constitutional designation of the persons who may be made slaves.

The constitutions of Tennessee and Louisiana make no direct
mention of slaves; and have no provisions in favor of slavery,
unless the general one for continuing existing laws in force, be
such an one. But both have specific provisions inconsistent with
slavery. Both purport to be established by "the people;" both
have provisions for the writ of *habeas corpus.* Indeed, the constitutions of most of the slave States have provisions for this writ,
which, as has been before shown, denies the right of property in
man. That of Tennessee declares also "that all courts shall be
open, and *every man,* for an injury done him in his lands, goods.
person or reputation, shall have remedy by due course of law, and
right and justice administered without sale, denial or delay."
Tennessee also was formerly a part of North Carolina; was set
off from her while the constitution of North Carolina was a free
one. Of course there has never been any legal slavery in Ten
nessee.

The constitutions of the States of Kentucky, Missouri, Arkan-
sas, Mississippi, and Alabama, all have provisions about slaves;
yet none of them tell us who may be slaves. Some of them
indeed provide for the admission into their State of such persons
as are slaves under the laws, (which of course means only the

constitutional laws,) *of other States.* But when we go to those other States, we find that their constitutions have made no designation of the persons who may be made slaves; and therefore we are as far from finding the actual persons of the slaves as we were before.

The principal provision, in the several State constitutions, recognizing slavery, is, in substance, this, that the legislature shall have no power to *emancipate* slaves without the consent of their owners, or without making compensation. But this provision is of no avail to legalize slavery, for slavery must be *constitutionally established*, before there can be any legal slaves to be emancipated; and it cannot be established without describing the persons who may be made slaves.

Kentucky was originally a part of Virginia, and derived her slaves from Virginia. As the constitution of Virginia was always a free one, it gave no authority for slavery in that part of the State which is now Kentucky. Of course Kentucky never had any legal slavery.

Slavery was positively prohibited in all the States included in the Louisiana purchase, by the third article of the treaty of cession —which is in these words:—

Art. 3. "The *inhabitants*" (that is, *all* the inhabitants,) "of the ceded territory shall be incorporated in the Union of the United States, and admitted as soon as possible, *according to the principles of the federal constitution*, to the enjoyment of all the rights, advantages, and immunities of *citizens* of the United States; and, in the mean time, they shall be maintained and protected in the free enjoyment of their liberty, property, and the religion which they profess."

The cession of Florida to the United States was made on the same terms. The words of the treaty, on this point are as follows:—

"Art. 6. The *inhabitants* of the territories, which his Catholic majesty cedes to the United States by this treaty, shall be incorporated in the Union of the United States, as soon as may be consistent with the principles of the federal constitution, and admitted to the enjoyment of all the privileges, rights and immunities of the *citizens* of the United States."

To allow *any* of the "inhabitants," included in those treaties, to be held as slaves, or denied the rights of citizenship under the United States constitution, is a plain breach of the treaties.

The constitutions of some of the slave States have provisions like this, viz., that all laws previously in force, shall remain in force until repealed, unless repugnant to this constitution. But I think there is no instance, in which the slave acts, then on their statute books, could be perpetuated by this provision—and for two reasons; 1st. These slave acts were previously unconstitutional, and therefore were not, legally speaking, "laws in force."* 2d. Every constitution, I think, that has this provision, has one or more other provisions that *are* "repugnant" to the slave acts

---

CHAPTER XIII.

THE CHILDREN OF SLAVES ARE BORN FREE.

THE idea that the children of slaves are necessarily born slaves, or that they necessarily follow that *natural law* of property, which gives the natural increase of property to the owner of the original stock, is an erroneous one.

It is a principle of natural law in regard to property, that a calf belongs to the owner of the cow that bore it; fruit to the owner of the tree or vine on which it grew; and so on. But the principle of *natural law*, which makes a calf belong to the owner of the cow, does not make the child of a slave belong to the owner of the slave—and why? Simply because both cow and calf are *naturally* subjects of property; while neither men nor children are *naturally* subjects of property. The law of nature gives no aid to anything inconsistent with itself. It therefore gives no aid to the transmission of property in man—while it does give aid to the transmission of property in other animals and in things.

Brute animals and things being *naturally* subjects of property, there are obvious reasons why the natural increase should belong to the owner of the original stock. But men, not being *naturally* subjects of property, the law of nature will not transmit any right of property acquired in violation of her own authority. The law

---

* This principle would apply, as we have before seen, where the change was from the *colonial* to a state government. It would also apply to all cases where the change took place, under the constitution of the United States, from a *territorial* to a state government. It needs no argument to prove that all our territorial statutes that have purported to authorize slavery, were unconstitutional.

of nature denies all rights not derived from herself. Of course she cannot perpetuate or transmit such rights — if rights they can be called.

One important reason why a calf belongs to the owner of the cow that bore it, is, *that there is no principle of natural law that can be opposed to that ownership.* For the calf is naturally a subject of property, and if it were not given to the owner of the cow, it would be lawful for any other person to assume the ownership. No wrong would be done to the animal by so doing. But as man is not naturally a subject of property, and as each separate individual is, on principles of natural law, entitled to the control of his own person, it is as much a wrong, and as much a violation of natural law, to make a slave of the child of a slave, as to make a slave of any other person. The natural rights of the child to the control of his own person, rise up, from the moment of his birth, in opposition to the transmission to him of any ownership, which, in violation of natural law, has been asserted to the parent.

Natural law may be overborne by arbitrary institutions; but she will never aid or perpetuate them. For her to do so, would be to resist, and even deny her own authority. It would present the case of a principle warring against and overcoming itself. Instead of this, she asserts her own authority on the first opportunity. The moment the arbitrary law expires by its own limitation, natural law resumes her reign. If, therefore, the government declare A to be a slave, natural law may be practically overborne by this arbitrary authority; but she will not herself perpetuate it beyond the person of A — for that would be acting in contradiction to herself. — She will therefore suffer this arbitrary authority to expend itself on the person of A, according to the *letter* of the arbitrary law: but she will assert her own authority in favor of the child of A, to whom the letter of the law enslaving A, does not apply.

Slavery is a wrong to each individual enslaved; and not merely to the first of a series. Natural law, therefore, as much forbids the enslaving of the child, as if the wrong of enslaving the parent had never been perpetrated.

Slavery, then, is an arbitrary institution throughout. It depends from first to last, upon the letter of the arbitrary law. Natural law gives it no aid, no extension, no new application, under any circumstances whatever. Unless, therefore, the letter of the arbitrary law explicitly authorize the enslavement of the child, the child is born free, though the parent were a slave.

If the views that have already been taken of our written constitutions, be correct, no parent has ever yet been legally enslaved in this country; and of course no child. If, however, any one thinks he can place his finger upon any *constitutional* law, that has enslaved a parent, let him follow that law, and see whether it also expressly authorized the enslavement of the child. If it did not, the child would be free.

It is no new principle that the child of a slave would be born free, but for an express law to the contrary. Some of the slave codes admit the principle—for they have special provisions that the child shall follow the condition of the mother; thus virtually admitting that, but for such a provision, the child would be free, though the mother were a slave.

Under the constitutions of the States and the United States, it requires as explicit and plenary *constitutional* authority, to make slaves of the children of slaves, as it would to make slaves of anybody else. Is there, in any of the constitutions of this country, any general authority given to the governments, to make slaves of whom they please? No one will pretend it. Is there, then, any particular authority for making slaves of the children of those, who have previously been held in slavery? If there be, let the advocates of slavery point it out. If there be no such authority all their statutes declaring that the children of slaves shall follow the condition of their mothers, are unconstitutional and void; and those children are free by force of the law of nature.

This law of nature, that all men are born free, was recognized by this country in the Declaration of Independence. But it was no new principle then. Justinian says, " Captivity and servitude are both contrary to the law of nature ; for by that law all men are born free." But the principle was not new with Justinian; it exists in the nature of man, and is as old as man—and the race of man generally has acknowledged it. The exceptions have been special; the rule general.

The constitution of the United States recognizes the principle that all men are born free ; for it recognizes the principle that natural birth in the country gives citizenship *—which of course

---

* Art. 2, Sec. 1, Clause 5 : " No person, except a *natural born* citizen, * * * shall be eligible to the office of President."

implies freedom. And no exception is made to the rule. Of
course all born in the country since the adoption of the constitution
of the United States, have been born free, whether there were, or
were not any legal slaves in the country before that time.

Even the provisions, in the several State constitutions, that the
legislatures shall not *emancipate* slaves, would, if allowed their full
effect, unrestrained by the constitution of the United States, hold
in slavery only those who were then slaves; it would do nothing
towards enslaving their children, and would give the legislatures
no authority to enslave them.

It is clear, therefore, that, on this principle alone, slavery would
now be extinct in this country, unless there should be an exception
of a few aged persons.

THE

UNCONSTITUTIONALITY

OF

SLAVERY:

PART SECOND.

BY LYSANDER SPOONER.

BOSTON:
PUBLISHED BY BELA MARSH,
NO. 25 CORNHILL.

Stereotyped by
GEORGE A. CURTIS.
NEW ENGLAND TYPE AND STEREOTYPE FOUNDRY.

CONTENTS OF PART SECOND.

		PAGE
CHAPTER XIV. — THE DEFINITION OF LAW,	- -	137
" XV. — OUGHT JUDGES TO RESIGN THEIR SEATS?	• - • • • •	147
" XVI. — "THE SUPREME POWER OF A STATE,"		153
" XVII. — RULES OF INTERPRETATION,	- -	155
First Rule,	• • • • •	157
Second Rule,	- • • • •	161
Third Rule,	- • • • •	165
Fourth Rule,	• • • • •	168
Fifth Rule,	• • • • •	180
Sixth Rule,	• • • • •	182
Seventh Rule,	• • • • •	189
Eighth Rule,	• • • • •	196
Ninth Rule,	• • • • •	198
Tenth Rule,	• • • • •	199
Eleventh Rule,	- • • • •	200
Twelfth Rule,	• • • • •	200
Thirteenth Rule,	- • • • •	201
Fourteenth Rule,	- • • • .	204
RULES CITED FOR SLAVERY,	- • • •	205
First Rule cited for Slavery,	- • • •	205
Second Rule do. do.	• • • •	213
Third Rule do. do.	• • • •	217
Fourth Rule do. do.	• • • •	219
" XVIII. — SERVANTS COUNTED AS UNITS,	- -	237
" XIX. — SLAVE REPRESENTATION,	- -	238
" XX. — ALIENS COUNTED AS THREE FIFTHS,		242
" XXI. — WHY THE WORDS "FREE PERSONS" WERE USED,	- - • •	247
" XXII. — "ALL OTHER PERSONS,"	- -	257
" XXIII. — ADDITIONAL ARGUMENTS ON THE WORD "FREE,"	- - -	264
" XXIV. — POWER OF THE GENERAL GOVERNMENT OVER SLAVERY,	- -	269

APPENDIX.

A. FUGITIVE SLAVES,	- - - - - - - -	279
B. SUGGESTIONS TO ABOLITIONISTS,	- - - - -	290

UNCONSTITUTIONALITY OF SLAVERY.

PART SECOND.

CHAPTER XIV.

THE DEFINITION OF LAW.

It has been alleged, by way of objection to the definition of law given in chapter first, that under it the law would be uncertain, and government impracticable. Directly the opposite of both these allegations is true. Let us see.

1. Natural law, so far from being uncertain, when compared with statutory and constitutional law, is the only thing that gives any certainty at all to a very large portion of our statutory and constitutional law. The reason is this. The words, in which statutes and constitutions are written, are susceptible of so many different meanings,—meanings widely different from, often directly opposite to, each other, in their bearing upon men's rights, —that, unless there were some rule of interpretation for determining which of these various and opposite meanings are the true ones, there could be no certainty at all as to the meaning of the statutes and constitutions themselves. Judges could make almost anything they should please out of them. Hence the necessity of a rule of interpretation. *And this rule is, that the language of statutes and constitutions shall be construed, as nearly as possible, consistently with natural law.*

The rule assumes, what is true, that natural law is a thing certain in itself; also that it is capable of being learned. It assumes, furthermore, that it actually is understood by the legislators and judges who make and interpret the written law. Of necessity, therefore, it assumes further, that they (the legislators and judges) are *incompetent* to make and interpret the *written* law, unless they previously understand the natural law applicable to the

12*

same subject. It also assumes that the *people* must understand the natural law, before they can understand the written law.

It is a principle perfectly familiar to lawyers, and one that must be perfectly obvious to every other man that will reflect a moment, that, as a general rule, *no one can know what the written law is, until he knows what it ought to be;* that men are liable to be constantly misled by the various and conflicting senses of the same words, unless they perceive the true legal sense in which the words *ought to be taken.* And this true legal sense is the sense that is most nearly consistent with natural law of any that the words can be made to bear, consistently with the laws of language, and appropriately to the subjects to which they are applied.

Though the words *contain* the law, the *words* themselves are not the law. Were the words themselves the law, each single written law would be liable to embrace many different laws, to wit, as many different laws as there were different senses, and different combinations of senses, in which each and all the words were capable of being taken.

Take, for example, the Constitution of the United States. By adopting one or another sense of the single word "*free*," the whole instrument is changed. Yet, the word *free* is capable of some ten or twenty different senses. So that, by changing the sense of that single word, some ten or twenty different constitutions could be made out of the same written instrument. But there are, we will suppose, a thousand other words in the constitution, each of which is capable of from two to ten different senses. So that, by changing the sense of only a single word at a time, several thousands of different constitutions would be made. But this is not all. Variations could also be made by changing the senses of two or more words at a time, and these variations could be run through all the changes and combinations of senses that these thousand words are capable of. We see, then, that it is no more than a literal truth, that out of that single instrument, as it now stands, without altering the location of a single word, might be formed, by construction and interpretation, more different constitutions than figures can well estimate.

But each written law, in order to be a law, must be taken only in some *one* definite and distinct sense; and that definite and distinct sense must be selected from the almost infinite variety of senses which its words are capable of. How is this selection to be made? It can be only by the aid of that perception of natural law, or natural justice, which men naturally possess.

Such, then, is the comparative certainty of the natural and the written law. Nearly all the certainty there is in the latter, so far as it relates to principles, is based upon, and derived from, the still greater certainty of the former. In fact, nearly all the uncertainty of the laws under which we live,—which are a mixture of natural and written laws,—arises from the difficulty of construing, or, rather, from the facility of misconstruing, the *written* law. While natural law has nearly or quite the same certainty as mathematics. On this point, Sir William Jones, one of the most learned judges that have ever lived, learned in Asiatic as well as European law, says,—and the fact should be kept forever in mind, as one of the most important of all truths :—" *It is pleasing to remark the similarity, or, rather, the identity of those conclusions which pure, unbiassed reason, in all ages and nations, seldom fails to draw, in such juridical inquiries as are not fettered and manacled by positive institutions.*"* In short, the simple fact that the written law must be interpreted by the natural, is, of itself, a sufficient confession of the superior certainty of the latter.

The written law, then, even where it can be construed consistently with the natural, introduces labor and obscurity, instead of shutting them out. And this must always be the case, because words do not create ideas, but only recall them ; and the same word may recall many different ideas. For this reason, nearly all abstract principles can be seen by the single mind more clearly than they can be expressed by words to another. This is owing to the imperfection of language, and the different senses, meanings, and shades of meaning, which different individuals attach to the same words, in the same circumstances.†

Where the written law cannot be construed consistently with the natural, there is no reason why 't should ever be enacted at all. It may, indeed, be sufficiently plain and certain to be easily understood ; but its certainty and plainness are but a poor compen-

---

* Jones on Bailments, 133.

† Kent, describing the difficulty of construing the written law, says :—

" Such is the imperfection of language, and the want of technical skill in the makers of the law, that statutes often give occasion to the most perplexing and distressing doubts and discussions, arising from the ambiguity that attends them. It requires great experience, as well as the command of a perspicuous diction, to frame a law in such clear and precise terms, as to secure it from ambiguous expressions, and from all doubts and criticisms upon its meaning."— *Kent*, 460

sation for its injustice. Doubtless a law forbidding men to drink water, on pain of death, might be made so intelligible as to cut off all discussion as to its meaning; but would the intelligibleness of such a law be any equivalent for the right to drink water? The principle is the same in regard to all unjust laws. Few persons could reasonably feel compensated for the arbitrary destruction of their rights, by having the order for their destruction made known beforehand, in terms so distinct and unequivocal as to admit of neither mistake nor evasion. Yet this is all the compensation that such laws offer.

Whether, therefore, written laws correspond with, or differ from, the natural, they are to be condemned. In the first case, they are useless repetitions, introducing labor and obscurity. In the latter case, they are positive violations of men's rights.

There would be substantially the same reason in enacting mathematics by statute, that there is in enacting natural law. Whenever the natural law is sufficiently certain to all men's minds to justify its being enacted, it is sufficiently certain to need no enactment. On the other hand, until it be thus certain, there is danger of doing injustice by enacting it; it should, therefore, be left open to be discussed by anybody who may be disposed to question it, and to be judged of by the proper tribunal, the judiciary.*

It is not necessary that legislators should enact natural law in order that it may be known to *the people*, because that would be presuming that the legislators already understand it better than the people,—a fact of which I am not aware that they have ever heretofore given any very satisfactory evidence. The same sources of knowledge on the subject, are open to the people, that are open to the legislators, and the people must be presumed to know it as well as they.†

---

* This condemnation of written laws must, of course, be understood as applying only to cases where principles and rights are involved, and not as condemning any governmental arrangements, or instrumentalities, that are consistent with natural right, and which must be agreed upon for the purpose of carrying natural law into effect. These things may be varied, as expediency may dictate, so only that they be allowed to infringe no principle of justice. And they must, of course, be written, because they do not exist as fixed principles, or laws in nature.

† The objections made to natural law, on the ground of obscurity, are wholly unfounded. It is true, it must be learned, like any other science, but it is equally true, that it is very easily learned. Although as illimitable in its applications as the infinite relations of men to each other, it is, nevertheless, made up of simple elementary principles, of the truth and justice of which every ordinary mind has

2. But it is said further, that government is not *practicable* under this theory of natural law. If by this is meant only that government cannot have the same arbitrary and undisputed supremacy over men's rights, as under other systems — the same absolute

---

an almost intuitive perception. *It is the science of justice,* — and almost all men have the same perceptions of what constitutes justice, or of what justice requires, when they understand alike the facts from which their inferences are to be drawn. Men living in contact with each other, and having intercourse together, *cannot avoid* learning natural law, to a very great extent, even if they would. The dealings of men with men, their separate possessions, and their individual wants, are continually forcing upon their minds the questions, — Is this act just? or is it unjust? Is this thing mine? or is it his? And these are questions of natural law ; questions, which, in regard to the great mass of cases, are answered alike by the human mind everywhere.

Children learn many principles of natural law at a very early age. For example : they learn that when one child has picked up an apple or a flower, it is his, and that his associates must not take it from him against his will. They also learn that if he voluntarily exchange his apple or flower with a playmate, for some other article of desire, he has thereby surrendered his right to it, and must not reclaim it. These are fundamental principles of natural law, which govern most of the greatest interests of individuals and society ; yet, children learn them earlier than they learn that three and three are six, or five and five, ten. Talk of enacting natural law by statute, that it may be known! It would hardly be extravagant to say, that, in nine cases in ten, men learn it before they have learned the language by which we describe it. Nevertheless, numerous treatises are written on it, as on other sciences. The decisions of courts, containing their opinions upon the almost endless variety of cases that have come before them, are reported ; and these reports are condensed, codified, and digested, so as to give, in a small compass, the facts, and the opinions of the courts as to the law resulting from them. And these treatises, codes, and digests are open to be read of all men. And a man has the same excuse for being ignorant of arithmetic, or any other science, that he has for being ignorant of natural law. He can learn it as well, if he will, without its being enacted, as he could if it were.

If our governments would but themselves adhere to natural law, there would be little occasion to complain of the ignorance of the people in regard to it. The popular ignorance of law is attributable mainly to the innovations that have been made upon natural law by legislation ; whereby our system has become an incongruous mixture of natural and statute law, with no uniform principle pervading it. To learn such a system, — if system it can be called, and if learned it can be,—is a matter of very similar difficulty to what it would be to learn a system of mathematics, which should consist of the mathematics of nature, interspersed with such other mathematics as might be created by legislation, in violation of all the natural principles of numbers and quantities.

But whether the difficulties of learning natural law be greater or less than here represented, they exist in the nature of things, and cannot be removed. Legislation, instead of removing, only increases them. This it does by innovating upon natural truths and principles, and introducing jargon and contradiction, in the place of order, analogy, consistency, and uniformity.

Further than this ; legislation does not even profess to remove the obscurity of natural law. That is no part of its object. It only professes to substitute some-

authority to do injustice, or to maintain justice, at its pleasure — the allegation is of course true ; and it is precisely that, that constitutes the merits of the system. But if anything more than that is meant, it is untrue. The theory presents no obstacle to the use of all *just* means for the maintenance of justice ; and this is all the power that government ought ever to have. It is all the power that it can have, consistently with the rights of those on whom it is to operate. To say that such a government is not practicable, is equivalent to saying that no governments are practicable but arbitrary ones ; none but those that are licensed to do injustice, as well as to maintain justice. If these latter governments only are practicable, it is time that all men knew it, in order that those who are to be made victims may stand on their defence, instead of being cheated into submission by the falsehood that government is their protector, and is licensed to do, and intends to do, nothing but justice to any.

If we say it is impracticable to limit the constitutional power of government to the maintenance of natural law, we must, to be consistent, have done with all attempts to limit government at all by written constitutions ; for it is obviously as easy, by written constitutions, to limit the powers of government to the maintenance of natural law, as to give them any other limit whatever. And if they were thus limited expressly, it would then, for the reasons before given, be as easy, and even altogether more easy, for the judiciary to determine what legislation was constitutional, and what not, than it is under a constitution that should attempt to define the powers of government arbitrarily.

---

thing arbitrary in the place of natural law. Legislators generally have the sense to see that legislation will not make natural law any clearer than it is.

Neither is it the object of legislation to establish the authority of natural law. Legislators have the sense to see that they can add nothing to the authority of natural law, and that it will stand on its own authority, unless they overturn it.

The whole object of legislation, excepting that legislation which merely makes regulations, and provides instrumentalities for carrying other laws into effect, is to overturn natural law, and substitute for it the arbitrary will of power. In other words, the whole object of it is to destroy men's rights. At least, such is its only effect ; and its design must be inferred from its effect. Taking all the statutes in the country, there probably is not one in a hundred, — except the auxiliary ones just mentioned, — that does not violate natural law ; that does not invade some right or other.

Yet, the advocates of arbitrary legislation are continually practising the fraud of pretending, that unless the legislature *make* the laws, the laws will not be known. The whole object of the fraud is to secure to the government the authority of making laws that never ought to be known.

On what ground it can seriously be said that such a government is impracticable, it is difficult to conceive. Protecting the rights of all, it would naturally secure the cordial support of all, instead of a part only. The *expense* of maintaining it would be far less than that of maintaining a different one. And it would certainly be much more practicable to live under it, than under any other. Indeed, this is the *only* government which it is practicable to establish by the consent of all the governed; for an unjust government must have victims, and the victims cannot be supposed to give their consent. All governments, therefore, that profess to be founded on the consent of the governed, and yet have authority to violate natural laws, are necessarily frauds. It is not a supposable case, that all, or even any very large part, of the governed, can have agreed to them. Justice is evidently the only principle that *everybody* can be presumed to agree to, in the formation of government.

It is true that those appointed to administer a government founded on natural law, might, through ignorance or corruption, depart from the true theory of the government in particular cases, as they do under any other system; and these departures from the system would be departures from justice. But departures from justice would occur only through the errors of the men; such errors as systems cannot wholly prevent; they would never, as under other systems, be authorized by the constitution. And even errors arising from ignorance and corruption would be much less frequent than under other systems, because the powers of government would be much more definite and intelligible; they could not, as under other systems, be stretched and strained by construction, so as to afford a pretext for anything and everything that corruption might desire to accomplish.

It is probable that, on an average, three fourths, and not unlikely nine tenths, of all the law questions that are decided in the progress of every trial in our courts, are decided on natural principles; such questions, for instance, as those of evidence, crime, the obligation of contracts, the burden of proof, the rights of property, &c., &c.* If government be practicable, as we thus see it to be, where three fourths or nine tenths of the law administered

---

* Kent says, and truly, that "A great proportion of the rules and maxims, which constitute the immense code of the common law. grew into use by gradual adoption, and received the sanction of the courts of justice, without any legislative act or interference. *It was the application of the dictates of natural justice and cultivated reason to particular cases.*" 1 *Kent*, 470.

is natural, it would be equally practicable where the whole was
so.

So far from government being impracticable on principles of
natural law, it is wholly impracticable to have a government of
law, applicable to all cases, unless the great body of the law administered be natural; because it is impossible for legislation to
anticipate but a small portion of the cases that must arise in regard
to men's rights, so as to enact a law for them.   In all the cases
which the legislature cannot anticipate and provide for, natural law
must prevail, or there can be no law for them, and, consequently,
— so far as those cases are concerned — no government.

Whether, therefore, we regard the certainty of the law, or the
practicability of a government applicable to all cases, the preference
is incomparably in favor of natural law.

But suppose it were not so.   Suppose, for the sake of the argument, that the meaning of the arbitrary commands of power were,
in the majority of cases, more easily ascertained than the principles
of natural justice; is that any proof that the former are law, and
the latter not?   Does the comparative intelligibility of the two
determine which is to be adopted as the true definition of law?   It
is very often easier to understand a lie than to ascertain a truth;
but is that any proof that falsehood is synonymous with fact? or
is it any reason why falsehood should be held to be fact?   As
much reason would there be in saying this, as there is in saying
that the will of the supreme power of the state is law, or should
be held to be law, rather than natural justice, because it is easier
to understand the former than to ascertain the latter.

Or suppose, further, that government were *impracticable*, under
such a definition of law as makes law synonymous with natural
justice; would that be any argument against the definition? or only
against government?

The objection to the practicability of government under such a
definition of law, assumes, 1st, that government must be sustained,
whether it administer justice or injustice; and, 2d, that its commands must be called law, whether they really are law or not.
Whereas, if justice be not law, it may certainly be questioned
whether government ought to be sustained.   And to this question
all reasonable men must answer, that we receive such an abundance
of injustice from private persons, as to make it inexpedient to
maintain a government for the sole purpose of increasing the supply.   But even if unjust government must be sustained, the ques-

tion will still remain, whether its commands ought to be called law ? If they are not law, they should be called by their right name, whatever it may be.

In short, the definition of law involves a question of truth or falsehood. Natural justice either is law, or it is not. If it be law, it is always law, and nothing inconsistent with it can ever be made law. If it be not law, then we have no law except what is prescribed by the reigning power of the state ; and all idea of justice being any part of our system of law, any further than it may be specially prescribed, ought to be abandoned ; and government ought to acknowledge that its authority rests solely on its power to compel submission, and that there is not necessarily any moral obligation of obedience to its mandates.

If natural justice be *not* law, then all the decisions that are made by our courts on natural principles, without being prescribed by statute or constitution, are unauthorized, and not law. And the decisions of this kind, as has already been supposed, comprise probably three fourths, or more likely nine tenths, of all the decisions given by our courts as law.*

If natural justice *be* law, then all statutes and constitutions inconsistent with it are no law, and courts are bound to say so. Courts must adopt some definition of law, and adhere to it. They cannot make it mean the two opposite principles of justice and injustice at once. White cannot be made white and black at the same time, by the assertions of all the courts on the globe. Neither can law be made two opposite things at once. It must be either one thing or the other.   •

No one doubts that there is such a principle as natural law ; and natural law is natural justice. If natural justice be law, natural injustice cannot be made law, either by "the supreme power of the

---

* That is, these decisions are unauthorized, on the supposition that justice is *not* necessarily law, unless the *general* requirement, made upon courts by some of our constitutions, that they "administer right and justice," or some other requirement contained in them equivalent to that, be considered as arbitrarily prescribing these principles as law, and thus authorizing the decisions. But if these requirements, instead of being regarded, as they doubtless ought to be, as an acknowledgment that "right and justice" are law of themselves, be considered only as arbitrarily prescribing them as law, it is at least an admission that the simple words "right and justice" express, with legal accuracy, an infinite variety of fixed, definite, and certain principles, that are properly applicable, *as law*, to the relations of man with man. But wherever a constitution makes no such requirement, the decisions are illegal, as being made without authority, unless justice itself be law.

state," or by any other power; and it is a fraud to call it by that name.

"The supreme powers of states," whether composed of majorities or minorities, have alike assumed to dignify their unjust commands with the name of law, simply for the purpose of cheating the ignorant into submission, by impressing them with the idea that obedience was a duty.

The received definition of law, viz., that it is "a rule of civil conduct prescribed by the supreme power of a state," had its origin in days of ignorance and despotism, when government was founded in force, without any acknowledgment of the natural rights of men. Yet even in those days the principle of justice competed, as now, with the principle of power, in giving the definition of law; for justice was conceded to be the law in all, or very nearly all, the cases where the will of the supreme power had not been explicitly made known; and those cases comprised, as now, a very large portion of all the cases adjudicated.

What a shame and reproach, nay, what an unparalleled crime is it, that at this day, *and in this country*, where men's natural rights are universally acknowledged, and universally acknowledged to be inalienable, and where government is acknowledged to have no just powers except what it derives from the consent of the governed, (who can never be supposed to consent to any invasion of their rights, and who can be supposed to establish government only for their protection,) a definition of law should be adhered to, that denies all these self-evident and glorious truths, blots out all men's natural rights, founds government on force, buries all present knowledge under the ignorance and tyranny of the past, and commits the liberties of mankind to the custody of unrestrained power!

The enactment and enforcement of unjust laws are the greatest crimes that are committed by man against man. The crimes of single individuals invade the rights of single individuals. Unjust laws invade the rights of large bodies of men, often of a majority of the whole community; and generally of that portion of community who, from ignorance and poverty, are least able to bear the wrong, and at the same time least capable of resistance.*

---

* We add the following authorities to those given in the note to chapter first, on the true nature and definition of law: — Cicero says, "There is a true law, a right reason, conformable to nature, universal, unchangeable, eternal. * * * * This law cannot be contradicted by any other law, and is not liable either to derogation

CHAPTER XV.

OUGHT JUDGES TO RESIGN THEIR SEATS?

It being admitted that a judge can rightfully administer injustice as law, in no case, and on no pretence whatever ; that he has no right to assume an oath to do so ; and that all oaths of that kind

---

or abrogation. Neither the senate nor the people can give us any dispensation for not obeying this universal law of justice. * * * * It is not one thing at Rome, and another at Athens ; one thing to-day, and another to-morrow ; but in all times and nations, this universal law must forever reign, eternal and imperishable. * * * * He who obeys it not, flies from himself, and does violence to the very nature of man." — *Cicero's Republic, Barham's Translation, B. 3, p.* 270.

"This justice is the very foundation of lawful government in political constitu tions." — *Same, B.* 3, *p.* 272.

"To secure to the citizens the benefits of an honest and happy life, is the grand object of all political associations." — *Same, B.* 4, *p.* 283.

"There is no employment so essentially royal as the exposition of equity, which comprises the true meaning of all laws." — *Same, B.* 5, *p.* 290.

"According to the Greeks, the name of law implies an equitable distribution of goods ; according to the Romans, an equitable discrimination between good and evil. The true definition of law should, however, include both these character-istics. And this being granted as an almost self-evident proposition, the origin of justice is to be sought in the divine law of eternal and immutable morality." — *Cicero's Treatise on the Laws, Barham's Translation, B.* 1, *p.* 37.

"Of all the questions which our philosophers argue, there is none which it is more important thoroughly to understand than this, — *that man is born for justice, and that law and equity are not a mere establishment of opinion, but an institution of nature.*" — *Same, B.* 1, *p.* 45.

"Nature hath not merely given us reason, but right reason, and, consequently, that law, which is nothing else than right reason, enjoining what is good, and for-bidding what is evil.

"Now, if nature hath given us law, she hath also given us justice ; for, as she has bestowed reason on all, she has equally bestowed the sense of justice on all." — *Same, B.* 1, *p.* 48.

"Nature herself is the foundation of justice." — *Same, B.* 1, *p.* 49.

"It is an absurd extravagance, in some philosophers, to assert that all things are necessarily just, which are established by the civil laws and the institutions of the people. Are, then, the laws of tyrants just, simply because they are laws ? If the thirty tyrants of Athens imposed certain laws on the Athenians, and if these Atheni-ans were delighted with these tyrannical laws, are we, therefore, bound to consider these laws as just? For my own part, I do not think such laws deserve any greater estimation than that passed during our own interregnum, which ordained that the dictator should be empowered to put to death with impunity, whatever citizens he pleased, without hearing them in their own defence.

"There can be but one essential justice which cements society, and one law which establishes this justice. This law is right reason, which is the true rule of all commandments and prohibitions. Whoever neglects this law, whether written or unwritten, is necessarily unjust and wicked.

are morally void; the question arises, whether a judge, who has
actually sworn to support an unjust constitution, be morally bound

---

"But if justice consist in submission to written laws and customs, and if, as the
Epicureans persist in affirming, everything must be measured by utility alone, he
who wishes to find an occasion of breaking such laws and customs, will be sure to
discover it. So that real justice remains powerless if not supported by nature,
and this pretended justice is overturned by that very utility which they call its
foundation." — *Same, B.* 1, *p.* 55-6.

"If nature does not ratify law, all virtues lose their sway." — *Same, B.* 1, *p.* 56.

"If the will of the people, the decrees of the senate, the adjudications of magis-
trates, were sufficient to establish justice, the only question would be how to gain
suffrages, and to win over the votes of the majority, in order that corruption and
spoliation, and the falsification of wills, should become lawful. But if the opinions
and suffrages of foolish men had sufficient weight to outbalance the nature of
things, might they not determine among them, that what is essentially bad and
pernicious should henceforth pass for good and beneficial? Or why should not a
law, able to enforce injustice, take the place of equity? Would not this same law
be able to change evil into good, and good into evil?

"As far as we are concerned, we have no other rule capable of distinguishing
between a good or a bad law, than our natural conscience and reason. These, however, enable us to separate justice from injustice, and to discriminate between the
honest and the scandalous. For common sense has impressed in our minds the
first principles of things, and has given us a general acquaintance with them, by
which we connect with virtue every honorable and excellent quality, and with vice
all that is abominable and disgraceful.

"Now we must entirely take leave of our senses, ere we can suppose that law
and justice have no foundation in nature, and rely merely on the transient opinions of men." — *Same, B.* 1, *p.* 56-7.

"Whatever is just is always the true law; nor can this true law either be originated or abrogated by any written enactments." — *Same, B.* 2, *p.* 83.

"As the divine mind, or reason, is the supreme law, so it exists in the mind of
the sage, so far as it can be perfected in man. With respect to civil laws, which
differ in all ages and nations, the name of law belongs to them not so much by
right as by the favor of the people. For every law which deserves the name of
a law ought to be morally good and laudable, as we might demonstrate by the
following arguments. It is clear, that laws were originally made for the security of
the people, for the preservation of cities, for the peace and benefit of society.
Doubtless, the first legislators persuaded the people that they would write and pub-
lish such laws only as should conduce to the general morality and happiness, if
they would receive and obey them. Such were the regulations, which being settled and sanctioned, they justly entitled *laws*. From which, we may reasonably
conclude, that those who made unjustifiable and pernicious enactments for the people, counteracted their own promises and professions, and established anything
rather than *laws*, properly so called, since it is evident that the very signification
of the word *law* comprehends the essence and energy of justice and equity." —
Same, B. 2, *p.* 83-4.

"*Marcus.* If then, in the majority of nations, many pernicious and mischievous
enactments are made, as far removed from the law of justice we have defined as
the mutual engagements of robbers, are we bound to call them laws? For as we
cannot call the recipes of ignorant empirics, who give poisons instead of medicines,
the prescriptions of a physician, we cannot call that the true law of the people,
whatever be its name, if it enjoins what is injurious, let the people receive it as
they will. For law is the just distinction between right and wrong, conform-

to resign his seat? or whether he may rightfully retain his office, administering justice, instead of injustice, regardless of his oath?

---

able to nature, the original and principal regulator of all things, by which the laws of men should be measured, whether they punish the guilty, or protect the innocent.

"*Quintus.* I quite agree with you, and think that no law but that of justice should either be proclaimed as a law, or enforced as a law.

"*Marcus.* Then you regard as nullable and voidable, the laws of Titius and Apuleius, because they are unjust.

"*Quintus.* You may say the same of the laws of Livius.

"*Marcus.* You are right; and so much the more, since a single vote of the senate would be sufficient to abrogate them in an instant. But that law of justice which I have explained can never be rendered obsolete or inefficacious.

"*Quintus.* And, therefore, you require those laws of justice the more ardently, because they would be durable and permanent, and would not require those perpetual alterations which all injudicious enactments demand." — *Same, B.* 2, *p.* 85-6.

"Long before positive laws were instituted, the moral relations of justice were absolute and universal." — *Montesquieu.*

"All the tranquillity, the happiness, and security of the human race, rests on justice; on the obligation of paying a regard to the rights of others." — *Vattel, B.* 2, *chap.* 12, *sec.* 163.

"Justice is the basis of all society." — *Vattel, B.* 1, *chap.* 5, *sec.* 63.

Bacon says, "There are in nature certain fountains of justice, whence all civil laws are derived but as streams." — *Bacon's Tract on Universal Justice.*

"Let no man weakly conceive that just laws, and true policy, have any antipathy, for they are like the spirits and sinews, that one moves with the other." — *Bacon's Essay on Judicature.*

"Justice is the end of government. It is the end of civil society." — *Federalist, No.* 51.

About half our state constitutions specially require of our courts that they administer "right and justice" to every man.

The national constitution enumerates among its objects, the establishment of "justice," and the security of "liberty."

Judge Story says, "To establish justice must forever be one of the greatest ends of every wise government; and even in arbitrary governments it must, to a great extent, be practised, at least in respect to private persons, as the only security against rebellion, private vengeance, and popular cruelty. But in a free government, it lies at the very basis of all its institutions. Without justice being freely, fully, and impartially administered, neither our persons, nor our rights, nor our property, can be protected." — 1 *Story's Com. on Const.,* 463.

"It appears in our books, that, in many cases, the common law will control acts of parliament, and sometimes adjudge them to be utterly void; for when an act of parliament is against common right or reason, the common law will control it, and adjudge such act to be void." — *Coke, in Bonham's case; 4 Coke's Rep., part* 8, *p.* 118.

Kent also, although he holds that, *in England,* "the will of the legislature is the supreme law of the land, and demands perfect obedience," yet says: "But while we admit this conclusion of the English law, we cannot but admire the intrepidity and powerful sense of justice which led Lord Coke, when Chief Justice of the King's bench, to declare, as he did in *Doctor Bonham's* case, that the common law doth control acts of parliament, and adjudges them void when against common right and reason. The same sense of justice and freedom of opinion led Lord

The prevalent idea is, that he ought to resign his seat; and high authorities may be cited for this opinion. Nevertheless, the opinion is probably erroneous; for it would seem that, however wrong it may be to take the oath, yet the oath, when taken, being morally void to all intents and purposes, can no more bind the taker to resign his office, than to fulfil the oath itself.

The case appears to be this : The office is simply *power*, put into a man's hands, on the condition, based upon his oath, that he will use that power to the destruction or injury of some person's rights. This condition, it is agreed, is void. He holds the power, then, by the same right that he would have done if it had been put into his hands *without the condition*. Now, seeing that he cannot fulfill, and is under no obligation to fulfill, this void condition, the question is, whether he is bound to resign the power, in order that it may be given to some one who will fulfill the condition ? or whether he is bound to hold the power, not only for the purpose of using it himself in *defence* of justice, but also for the purpose of withholding it from the hands of those who, if he surrender it to them, will use it unjustly ? Is it not clear that he is bound to retain it for both of these reasons ?

Suppose A put a sword into the hands of B, on the condition of B's taking an oath that with it he will murder C. Now, however immoral the taking of this oath may be, yet, when taken, the oath and the condition are utterly void. They are incapable of raising the least moral obligation, of any kind whatever, on the part of B towards A. B then holds the sword on the same principle, and by the same right, that he would have done if it had

---

Chief Justice Hobart, in *Day* vs. *Savage*, to insist that an act of parliament, made against natural equity, as to make a man judge in his own case, was void; and induced Lord Chief Justice Holt to say, in the case of the *City of London* vs. *Wood*, that the observation of Lord Coke was not extravagant, but was a very reasonable and true saying." — 1 *Kent*, 448.

"A treaty made from an unjust and dishonest intention is absolutely null, nobody having a right to engage to do things contrary to the law of nature." — *Vattel*, B. 2, *chap*. 12, *sec*. 161.

That definition which makes law to be "a rule of civil conduct, prescribed by the supreme power of a state, commanding what its subjects are to do, and prohibiting what they are to forbear," is manifestly a false definition, inasmuch as it does not include the law of nations. The law of nations has never been "prescribed" by any "supreme power," that regards the nations as its "subjects," and rules over them as other governments rule over individuals. Nations acknowledge no such supreme power. The law of nations is, in reality, nothing else than the law of nature, applicable to nations. Yet it is a law which all civilized nations acknowledge, and is all that preserves the peace of nations; and no definition of law that excludes so important a portion of the law of the world, can reasonably be for a moment regarded as true.

been put into his hands without any oath or condition whatever. Now the question is, whether B, on refusing to fulfil the condition, is bound to retain the sword, and use it, if necessary, in *defence* of C? or whether he is bound to return it to A, in order that A may give it to some one who will use it for the murder of C? The case seems to be clear. If he were to give up the sword, under these circumstances, knowing the use that was intended to be made of it, and it should then be used, by some other person, for the murder of C, he would be, on both moral and legal principles, as much accessary to the murder of C, as though he had furnished the sword for that specific purpose, under any other circumstances whatever.

Suppose A and B come to C with money, which they have stolen from D, and intrust it to him, on condition of his taking an oath to restore it to them when they shall call for it. Of course, C ought not to take such an oath in order to get possession of the money; yet, if he have taken the oath, and received the money, his duty, on both moral and legal principles, is then the same as though he had received it without any oath or condition; because the oath and condition are both morally and legally void. And if he were to restore the money to A and B, instead of restoring it to D, the true owner, he would make himself their accomplice in the theft — a receiver of stolen goods. It is his duty to restore it to D.

Suppose A and B come to C, with a captive, D, whom they have seized with the intention of reducing him to slavery; and should leave him in the custody of C, on condition of C's taking an oath that he will restore him to them again. Now, although it is wrong for C to take such an oath for the purpose of getting the custody of D, even with a view to set him free, yet, if he have taken it, it is void, and his duty then is, not to give D up to his captors, but to set him at liberty — else he will be an accomplice in the crime of enslaving him.

The principle, in all these cases, appears to be precisely similar to that in the case of a judge, who has sworn to support an unjust constitution. He is intrusted with certain power over the rights of men, on condition of his taking an oath that he will use the power for the violation of those rights. It would seem that there can hardly be a question, on either moral or legal principles, that this power, which he has received on the condition that he shall use it for the destruction of men's rights, he is bound to retain and use for their defence.

If there be any difference of principle in these several cases, I should like much to see it pointed out. There probably is none. And if there be none, the principle that would induce a judge to resign his power; is only a specimen of the honor that is said to prevail among thieves; it is no part of the morality that should govern men claiming to be just towards all mankind. It is indeed but a poor specimen even of the honor of thieves, for that honor, I think, only forbids the exposure of one's accomplices, and the seizure, for one's own use, of more than his agreed share of the spoils; it hardly forbids the restoration of stolen property to its rightful owners.

As long as the dogma is sustained that a judge is morally bound either to fulfil his oath to support an unjust constitution, or to surrender the power that has been entrusted to him for that purpose, so long those, who wish to establish such constitutions, will be encouraged to do so; because they will know that they can always find creatures enough, who will accept the office for its honors and emoluments, and will then execute it, *if they must*, rather than surrender them. But let the principle be established that such oaths are void, and that the power conferred is therefore held on the same grounds as though the oath had not been taken at all, and one security, at least, for the execution of unjust constitutions is taken away, and the inducement to establish them is consequently weakened.

Judges and other public officers habitually appeal to the pretended obligation of their oaths, when about to perform some act of iniquity, for which they can find no other apology, and for which they feel obliged to offer some apology. Hence the importance of the doctrine here maintained, if it be true.

Perhaps it will be said that a judge has no right to set up his own notions of the validity of a statute, or constitution, against the opinions of those who enact or establish it; that he is bound to suppose that they consider the statute or constitution entirely just, whatever may be his own opinion of it; and that he is therefore bound to yield his opinion to theirs, or to resign his seat. But this is only saying that, though appointed judge, he has no right to be judge. It is the prerogative of a judge to decide everything that is involved in the question of law, or no law. His own mind alone is the arbiter. To say that it is not, is to say that he is not judge. He may err, like other men. Those who appoint him, take the risk of his errors. He is bound only by his own convictions.

But there is no reason in presuming that legislators, or constitution makers, when they violate natural law, do it in the belief that they are conforming to it. Everybody is presumed to know the law, especially natural law. And legislators must be presumed to know it, as well as other men; and if they violate it, (which question the judge must decide,) they, like other men, must be presumed to have done it intentionally.

CHAPTER XVI.

"THE SUPREME POWER OF A STATE."

If any additional argument were needed to enforce the authority of natural law, it would be found in the nature of the only opposing authority, to wit, the authority of "the supreme power of the state," as it is called.

In most "states," "the supreme power" is obtained by force, and rests upon force; and its mandates do not necessarily have any other authority than what force can give them.

, But in this country, "the supreme power" is acknowledged, *in theory*, to rest with the people. Our constitutions purport to be established by "the people," and, *in theory*, "all the people" *consent* to such government as the constitutions authorize. But this consent of "the people" exists only in theory. It has no existence in fact. Government is in reality established by the few; and these few *assume* the consent of all the rest, without any such consent being actually given. Let us see if such be not the fact.

Only the male adults are allowed to vote either in the choice of delegates to form constitutions, or in the choice of legislators under the constitutions. These voters comprise not more than *one fifth* of the population. A bare *majority* of these voters,—that is, a little more than *one tenth* of the whole people,—choose the delegates and representatives. And then a *bare majority of these delegates and representatives*, (which *majority* were chosen by, and, consequently, represent but little more than *one twentieth* of the whole people,) adopt the constitution, and enact the statutes. Thus the actual makers of constitutions and statutes cannot be said to be the representatives of but little more than *one twentieth* of the people whose rights are affected by their action.

In fact, not one twentieth, but only a little more than *one forti-*

eth, of the people, are *necessarily* represented in our *statutory* legislation, state and national; for, in the national legislature, and in nearly all the state legislatures, a bare majority of the legislative bodies constitute a quorum, and a bare majority of that quorum are sufficient to enact the laws. The result, then, is substantially this. Not more than *one fifth* of the people vote. A bare majority of that fifth, (being about one tenth of the whole,) choose the legislators. A bare majority of the legislators, (representing but about one twentieth of the people,) constitute a quorum. A bare majority of the quorum, (representing but about one fortieth of the people,) are sufficient to make the laws.

Finally. Even the will of this *one fortieth* of the people cannot be said to be represented in the general legislation, because the representative is necessarily chosen for his opinions on one, or at most a few, important topics, when, in fact, he legislates on an hundred, or a thousand others, in regard to many, perhaps most, of which, he differs in opinion from those who actually voted for him. He can, therefore, with certainty, be said to represent nobody but himself.

Yet the statutory and constitutional law, that is manufactured in this ridiculous and fraudulent manner, is claimed to be the will of "the supreme power of the state;" and even though it purport to authorize the invasion, or even the destruction, of the natural rights of large bodies of the people, — men, women, and children, — it is, nevertheless, held to have been established by the consent of the whole people, and to be of higher authority than the principles of justice and natural law. And our judges, with a sanctimony as disgusting as it is hypocritical, continually offer these statutes and constitutions as their warrant for such violations of men's rights, as, if perpetrated by them in their private capacities, would bring upon them the doom which they themselves pronounce upon felons.*

---

* The objection stated in the text, to our present system of legislation, will not be obviated *in principle*, by assuming that the male adults are natural guardians of women and children, as they undoubtedly are of children, and perhaps, also, in some sense, of women. But if they are their natural guardians, they are their guardians only for the purpose of *protecting* their rights; not for the purpose of taking them away. Nevertheless, suppose, for the sake of the argument, that the women and children are really and rightfully represented through the male adults, the objection will still remain that the legislators are chosen by a bare majority of the voters, (representing a bare majority of the people ;) and then, a bare majority of the legislators chosen constitute a quorum ; and a bare majority of this quorum

CHAPTER XVII.

RULES OF INTERPRETATION.*

THE three preceding chapters, as also chapter first, although their principles are claimed to be of paramount authority, as law, to all statutes and constitutions inconsistent with them, are nevertheless *not* claimed to have anything to do with the question of the constitutionality or unconstitutionality of slavery, further than this, viz., that they indicate the rule of interpretation that should be adopted in construing the constitution. They prove the reasonableness, propriety, and therefore truth, of the rule, quoted from the supreme court of the United States, and adopted in the prior argument, as the fundamental rule of interpretation; a rule which, if adhered to, unquestionably proves that slavery is unconstitutional. That rule is this.

" Where rights are infringed, where fundamental principles are overthrown, where the general system of the laws † is departed from, the legislative intention must be *expressed with irresistible clearness,* to induce a court of justice to suppose a design to effect such objects." 2 *Cranch,* 390.

The whole question of the constitutionality or unconstitutionality

---

make the laws. So that, even then, the actual law-makers represent but little more than *one eighth* of the people.

If the principle is to be acted upon, that the majority have a right to rule arbitrarily, there is no legitimate way of carrying out that principle, but by requiring, either that a majority of the whole people, (or of the voters,) should vote in favor of every separate law, or by requiring entire unanimity in the representative bodies, who actually represent only a majority of the people.

But the principle is utterly false, that a majority, however large, have any right to rule so as to violate the natural rights of any single individual. It is as unjust for millions of men to murder, ravish, enslave, rob, or otherwise injure a single individual, as it is for another single individual to do it.

* Two things are necessary to a good lawyer. 1. *A knowledge of natural law.* This knowledge, indispensable to the peace and security of mankind, in their dealings, intercourse, and neighborhood with each other, is possessed, in some good measure, by mankind at large. 2. *A knowledge of the rules of interpreting the written law.* These are few, simple, natural, reasonable, just, and easily learned. These two branches of knowledge comprise substantially all the science, and all " the reason," there are in the law. I hope these considerations, in addition to that of understanding the constitution, may induce all, who read any portion of this book, to read with patience this chapter on the rules of interpretation, however tedious it may be.

† In " The Unconstitutionality of Slavery," the word *laws*, in this rule, was printed *law*, through my inadvertence in copying the rule. The error was not dis-

of slavery, is one of construction. And the real question is only whether the rules, applicable to the interpretation of statutes, and all other legal instruments, that are enforced by courts as obligatory, shall be applied also to the interpretation of the constitution? or whether these rules are to be discarded, and the worst possible meaning of which the words are capable put upon the instrument arbitrarily, and for no purpose *but to sustain slavery?* This is the question, and the whole of it.

The validity of the rule, quoted from the supreme court, has not, so far as I am aware, been denied. But some of the explanations given of the rule, in the prior argument, have been called in question. As the whole question at issue, in regard to the constitutionality of slavery, is one solely of interpretation, it becomes important to sustain, not only the explanations given of this rule,

---

covered until it was pointed out by Wendell Phillips. I am obliged to him for the correction. A case might be supposed, in which the difference would be important. But I am not aware that the correction affects any of the arguments on which the rule has *thus far* been, or will hereafter be, brought to bear ; because, in construing the constitution by this rule, " the general system of the laws " must be presumed to be " the general system of the laws " authorized by the constitution itself, and not " the general system of the laws " previously prevailing in the country, if the two systems should happen to differ. The constitution being the supreme law, anything in the constitutions or laws of the states to the contrary notwithstanding, those constitutions and laws must be construed with reference to *it;* instead of *its* being construed with reference to them, whenever the two may appear to conflict.

Mr. Phillips, however, seems to think the difference important to this discussion ; because he says " the general system of the *law* might refer to the general system of law, as a science ;" whereas " the general system of the *laws* clearly relates to the general spirit of the *laws of this nation,* which is quite a different thing." But he here assumes the very point in dispute, viz., that " the general spirit of the *constitutional* laws of this nation, (which are, in reality, its only *laws,*) *are* a very different thing " from " the general system of law, as a science." So far as they relate to slavery, we claim that all our *constitutional* laws are perfectly accordant with " the general system of law, as a science," and this is the question to be determined.

That " the general system of the laws," *authorized by the constitution,* and relating to other subjects than slavery, is, for the most part, at least, if not entirely, accordant with " law, as a science," Mr. Phillips will probably not deny, whatever he may think of those it authorizes in relation to slavery. But the rule of the court forbids that, in the matter of slavery, any construction of the constitution be adopted, at variance with " the general system of the laws " authorized by the constitution, *on all other subjects,* unless such intention " be expressed with irresistible clearness." " The general system of the laws," authorized by the constitution, on all other subjects than slavery, is a very important guide for the interpretation of those clauses that have been claimed for slavery. If this guide be followed, it extinguishes all pretended authority for slavery — instead of supporting it, as Mr. Phillips' remark would imply.

out also some of the other rules laid down in that argument. And hence the necessity of going more fully into the question of interpretation.

The first rule, in the interpretation of the constitution, as of all other laws and contracts, is, " *that the intention of the instrument must prevail.*"

The reason of this rule is apparent; for unless the intention of the instrument prevail, wherefore was the instrument formed? or established as law? If any other intention is to prevail over the instrument, the instrument is not the law, but a mere nullity.

The intentions of a statute or constitution are always either declared, or *presumed.*

The *declared* intentions of a statute or constitution are the intentions that are clearly expressed in terms in the statute or constitution itself.

Where the intentions of statutes and constitutions are not clearly expressed in the instruments themselves, the law always *presumes* them. And it always presumes the most just and beneficial intentions. which the words of the instruments, taken as a whole, can fairly be made to express, or imply.

Statutes and constitutions, in which no intentions were declared, and of which no reasonable intentions could be presumed, would be of no legal validity. No intentions that might be attributed to them by mere force of conjecture, and exterior history, could be legally ascribed to them, or enforced as law.

The intentions, which individuals, in discussions, conversations, and newspapers, may attribute to statutes and constitutions, are no part of the instruments themselves. And they are not of the slightest importance as evidence of their intentions, especially if they are in opposition, either to the declared, or the *presumed*, intentions of the instruments. If the intentions of statutes and constitutions were to be gathered from the talk of the street, there would be no use in writing them in terms. The talk of the street, and not the written instruments, would constitute the laws. And the same instrument would be as various and contradictory in its meanings, as the various conjectures, or assertions, that might be heard from the mouths of individuals; for one man's conjecture or assertion would be of as much legal value as another's; and effect would therefore have to be given to all, if to any.

14

Those who argue for slavery, hold that "the intentions of *the people*" must prevail, instead of "the intentions of *the instrument;*" thus falsely assuming that there is a legal distinction between the intentions of the instrument and the intentions of the people. Whereas the only object of the instrument is to express the intentions of the people. That is the only motive that can be attributed to the people, for its adoption. *The people established the constitution solely to give written and certain evidence of their intentions.* Having their written instrument, we have their own testimony, their own declaration, of what their intentions are. The intentions of the instrument, then, and the intentions of the people, are identical. And it is legally a matter of indifference which form of expression is used; for both legally express the same idea.

But the same class of persons, who assume a distinction between the intentions of the instrument and the intentions of the people, labor to prove, *by evidence extraneous to the instrument*, that the intentions of the people were different from those the instrument expresses; and then they infer that the instrument must be warped and twisted, and made to correspond to these *unexpressed* intentions of the people.

The answer to all this chicanery is this. The people, assuming that they have the right to establish their will as law, have, in theory, agreed upon an instrument to express their will, or their intentions. They have thus said that the intentions expressed in that instrument are *their* intentions. Also that their intentions, *as expressed in the instrument*, shall be the supreme law of the land.

"The people," by thus agreeing that the intentions, *expressed by their joint instrument*, shall be the supreme law of the land, have virtually and legally contracted with each other, that, for the sake of having these, their *written* intentions, carried into effect, they will severally forego all other intentions, of every name and nature whatsoever, that *conflict* with the written ones, in which they are all agreed.

Now this written instrument, which is, in theory, the voluntary contract of each and every individual with each and every other, is *the highest legal evidence* of their intentions. It is the specific evidence that is required of all the parties to it. It is the *only* evidence that is required, or accepted, of any. It is equally valid and sufficient, in favor of all, and against all. It is the only evidence that is common to all. The intentions it expresses must, therefore, stand as the intentions of all, and be carried into effect as law, in preference to any contrary intentions, that may have been separately, individually, and informally expressed by any one or all the parties on other occasions; else the contract is broken.

As long as the parties acknowledge the instrument as being their contract, they are each and all estopped by it from saying that they have any intentions adverse to it. *Its* intentions and their intentions are identical, else the parties individually contradict themselves. To acknowledge the contract, and yet disavow its intentions, is perfect self-contradiction.

If the parties wish to repudiate the intentions of the instrument, they must repudiate or abolish the instrument itself. If they wish to *change* the intentions of the instrument, in any one or more particulars, they must change its language in those particulars, so as to make it express the intentions they desire. But no change can be wrought by exterior evidence; because the *written* instrument, to which, and to which only, all have, in theory, agreed, must always be the *highest evidence* that the courts can have of the intentions of the whole people.

If, therefore, the fact were *historically* well authenticated, *that every man in the nation* had publicly asserted, within one hour after the adoption of the constitution, (that is, within one hour after he had, in theory, agreed to it,) that he did not agree to it intending that any or all of the principles expressed by the instrument should be established as law, all those assertions would not be of the least legal consequence in the world; and for the very sufficient reason, that what they have said *in the instrument* is the law; and what they have said out of it is no part of it, and has no legal bearing upon it.

Such assertions, if admitted to be true, would only prove that the parties had lied when they agreed to the instrument; and if they lied then, they may be lying now. If we cannot believe their first and formal assertion of their intentions, we cannot believe their second and informal one.

The parties cannot claim that they did not *understand* the language of the instrument; for if they did not understand the language then, when they agreed to it, how can we know that they understand it now, when they dissent from it? Or how can we know that they so much as understand the very language they are now using in making their denial? or in expressing their contrary intentions?

They cannot claim that they did not understand *the rules, by which their language, used in the instrument, would be interpreted;* for if they did not understand them then, how can we know that they understand them now? Or how do we know that they understand the rules, by which their present declarations of their intentions will be interpreted?

The consequence is, that every man must be presumed to understand a contract to which he agrees, whether he actually does understand it or not. He must be presumed to understand the meaning of its words; the rules by which its words will be interpreted; and the intentions, which its words, thus interpreted, express. Otherwise men can never make contracts that will be binding upon them; for a man cannot bind himself by a contract which he is not presumed to understand; and it can seldom, or never, be proved whether a man actually does understand his contract, or not. If, therefore, at any time, through *ignorance*, carelessness, mental reservations, or fraudulent designs, men agree to instruments that express intentions different from their own, they must abide the consequences. The instrument must stand, as expressing their intentions, and their adverse intentions must fail of effect.

Every one, therefore, when he agrees to a contract, judges for himself, *and takes his own risk*, whether he understands the instrument to which he gives his assent. It is plainly impossible to have constitutions established by contract of the people with each other on any other principle than this; for, on any other principle, it could never be known what the people, as a whole, had agreed to. If every individual, after he had agreed to a constitution, could set up his own intentions, his own understandings of the instrument, or his own mental reservations, in opposition to the intentions expressed by the instrument itself, the constitution would be liable to have as many different meanings as there were different individuals who had agreed to it. And the consequence would be, that it would have no obligation at all, as a *mutual* and binding contract, for, very likely, no two of the whole would have understood the instrument alike in every particular, and therefore no two would have agreed to the same thing.

Each man, therefore, before he agrees to an instrument, must judge for himself, *taking his own risk* whether he understands it.

After he has agreed to it, he is estopped, by his own instrument, from denying that his intentions were identical with the intentions expressed by the instrument.

The constitution of the United States, therefore, until its language is altered, or the instrument itself abolished, by the people of the United States, must be taken to express the intentions of the whole people of the United States, whether it really do express their intentions or not. It is the highest evidence of their intentions. It is the only evidence which they have *all* agreed to furnish of their intentions. All other *adverse* evidence is, therefore, legally worthless and inadmissible. The intentions of the instrument, then, must prevail, *as being the intentions of the people*, or the constitution itself is at an end.

SECOND RULE.

The second rule of interpretation is, that " the intention of the constitution must be collected from its words."*

This rule is, in reality, nearly synonymous with the preceding one ; and *its* reason, like that of the other, is apparent; for why are words used in writing a law, unless it is to be taken for granted

---

* The Supreme Court of the United States say : " The intention of the instrument must prevail ; *this intention must be collected from its words.*" — 12 *Wheaton,* 332.

" The intention of the legislature is to be searched for in the words which the legislature has employed to convey it." — 7 *Cranch*, 60.

Story says, " We must take it to be true, that the legislature intend precisely what they say." — 2 *Story's Circuit Court Rep.*, 653.

Rutherforth says, " A promise, or a contract, or a will, gives us a right to whatever the promiser, the contractor, or the testator, designed or intended to make ours. But his design or intention, if it is considered merely as an act of his mind, cannot be known to any one besides himself. When, therefore, we speak of his design or intention as the measure of our claim, we must necessarily be understood to mean the design or intention which he has made known or expressed by some outward mark ; because, a design or intention which does not appear, can have no more effect, or can no more produce a claim, than a design or intention which does not exist.

" In like manner, the obligations that are produced by the civil laws of our country arise from the intention of the legislator ; not merely as this intention is an act of the mind, but as it is declared or expressed by some outward sign or mark, which makes it known to us. For the intention of the legislator, whilst he keeps it to himself, produces no effect, and is of no more account, than if he had no such intention. Where we have no knowledge, we can be under no obligation. We cannot, therefore, be obliged to comply with his will, where we do not know what his will is. And we can no otherwise know what his will is, than by means of some outward sign or mark, by which this will is expressed or declared." — *Rutherforth, B.* 2, *chap.* 7, *p.* 307-8.

14*

that when written they contain the law? If more was meant, why was not more said? If less was meant, why was so much said? If the contrary was meant, why was this said, instead of the contrary?

To go *beyond* the words of a law, (including their necessary or reasonable implications,) *in any case*, is equivalent to saying that the *written* law is incomplete; that it, in reality, is not a law, but only a part of one; and that the remainder was left to be guessed at, or rather to be *made*, by the courts.

It is, therefore, a violation of legal rules, to go *beyond* the words of a law, (including their necessary or reasonable implications,) in any case whatever.*

To go *contrary* to the words of a law, is to abolish the law itself, by declaring its words to be false.

But it happens that the same words have such various and opposite meanings in common use, that there would be no certainty as to the meaning of the laws themselves, unless there were some *rules* for determining which one of a word's various meanings was to be attached to it, when the word was found in a particular connection. Hence the necessity of rules of interpretation. Their office is to determine the legal meaning of a word, or, rather, to *select* the legal meaning of word, out of all the various meanings which the word bears in common use. Unless this selection were made, a word might have two or more different and contradictory meanings in the same place. Thus the law would be mere jargon, instead of being a certain and precise rule of action.

These rules of interpretation have never been specially enacted by statute, or constitutions, for even a statute or constitution enacting them would be unintelligible or uncertain, until interpreted by them. They have, therefore, originated in the necessity of the case; in the inability of words to express single, definite, and clear ideas, such as are indispensable to certainty in the law, unless some one of their several meanings be selected as the legal one.

Men of sense and honesty, who have never heard of these rules as legal ones, but who, nevertheless, assume that written laws and contracts are made for just and reasonable ends, and then judge of

---

* This rule, that forbids us to go *beyond* the words of the law, must not be understood as conflicting with the one that allows us, in certain cases, to go out of an instrument *to find the meaning of the words used in the instrument.* *We may, in certain cases,* (not in all,) and under certain limitations, as will hereafter be explained, go out of an instrument *to find the meaning of its words;* but we can never go *beyond* their meaning, when found.

their meaning accordingly, *unconsciously* act upon these rules in so doing. Their perception of the fact, that unless the meaning of words were judged of in this manner, words themselves could not be used for writing laws and contracts, without being liable to be perverted to subserve all manner of injustice, and to defeat the honest intentions of the parties, forces upon them the conviction, that the *legal* meaning of the words must be such, and only such, as (it will hereafter be seen) these rules place upon them. The rules, then, are but the dictates of common sense and common honesty, applied to determining the meaning of laws and contracts. And common sense and common honesty are all that is necessary to enable one to judge of the necessity and soundness of the rules.

Rules of interpretation, then, are as old as the use of words, in prescribing laws, and making contracts. They are as necessary for defining the words as the words are for describing the laws and contracts. The words would be unavailable for writing laws and contracts, without the aid of the rules for interpreting them. The rules, then, are as much a part of the *language* of laws and contracts as are the words themselves. Their application to the words of laws and contracts is as much presumed to be understood, by all the parties concerned, as is the meaning of the words themselves. And courts have no more right to depart from, or violate, these rules, than to depart from, or contradict, the words themselves.

The people must always be presumed to understand these rules, and to have framed all their constitutions, contracts, &c., with reference to them, as much as they must be presumed to understand the common meanings of the words they use, and to have framed their constitutions and contracts with reference to them. And why? Because men's contracts and constitutions would be no contracts at all, unless there were some rules of interpretation understood, or agreed upon, for determining which was the legal meaning of the words employed in forming them. The received rules of interpretation have been acted upon for ages ;* indeed, they must have been acted upon through all time, since men first attempted to make honest contracts with each other. As no other rules than these received ones can be presumed against the parties, *and as these are the only ones that can secure men's honest*

---

* *Kent* says, these rules " have been accumulated by the experience, and ratified by the approbation, of ages."—1 *Kent,* 461.

rights, under their honest contracts; and, as everybody is bound
to know that courts must be governed by fixed rules, applying the
same to all contracts whatsoever, it must always be presumed, in
each particular case, that the parties intended their instruments
should be construed by the same rules by which the courts construe all others.

Another reason why the people must be presumed to know
these rules, at least in their application to cases where a question
of right and wrong is involved, is, that the rules are but a transcript
of a common principle of morality, to wit, the principle which
requires us to attribute good motives and good designs to all the
words and actions of our fellow-men, that can reasonably bear such
a construction. This is a rule by which every man claims that
his own words and actions should be judged. It is also a principle of law, as well as of morals, and one, too, of which every
man who is tried for an offence claims the benefit. And the law
accords it to him. So long as there be so much as " *a reasonable
doubt* " whether his words or actions evince a criminal intent, the
law presumes a good intent, and gives him the benefit of it. Why
should not the same rule be observed, in inferring the intent of the
whole community, from the language of their laws and constitutions, which is observed in inferring the intent of each individual
of that community from his language and conduct? It should
clearly require as strong proof to convict the whole community of
a crime, (and an unjust law or constitution is one of the highest
of all possible crimes,) as it does to convict a single individual.
The principle, then, is the same in both cases; and the practice of
those who infer a bad intent from the language of the constitution,
so long as the language itself admits of a reasonable doubt
whether such be its intent, goes the length of overthrowing an
universally recognized principle of law, on which the security
of every accused person is liable to depend.*

For these, and perhaps other reasons, the people are presumed

---

* *Vattel* says, " The interpretation of every act, and of every treaty, ought to be
made according to certain rules proper to determine the sense of them, such as the
parties concerned must naturally have understood when the act was prepared and
accepted.

" As these rules are founded on right reason, and are consequently approved and
prescribed by the law of nature, every man, every sovereign, is obliged to admit
and follow them. If princes were to acknowledge no rules that determined the
sense in which the expressions ought to be taken, treaties would be only empty
words; nothing could be agreed upon with security, and it would be almost ridiculous to place any dependence on the effect f conventions." — *Vattel, B.* 2, *chap.*
17, *sec.* 268.

to understand the reason and justice of these rules, and therefore, to understand that their contracts will be construed by them. If, therefore, men ever frame constitutions or contracts with the intention that they shall be construed contrarily to these rules, their intention must be defeated; and for the same reason that they would have to be defeated if they had used words in a directly opposite sense to the common ones, such, for example, as using white when they meant black, or black when they meant white.

For the sake of having a case for the rules to apply to, we will take the representative clause, embracing the word " free," (Art. 1, sec. 2,) which is the first and the *strongest* of all the clauses in the constitution that have been claimed as recognizing and sanctioning slavery. Indeed, unless this clause do recognize and sanction it, nobody would pretend that either of the other clauses do so. The same rules, if any, that prevent the representative clause and the word " free " from having any legal reference to slavery, will also have the same effect upon the other clauses. If, therefore, the argument for slavery, based upon the word " free," falls to the ground, the arguments based upon the words " importation of persons," " service and labor," &c., must also fall; for they can stand, if at all, only by means of the support they obtain from the argument drawn from the word " free."

A third rule is, that we are always, if possible, to give a word some meaning appropriate to the subject matter of the instrument itself.*

This rule is indispensable, to prevent an instrument from degenerating into absurdity and nonsense.

In conformity with this rule, words which purport to describe certain classes of persons existing under the constitution, must be taken in a sense that will aptly describe such persons as were actually to exist under it, and not in a sense that will only describe those who were to have no existence under it.

It would, for instance, be absurd for the constitution to provide that, in every ten years, there should be "added to the whole num-

---

* Blackstone says, " As to the *subject matter*, words are always to be understood as having regard thereto."—1 *Blackstone*, 60.

" We ought always to give to expressions the sense most suitable to the subject, or to the matter, to which they relate."—*Vattel*, B. 2., chap. 17, sec. 280.

Other authorities on this point are given in the note at the end of this chapter.

ber of *free* persons three fifths of all *other* persons," if there were really to be no other persons than the free.

If, therefore, a sense correlative with slavery were given to the word *free*, it would make the word inappropriate to the subject matter of the constitution, *unless there were really to be slaves under the constitution.*

It is, therefore, inadmissible to say that the word *free* is used in the constitution as the correlative of slaves, *until it be first proved that there were to be slaves under the constitution.*

We must find out what classes of persons were to exist under the constitution, before we can know what classes of persons the terms used in the constitution apply to.

If the word *free* had but one meaning, we might infer, *from the word itself*, that such persons as that word would necessarily describe were to exist under the constitution. But since the word has various meanings, we can draw no certain inference *from it alone*, as to the class of persons to whom it is applied. We must, therefore, fix its meaning in the constitution, by ascertaining, *from other parts of the instrument*, what kind of "free persons," and also what kind of "other persons," were really to exist under the constitution. Until this is done, we cannot know the meaning of the word *free*, as it is used in the constitution.

Those who say that the word *free* is used, in the constitution, in a sense correlative with slavery, assume the very point in dispute ; viz., that there were to be slaves under the constitution. *This is the point to be proved, and cannot be assumed. And until it be proved*, it is making nonsense of the constitution, to say that the word *free* is used as the correlative of slavery.

There is no language in the constitution, that expressly declares, or necessarily implies, that slavery was to exist under the constitution. To say, therefore, that the word *free* was used as the correlative of slaves, is begging the question that there were to be slaves ; it is assuming the whole ground in dispute. Those who argue for slavery, must first prove, *by language that can mean nothing less*, that slavery was to be permitted under the constitution. *Then* they may be allowed to infer that the word *free* is used as its correlative. But until then, a different meaning must be given to the word, else the clause before cited is converted into nonsense.

On the other hand, in giving the word *free* the sense common at that day, to wit, a sense correlative with persons not naturalized, and not possessed of equal political privileges with others, we assume the existence of no class of persons except those whom the constitution itself especially recognizes, to wit, those possessing full political rights, as citizens, or members of the state, and those unnaturalized persons who will not possess full political rights. The constitution explicitly recognizes these two classes, because it makes a distinction between them in the matter of eligibility to certain offices, and it also explicitly authorizes Congress to pass laws for the naturalization of those who do not possess full rights as citizens.

If, then, we take the word *free* in the sense correlative with unnaturalized persons, the word has a meaning that is already appropriate to the subject matter of the instrument, and requires no illegal assumptions to make it so.

On the other hand, if we use the word in the sense correlative with slaves, we either make nonsense of the language of the constitution, or else we assume the very point in dispute, viz., that there were to be slaves under the constitution; neither of which have we any right to do.

This argument is sufficient, of itself, to overthrow all the arguments that were ever made in favor of the constitutionality of slavery.

Substantially the whole argument of the advocates of slavery is founded on the assumption of the very fact in dispute, viz., that there was to be slavery under the constitution. Not being able to *prove*, by the words of the constitution, that there was to be any slavery under it, they *assume* that there was to be slavery, and then use that assumption to prove the meaning of the constitution itself. In other words, not being able to prove slavery by the constitution, they attempt to prove the meaning of the constitution by slavery. Their whole reasoning on this point is fallacious, simply because the legality of slavery, under the constitution, is itself a thing to be proved, and cannot be assumed.

The advocates of slavery cannot avoid this dilemma, by saying that slavery existed at the time the constitution was adopted; for many things existed at the time, such as theft, robbery, piracy, &c., which were not therefore to be legalized by the constitution. And slavery had no better constitutional or legal existence than either of these crimes.

Besides, even if slavery had been legalized (as it was not) by any of the then existing *state* constitutions, its case would have been no better; for the United States constitution was to be the supreme law of the land, *anything in the constitution or laws of any state to the contrary notwithstanding.* The constitution being the supreme law, operating directly upon the people, and securing to them certain rights, it necessarily annulled everything that might be found in the state constitutions that was inconsistent with the freedom of the people to enjoy those rights. It of course would have annulled the legality of slavery, if slavery had then had any legal existence; because a slave cannot enjoy the rights secured by the United States constitution.

Further. The constitution is a *political* instrument, treating of men's political rights and privileges. Its terms must therefore be taken in their political sense, in order to be appropriate to the subject matter of the instrument. The word *free*, in its political sense, appropriately describes men's political rank as free and equal members of the state, entitled, *of right*, to the protection of the laws. On the other hand, the word *free*, in the sense correlative with slavery, has no appropriateness to the subject matter of such an instrument — and why? Because slavery is not, *of itself*, a political relation, or a political institution; although political institutions may, and sometimes do, recognize and legalize it. But, *of itself*, it is a merely private relation between one man and another, created by *individual force*, and not by political authority. Thus a strong man beats a weaker one, until the latter will obey him. This is slavery, and the whole of it; *unless it be specially legalized.* The United States constitution does not specially legalize it; and therefore slavery is no part of the *subject matter* of *that* instrument. The word *free*, therefore, in the constitution, cannot be said to be used as the correlative of slavery; because that sense would be entirely inappropriate to anything that is the subject matter of the instrument. It would be a sense which no other part of the constitution gives any occasion or authority for.

FOURTH RULE.

A fourth rule is, that where *technical* words are used, a technical meaning is to be attributed to them.

This rule is commonly laid down in the above general terms. It is, however, subject to these exceptions, viz., that where the technical sense would be inconsistent with, or less favorable to, justice, or not consonant to the context, or not appropriate to the nature of the subject, some other meaning may be adopted. Subject to these exceptions, the rule is of great authority, for reasons that will hereafter appear.

Thus, in commercial contracts, the terms and phrases used in them are to be taken in the technical or professional sense common among merchants, if that sense be consonant to the context, and appropriate to the nature of the contracts.

In political contracts, the terms and phrases used in them are to be taken in the political and technical sense common in such instruments, if that sense be consonant to the context, and appropriate to the subject matter of the contracts.

Terms common and proper to express political rights, relations, and duties, are of course to be taken in the technical sense natural and appropriate to those rights, relations, and duties.

Thus, in political papers, such terms as liberty, allegiance, representation, citizenship, citizens, denizens, freemen, free subjects, free-born subjects, inhabitants, residents, people, aliens, allies, enemies, are all to be understood in the technical sense appropriate to the subject matter of the instrument, unless there be something else, *in the instrument itself*, that shows that some other meaning is intended.

Terms which, by common usage, are properly descriptive of the parties to, or members of, the compact, as distinguished from others, are to be taken in the technical sense, which describes them, as distinguished from others, unless there be, in the instrument itself, some unequivocal evidence that they are to be taken in a different sense.

The authority of this rule is so well founded in nature, reason, and usage, that it is almost strange that it should be questioned. It is a rule which everybody, *by their common practice*, admit to be correct; for everybody more naturally understands a word in its technical sense than in any other, unless that sense be inconsistent with the context.

Nevertheless, an attempt has been made by some persons to deny the rule, and to lay down a contrary one, to wit, that where a word has what they *choose to call* a common or popular meaning, and also a technical one, the *former* is to be preferred, unless there be something, in other parts of the instrument, that indicates that the technical one should be adopted.

The argument for slavery virtually claims, not only that this so called common and popular meaning of a word, (and especially of the word " free,") is to be preferred to the technical one, but also that this simple preference is of sufficient consequence to out-

15

weigh all considerations of justice and injustice, and indeed all, or nearly all, the other considerations on which legal rules of interpretation are founded. Nevertheless I am not aware that the advocates of slavery have ever had the good fortune to find a single instance where a court has laid it down, *as a rule*, that any other meaning is, *of itself*, preferable to the technical one ; much less that that preference was sufficient, in cases where right and wrong were involved, to turn the scale in favor of the wrong. And if a court were to lay down such a rule, every one is at liberty to judge for himself of its soundness.

But inasmuch as this pretended rule is one of the main pillars, if not *the* main pillar, in support of the constitutionality of slavery, it is entitled to particular consideration.

The falsehood of this pretended rule will be evident when it is considered that it assumes that the technical meaning of a word is *not* the common and popular one ; *whereas it is the very commonness, approaching to uniformity, with which a word is used in a particular sense, in relation to particular things, that makes it technical.**

A technical word is a word, which in one profession, art, or trade, or in reference to particular subjects, is generally, or uniformly, used in a particular sense, and that sense a somewhat different one from those in which it is generally used out of that profession, art, or trade, or in reference to other subjects.

There probably is not a trade that has not its technical words. Even the cobbler has his. His *ends* are generally quite different things from the ends of other people. If we hear a cobbler speak of *his* ends, we naturally suppose he means the ends of his threads, because he has such frequent occasion to speak of and use them. If we hear other people speak of their ends, we naturally suppose that they mean the objects they have in view. With the cobbler, then, *ends* is a technical word, because he frequently or generally uses the word in a different sense from that in which it is used by other people.

Mechanics have very many technical words, as, for instance, to describe particular machines, parts of machines, particular processes

* It was, for example, the commonness, or rather the uniformity, with which the word "free" had been used — *up to the time the constitution was adopted* — to describe persons possessed of political and other legal franchises, as distinguished from persons not possessed of the same franchises, that made the word "free" a technical one in the law.

of labor, and particular articles of manufacture. And when we hear a mechanic use one of these words, we naturally suppose that he uses it in a technical sense — that is, with reference to his particular employment, machinery, or production. And why do we suppose this? Simply because it is more common for *him* to use the word in that sense than in any other, especially if he is talking of anything in regard to which that sense would be appropriate. If, however, his talk is about some other subject, in relation to which the technical sense of the word would not be appropriate, then we conclude that he uses it, not in the technical sense appropriate to his art, but in some other sense more appropriate to the subject on which he is speaking.

So, if we were to hear a banker speak of " the days of grace having expired," we should naturally attach a very different meaning to the words from what we should if we were to hear them from the pulpit. We should suppose, of course, that he used them in the technical sense appropriate to his business, and that he had reference only to a promissory note that had not been paid when due.

If we were to hear a banker speak of a *check*, we should suppose he used the word in a technical sense, and intended only an order for money, and not a stop, hindrance, or restraint.

So, if one farmer were to say of another, He is a *good husband*, we should naturally infer that he used the word *husband* in the technical sense appropriate to his occupation, meaning that he cultivated and managed his farm judiciously. On the other hand, if we were to hear lawyers, legislators, or judges, talking of husbands, we should infer that the word was used only in reference to men's *legal* relations to their wives. The word would be used in a technical sense in both cases.

So, if we were to hear a man called a Catholic priest, we should naturally infer that the word *Catholic* was used in its technical sense, that is, to describe a priest of the Catholic persuasion, and not a priest of a catholic, liberal, and tolerant spirit.

These examples might be multiplied indefinitely. But it will be seen from those already given that, so far from the technical sense and the common sense of words being opposed to each other, *the technical sense is itself the common sense in which a word is used with reference to particular subjects.*

These examples also show how perfectly natural, instead of unnatural, it is for us to attribute the technical meaning to a word.

whenever we are talking of a subject in relation to which that meaning is appropriate.

Almost every word of substantive importance, that is of frequent use in the law, is used in a technical sense — that is, in a sense having some special relation either to natural justice, or to men's rights or privileges under the laws.

The word *liberty*, for instance, has a technical meaning in the law. It means, not freedom from all restraint, or obligation; not a liberty to trespass with impunity upon other men's rights; but only that degree of liberty which, of natural right, belongs to a man; in other words, the greatest degree of liberty that he can exercise, without invading or immediately endangering the rights of others.

Unless nearly all words had a technical meaning in the law, it would be impossible to describe laws by words; because words have a great variety of meanings in common use; *whereas the law demands certainty and precision.* We *must* know the *precise* meaning of a word, before we can know what the law is. And the technical meaning of a word is nothing more than a *precise* meaning, that is appropriate, and commonly applied, to a particular subject, or class of subjects.

How would it be possible, for instance, to have laws against murder, unless the word murder, or some other word, were understood, in a technical sense, to describe that particular mode of killing which the law wishes to prohibit, and which is morally and legally distinguishable from all other modes of killing?

So indispensable are precision and certainty, as to the meaning of words used in laws, that where a word has not a technical meaning already known, the legislature frequently define the meaning they intend it shall bear in particular laws. Where this is not done, the *courts* have to give it a precise and definite meaning, before the law can be administered; and this precise meaning they have to conjecture, by reference to the context, and to the presumed object of all laws, justice.

What perfect chaos would be introduced into all our existing laws and contracts, if the technical meanings of all the words used in them were obliterated from our minds. A very large portion of the laws and contracts themselves would be substantially abolished, because all certainty as to their meaning would be extinguished. Suppose, for instance, the technical meanings of liberty, trial by jury, *habeas corpus*, grand jury, petit jury, murder, rape arson, theft, indictment, trial, oath, testimony, witness, court, verdict, judgment, execution, debt, dollar, bushel, yard, foot, cord, acre, rod, pound, check, draft, order, administrator, executor, guardian, apprentice, copartner, company, husband, wife, marriage, lands, goods, real estate, personal estate, highway, citizen, alien, subject, and an almost indefinite number of other words, as they now stand in our laws and contracts, were at once erased from our minds, and the legal meanings of the same words could only be conjectured by the courts and people from the context, and such other circumstances as might afford grounds for conjecture. Suppose all this, and where would be our existing laws and contracts, and the rights dependent upon them? We might nearly as well throw our statute-books, and all our deeds, notes, and other contracts, into the fire, as to strike out the technical meanings of the words in which they are written. Yet for the courts to disregard these technical meanings, is the same thing as to strike them out of existence.

If all our constitutions, state and national, were to be annulled at a blow, with all the statutes passed in pursuance of them, it would hardly create greater confusion as to men's rights, than would be created by striking out from men's minds all knowledge of the technical meanings of the words now used in writing laws and contracts. And the reconstruction of the governments, after such an abolition of them, would be a much less labor than the reconstruction of a legal language, in which laws and contracts could be written with the same conciseness and certainty as now. The former would be the work of years, the latter of centuries.

The foregoing considerations show in what ignorance and folly are founded the objections to the technical meanings of words used in the laws.

The real difference between the technical meaning of a word, and any other meaning, is just the difference between a meaning that is common, certain, and precise, and one that is, at best, less common, less certain, and less precise, and perhaps neither common, certain, nor precise.

The authorities in favor of the technical meaning, are given in the note, and are worthy of particular attention.*

---

* "Terms of art, or technical terms, must be taken according to the acceptation of the learned in each art, trade, and science." — 1 *Blackstone*, 59.

"When technical words are used, they are to be understood in their technical sense and meaning, *unless the contrary clearly appears*." — 9 *Pickering*, 514.

"The words of a statute are to be taken in their natural and ordinary significa-

The argument, and the whole argument, so far as I know, in favor of what is called the common or popular meaning, is, that that meaning is supposed to be better known by the people, and therefore it is more probable they would use it, than the other.

---

tion and import ; and if technical words are used, they are to be taken in a technical sense." — 1 *Kent*, 461.

Lord Ellenborough says, " An agreement is to be construed according to its sense and meaning, as collected in the first place from the terms used in it, which terms are themselves to be understood in their plain, ordinary, and popular sense, *unless they have generally, in respect to the subject matter, as by the known usage of trade or the like, acquired a peculiar sense, distinct from the popular sense of the same words ; or unless the context evidently points out that they must, in the particular instance, and in order to effect the immediate intention of the parties to that contract, be understood in some other special and peculiar sense.*" — 4 *East*, 135 ; *cited in Chitty on Contracts*, 80.

Chitty adds, " The same rule applies to the construction of acts of parliament," and cites several authorities.

" In the enactment of laws, when terms of art, or peculiar phrases, are made use of, it must be supposed that the legislature have in view the subject matter about which such terms or phrases are commonly employed." — 1 *Pickering*, 261.

" If a statute make use of a word, the meaning of which is well known at the common law, the word shall be understood in the same sense it was understood as the common law." — *Bacon's Abridg. Stat., I.*, 29.

" Technical terms, or terms proper to the arts and sciences, ought commonly to be interpreted according to the definition given of them by the masters of the art, the person versed in the knowledge of the art or science to which the term belongs. I say commonly ; for this rule is not so absolute, that we cannot, or even ought not, to deviate from it, when we have good reasons to do it ; as, for instance, if it was proved that he who speaks in a treaty, or in any other public piece, did not understand the art or science from which he borrowed the term, that he knows not its force as a technical word : that he has employed it in a vulgar sense, &c." — *Vattel, B.* 2, *ch.* 17, *sec.* 276.

" In things favorable," (" things favorable " he defines to mean " things useful and salutary to human society,") " the terms of art ought to be taken in the fullest extent they are capable of ; not only according to common use, but also as technical terms, if he who speaks understands the art to which those terms belong, or if he conducts himself by the advice of men who understand that art.

" But we ought not from this single reason, that a thing is favorable, to take the terms in an improper signification ; this is only allowable to be done, to avoid absurdity, injustice, or the nullity of the act, as is practised on every subject. For we ought to take the terms of an act in their proper sense, conformable to custom, at least, if we have not very strong reasons for deviating from it." — *Vattel, B.* 2, *ch.* 17, *sec.* 307.

" Where technical words are used, the technical meaning is to be applied to them, *unless it is repelled by the context.* But the same word often possesses a technical and a common sense. In such a case the latter is to be preferred, *unless some attendant circumstance points clearly to the former.*" — 1 *Story's Comm. on Const.*, 433.

It will be observed that every one of these authorities, except the single one from Story, gives the preference to the technical meaning, over any of the other meanings which a word may have. *The latter branch* of Story's rule gives the preference to the other meaning over the technical one.

Admitting, for the sake of the argument, that the latter branch of Story's rule is

But this argument, if not wholly false, is very shallow and frivolous; for everybody is presumed to know the laws, and therefore
they are presumed to be familiar with the technical meanings of
all the technical words that are of frequent use in writing the laws.

---

correct, still the meaning of the word "free," in the constitution, is not thereby
altered; because his rule admits that if "*some attendant circumstance* points
clearly to the technical meaning," that meaning is to be adopted. Now *every*
"attendant circumstance" that can *legally* be taken into consideration, "points
clearly to the technical meaning" — and why? Because that meaning alone is
consistent with justice, appropriate to the subject matter of the instrument, consistent with the idea that all the parties to the instrument could have reasonably
agreed to it, (an essential point, as will hereafter be seen,) consistent with all the
general provisions of the instrument. If the other meaning be adopted, all the
general provisions of the instrument are either contradicted outright, or have to be
taken subject to limitations and exceptions which are nowhere expressed, and
which would not only exclude one sixth of "the people of the United States" from
the operation of the constitution, established in their name, and for their benefit,
but would actually sanction the greatest wrongs against them.

The result, then, is, not merely that "*some* attendant circumstance," (although
the rule admits that that would be sufficient to turn the scale,) but that *every* attendant circumstance, points to the technical meaning as the true one.

There is, also, in the *same clause* with the word "free," *one* attendant circumstance which points clearly to the technical meaning; and that is, that "all other
persons" than the free, are to be represented and taxed as three fifths units. Now
there is no propriety in representing or taxing *slaves* at all, *as persons;* but there
is a special propriety in representing and taxing aliens as three fifths units, as will
more fully appear hereafter.

But, in point of fact, Story's rule destroys itself, for the two branches of it flatly
contradict each other. The *first* branch says, that "where technical words are
used, the *technical* meaning is to be applied to them, unless it is *repelled* by the
context." The second branch says, that "the same word often possesses a technical and a common sense. In such case the *latter* is to be preferred, unless
some attendant circumstance points clearly to the former."

It might be thought, on a careless reading of this rule, that there was no contradiction in it; that the first branch of it referred to a case where a word had only
one meaning, and that a *technical* one; and that the latter branch referred to a case
where a word had two or more meanings. But, in reality, there is probably not a
single technical word in the language, that has not one or more other meanings
beside the technical one; and it seems impossible there should be such a word,
because the very meaning of a technical word is a word which, in one profession,
art, or trade, is used in a somewhat different sense from what it is out of that profession, art, or trade. But be this as it may, it is evident that the first branch of
the rule as much refers to a word having two meanings, as does the latter branch
of it; for it says "the technical meaning is to be applied, *unless it be repelled by
the context.*" What is the inference from this proviso? Why, plainly, that if
the technical meaning "be repelled by the context," the other meaning is to be
adopted. This of course implies that the word has another meaning which may
be adopted if the context require it.

If, then, there are two meanings to the words in each case, the two branches of
this rule flatly contradict each other.

The first branch of the rule is given by Story, and is sustained by all the other

And this presumption of law corresponds with the general fact. The mass of the people, who are not learned in the law, but who nevertheless have general ideas of legal matters, naturally understand the words of the laws in their legal senses, and attach their legal senses to them without being aware that the legal sense is a technical one. They have been in the habit of thinking that the technical meaning of words was something dark and recondite, (simply because some few technical terms are in another language than the English,) when in reality they themselves are continually using a great variety of words, indeed, almost all important words, in a technical or legal sense, whenever they are talking of legal matters.

But whether the advocates of slavery can, or cannot, reconcile themselves to the technical meaning of the word " free," they cannot, *on their own construction of the constitution,* avoid giving the word a precise and technical sense, to wit, as the correlative of *slavery,* as distinguished from all other forms of restraint and servitude.

---

authorities cited. The second branch is Story's own, sustained by nobody. The reader will judge which is sustained by reason.

But, in truth, Story has himself laid down the true rule more accurately in another place, as follows:

" Where the words admit of two senses, each of which is conformable to common usage, that sense is to be adopted which, without departing from the literal import of the words, best harmonizes with the nature and objects, the scope and design, of the instrument." — 1 *Comm. on Const.,* 387.

One other authority, which has fallen under my eye, ought to be noticed, lest it be misunderstood. It is this:

" The language of a statute is not to be construed according to technical rules, unless such be the apparent meaning of the legislature." — 14 *Mass. Rep.,* 92.

This language, taken independently of the context, would convey the idea that the adoption of the technical meaning was a matter of indifference; or perhaps even that another meaning was rather to be preferred to the technical one.

But it will be seen, on examining the report from which this extract is taken, that the court did not at all intend to deny, but on the contrary to admit, that the *general* rule was, that the *technical* meaning was to be preferred; and that they only intended to assert that the rule in favor of the technical meaning was not so imperative that it could not be departed from in a case where " manifest justice " would be promoted by the departure; for they plead, *as a justification for departing from the technical meaning,* that in that particular case, " manifest justice " will be subserved by a different construction.

Thus have been presented all the authorities on this point, that happen now to be within my knowledge. Many more of the same kind might doubtless be found. I am aware of no contrary one, unless the single one cited from Story be so esteemed.

The conclusion, both from reason and authority, evidently is, that the technical meaning is the preferable one in all cases, except where justice, or some other legal object, will be promoted by adopting some other.

The word *slaves,* if it had been used in the constitution, (instead
of the words " all other persons,") would have itself been held to
be used in a technical sense, to wit, to designate those persons who
were held as *chattels,* as distinguished from serfs, villeins, apprentices, servants for years, persons under twenty-one years of age,
prisoners of war, prisoners for debt, prisoners for crime, soldiers,
sailors, &c., &c.   The word *slaves,* then, being technical, the word
free must necessarily have been taken in a technical sense, to wit,
as the precise correlative of *chattel slaves,* and not as the correlative
of persons held under any of these other forms of restraint or servitude.   So that on the score of technicality, (even if that were an
objection,) nothing would be gained by adopting the sense correlative with slaves.

*But it is a wholly erroneous assumption that the use of the word
" free," in a sense correlative with slaves, was either a common or
popular use of the word.*   It was neither common nor popular, if
we may judge of that time by the present; for now such a use of
it is seldom or never heard, unless made with special reference to
the classification which it is *assumed* that the constitution has
established on that point.

The common and popular classification of the people of this
country, with reference to slavery, is by the terms, *white, free colored,* and *slaves.*   We do not describe anybody as *free,* except the
free colored.   The term *white* carries with it the idea of liberty ;
and it is nearly or quite universally used in describing the white
people of the South, as distinguished from the slaves.

But it will be said by the advocates of slavery, that the term
white was not used in the constitution, because it would not include
all the *free ;* that the term *free* was used in order to include both
white and free colored.   But this assertion is but another wholly
gratuitous assumption of the facts, that there were to be slaves
under the constitution, and that representation and taxation were
to be based on the distinction between the slaves and the free ; both
of which points are to be proved, not assumed.

If there were to be slaves under the constitution, and *if* representation and taxation were to be based upon the distinction between
the slaves and the free, *then* the constitution undoubtedly used the
word *free,* instead of *white,* in order to include both the white and
free colored in the class of units.   But if, as we are bound to presume until the contrary is proved, there were to be no slaves under
the constitution, or if representation and taxation were not founded

on the distinction between them and the free, then the constitution did *not* use the word *free* for such a purpose. The burden is upon the advocates of slavery to prove, first, that there were to be slaves under the constitution, and, secondly, that representation and taxation were to be based on the distinction between them and the free, before they can say that the word *free* was used for the purpose of including the white and free colored.

Now the whole argument, or rather assertion, which the advocates of slavery can offer in support of these points, which they are necessitated to prove, is, that the word *free* is commonly and popularly used as the correlative of slaves. That argument, or assertion, is answered by the fact that the word *free* is *not* commonly or popularly used as the correlative of slaves; that the terms *white* and *free colored* are the common terms of distinction between the free and the slaves. Now these last named facts, and the argument resulting from them, are not met at all, by saying that *if* there were to be slaves, and *if* representation and taxation were to be based on the distinction between them and the free, the word *free* would *then* have been used, in preference to any other, in order to include the free colored in the same class with the whites.

It must first be proved that there were to be slaves under the constitution, and that representation and taxation were to be based on the distinction between them and the free, before it can be said that the word *free* was used in order to include both white and free colored. Those points not being proved, the allegation, founded on the assumption of them, is good for nothing.

The use of the word *free*, then, in a sense correlative with slavery, *not* being the common and popular use of the word at the time the constitution was adopted, all the argument, founded on that assumption, falls to the ground.

On the other hand, the use of the word *free*, in a political sense, as correlative either with aliens, or with persons not possessed of equal political privileges with others, *was* the *universal* meaning of the word, in all documents of a fundamental and constitutional character, up to the time when the constitution of the United States was adopted — (that is, when it was used, as it is in the United States constitution, to describe one person, as distinguished from another living under the same government.) Such was the meaning of the word in the colonial charters, in several of the State constitutions existing in 1789, and in the articles of confederation Furthermore, it was a term that had very recently been in common use in political discussions, and had thus been made perfectly familiar to the people. For example, the discussions immediately preceding the revolution, had all, or nearly all, turned upon the rights of the colonists, as "*free* British subjects." In fact, the political meaning of the word *free* was probably as familiar to the people of that day as the meaning of the word *citizen* is now; perhaps, indeed, more so, for there is some controversy as to the legal meaning of the word *citizen*. So that all the argument against the technical sense of the term, on the ground of its not being the common sense, is founded in sheer ignorance or fraud.*

Finally; unless the word *free* be taken in the technical sense common at that day, it is wholly an unsettled matter what sense should be given to it, in the constitution. The advocates of slavery *take it for granted* that, if it be not taken in its common and technical sense, it *must* be taken in the sense correlative with slavery. But that is all gratuitous. There are many kinds of freedom besides freedom from chattel slavery; and many kinds of restraint besides chattel slavery; restraints, too, more legitimate in their nature, and better legitimated under the laws then existing, than slavery. And it may require a great deal more argument than some persons imagine, to settle the meaning of the word *free*, as used in the constitution, if its technical meaning be discarded.

I repeat, it is a wholly gratuitous assumption that, if the technical meaning of the word *free* be discarded, the sense correlative with slavery must be adopted. The word "*free*," *in its common and popular sense*, does not at all imply, as its correlative, either property in man, or even involuntary service or labor. It, therefore, does not imply slavery. It implies, as its correlative, simply *restraint*. It is, *of itself*, wholly indefinite as to the *kind* of restraint implied. It is used as the correlative of all kinds of restraint, imprisonment, compulsion, and disability, to which mankind are liable. Nothing, therefore, can be inferred from the word alone, as to the particular kind of restraint implied, in any case. It is indispensable to know the subject matter, about which the word is used, in order to know the kind of restraint implied. And

---

* *Vattel* says, "Languages vary incessantly, and the signification and force of words change with time. When an ancient act is to be interpreted, we should know the common use of the terms at the time when it was written." — *B.* **2,** *ch.* 17, *sec.* 272.

He also says, "In the interpretation of treaties, pacts, and promises, we ought not to deviate from the common use of language, at least, if we have not very strong reasons for it." — *Same sec.*

if the word had had no technical meaning appropriate to the subject matter of the constitution, and if no other part of the constitution had given us any light as to the sense of the word in the
representative clause, we should have been obliged to conjecture its
correlative.   And slavery is one of the last correlatives that we
should have been at liberty to adopt.   In fact, we should have
been obliged to let the implication remain inoperative for ambiguity, and to have counted all men as " free," (for reasons given
under rule seventh,) rather than have adopted slavery as its correlative.

FIFTH RULE.

A fifth rule of interpretation is, that the sense of every word,
that is ambiguous in itself, must, *if possible*, be determined by
reference to the rest of the instrument.

The importance of this rule will be seen, when it is considered
that the only alternatives to it are, that we must go out of the
instrument, and resort to conjecture, for the meaning of ambiguous
words.

The rule is an universal one among courts, and the reasons of
it are as follows : —

Vattel says, " If he who has expressed himself in an obscure or
equivocal manner, has spoken elsewhere more clearly on the same
subject, he is the best interpreter of himself.   *We ought to interpret
his obscure and vague expressions, in such a manner, that they may
agree with those terms that are clear and without ambiguity,
which he has used elsewhere, either in the same treaty, or in some
other of the like kind.*   In fact, while we have no proof that a man
has changed his mind, or manner of thinking, it is presumed that
his thoughts have been the same on the same occasions ; so that
if he has anywhere clearly shown his intention, with respect to
anything, we ought to give the same sense to what he has elsewhere said obscurely on the same affair."—*B. 2, ch.* 17, *sec.*
284.

Also ; " Frequently, in order to abridge, people express imperfectly, and with some obscurity, what they suppose is sufficiently
elucidated by the things that preceded it, or even what they propose to explain afterwards ; and, besides, the expressions have a
force, and sometimes even an entirely different signification, according to the occasion, their connection, and their relation to other
words.   The connection and train of the discourse is also another
source of interpretation.   *We ought to consider the whole discourse
together, in order perfectly to conceive the sense of it, and to give
to each expression, not so much the signification it may receive in*

itself, as that it ought to have from the thread and spirit of the discourse. This is the maxim of the Roman law : *Incivile est, nisi tota lege perspecta una aliqua particula ejus proposita, judicare, vel respondere.*" (It is improper to judge of, or answer to, any one thing proposed in a law, unless the whole law be thoroughly examined.) — *Same, sec.* 285.

Also ; " The connection and relation of things themselves, serve also to discover and establish the true sense of a treaty, or of any other piece. *The interpretation ought to be made in such a manner, that all the parts appear consonant to each other ; that what follows agree with what went before ; at least, if it does not manifestly appear, that by the last clauses, something is changed that went before.* For it is presumed that the authors of the treaty have had an uniform and steady train of thought ; that they did not desire things which ill agreed with each other, or contradictions ; but rather that they have intended to explain one thing by another ; and, in a word, that one and the same spirit reigns throughout the same work, or the same treaty." — *Same, sec.* 286.

The Sup. Court of Mass. says, " When the meaning of any particular section or clause of a statute is questioned, it is proper to look into the other parts of the statute ; otherwise, the different sections of the same statute might be so construed as to be repugnant."— 1 *Pickering,* 250.

Coke says, " It is the most natural and genuine exposition of a statute to construe one part of the statute by another part of the same statute." — *Co. Lit.*, 381, *b.*

The foregoing citations indicate the absolute necessity of the rule, to preserve any kind of coherence or congruity between the different parts of an instrument.

If we were to go out of an instrument, instead of going to other parts of it, to find the meaning of every ambiguous word, we should be liable to involve the whole instrument in all manner of incongruities, contradictions, and absurdities. There are hardly three consecutive lines, of any legal instrument whatever, the sense of which can be understood without reference to other parts of the instrument.

To go out of an instrument, instead of going to other parts of it, to find the sense of an ambiguous word, is also equivalent to saying that the instrument itself is incomplete.

Apply this rule, then, to the word " *free,*" and the words " *all other persons.*" The sense of these words being ambiguous in themselves, the rest of the instrument must be examined to find the persons who may properly be denominated " *free* persons," and " all other persons." In making this examination, we shall

16

find no classes mentioned answering to these descriptions, but the native and naturalized persons on the one hand, and those not naturalized on the other.

SIXTH RULE.

A sixth rule of interpretation, and a very important, inflexible, and universal one, applicable to *contracts*, is, that a contract must never, if it be possible to avoid it, be so construed, as that any one of the parties to it, assuming him to understand his rights, and to be of competent mental capacity to make *obligatory** contracts, may not reasonably be presumed to have consented to it.

If, for instance, two men were to form a copartnership in business, their contract, if its language will admit of any other possible construction, must not be so construed as to make it an agreement that one of the partners shall be the slave of the other; because such a contract would be unnatural, unreasonable, and would imply that the party who agreed to be a slave was incompetent to make a reasonable, and therefore obligatory, contract.†

This principle applies to the constitution of the United States, and to all other constitutions that purport to be established by "the people;" for such constitutions are, in theory, but contracts of the people with each other, entered into by them severally for their individual security and benefit. It also applies equally to all statutes made in pursuance of such constitutions, because the statutes derive their authority from the constitutional consent or contract of the people that such statutes may be enacted and enforced. The authority of the statutes, therefore, as much rests on contract, as does the authority of the constitutions themselves. To deny that constitutions and statutes derive their authority from contract, is to found the government on arbitrary power.

By the rule laid down, these statutes and constitutions, therefore, must not be construed, (unless such construction be unavoidable,) so as to authorize anything whatever *to which every single individual of "the people"* may not, as competent men, knowing

---

* Contracts made by persons mentally incompetent to make *reasonable* contracts, are not "obligatory."

† Although the greatest discretion that is within the limits of reason, is allowed to parties in making contracts, yet contracts manifestly unreasonable are not held obligatory. And all contracts are unreasonable that purport to surrender one's natural rights. Also, all contracts that purport to surrender any valuable acquired rights, as property, for example, without any equivalent, or reasonable motive.

their rights, reasonably be presumed to have freely and voluntarily assented.

Now the *parties* to the contract expressed in the constitution of the United States, are " the people of the United States," that is, the *whole* people of the United States. The description given of the parties to the constitution, as much includes those " people of the United States" who were at the time treated as slaves, as those who were not. The adoption of the constitution was not, *in theory*, the exercise of a right granted to the people by the State legislatures, but of the *natural* original right of the people themselves, as individuals. (This is the doctrine of the supreme court, as will presently appear.) The slaves had the same *natural* competency and right to establish, or consent to, government, that others had; and they must be presumed to have consented to it equally with others, if the language of the constitution implies it. *We certainly cannot go out of the constitution to find the parties to it.* And the constitution affords no legal ground whatever for separating the then " people of the United States " into two classes, and saying that one class were parties to the constitutional contract, and that the other class were not. There would be just as much reason in saying that the terms " the people " used in the constitutions of Massachusetts, Maine, New Hampshire, and Vermont, to describe the parties to those constitutions, do not include *all* " the people " of those States, as there is for saying that *all* " the people of the United States " are not included in the constitutional description of them, and are not, therefore, parties to the constitution of the United States.

We are obliged to take this term, " the people," in its broadest sense, unless the instrument itself have clearly and palpably imposed some restriction upon it.

It is a universal rule of courts, that where justice will be promoted by taking a word in the most comprehensive sense in which it can be taken consistently with the rest of the instrument, it must be taken in that sense, in order that as much justice as possible may be accomplished. On the other hand, where a word is unfavorable to justice, it must be taken in its most restricted sense, in order that as little injustice as possible may be accomplished.*

* Vattel says, " When the subject relates to things favorable "— (in sec. 302, he defines "things favorable " to be things "useful and salutary to human society,") ···" we ought to give the terms all the extent they are capable of in common use ;

In conformity with this rule, the words, "the people of the United States," would have to be taken in their most extensive sense, even though they stood but on an equal ground with other words in the instrument.   But, in fact, they stand on privileged ground.   *Their meaning is to be determined before we proceed to the interpretation of the rest of the instrument.*   The first thing to be ascertained, in regard to an instrument, always is, *who are the parties to it ;* for upon that fact may depend very many important things in the construction of the rest of the instrument.   In short, the body of the instrument is to be interpreted with reference to the parties, and not the parties conjectured by reference to the body of the instrument.   We must first take the instrument's own declaration as to who the parties are ; and then, if possible, make the body of the instrument express such, and only such, intentions, as *all* the parties named may reasonably be presumed to have agreed to.

Assuming, then, that *all* "the people of the United States" are parties to the constitutional contract, it is manifest, that it cannot reasonably be presumed that any, even the smallest, portion of them, knowing their natural rights, and being competent to make a reasonable contract of government, would consent to a constitution that should either make them slaves, or assist in keeping them in slavery.   Such a construction, therefore, must not be put upon the contract, if the language admits of any other.   This rule alone, then, is sufficient to forbid a construction sanctioning slavery.

It may, perhaps, be argued that the slaves were not parties to the constitution, inasmuch as they never, *in fact*, consented to it.   But this reasoning would disfranchise half the population; for there is not a single constitution in the country—state, or national —to which one half of the people who are, *in theory*, parties to it, ever, *in fact and in form*, agreed.   Voting for and under a constitution, are almost the only acts that can, with any reason at all, be considered a *formal* assent to a constitution.   Yet a bare majority

and if a term has many significations, the most extensive ought to be preferred."—*B.* 2, *ch.* 17, *sec.* 307.

" In relation to things favorable, the most extensive signification of the terms is more agreeable to equity than their confined signification." — *Same.*

" We should, in relation to things *odious*," — (in sec. 302, he defines "as *odious*, everything that, in its own nature, is rather hurtful than of use to the human race,") — " take the terms in the most confined sense, and even, to a certain degree, may admit the figurative, to remove the burdensome consequences of the proper and literal sense, or what it contains that is odious." — *Same, sec.* 303.

of the adult males, or about one tenth of the whole people, is the largest number of "the people" that has ever been considered necessary, in this country, to establish a constitution. And after it is established, only about one fifth of the people are allowed to vote under it, even where suffrage is most extended. So that no formal assent to a constitution is ever given by the people at large. Yet the constitutions themselves assume, and virtually *assert*, that *all* "the people" have agreed to them. They must, therefore, be construed on the theory that all have agreed to them, else the instruments themselves are at once denied, and, of course, invalidated altogether. No one, then, who upholds the validity of the constitution, can deny its own assertion, that all "the people" are parties to it. Besides, no one, unless it be the particular individuals who have *not* consented, can take advantage of the fact that they have not consented.

And, in practice, we do not allow even such individuals to take advantage of the fact of their non-consent, *to avoid the burdens imposed by the instrument ;* and not allowing the individuals themselves to take advantage of it for that purpose, no other person, certainly, can be allowed to take advantage of it to shut them out from its protection and benefits.

The consent, then, of "the people" at large is *presumed*, whether they ever have really consented, or not. Their consent is presumed only on the assumption that the rights of citizenship are valuable and beneficial to them, and that if they understood that fact, they would willingly give their consent in form. Now, the slaves, if they understood that the legal effect of their consenting to the constitution would be "to secure the blessings of liberty to themselves and their posterity," would doubtless all be as ready to give their actual assent to it, as any other portion of "the people" can be. Inasmuch, then, as such would be the legal effect of their consent, there is no other class of "the people of the United States," whose consent to the constitution may, with so much reason, be presumed; because no other class have so much to gain by consenting to it. And since the consent of all is presumed, solely on the ground that the instrument is beneficial to them, regardless of their actual assent, there is no ground for excluding, *or for not presuming*, the consent of those, whose consent, on account of its beneficial operation upon their interests and rights, can be most reasonably and safely presumed.

But it may, perhaps, be said that it cannot reasonably be pre-

16*

sumed that the *slaveholders* would agree to a constitution, which would destroy their right to their slave property.

One answer to this argument is, that the slaveholders had, at the time, no legal or constitutional right to their slaves, under their State constitutions, as has already been proved ; and they must be presumed to have known that such was the fact, for every one is presumed to know the law.

A second answer is, that it is, *in law*, considered reasonable — as it is, in fact, one of the highest evidences of reason — for a man voluntarily to do justice, against his apparent pecuniary interests.

Is a man considered *non compos mentis* for restoring stolen property to its rightful owner, when he might have retained it with impunity ?   Or are all the men, who have voluntarily emancipated their slaves, presumed to have been fools ? incompetent to make reasonable contracts ? or even to have had less reason than those who refuse to emancipate ?   Yet this is the whole argument of those, who say that it cannot be supposed that the slaveholders would agree to a free constitution.   The argument would have been good for nothing, even if the then existing State constitutions had authorized slavery.

There would be just as much reason in saying that it cannot be supposed that thieves, robbers, pirates, or criminals of any kind, would consent to the establishment of governments that should have authority to suppress *their* business, as there is in saying that slaveholders cannot be supposed to consent to a government that should have power to suppress slaveholding.   If this argument were good for anything, we should have to apply it to the state constitutions, and construe them, if possible, so as to sanction all kinds of crimes which men commit, on the ground that the criminals themselves could not be supposed to have consented to any government that did not sanction them.

The truth is, that however great a criminal a man may have been, it is considered a very reasonable act for him to agree to do justice in future ; and therefore, when communities establish governments for the purpose of maintaining justice and right, the assent of all the thieves, robbers, pirates, and slaveholders, is as much presumed, as is the assent of the most honest portion of community.   Governments for the maintenance of justice and liberty could not be established by the consent of the whole people on any other ground.

It would be a delectable doctrine, indeed, for courts to act upon, in construing a constitution, to presume that it was intended to subserve the criminal purposes of a few of the greatest villains in community; and then to force all its honest words to yield to that presumption, on the ground that otherwise these villains could not be presumed to have agreed to it. Yet this is the doctrine practised upon by all who uphold the constitutionality of slavery. They know that the whole people, honest and dishonest, slaveholders and non-slaveholders alike, must be presumed to have agreed either to an honest or a dishonest constitution; and they think it more reasonable to presume that all the honest people agreed to turn knaves, than that all the knaves agreed to become honest. This presumption is the polar star of all their reasonings in favor of the constitutionality of slavery. If this presumption be a true guide in the interpretation of all other constitutions, laws, and contracts, it is, of course, a correct one for interpreting the constitution of the United States; otherwise not.

The doctrine, that an instrument, capable of an honest meaning, is to be construed into a dishonest one, merely because one in forty of the parties to it has been a dishonest man up to the time of making the agreement, (and probably not more than one in forty of "the people of the United States" were slaveholders,) would not only put it nearly or quite out of the power of dishonest men to make contracts with each other that would be held honest in the sight of the law, but it would even put it nearly or quite out of the power of honest men to make contracts with dishonest ones, that would be held honest in the sight of the law. All their contracts, susceptible of a dishonest meaning, would have to be so construed; and what contract is ever entered into by honest with dishonest men, that is not susceptible of such a construction, especially if we may go out of the contract, and inquire into the habits, character, and business of each of the parties, in order to find that one of them is a man who may be suspected of a dishonest motive, and this suspected motive of the one may then be attributed to the others as their true motive.

Such a principle of law would virtually cut off dishonest men from all right to make even honest contracts with their fellowmen, and would be a far greater calamity to themselves than the doctrine that holds all their contracts to be honest, that are susceptible of an honest construction; because it is indispensable to a dishonest man's success and well-being in life that a large portion of his contracts should be held honest and valid.

Under a principle of law, that presumes everybody *dishonest*, and construes their constitutions, laws, and contracts accordingly, pandemonium would be established at once, in which dishonest men would stand no better chance than others ; and would therefore have no more motive than others for sustaining the government.

In short, it is obvious that government would not, and could not, be upheld for an instant, by *any* portion of society, honest or dishonest, if such a presumption were to be adopted by the courts as a general rule for construing either constitutions, laws, or private contracts. Yet, let it be repeated, and never forgotten, that this presumption is indispensable to such a construction of the constitution as makes slavery constitutional. It is the *sine qua non* to the whole fabric of the slaveholding argument.

There is, then, no *legal* ground whatever for not presuming the consent of slaves, slaveholders, and non-slaveholders to the constitution of the United States, on the supposition that it prohibits slavery. Consequently, there is no legal ground for denying that the terms " the people of the United States," included the *whole* of the then people of the United States. And if the whole of the people are parties to it, it must, if possible, be so construed as to make it such a contract as each and every individual might reasonably agree to. In short, it must, if possible, be so construed as not to make any of the parties consent to their own enslavement. Such a construction is possible, and being possible, is necessarily the true construction.

The constitution of the United States, therefore, would have abolished slavery, by making the slaves parties to it, even though the state constitutions had previously supported it.*

---

* Story says, " Who, then, are the parties to this contract ?   *   *   * Let the instrument answer for itself. The people of the United States are the parties to the constitution."—1 *Story's Comm. on Const., p.* 355.

The supreme court of the United States says, " The government (of the U. S.) proceeds directly from the people ; is 'ordained and established' in the name of the people."—4 *Wheaton*, 403.

" The government of the Union is, emphatically and truly, a government of the people ; and in form and in substance it emanates from them. Its powers are granted by them, and are to be exercised directly on them, and for their benefit."—4 *Wheaton*, 404, 405.

" The constitution of the United States was ordained and established, *not* by the United States in their sovereign capacities, but emphatically, as the preamble of the constitution declares, by the *people* of the United States."—1 *Wheaton*, 324.

Story, commenting upon the words " We the people of the United States," says, ' We have the strongest assurances that this preamble was not adopted as a mere

SEVENTH RULE.

The seventh rule of interpretation is the one that has been repeatedly cited from the supreme court of the United States, to wit:

" Where rights are infringed, where fundamental principles are overthrown, where the general system of the laws is departed from, the legislative intention must be expressed with irresistible clearness, to induce a court of justice to suppose a design to effect such objects."

---

formulary; but as a solemn promulgation of a fundamental fact, vital to the character and operations of the government. The obvious object was to substitute a government of the people for a confederacy of states." — 1 *Comm., p.* 416.

Also, " The convention determined that the fabric of American empire ought to rest, and should rest, on the solid basis of the consent of the people. The streams of national power ought to flow, and should flow, immediately from the highest original fountain of all legitimate authority. * * * And the uniform doctrine of the highest judicial authority has accordingly been, that it was the act of the people, and not the act of the states; and that it bound the latter as subordinate to the people." — 1 *Story's Comm., p.* 447.

Kent says, " The government of the United States was erected by the free voice and the joint will of the people of America, for their common defence and general welfare." — 1 *Kent*, 189.

Chief Justice Jay said, " Every state constitution is a compact, made by and between the citizens of the state to govern themselves in a certain manner; and the constitution of the United States is likewise a compact, made by the people of the United States to govern themselves, as to general objects, in a certain manner." — 2 *Dallas*, 419; *cited by Story*, 1 *Comm., p.* 317.

Mr. Webster says, " It is the people's constitution, the people's government; made for the people; made by the people; and answerable to the people. The people of the United States have declared that this constitution shall be the supreme law. We must either admit the proposition, or dispute their authority. * * * We are all agents of the same supreme power, the people. The general government and the state governments derive their authority from the same source." — *Webster's Speeches, vol.* 1, *p.* 410.

Also, " I hold it to be a popular government, erected by the people; those who administer it, responsible to the people; and itself capable of being amended and modified, just as the people choose it should be. It is as popular, just as truly emanating from the people, as the state governments. It is created for one purpose; the state governments for another. It has its own powers; they have theirs." — *Same, p.* 419.

Also, " This government is the independent offspring of the popular will." — *Same*, 419.

If the constitution were not established by " the people," there is no information given in the constitution, as to whom it was established by. We must, of necessity, therefore, accept its own declaration, that it was established by the people. And if we accept its declaration that it was established by " the people," we must also accept its virtual declaration that it was established by the whole people, for it gives no information of its being established by one portion of the people, any more than by another. No separation can therefore be made between different portions of the people.

The pith of this rule is, that any *unjust* intention must be "*expressed with irresistible clearness*," to induce a court to give a law an unjust meaning.

The word "*expressed*" is a very important one, in this rule. It is necessary, therefore, for the benefit of the unprofessional reader, to define it.

In law, a thing is said to be " expressed," only when it is *uttered, or written out, embodied in distinct words*, in contradistinction to its being inferred, *implied*, or gathered from evidence exterior to the words of the law.

The amount of the rule, then, is, that the court will never, *through inference, nor implication*, attribute an unjust intention to a law ; *nor seek for such an intention in any evidence exterior to the words of the law.* They will attribute such an intention to the law, only when such intention is *written out in actual terms ;* and in terms, too, of " irresistible clearness."

The rule, it will be observed, does not forbid a resort to inference, implication, or exterior evidence, to help out the supposed meaning of, or to solve any ambiguities in, *a law that is consistent with justice.* It only forbids a resort to such means to help out the supposed meaning of, or to solve any ambiguities in, *an unjust law.* It virtually says that if an ambiguous law can possibly be interpreted favorably to justice, it shall be thus interpreted. But if it cannot be thus interpreted, it shall be suffered to remain inoperative — void for its ambiguity — rather than the court will help out its supposed meaning by inference, implication, or exterior evidence.

Is this rule a sound one ? It is ; and for the following reasons :

Certainty is one of the vital principles of law. Properly speaking, nothing is law that is uncertain. A written law is only what is written. It is not certain, any further than it is written. If, then, we go out of the written law, we necessarily go into the region of uncertainty. It must, also, generally be presumed, that the legislature intend nothing more than they have chosen to communicate. It is therefore straining matters, and going beyond *strict* legal principles, to go out of the words of a law, to find its meaning, *in any case whatever, whether for a good purpose, or a bad one.*

It will be asked, then, " Why resort to inference, implication, and exterior evidence, to solve the ambiguities in a *just* law ?" The answer is this : Such is the variety of senses in which language is used by different persons, and such the want of skill in many of those who use it, that laws are very frequently left in some ambiguity. Men, nevertheless, act upon them, assuming to understand them. Their rights thus become involved in the efficacy of the law, and will be sacrificed unless the law be carried into effect. *To save these rights, and for no other purpose,* the courts will venture to seek the meaning of the law in exterior evidence, when the intent of the law is good, and the apparent ambiguity not great. *Strictly speaking, however, even this proceeding is illegal.* Nothing but the necessity of saving men's rights, affords any justification for it. But where a law is ambiguous and *unjust,* there is no such necessity for going out of its words to settle its probable meaning, because men's rights will not be saved, but only sacrificed, by having its uncertainty settled, and the law executed. It is, therefore, *better* that the law should perish, be suffered to remain inoperative for its uncertainty, than that its uncertainty should be removed, (or, rather, attempted to be removed, for it cannot be removed absolutely, by exterior evidence,) and the law carried into effect for the destruction of men's rights.

Assuming, then, the rule of the court to be sound, are the rules laid down in the " Unconstitutionality of Slavery,"* that have since been somewhat questioned,† embraced in it? Those rules are as follows :

1. " One of them is, that where words are susceptible of two meanings, one consistent, and the other inconsistent, with justice and natural right, that meaning, *and only that meaning,* which is consistent with right, shall be attributed to *them,* unless other parts of the instrument overrule that interpretation."

This rule is clearly embraced in the rule of the court; for the rule of the court requires *the unjust* meaning to be " expressed with irresistible clearness," before it can be adopted ; and an unjust meaning certainly cannot be said to be " expressed with irresistible clearness," when it is expressed only by words, which, consistently with the laws of language, and the rest of the instrument, are susceptible of an entirely different—that is, a perfectly innocent—meaning.

2. " Another rule, (if, indeed, it be not the same,) is, that no language except that which is peremptory, and no implication,

---

* Page 62, Second Edition.   † By Wendell Phillips.

except one that is inevitable, shall be held to authorize or sanction anything contrary to natural right."

This rule is also clearly embraced in the rule of the court; for the rule of the court requires that the unjust intention be "*expressed*," that is, *uttered, written out in terms*, as distinguished from being *inferred*, or *implied*. The requirement, also, that it be "*expressed with irresistible clearness*," is equivalent to the requirement that the language be "peremptory."

3. "Another rule is, that *no extraneous or historical evidence* shall be admitted to fix upon a statute an unjust or immoral meaning, when the words themselves of the act are susceptible of an innocent one."

This rule is also clearly embraced in the rule of the court; for the rule of the court requires, not only that the unjust intention be "*expressed*," written out, embodied in words, as distinct from being inferred, implied, *or sought in exterior historical evidence*, but also that it be embodied in words of "irresistible clearness." Now, words that *express* their intention with "*irresistible clearness*," can of course leave no necessity for going out of the words, to "*extraneous or historical evidence*," to find their intention.

But it is said that these rules are in conflict with the general rule, that where a law is ambiguous, the probable intent of the legislature may be ascertained by extraneous testimony.

It is not an *universal* rule, as has already been shown, that even where a law, *as a whole*, is ambiguous, the intentions of the legislature may be sought in exterior evidence. It is only where a *just* law is ambiguous, that we may go out of its words to find its probable intent. We may never do it to find the probable intent of an *unjust* one that is ambiguous; for it is better that an unjust law should perish for uncertainty, than that its uncertainty should be solved by exterior evidence, and the law then be executed for the destruction of men's rights.

Where only single words or phrases in a law are ambiguous, as is the case with the constitution of the United States, the rule is somewhat different from what it is where the law, *as a whole*, is ambiguous. In the case of single words and phrases that are ambiguous, all the rules applicable to ambiguous words and phrases must be exhausted in vain, before resort can be had to evidence exterior to the law, or the words and phrases be set down as sanctioning injustice. For example; to settle the meaning of an ambiguous word or phrase, we must, before going out of the instrument, refer to all the other parts of the instrument itself, to its preamble, its general spirit and object, its subject matter, and, in the case of the constitution, to "the general system of the laws" authorized and established by it. And the ambiguous word or phrase must be construed in conformity with these, if possible, especially when these are favorable to justice. And it is only when all these sources of light have failed to suggest a just, reasonable, and consistent meaning, that we can go out of the instrument to find the probable meaning.

If, when a single word or phrase were ambiguous, we could *at once* go out of the instrument, (*before going* to other parts of it,) to find the probable intent of that single word or phrase, and could determine its intent, independently of its relation to the rest of the instrument, we should be liable to give it a meaning irrelevant to the rest of the instrument, and thus involve the whole instrument in absurdity, contradiction, and incongruity.

There are only four or five single words and phrases in the constitution, that are claimed to be ambiguous in regard to slavery. All the other parts of the instrument, its preamble, its prevailing spirit and principles, its subject matter, "the general system of the laws" authorized by it, all repel the idea of its sanctioning slavery. If, then, the ambiguous words and phrases be construed with reference to the rest of the instrument, there is no occasion to go out of the instrument to find their meaning.

But, in point of fact, the words of a law *never are ambiguous, legally speaking*, where the alternative is only between a meaning that is consistent, and one that is inconsistent, with natural right; for the rule that requires the right to be preferred to the wrong, is imperative and universal in all such cases; *thus making the legal meaning of the word precisely as certain, as though it could, in no case, have any other meaning. It thus prevents the ambiguity, which, but for the rule, might have existed.*

This rule, that a just, in preference to an unjust, meaning must be given to a word, wherever it is possible, consistently with the rest of the instrument, obviously *takes precedence* of the rule that permits a resort to exterior evidence; and for the following reasons: —

1. Otherwise, the rule in favor of the just meaning could seldom or never be applied at all, because when we have gone out of the *words* of the law, we have gone away from those things to which the rule applies. The exterior evidence which we should

find, would not necessarily furnish any opportunity for the application of the rule. This rule, therefore, of preferring the just to
the unjust meaning of a word, could hardly have had an existence,
except upon the supposition that it was to be applied to the words
given in the law itself. And if applied to the words given in the
law itself, it of course settles the meaning, and there is then no
longer any occasion to go out of the law to find its meaning.

2. Nothing would be *gained* by going out of a law to find
evidence of the meaning of one of its words, when a *good* meaning
could be found in the law itself. Nothing better than a *good*
meaning could be expected to be found by going out of the law.
As nothing could be *gained*, then, by going out of the law, the
only object of going out of it would be to find an *unjust* meaning;
but that, surely, is no sufficient reason for going out of it. To go
out of a law to find an *unjust* meaning for its words, when a *just*
meaning could be found in the law itself, would be acting on the
principle of subverting all justice, if possible.

3. It would hardly be possible to have written laws, unless the
legal meaning of a word were considered certain, instead of ambiguous, in such cases as this ; because there is hardly any word
used in writing laws, which has not more than one meaning, and
which might not therefore be held ambiguous, if we were ever to
lose sight of the fact, or abandon the presumption, that justice is
the design of the law. To depart from this principle would be
introducing universal ambiguity, and opening the door to universal
injustice.

4. Certainty and right are the two most vital principles of the
law. Yet certainty is *always* sacrificed by going out of the words
of the law ; and right is always *liable* to be sacrificed, if we go
out of the words, with liberty to choose a bad meaning, when a
good meaning can be found in the words themselves ; while both
certainty and right are secured by adhering uniformly to the rule
of preferring the just to the unjust meaning of a word, wherever
the two come in collision. Need anything more be said to prove
the soundness of the rule ?

The words of a law, then, are never *ambiguous, legally speaking*, when the only alternative is between a just and an unjust
meaning. They are ambiguous only when both meanings are
consistent with right, or both inconsistent with it.

In the first of these two cases, viz., where both meanings are
consistent with right, it is allowable, for the sake of saving the

rights dependent on the efficacy of the law, to go to extraneous history to settle the probable intention of the legislature. But in the latter case, viz., where both meanings are *inconsistent* with right, it is *not* allowable to go out of the words of the law itself, to ascertain the legislative intention. The law must rather be suffered to remain inoperative for its uncertainty.

The rule, quoted from the supreme court, comes fully up to these principles; for that rule requires, in order that an unjust law may be carried into effect, that the unjust intent be " expressed," as distinguished from being inferred, implied, or sought in exterior evidence. It must also be " expressed with irresistible clearness." If it be left in an uncertainty, the law will be construed in favor of the right, if possible ; if not, it will be suffered to perish for its ambiguity.

Apply, then, this rule of the court, in all its parts, to the word " free," and the matter will stand thus.

1. A sense correlative with aliens, makes the constitution consistent with natural right. A sense correlative with slaves, makes the constitution inconsistent with natural right. The choice must therefore be made of the former sense.

2. A sense correlative with aliens, is consistent with " the general system of the laws " established by the constitution. A sense correlative with slavery, is inconsistent with that system. The former sense then must be adopted.

3. If a sense correlative with aliens be adopted, the constitution itself designates the individuals to whom the word " free," and the words " all other persons " apply. If a sense correlative with slaves be adopted, the constitution itself has not designated the individuals to whom either of these descriptions apply, and we should have to go out of the constitution and laws of the United States to find them. This settles the choice in favor of the former sense.

4. *Even if it were admitted that the word " free" was used as the correlative of slaves, still, inasmuch as the constitution itself has not designated the individuals who may, and who may not, be held as slaves, and as we cannot go out of the instrument to settle any ambiguity in favor of injustice, the provision must remain inoperative for its uncertainty ; and all persons must be presumed free, simply because the constitution itself has not told us who may be slaves.*

Apply the rule further to the words " importation of persons," and "service and labor," and those words wholly fail to recognize slavery.

Apply the rule only to the word "free," and slavery is unconstitutional; for the words "importation of persons," and "service and labor," can have no claims to be considered recognitions or sanctions of slavery, unless such a signification be *first* given to the word "free."

An eighth rule of interpretation is, that where the prevailing principles and provisions of a law are favorable to justice, and general in their nature and terms, no *unnecessary exception* to them, or to their operation, is to be allowed.

It is a dictate of law, as of common sense — or rather of law, because of common sense — that an exception to a rule cannot be established, unless it be stated with at least as much distinctness and certainty as the rule itself, to which it is an exception ; because otherwise the authority of the rule will be more clear and certain, and consequently more imperative, than that of the exception, and will therefore outweigh and overbear it. This principle may justly be considered a strictly mathematical one. It is founded simply on the necessary preponderance of a greater quantity over a less. On this principle, an exception to a general *law* cannot be established, unless it be expressed with at least as much distinctness as the law itself.

In conformity with this principle, it is the ordinary practice, in the enactment of laws, to state the exceptions with the greatest distinctness. They are usually stated in a separate sentence from the rest of the law, and in the form of a *proviso*, or *exception*, commencing with the words "*Provided, nevertheless*," "*Excepting, however*," or words of that kind. And the language of the proviso is generally even more emphatic than that of the law, as it, in reality, ought to be, to preponderate against it.

This practice of stating exceptions has been further justified, and apparently induced, by that knowledge of human nature which forbids us to understand a man as contradicting, in one sentence what he has said in another, unless his language be incapable of any other meaning. For the same reason, a law, (which is but the expression of men's intentions,) should not be held to contradict, in one sentence, what it has said in another, except the terms be perfectly clear and positive.

The practice of stating exceptions in this formal and emphatic manner, shows also that legislators have usually, perhaps unconsciously, recognized, and virtually admitted, the soundness of the rule of interpretation, that requires an exception to be stated with at least as much clearness as the law to which it is an exception.

This practice of stating exceptions in a clear and formal manner, is common even where no violation of justice is involved in the exception ; and where an exception therefore involves less violation of reason and probability.

This rule of interpretation, in regard to exceptions, corresponds with what is common and habitual, if not universal, in common life, and in ordinary conversation. If, for instance, a man make an exception to a general remark, he is naturally careful to express the exception with peculiar distinctness ; thus tacitly recognizing the right of the other party not to notice the exception, and the probability that he *will not* notice it, unless it be stated with perfect distinctness.

Finally. Although an exception is not, in law, a contradiction, it nevertheless partakes so strongly of the nature of a contradiction — especially where there is no legitimate or rightful reason for it — that it is plainly absurd to admit such an exception, except upon substantially the same terms that we admit a contradiction, viz., irresistible clearness of expression.

The question now is, whether there is, in the constitution, any compliance with these principles, in making exceptions in favor of slavery ? Manifestly there is none. There is not even an approach to such a compliance. There are no words of exception ; no words of proviso ; no words necessarily implying the existence or sanction of anything in conflict with the general principles of the instrument.

Yet the argument for slavery, (I mean that founded on the representative clause,) makes *two* exceptions — not *one* merely, but *two* — and both of the most flagitious and odious character — without the constitution's having used any words of proviso or exception ; without its having devoted any separate sentence to the exception ; and without its having used any words which, even if used in a separate sentence, and also preceded by a " *Provided, nevertheless*," would have necessarily implied any *such* exceptions as are claimed. The exceptions are claimed as having been established merely *incidentally* and casually, in describing the *manner of counting the people* for purposes of representation and taxation; when, what is worse, the words used, if not the *most* common and proper that could have been used, are certainly both common and proper for describing the people, where no exception to " the general system of the laws" established by the constitution is intended.

It is by this process, and this alone, that the argument for slavery makes *two* exceptions to the constitution ; and both, as has already been said, of the most flagitious and odious character.

One of these exceptions is an exception of *principle*, substituting injustice and slavery, for " justice and liberty."

The other is an exception of *persons ;* excepting a part of " the people of the United States " from the rights and benefits, which the instrument professes to secure to the whole ; and exposing them to wrongs, from which the people generally are exempt.

An exception of *principle* would be less odious, if the injustice were of a kind that bore equally on all, or applied equally to all. But these two exceptions involve not only injustice in principle, but partiality in its operation. This double exception is doubly odious, and doubly inadmissible.

Another insuperable objection to the allowance of these exceptions, is, that they are *indefinite* — especially the latter one. The persons who may be made slaves are not designated. The persons allowed to be made slaves being left in uncertainty, the exception must fail for uncertainty, if for no other reason. We cannot, for the reasons given under the preceding rule, *go out of the instrument* to find the persons, because it is better that the exception should fail for its uncertainty, than that resort should be had to exterior evidence for the purpose of subjecting men to slavery.

NINTH RULE.

A ninth rule of interpretation is, to be guided, in doubtful cases, by the preamble.

The authority of the preamble, as a guide to the meaning of an instrument, where the language is ambiguous, is established. In fact, the whole object of the preamble is to indicate the objects had in view in the enacting clauses ; and of necessity those objects will indicate the construction to be given to the words used in those clauses. Any other supposition would either make the preamble worthless, or, worse than that, deceitful.

If we are guided by the preamble in fixing the meaning of those clauses that have been claimed for slavery, it is plain that no sanction or recognition of slavery will be found in them; for the preamble declares the objects of the constitution to be, among other things, "justice" and "liberty." *

TENTH RULE.

A tenth rule of interpretation is, that one part of an instrument must not be allowed to contradict another, unless the language be so explicit as to make the contradiction inevitable.

---

* Story says, "The importance of examining the preamble, for the purpose of expounding the language of a statute, has been long felt, and universally conceded in all juridical discussions. It is an admitted maxim in the ordinary course of the administration of justice, that the preamble of a statute is a key to open the mind of the makers, as to the mischiefs which are to be remedied, and the objects which are to be accomplished by the provisions of the statute. We find it laid down in some of our earliest authorities in the common law, and civilians are accustomed to a similar expression, *cessante legis præmio, cessal el ipsa lex.* (The preamble of the law ceasing, the law itself also ceases.) Probably it has a foundation in the exposition of every code of written law, from the universal principle of interpretation, that the will and intention of the legislature is to be regarded and followed. It is properly resorted to where doubts or ambiguities arise upon the words of the enacting part; for if they are clear and unambiguous, there seems little room for interpretation, except in cases leading to an absurdity, or to a direct overthrow of the intention expressed in the preamble.

"There does not seem any reason why, in a fundamental law or constitution of government, an equal attention should not be given to the intention of the framers, as expressed in the preamble. And accordingly we find that it has been constantly referred to by statesmen and jurists to aid them in the exposition of its provisions." — 1 *Story's Comm. on Const.*, p. 443-4.

Story also says, "Its true office is to expound the nature, and extent, and application of the powers actually conferred by the constitution, and not substantively to create them." — *Same*, 445.

"Though the preamble cannot control the enacting part of a statute which is expressed in clear and unambiguous terms, yet, if any doubt arise on the words of the enacting part, the preamble may be resorted to, to explain it." — 7 *Bacon's Abr.*, 435, *note.* 4 *Term Rep.*, 793. 13 *Vesey*, 36. 15 *Johnson, N. Y. Rep.*, 116.

"A statute made *pro bono publico* (for the public good) shall be construed in such manner that it may as far as possible attain the end proposed." — 7 *Bacon's Abr.*, 461.

The constitution of the United States avows itself to be established for the public good — that is, for the good of "the people of the United States" — to establish justice and secure the blessings of liberty to themselves and their posterity. It must of course "be construed in such manner that it may, as far as possible, attain that end."

Story says, "Was it not framed for the good of the people, and by the people?" — 1 *Story's Comm.*, 394.

Chief Justice Jay dwells at length upon the authority of the preamble, as a guide for the interpretation of the constitution. — 2 *Dallas*, 419. Also Justice Story, in his Commentaries on the Constitution, *vol.* 1, *book* 3, *ch.* 6.

Now the constitution would be full of contradictions, if it toler‑
ated slavery, unless it be shown that the constitution itself has
established an *exception* to all its general provisions, limiting their
operation and benefits to persons *not* slaves. Such an exception
or limitation would *not, legally speaking*, be a contradiction. But
I take it for granted that it has already been shown that no such
exception can be made out from its words. If no such exception
be made out from its words, such a construction must. if possible,
be given to each clause of the instrument, as will not amount to a
contradiction of any other clause. There is no difficulty in mak‑
ing such a construction; but when made it will exclude slavery.

ELEVENTH RULE.

An eleventh rule is one laid down by the supreme court of the
United States, as follows:

"An act of congress" (and the rule is equally applicable to the
constitution) "ought never to be construed to violate the law of
nations, if any other *possible* construction remains."*

This rule is specially applicable to the clause relative to "the
importation of persons." If that clause were construed to sanction
the kidnapping of the people of foreign nations, and their importa‑
tion into this country as slaves, it would be a flagrant violation of
that law.

TWELFTH RULE.

A twelfth rule, universally applicable to questions both of *fact
and law*, and sufficient, *of itself alone*, to decide, *against slavery*,
every possible question that can be raised as to the meaning of the
constitution, is this, "*that all reasonable doubts must be decided in
favor of liberty.*" †

All the foregoing rules, it will be observed, are little other than
varied and partial expressions of the rule so accurately, tersely,
comprehensively, and forcibly expressed by the supreme court of
the United States, viz.:

---

* 2 *Cranch*, 64.

† The Supreme Court of Mississippi say, referring to the claim of freedom, set
up before it, "Is it not an unquestioned rule that, in matters of doubt, courts
must lean *in favorem vitæ et libertatis?*" (in favor of life and liberty.) — *Harvey
vs. Decker, Walker's Mississippi Reports*, 36.
I cite this authority from Mr. Chase's argument in the Van Zandt case.

"Where rights are infringed, where fundamental principles are overthrown, where the general system of the laws is departed from, the legislative intention must be expressed with *irresistible clearness*, to induce a court of justice to suppose a design to effect such objects."

THIRTEENTH RULE.

A thirteenth rule, and one of great importance, is, *that instruments must be so construed as to give no shelter or effect to fraud.*

This rule is especially applicable for deciding what meaning we are to give to the word *free* in the constitution; for if a sense correlative with slavery be given to that word, it will be clearly the result of fraud.

We have abundant evidence that this fraud was intended by some of the *framers* of the constitution. They knew that an instrument legalizing slavery could not gain the assent of the north. They therefore agreed upon an instrument honest in its terms, with the intent of misinterpreting it after it should be adopted.

The fraud of the framers, however, does not, of itself, implicate the people. But when any portion of the people adopt this fraud in practice, they become implicated in it, equally with its authors. And any one who claims that an ambiguous word shall bear a sense inappropriate to the subject matter of the instrument, contrary to the technical and common meaning of the word, inconsistent with any intentions that *all* the parties could reasonably be presumed to agree to, inconsistent with natural right, inconsistent with the preamble, and the declared purpose of the instrument, inconsistent with "the general system of the laws" established by the instrument; any one who claims such an interpretation, becomes a participator in the fraud. It is as much fraudulent, *in law*, for the people of the present day to claim such a construction of the word *free*, as it was for those who lived at the time the instrument was adopted.

Vattel has laid down two very correct principles to be observed as preventives of fraud. They are these:

1. That it is not permitted to interpret what has no need of interpretation.

2. That if a party have not spoken plainly, when he ought to have done so, that which he has *sufficiently* declared, shall be taken for true against him.

Vattel's remarks in support of, and in connection with, these principles, are so forcible and appropriate that they will be given

somewhat at length.   If he had had in his mind this very fraud
which the slaveholders and their accomplices intended to perpe-
trate by means of the word *free* in the constitution, he could
hardly have said anything better fitting the case.

He says, " That fraud seeks to take advantage even of the
imperfection of language ; that men designedly throw obscurity
and ambiguity into their treaties, to obtain a pretence for eluding
them upon occasion.   It is then necessary to establish rules
founded on reason, and authorized by the law of nature, capable
of frustrating the attempts of a contracting power void of good
faith.   Let us begin with those that tend particularly to this end;
with those maxims of justice and equity destined to repress fraud
and prevent the effect of its artifices.

" The first general maxim of interpretation is, *that it is not permitted to interpret what has no need of interpretation.**   When
an act is conceived in clear and precise terms, when the sense is
manifest and leads to nothing absurd, there can be no reason to
refuse the sense which this treaty naturally presents.   *To go elsewhere in search of conjectures in order to restrain or extinguish
it, is to endeavor to elude it.*   If this dangerous method be once
admitted, there will be no act which it will not render useless.
Let the brightest light shine on all the parts of the piece, let it be
expressed in terms the most clear and determinate ; all this shall
be of no use, if it be allowed to search for foreign reasons in order
to maintain what cannot be found in the sense it naturally presents.

" The cavillers who dispute the sense of a clear and determinate
article, are accustomed to draw their vain subterfuges from the
pretended intention and views of the author of that article.   It
would often be very dangerous to enter with them into the discussion of these supposed views, that are not pointed out in the piece
itself.   *This rule* is more proper to repel them, and which cuts off
all chicanery ; *if he who can and ought to have explained himself
clearly and plainly, has not done it, it is the worse for him ; he
cannot be allowed to introduce subsequent restrictions which he has*

---

* This rule is fairly applicable to the word *free.* The sense correlative with
aliens is a sense appropriate to the subject matter of the instrument ; it accurately
and properly describes a class of persons, which the constitution presumes would
exist under it ; it was, at the time, the received and *technical* sense of the word in
all instruments of a similar character, and therefore its *presumptive* sense in the
constitution ; it is consistent with intentions reasonably attributable to *all* the parties to the constitution ; it is consistent with natural right, with the preamble, the
declared purpose of the constitution, and with the general system of the laws
established by the constitution.   Its *legal* meaning, in the constitution, was therefore plain, manifest, palpable, and, at the time of its adoption, *had no need of interpretation.*   It needs interpretation *now*, only to expose the fraudulent interpretation
of the past ; and because, in pursuance of that fraudulent interpretation, usage has
now somewhat changed the received meaning of the word.

not expressed. This is the maxim of the Roman law; *Pactionem obscuram iis nocere, in quorum fuit potestate legem apertius conscribere.* (The harm of an obscure compact shall fall upon those in whose power it was to write the rule plainly.) The equity of this rule is extremely visible, and its necessity is not less evident. There can be no secure conventions, no firm and solid concession, if these may be rendered vain by subsequent limitations that ought to have been mentioned in the piece, if they were included in the intentions of the contracting powers."— *Vattel, b.* 2, *ch.* 17, *secs.* 262, 263, 264.

" *On every occasion when a person has, and ought to have shown his intention, we take for true against him what he has* SUFFICIENT-LY *declared.* This is an incontestible principle applied to treaties; for if they are not a vain play of words, the contracting parties ought to express themselves with truth, and according to their real intentions. If the intention *sufficiently declared,* was not taken for the true intention of him who speaks and binds himself, it would be of no use to contract and form treaties."— *Same, sec.* 266.

" Is it necessary, in an enlightened age, to say that mental reservations cannot be admitted in treaties? This is manifest, since by nature even of the treaty, the parties ought to declare the manner in which they would be reciprocally understood. There is scarcely a person at present, who would not be ashamed of building upon a mental reservation. What can be the use of such an artifice, if it was not to lull to sleep some other person under the vain appearance of a contract? It is, then, a real piece of knavery." — *Same, sec.* 275.

" There is not perhaps any language that has not also words which signify two or many different things, or phrases susceptible of more than one sense. Thence arise mistakes in discourse. *The contracting powers ought carefully to avoid them.* To employ them with design, in order to elude engagements, is a real perfidy, since the faith of treaties obliges the contracting parties to express their intentions clearly. But if the equivocal term has found admission into a public treaty, the interpretation is to make the uncertainty produced by it disappear.

" This is the rule that ought to direct the interpretation in this case. *We ought always to give to expressions the sense most suitable to the subject, or to the matter to which they relate.* For we endeavor by a true interpretation, to discover the thoughts of those who speak, or of the contracting powers in a treaty. Now it ought to be presumed that he who has employed a word capable of many different significations, has taken it in that which agrees with the subject. In proportion as he employs himself on the matter in question, the terms proper to express his thoughts present themselves to his mind; this equivocal word could then only offer itself in the sense proper to express the thought of him who makes use of it, that is, in the sense agreeable to the subject. *It would be to no purpose to object, that we sometimes have recourse to equivocal expressions, with a view of exhibiting something very different from what one has truly in the mind, and that then the sense which agrees with the subject is not that which answers to the intention of the man who speaks. We have already observed, that whenever a man can and ought to have made known his intention, we may take for true against him what he has sufficiently declared. And as good faith ought to preside in conventions, they are always interpreted on the supposition that it actually did preside in them."* — *Same, sec.,* 279, 80.

"*The reason of the law, or the treaty,* that is, the motive which led to the making of it, and the view there proposed, is one of the most certain means of establishing the true sense, and great attention ought to be paid to it whenever it is required to explain an obscure, equivocal and undetermined point, either of a law, or of a treaty, or to make an application of them to a particular case. *As soon as we certainly know the reason which alone has determined the will of him who speaks, we ought to interpret his words, and to apply them in a manner suitable to that reason alone.* Otherwise he will be made to speak and act contrary to his intention, and in a manner opposite to his views.

But we ought to be very certain that we know the true and only reason of the law, the promise, or the treaty. It is not here permitted to deliver ourselves up to vague and uncertain conjectures, and to suppose reason and views where there are none certainly known. If the piece in question is obscure in itself; if in order to know the sense, there are no other means left but to search for the reason of the act, and the views of the author; we must then have recourse to conjecture, and in the want of certainty, receive for true, what is most probable. But it is a dangerous abuse to go, without necessity, in search of reasons and uncertain views, in order to turn, restrain, or destroy, the sense of a piece that is clear enough in itself, and that presents nothing absurd ; this is to offend against this incontestible maxim, that it is not permitted to interpret what has no need of interpretation. *Much less is it permitted, when the author of a piece has himself there made known his reasons and motives, to attribute to him some secret reason, as the foundation to interpret the piece contrary to the natural sense of the terms. Though he had really the view attributed to him, if he has concealed it, and made known others, the interpretation can only be founded upon these, and not upon the views which the author has not expressed ; we take for true against him what he has sufficiently expressed.*" — *Same, sec.* 287.

FOURTEENTH RULE.

In addition to the foregoing particular rules of interpretation, this general and sweeping one may be given, to wit, *that we are never unnecessarily to impute to an instrument any intention whatever which it would be unnatural for either reasonable or honest men to entertain.* Such intention can be admitted only when the language will admit of no other construction.

Law is "a rule of conduct." The very idea of law, therefore, necessarily implies the ideas of reason and right. Consequently, every instrument, and every man, or body of men, that profess to establish a law, impliedly assert that the law they would establish is reasonable and right. The law, therefore, must, if possible, be construed consistently with that implied assertion.

RULES CITED FOR SLAVERY.

The rules already given (unless perhaps the fourth) *take precedence* of all the rules that can be offered on the side of slavery; and, taking that precedence, they decide the question without reference to any others.

It may, however, be but justice to the advocates of slavery, to state the rules relied on by them. The most important are the following :

FIRST RULE CITED FOR SLAVERY.

One rule is, that the most common and obvious sense of a word is to be preferred.

This rule, so far as it will apply to the word *free* in the constitution, is little or nothing more than a repetition of the rule before given, (under rule fourth,) in favor of the technical meaning of words. It avails nothing for slavery; and for the following reasons :

1. In determining, in a particular case, what *is* "the most common and obvious meaning" of a word, reference must be had not alone to the sense in which the word is most frequently used in the community, without regard to the context, or the subject to which it is applied ; but only to its most common meaning, when used in a similar connection, for similar purposes, and with reference to the same or similar subjects. For example. In a law relative to vessels navigating Massachusetts Bay, or Chesapeake Bay, we must not understand the word bay in the same sense as when we speak of a bay horse, a bay tree, or of a man standing at bay. Nor in a law regulating the rate of discount, or the days of grace, on checks, notes, drafts and orders, must we understand

18

the word *check* in the same sense as when we speak of a man's being checked in his career; nor the word *note* in the same sense as when we speak of notes in music, or of a man of note; nor the word *draft* in the same sense as when we speak of a ship's draft of water, or of a sketch, plan, or drawing on paper; nor the word *order* in the same sense as when we speak of a military order, or orders in architecture, or of different orders of men, as the order of dukes, the order of knights, the order of monks, the order of nuns, &c., &c.

All can see that the meanings of the same words are so different when applied to different subjects, and used in different connections, that written laws would be nothing but jargon, and this rule utterly ridiculous, unless, in determining the most common and obvious meaning of a word, in any particular case, reference be had to its most common use in similar connections, and when applied to similar subjects, and with similar objects in view.

To ascertain, then, the most "common and obvious meaning" of the word "*free*," *in such a connection as that in which it stands in the constitution*, we must *first* give it a meaning that appropriately describes a class, which the constitution certainly presumes will exist under the constitution. *Secondly*, a meaning which the *whole* "people of the United States," (slaves and all,) who are parties to the constitution, may reasonably be presumed to have voluntarily agreed that it should have. *Thirdly*, we must give it a meaning that will make the clause in which it stands consistent with the intentions which "the people," in the preamble, declare they have in view in ordaining the constitution, viz., "to establish justice," and "secure the blessings of liberty to themselves, (the whole people of the United States,) and their posterity." *Fourthly*, we must give it a meaning harmonizing with, instead of contradicting, or creating an exception to, all the general principles and provisions of the instrument. *Fifthly*, such a meaning must be given to it as will make the words, "all other persons," describe persons who are proper subjects of "representation" and of taxation *as persons*. No one can deny that, at the time the constitution was adopted, the most "common and obvious meaning" of the word "free," *when used by the whole people of a state or nation, in political instruments of a similar character to the constitution, and in connection with such designs, principles, and provisions as are expressed and contained in the constitution*, was such as has been claimed for it in this argument, viz., a meaning describing citizens,

or persons possessed of some political franchise, as distinguished
from aliens, or persons not possessed of the same franchise.   Nobody can deny this.   On the contrary, everybody who argues that
it describes free persons, as distinguished from slaves, admits, and
is obliged to admit, that this meaning is either in conflict with, or
an exception to, the professed intent, and all the general principles
and provisions of the instrument.

If the constitution had purported to have been instituted by a
part of the people, instead of the whole ; and for purposes of injustice and slavery, instead of "justice and liberty ;" and if "the
general system of the laws" authorized by the constitution, had
corresponded with that intention, there would then have been very
good reason for saying that " the most common and obvious meaning" of the word " free," *in such a connection*, was to describe free
persons as distinguished from slaves.   But as the constitution is,
in its terms, its professed intent, and its general principles and
provisions, directly the opposite of all this ; and as the word "free"
has a " common and obvious meaning," that accords with these terms,
intent, principles, and provisions, its *most* " common and obvious
meaning," *in such a connection*, is just as clearly opposite to what
it would have been in the other connection, as its most common
and obvious meaning, in the other connection, would be opposite
to the meaning claimed for it in this.   This position must either
be admitted, or else it must be denied that the connection in which
a word stands has anything to do with fixing its most " common
and obvious meaning." *

---

* " Story says, " Are we at liberty, upon any principles of reason or common
sense, to adopt a restrictive meaning which will defeat an avowed object of the
constitution, when another equally natural, and more appropriate to the subject, is
before us ? " — 1 *Story's Comm.*, p. 445.

Dane says, " With regard to the different parts of a statute, there is one general
rule of construction ; that is, the construction of each and every part must be made
on a full view of the whole statute ; and every part must have force and effect, if
possible ; *for the meaning of every part is found in its connection with other
parts.*" — 6 *Dane*, 593.

Vattel says, " Expressions have a force, and sometimes even an entirely different
signification, according to the occasion, their connection, and their relation to other
words.   The connection and train of the discourse is also another source of interpretation.   We ought to consider the whole discourse together, in order perfectly
to conceive the sense of it, and to give to each expression, not so much the signification it may receive in itself, as that it ought to have from the thread and spirit
of the discourse.   This is the maxim of the Roman law, *Incivile est, nisi tota lege
perspecta, una aliqua particula ejus proposita, judicare, vel respondere.*" (It is
improper to judge of, or answer to, any one particular proposed in a law, unless the
whole law be thoroughly examined.) — *B.* 2, ch. 17, sec. 285.

Also, " The connection and relation of things themselves, serve also to discover

Again.   It has already been shown that the most common, and
the nearly or quite universal meaning, given to the word *free*,
both in this country and in England, when used in laws of a fundamental character, like the constitution, or, indeed, in any other
laws, (for the purpose of designating one person, as distinguished
from another living under the same laws,) was not to designate a
free person, as distinguished from a slave, but to distinguish a
citizen, or person possessed of some franchise, as distinguished
from aliens, or persons not possessed of the same franchise.   The
authority of this rule, then, so far as it regards the most " common " meaning of this word *in the law*, is entirely in favor of the
argument for freedom, instead of the argument for slavery.

2. But the rule fails to aid slavery for another reason.   As has
before been remarked, the word " free " is seldom or never used,
even in common parlance, as the correlative of slaves, unless
when applied to *colored* persons.   A colored person, not a slave,
is called a "*free* colored person."   But the white people of the
south are never, in common parlance, designated as "*free* persons," but as *white* persons.   A slaveholder would deem it an
insult to be designated as a "*free* person," that is, using the word
free in a sense correlative with slavery, because such a designation would naturally imply the *possibility* of his being a slave.   It
would naturally imply that he belonged to *a race* that was sometimes enslaved.   Such an implication being derogatory to his race,
would be derogatory to himself.   Hence, where two races live
together, the one as masters, the other as slaves, the superior race
never habitually designate themselves as the " free persons," but
by the appropriate name of their race, thus avoiding the implication that they *can* be made slaves.

Thus we find, that the use of the word " free " *was* " common,"

---

and establish the true sense of a treaty, or of any other piece.   The interpretation
ought to be made in such a manner that all the parts appear consonant to each
other, that what follows agree with what went before ; at least, if it do not *manifestly* appear, that, by the last clauses, something is changed that went before." —
Same, sec. 286.

The way the advocates of slavery proceed in interpreting the constitution, is this.
Instead of judging of the meaning of the word *free* by its connection with the rest
of the instrument, they first separate that word entirely from all the rest of the instrument ; then, contrary to all legal rules, give it the worst meaning it is under any
circumstances capable of ; then bring it back into the instrument ; make it the
ruling word of the instrument ; and finally cut down all the rest of the instrument
so as to make it conform to the meaning thus arbitrarily and illegally given to this
one word *free*.

in the law, to describe those who were citizens, but it was *not*
" common," either in the law, or in common parlance, for describing the white people of the south, as distinguished from their
slaves. The rule, then, that requires the most common and obvious meaning of the word to be preferred, wholly fails to give to
the word *free*, as used in the constitution, a meaning correlative
with slaves.

3. But in point of fact, the rule that requires us to prefer the
most " common and obvious meaning," is of a wholly subordinate
and unauthoritative character, when compared with the rules
before laid down, except so far as it is necessary to be observed in
order to preserve a reasonable connection and congruity of ideas,
and prevent the laws from degenerating into nonsense. Further
than this, it has no authority to give an unjust meaning to a word
that admits of a just one, or to give to a word a meaning inconsistent with the preamble, the general principles, or any other provisions, of an instrument. In short, all the rules previously laid
down, (unless, perhaps, the fourth, which is nearly or quite synonymous with this,) *take precedence* of this, and this is of no consequence, in comparison with them, (except as before mentioned,)
when they come in conflict. In this case, however, of the word
free, there is no conflict. And the same may be said of the
words, " held to service or labor," and " the importation of persons." Neither of these two latter forms of expression had probably ever been used in the country, either in law or in common
parlance, to designate slaves or slavery. Certainly there had
been no *common* use of them for that purpose ; and such, therefore, cannot be said to be either their common or their obvious
meaning. But even if such were their common and obvious
meaning, it would not avail against the rule in favor of liberty or
right, or any of the other rules before laid down.

That the other rules take precedence of this, is proved by the
fact, that otherwise those rules could never have had an existence.
If this rule took precedence of those, it would *invariably* settle the
question ; no other rule of interpretation would ever be required ;
because, it is not a supposable case, that there can ever be two
meanings, without one being more common or obvious than the
other. Consequently, there could never be any opportunity to
apply the other rules, and they, therefore, could never have had
an existence.

If this rule took precedence of the others, all legal interpreta-
18*

tion would be resolved into the simple matter of determining
which was the most common and obvious meaning of words in
particular connections.   All questions of written law would thus
be resolved into a single question of fact; and that question of
fact would have to be decided by a judge, instead of a jury.
And a very slight preponderance of evidence, as to the senses in
which words are *most* commonly understood, would often have to
determine the question.   The judge, too, would have to be presumed omniscient as to the most common and obvious meaning of
words, *as used by the people at large*, each one of whom is known
to often use words in different senses, and with different shades
of meaning, from all others.   And the slightest preponderance of
evidence on this point, that should appear *to the judge's mind
alone*, would be sufficient to overrule all those palpable principles
of liberty, justice, right, and reason, which the people at large,
(who cannot reasonably be presumed to be very critical or learned
plilologists,) have in view in establishing government and laws.
In short, courts, acting on such a principle, would in practice be
little or nothing more than philological, instead of legal, tribunals.

Government and laws being established by the people at large,
not as philologists, but as plain men, seeking only the preservation of their rights, the words they use must be made to square
with that end, *if possible*, instead of their rights being sacrificed to
nice philological criticisms, to which the people are strangers.
Not that, in interpreting written laws, the plain and universal
principles of philology are to be *violated*, for the sake of making
the laws conform to justice ; for that would be equivalent to abolishing all written laws, and abolishing the use of words as a means
of describing the laws.   But the principle is, that great latitude
must be allowed in matters of philology, in accommodation of the
various senses in which different men use and understand the
same word in the same circumstances ; while a severe and rigid
adherence is required to principles of natural right, which are far
more certain in their nature, and in regard to which all men are
presumed to be agreed, and which all are presumed to have in
view in the establishment of government and laws.   It is much
more reasonable to suppose — because the fact itself is much more
common — that men differ as to the meaning of words, than that
they differ as to the principles which they try to express by their
words.

No two men, in drawing up the same law, would do it in the same words, owing to their different tastes, capacities, and habits, in the use of language. And yet a law, when written, must, in theory, mean the same to all minds. This necessity of having the law mean the same to all minds, imposes upon courts the necessity of disregarding men's different tastes and habits in the matter of words, and of construing the words of all laws so as to make them conform as nearly as possible to some general principle, which all men are presumed to have in view, and in regard to which all are presumed to be agreed. And that general principle is justice.

The result, then, is, that justice and men's rights—the preservation of which is the great object of all the government and laws to which it is a supposable case that the whole people can have agreed—must not be staked on the decision of such a nice, frivolous, and uncertain point, as is the one, whether this or that meaning of a word is the more common one in the community, or the more obvious one to the generality of minds, in particular cases, when, in fact, either meaning is grammatically correct, and appropriate to the subject. Instead of such folly and suicide, *any meaning*, that is consonant to reason in the connection in which the word stands, and that is consistent with justice, and is known and received by society, though less common or obvious than some others, must be adopted, rather than justice be sacrificed, and the whole object of the people in establishing the government be defeated.

So great is the disagreement, even among scholars and lexicographers, as to the meaning of words, that it would be plainly impossible for the most acute scholars to agree upon a code of written laws, having in view the preservation of their natural rights, unless they should also expressly or impliedly agree, that, out of regard to the different senses in which the different individuals of their number might have understood the language in which the laws were written, the courts, in construing those laws, should be allowed very great latitude whenever it should be necessary, for the purpose of finding a sense consistent with justice. And if this latitude would be required in construing an instrument agreed to only by scholars and critics, how much more is it required in construing an instrument agreed to by mankind at large.

This rule, then, that prefers the most common and obvious

meaning of words, is a very insignificant and unimportant one, compared with the previous ones; and it can legally be resorted to, only where the prior ones, (unless, perhaps, the fourth,) are either inapplicable to, or have failed to determine the question; as, for instance, in cases where there is involved no question of right or wrong, or of consistency or inconsistency with the preamble, the general principles, or other particular provisions of an instrument; where nothing more than questions of expediency or convenience are concerned. And even a clear case of serious *inconvenience* only, is sufficient to set aside the rule, unless the language be very explicit.*

This rule, in favor of the most common and obvious meaning of words, has never, so far as I am aware, been laid down as decisive, by the Supreme Court of the United States, in any cases where any question of right, consistency, or of great and manifest convenience, was involved. I think it has generally been cited as authoritative, in constitutional questions, only where the doubt was, whether a particular constitutional power had been vested in the general government, or reserved to the states. In such cases, where the power was admitted to be in one government or the other, and where no question of right, of consistency with other parts of the instrument, or of manifest convenience, was involved, the court, very properly assuming that the power might be as rightfully vested in one government as in the other, at the discretion of the people, have held that the doubt should be determined by taking the language of the constitution to have been used in its most common and obvious sense. But such a decision of a mere question as to which of two governments is the depository of a particular power, which is conceded to be vested

---

* No statute shall be construed in such manner as to be inconvenient, or against reason." — 7 *Bacon's Abridg.*, 465.

"Where the construction of a statute is doubtful, an argument from convenience will have weight." — 3 *Mass.*, 221.

Ch. J. Shaw says, "The argument from inconvenience may have considerable weight upon a question of construction, where the language is doubtful; it is not to be presumed, upon doubtful language, that the legislature intended to establish a rule of action, which would be attended with inconvenience." — 11 *Pickering*, 490.

Ch. J. Abbott says, "An exposition of these statutes, pregnant with so much inconvenience, ought not to be made, if they will admit of any other reasonable construction." — 3 *Barnwell, & A*, 271.

"The argument from inconvenience is very forcible in the law, as often hath been observed." — *Coke Lit.*, 383, *a. note.*

in one or the other, has nothing to do with cases where a question of right or wrong is involved, or of consistency with other parts of the instrument, or even where a serious and clear question of inconvenience is concerned.

If, however, that court have, at any time, laid greater stress upon the rule, they are not sustained, either by the reason of things, or by the practice of other courts; nor are they consistent or uniform in the observance of it themselves.*

SECOND RULE CITED FOR SLAVERY.

A second rule of interpretation, relied upon by the advocates of slavery, is that where laws are *ambiguous*, resort may be had to exterior circumstances, history, &c., to discover the probable intention of the law-givers.

But this is not an universal rule, as has before been shown, (under rule seventh,) and has no application to a question that can be settled by the rules already laid down, applicable to the words themselves. It is evident that we cannot go out of the words of a law, to find its meaning, until all the rules applicable to its words have been exhausted. To go out of a law to find the meaning of one of its words, when a meaning, and a good meaning, can be found in the law, is assuming gratuitously that the law is incomplete; that it has been but partially written; that, in reality, it is not a law, but only a part of a law; and that we have a right to make any additions to it that we please.

Again. When we go out of the words of the law, we necessarily go into the regions of conjecture. We therefore necessarily

---

* The Supreme Court United States say: "It is undoubtedly a well-established principle in the exposition of statutes, that every part is to be considered, and the intention of the legislature to be extracted from the whole. It is also true, that where *great inconvenience* will result from a particular construction, that construction is to be avoided, unless the meaning of the legislature be plain, in which case it must be obeyed." — 2 *Cranch*, 353.

"The natural import of the words of any legislative act, according to the common use of them, *when applied to the subject matter of the act*, is to be considered as expressing the intention of the legislature; *unless the intention, so resulting from the ordinary import of the words, be repugnant to sound, acknowledged principles of national policy. And if that intention be repugnant to such principles of national policy, then the import of the words ought to be enlarged or restrained, so that it may comport with those principles, unless the intention of the legislature be clearly and manifestly repugnant to them.*" — *Opinion of the Justices, including Parsons; 7 Mass.*, 523.

sacrifice certainty, which is one of the vital principles of the law. This cannot be done for any bad purpose. It can only be done to save *rights*, (not to accomplish wrongs,) depending on the efficacy of the law.

To go out of a law to find a bad meaning, when a good meaning can be found in the law, is also to sacrifice *right*, the other vital principle of law. So that both certainty and right would be sacrificed by going out of the constitution to find the meaning, or application, of the word *free ;* since an appropriate and good meaning is found in the instrument itself.

Further. It has before been shown, (under rule seventh,) that a word is not, *legally speaking*, " ambiguous," when the only question is between a just and an unjust meaning ; because the rule, which requires the right to be preferred to the wrong, being *uniform and imperative*, makes the meaning always and absolutely certain ; and thus prevents the ambiguity that might otherwise have existed.

It is true that, in a certain sense, such a word may be called " ambiguous," but not in a legal sense. Almost every word that is used in writing laws, might be called ambiguous, if we were allowed to lose sight of the fact, or unnecessarily abandon the presumption, that the law is intended for purposes of justice and liberty.

But this point has been so fully discussed in the former part of this chapter, (under rule seventh,) that it need not now be discussed at length.

It is not to be forgotten, however, that even if we go out of the constitution to find the meaning of the word *free*, and resort to all the historical testimony that is of a nature to be admissible at all, we shall still be obliged to put the same construction upon it as though we take the meaning presented by the constitution itself. The use of the word in all laws of a similar character, and even of a dissimilar character, to the constitution, fixes this meaning. The principles of liberty, prevailing in the country generally, as evidenced by the declaration of independence, and the several State constitutions, and constituting at least the *paramount*, the *preponderating*, law, in every State of the Union, require the same meaning to be given to the word.

The fact, that this prevailing principle of liberty, or this general principle of law, was, at that time, violated by a small portion, (perhaps one fortieth,) of the community, (the slaveholders,) fur-

nishes no *legal* evidence against this construction; because the
constitution, like every other law, presumes everybody willing to
do justice, unless the contrary explicitly appear in the instrument
itself. This is a reasonable presumption, both in fact and in law,
as has before been suggested, (under rule sixth.) What court
ever laid down the rule that an instrument was " *ambiguous*," or
that an unjust meaning must be given to it, because its just meaning was more just than the parties, or some few of the parties,
could reasonably be presumed to have intended the instrument
should be ? If this idea were admissible, as a rule of interpretation,
all our most just and equitable laws are liable to be held ambiguous,
and to have an unjust construction put upon them, (if their words
will admit of it,) on the ground of their present construction being
more just than some portion of the community, for which they
were made, could be presumed to desire them to be. The slaveholders, then, must be presumed to have been willing to do justice
to their slaves, if the language of the constitution implies it,
whether they were really willing or not. No unwillingness to do
justice can be presumed on the part of the slaveholders, any more
than on the part of any other of the parties to the constitution, as
an argument against an interpretation consistent with liberty.

Again. The real or presumed intentions of that particular portion
of the " people," who were slaveholders, are of no more legal consequence towards settling ambiguities in the constitution, than are
the real or presumed intentions of the same number of slaves; for
both slaves and slaveholders, as has been shown, (under rule
sixth,) were, in law, equally parties to the constitution. Now,
there were probably five or ten times as many slaves as slaveholders.
Their intentions, then, which can be presumed to have been only
for liberty, overbalance all the intentions of the slaveholders. The
intentions of all the non-slaveholders, both north and south, must
also be thrown into the same scale with the intentions of the slaves
— the scale of liberty.

But further. The intentions of all parties, slaves, slaveholders,
and non-slaveholders, throughout the country, must be presumed
to have been precisely alike, because, in theory, they all agreed to
the same instrument. There were, then, thirty, forty, or fifty,
who must be presumed to have intended liberty, where there was
but one that intended slavery. If, then, the intentions, principles,
and interests, of overwhelming majorities of " the people," who
" ordained and established the constitution," are to have any

weight in settling ambiguities in it, the decision must be in favor of liberty.*

But it will be said that, in opposition to this current of testimony, furnished by the laws and known principles of the nation at large, we have direct historical evidence of the intentions of particular individuals, *as expressed by themselves at or about the time.*

One answer to this argument is, that we have no *legal* evidence whatever of any such intentions having been expressed *by a single individual in the whole nation.*

Another answer is, that we have no authentic *historical* evidence of such intentions having been expressed by so many as *five hundred individuals.* If there be such evidence, where is it? *and who were the individuals? Probably not even one hundred such can be named.* And yet this is all the evidence that is to be offset against the intentions of the whole " people of the United States," as expressed in the constitution itself, and in the general current of their then existing laws.

It is the constant effort of the advocates of slavery, to make the constitutionality of slavery a historical question, instead of a legal one. In pursuance of this design, they are continually citing the opinions, or intentions, of Mr. A, Mr. B, and Mr. C, as handed down to us by some history or other; as if the opinions and intentions of these men were to be taken as the opinions and intentions of the whole people of the United States; and as if the irresponsible statements of historians were to be substituted for the constitution. If the people of this country have ever declared that these fugitive and irresponsible histories of the intentions and sayings of single individuals here and there, shall constitute the constitutional law of the country, be it so; but let us be consistent, burn

---

* There is one short and decisive answer to all the pretence that the slaveholders cannot be presumed to have agreed to the constitution, if it be inconsistent with slavery; and that is, that if the slaveholders cannot be presumed to have agreed to it, then *they,* and not the *slaves,* must be presumed to have been no parties to it, and must therefore be excluded from all rights in it. The *slaves* can certainly be presumed to have agreed to it, if it gives them liberty. And the instrument must be presumed to have been made by and for those who could reasonably agree to it. If, therefore, any body can be excluded from all rights in it, on the ground that they cannot be presumed to have agreed to such an instrument as it really is, it must be the slaveholders themselves. Independently of this presumption, there is just as much authority, in the constitution itself, for excluding slaveholders, as for excluding the slaves, from all rights in it. And as the slaves are some ten or fifteen times more numerous than the slaveholders, it is ten or fifteen times more important, on legal principles, that they be included among the parties to the constitution, than that the slaveholders should be.

the constitution, and depend entirely upon history. It is nothing but folly, and fraud, and perjury, to pretend to maintain, and swear to support, the constitution, and at the same time get our constitutional law from these irresponsible sources.

If every man in the country, at the time the constitution was adopted, had expressed the intention to legalize slavery, and that fact were *historically* well authenticated, it would be of no legal importance whatever — and why? Simply because such external expressions would be no part of the instrument itself.

Suppose a man sign a note for the payment of money, but at the time of signing it declare that it is not his intention to pay it, that he does not sign the note with such an intention, and that he never will pay it. Do all these declarations alter the legal character of the note itself, or his legal obligation to pay? Not at all — and why? Because these declarations are no part of that particular promise which he has expressed by signing the note. So if every man, woman, and child in the Union, at the time of adopting the constitution, had declared that it was their intention to sanction slavery, such declarations would all have been but idle wind — and why? Because they are no part of that particular instrument, which they have said shall be the supreme law of the land. If they wish to legalize slavery, they must say so in the constitution, instead of saying so out of it. By adopting the constitution, they say just what, and only what, the constitution itself expresses.

THIRD RULE CITED FOR SLAVERY.

A third rule of interpretation, resorted to for the support of slavery, is the maxim that "Usage is the best interpreter of laws."

If by this rule be meant only that the meaning to be applied to a word in a particular case ought to be the same that has usually been applied to it in other cases of a *similar nature*, we can, of course, have no objection to the application of the rule to the word "free;" for usage, as has already been shown, will fix upon it a meaning other than as the correlative of slaves.

Or if by this rule be meant that all laws must be interpreted according to those rules of interpretation which usage has established, that is all that the advocates of liberty can desire, in the interpretation of the constitution.

But if the rule requires that after a particular *law* has once,

19

twice, or any number of times, been adjudicated upon, it must
always be construed as it always has been, the rule is ridiculous ;
it makes the interpretation given to a law by the courts superior
to the law itself; because the law had a meaning of its own before
any "usage" had obtained under it, or any judicial construction
had been given to it.

It is the original meaning of the constitution itself that we are
now seeking for ; the meaning which the courts were *bound* to put
upon it from the beginning ; not the meaning they actually have
put upon it. We wish to determine whether the meaning which
they have hitherto put upon it be correct. To settle this point,
we must go back to the rules applicable to the instrument itself,
before any judicial constructions had been given to it. All constructions put upon it by the courts or the government, *since the
instrument was adopted*, come *too late* to be of any avail in settling the meaning the instrument had at the time it was adopted
—certainly unless it be impossible to settle its original meaning
by any rules applicable to the instrument itself.

We charge the courts with having misinterpreted the instrument
from the beginning ; with having violated the rules that were
applicable to the instrument before any practice or usage had obtained under it. This charge is not to be answered by saying that
the courts have interpreted it *as they have*, and that that interpretation is now binding, on the ground of usage, whether it were originally right or wrong. The constitution itself is the same now
that it was the moment it was adopted. It cannot have been
altered by all the false interpretations that may have been put
upon it.

If this rule were to be applied in this manner to the constitution,
it would deserve to be regarded as a mere device of the courts to
maintain their own reputations for infallibility, and uphold the
usurpations of the government on which they are dependent,
rather than a means of ascertaining the real character of the constitution.*

* In case *Ex parte* Bollman and Swartout, Justice Johnson, of the Sup. Court
U. S., said,—

" I am far, very far, from denying the general authority of adjudications. Uniformity in decisions is often as important as their abstract justice. (By no means.)
But I deny that a court is precluded from the right, or exempted from the necessity,
of examining into the correctness or consistency of its decisions, or those of any
other tribunal. If I need precedent to support me in this doctrine, I will cite the
example of this court, (Sup. Court U. S.) which, in the case of the United States
vs. Moore, February, 1805, acknowledged that in the case of the United States *vs.*

But perhaps it will be said, that by *usage* is meant the practice of the people. It would be a sufficient answer to this ground to say, that usage, against law and against right, can neither abolish nor change the law, in any case. And usage is worth nothing in the exposition of a law, except where the law is so uncertain that its meaning cannot be settled by the rules applicable to its words. Furthermore, it is only *ancient* usage that is, in any case, of any considerable importance.

This whole matter of usage is well disposed of in the note.*

FOURTH RULE CITED FOR SLAVERY.

A fourth rule of interpretation, relied on for the support of slavery, *is that the words of a law must be construed to subserve the intentions of the legislature.* So also the words of a contract

---

Sims, February, 1803, it had exercised a jurisdiction it did not possess. **Strange indeed would be the doctrine that an inadvertency, once committed by a court, shall ever after impose on it the necessity of persisting in its error.** *A case that cannot be tested by principle is not law, and in a thousand instances have such cases been declared so by courts of justice.*" — 4 *Cranch*, 103.

" *Nullius hominis authoritas tantum apud nos valere debet, ut meliora non sequeremur si quis attulerit.*" (The authority of no man ought to weigh so much with us, that if any one has offered anything better, we may not follow it.) — *Coke Lit.*, 383, *a, note.*

* In Vaughn's Reports, p. 169, 70, the court say, —

" The second objection is, that the king's officers by usage have had in several kings' times the duties of tonnage and poundage from wrecks.

" 1. We desired to see ancient precedents of that usage, but could see but one in the time of King James, and some in the time of the last king ; which are so new that they are not considerable, (not worthy to be considered.)

" 2. Where the penning of a statute is dubious, long usage is a just medium to expound it by ; for *jus et norma loquendi* (the rule and law of speech) is governed by usage. And the meaning of things spoken or written must be, as it hath constantly been received to be by common acceptation.

" But if usage hath been against the obvious meaning of an act of parliament, by the vulgar and common acceptation of the words, then it is rather an oppression of those concerned, than an exposition of the act, especially as the usage may be circumstanced.

" As, for instance, the customers seize a man's goods, under pretence of a duty against law, and thereby deprive him of the use of his goods, until he regains them by law, which must be by engaging in a suit with the king, rather than do so he is content to pay what is demanded for the king. By this usage all the goods in the land may be charged with the duties of tonnage and poundage ; for when the concern is not great, most men (if put to it) will rather pay a little wrongfully, than free themselves from it overchargeably.

" And in the present case, the genuine meaning of the words and purpose of the act, is not according to the pretended usage, but against it, as hath been shewed ; therefore usage in this case weighs not."

must be construed to subserve the intentions of the parties. And the constitution must be construed to subserve the intentions of " the people of the United States."

Those who quote this rule in favor of slavery, *assume* that it was the intention of " the people of the United States" to sanction slavery; and then labor to construe all its words so as to make them conform to that assumption.

But the rule does not allow of any such assumption. It does not supersede, or at all infringe, the rule that " the intention of the legislature is to be collected from the words they have used to convey it."* This last rule is obviously indispensable to make written laws of any value; and it is one which the very existence of written laws proves to be inflexible; for if the intentions could be assumed independently of the words, the words would be of no use, and the laws of course would not be written.

Nor does this rule, that words are to be construed so as to subserve intentions, supersede, or at all infringe, the rule, that the intentions of the legislature are to be taken to be just what their words express, whether such be really their intentions or not.†

---

* The Supreme Court United States say, " The intention of the legislature is to be searched for in the words which the legislature has employed to convey it." - 7 *Cranch*, 60.

Also, " The intention of the instrument (the constitution) must prevail; this intention must be collected from its words." — 12 *Wheaton*, 332.

† *Story* says, " We must take it to be true, that the legislature intend precisely what they say." — 1 *Story's C. C. Rep.*, 653.

Vattel says, " Much less is it permitted, when the author of a piece has himself there made known his reasons and motives, to attribute to him some secret reason, as the foundation to interpret the piece contrary to the natural sense of the terms. *Though he really had the view attributed to him, if he has concealed it, and made known others, the interpretation can only be founded upon these, (which he has made known,) and not upon the views which the author has not expressed ; we take for true against him what he has sufficiently declared.*" — *B.* 2, *ch.* 17, *sec.* 237.

Rutherforth says, " The safest ground for us to stand upon, is what the writer himself affords us ; when the legislator himself has plainly declared the reason (intention) of the law in the body of it, we may argue from thence with certainty." — *B.* 2, *ch.* 7, *p.* 330.

Rutherforth also says, " A promise, or contract, or a will, gives us a right to whatever the promiser, the contractor, or the testator, designed or intended to make ours. But his design or intention, if it is considered merely as an act of his mind, cannot be known to any one besides himself. When, therefore, we speak of his design or intention as the measure of our claim, we must necessarily be understood to mean the design or intention which he has made known or expressed by some outward mark ; because, a design or intention which does not appear, can have no more effect, or can no more produce a claim, than a design or intention which does not exist.

" In like manner, the obligations that are produced by the civil laws of our coun-

The two rules, that "words must be construed to subserve intentions," and that "intentions must be collected from the words," may, at first view, appear to conflict with each other. There is, however, no conflict between them. The rule, that words must be construed to subserve intentions, applies only to *ambiguous* words; to those words which, on account of their ambiguity, *need to be construed;** and it assumes that the intentions of the law have been made known by *other* words, that are *not* ambiguous. *The whole meaning of the rule, then, is, that the intentions of* AMBIGU- *ous words must be construed in conformity with the intentions expressed in those words that are explicit.*†

Where no intentions are explicitly revealed, the court will pre- sume the best intentions of which the words, taken as a whole, are capable; agreeably to the rule cited from the Supreme Court of Massachusetts, viz., "It is always to be presumed that the legisla- ture intend the most beneficial construction of their acts, when the design of them is not apparent." — 4 *Mass.*, 537.

This rule, then, that the ambiguous words of an instrument must be construed to subserve the intentions expressed by other words, that are explicit, requires that the ambiguous words in the constitution (if there are any such) be construed in favor of liberty, instead of slavery.

---

try arise from the intention of the legislator; not merely as this intention is an act of the mind, but as it is declared or expressed by some outward sign or mark, which makes it known to us. For the intention of the legislator, whilst he keeps it to himself, produces no effect, and is of no more account than if he had no such intention. Where we have no knowledge, we can be under no obligation. We cannot, therefore, be obliged to comply with his will, where we do not know what his will is. And we can no otherwise know what his will is, than by means of some outward sign or mark, by which this will is expressed or declared." — *B.* 2, *chap.* 7, *p.* 307.

* All rules of construction apply only to words *that need to be construed;* to those which are capable of more than one meaning, or of a more extended or restricted sense, and whose meanings in the law are therefore uncertain. Those words whose meanings are plain, certain, and precise, are not allowed to be construed at all. It is a fundamental maxim, as before cited, (under rule thirteenth,) that it is not ad- missible to interpret what needs no interpretation.

† *Vattel* says, "If he who has expressed himself in an obscure or equivocal man- ner, has spoken elsewhere more clearly on the same subject, he is the best inter- preter of himself. *We ought to interpret his obscure or vague expressions in such a manner that they may agree with those terms that are clear and without ambi- guity, which he has used elsewhere, either in the same treaty or in some other of the like kind.*" — *B.* 2, *ch.* 17, *sec.* 284.

And this is an universal rule with courts, to interpret the ambiguous words of an instrument by those that are explicit.

Thus have been stated and examined all the rules of interpretation, (with the exception of one, to be named hereafter,) that occur
to me as being of any moment in this discussion.   And I think
the soundness and permanent authority of those that make for
liberty and justice, if indeed they do not *all* make for liberty and
justice, have been shown.

But of the reason and authority of all these rules, the reader
must of necessity judge for himself; for their whole authority rests
on their reason, and on usage, and not on any statute or constitution enacting them.*   *And the way for the reader to judge of
their soundness, is, for him to judge whether they are the rules by
which he wishes his own contracts, and the laws on which he himself relies for protection, to be construed.   Whether, in fact, honest
contracts, honest laws, and honest constitutions, can be either agreed
upon, or sustained, by mankind, if they are to be construed on any
other principles than those contained in these rules.*

If he shall decide these questions in favor of the rules, he may
then properly consider further, that these were the received rules
of legal interpretation at the time the constitution was adopted, and
had been for centuries.   That they had doubtless been the received
rules of interpretation from the time that laws and contracts were
first formed among men; inasmuch as they are such as alone can
secure men's rights under their honest contracts, and under honest
laws, and inasmuch also as they are such as unprofessional and
unlearned men *naturally* act upon, under the dictates of common
sense, and common honesty.

If it now be still objected that the people, or any portion of
them, did not intend what the constitution, interpreted by the preceding rules, expresses, the answer is this.

We must admit that the constitution, *of itself, independently of
the actual intentions of the people*, expresses some certain, fixed,
definite, and legal intentions ; else the people themselves would
express no intentions by agreeing to it.   The instrument would,
in fact, contain nothing that the people *could* agree to.   Agreeing
to an instrument that had no meaning *of its own*, would only be
agreeing to nothing.

---

* It will not do to take these, or any other rules, on trust from courts ; for courts,
although they more generally disregard, or keep out of sight, all rules which stand
in the way of any unlawful decisions which they are determined to make, can yet
not very unfrequently lay down false rules to accomplish their purposes.   For these
reasons, only those of their rules that are plainly adapted to promote certainty and
justice, are to be relied on.

The constitution, then, must be admitted to have a meaning of its own, independently of the actual intentions of the people. And if it be admitted that the constitution has a meaning of its own, the question arises, What is that meaning? And the only answer that can be given is, that it can be no other than the meaning which its words, interpreted by sound legal rules of interpretation, express. That, and that alone, is the meaning of the constitution. And whether the people who adopted the constitution really meant the same things which the constitution means, is a matter which they were bound to settle, each individual with himself, before he agreed to the instrument; and it is therefore one with which we have now nothing to do. We can only take it for granted that the people intended what the constitution expresses, because, by adopting the instrument as their own, they declared that their intentions corresponded with those of the instrument. The abstract intentions, or meaning, of the instrument itself, then, is all that we have now any occasion to ascertain. And this we have endeavored to do, by the application of the foregoing rules of interpretation.

It is perfectly idle, fraudulent, and futile, to say that the people did not agree to the instrument *in the sense* which these rules fix upon it; for if they have not agreed to it in that sense, they have not agreed to it at all. The instrument itself, as a *legal* instrument, *has no other sense*, in which the people *could* agree to it. And if the people have not adopted it in that sense, they have not yet adopted the *constitution;* and it is not now, and never has been, the law of the land.

There would be just as much reason in saying that a man who signs a note for the payment of five hundred dollars, does not sign it in the legal sense of the note, but only in the sense that he will not pay, instead of the sense that he will pay, so much money, as there is in saying that the people did not agree to the constitution in its legal sense, but only in some other sense, which slaveholders, pirates, and thieves might afterwards choose to put upon it.

Besides, does any one deny that all the rest of the constitution, except what is claimed for slavery, was agreed to in the sense which these rules put upon it? No decent man will make such a denial. Well, then, did not the people intend that all parts of the same instrument should be construed by the same rules? Or do the advocates of slavery seriously claim that three or four millions of people, thinly scattered over thirteen states, and having no opportunity for concert, except by simply saying yea, or nay, to the

instrument presented to them, did, nevertheless, at the time of
agreeing to the instrument, agree, also, by means of some myste-
rious, invisible, miraculous intercourse, that the slave clauses, as
they are called, should be construed by directly opposite rules from
all the rest of the instrument? Even if they did so agree, such
agreement would be no part of the constitution; but if they did
not, they certainly did not agree to sanction slavery. No matter
what any, or all, of them said before, or after, *or otherwise than by*,
the adoption of the instrument. What they all said *by the single
act of adoption*, is all that had any effect in establishing the constitutional law of the country.

Certainly, the whole instrument must be construed by uniform
rules of interpretation. If, then, the slave clauses, as they are
called, are construed so as to sanction slavery, all the rest of the
instrument must be construed to sanction all possible iniquity and
injustice of which its words can be made to insinuate a sanction.
More than this. "*The laws passed in pursuance of the constitution*," must of course be construed by the same rules as the constitution itself. If, then, the constitution is to be construed as ad-
versely as possible to liberty and justice, all "the laws passed in
pursuance of it" must be construed in the same manner. Such
are the necessary results of the arguments for slavery.

Nothing can well be more absurd than the attempt to set up the
real or pretended intentions of a few individuals, in opposition to
the legal meaning of the instrument the whole people have adopted, and the presumed intentions of every individual who was a
party to it. Probably no two men, framers, adopters, or any others,
ever had the same intentions as to the whole instrument; and
probably no two ever will. If, then, one man's actual intentions
are of any avail against the legal meaning of the instrument, and
against his presumed intentions, any and every other man's actual
intentions are of equal importance; and consequently, in order to
sustain this theory of carrying into effect men's actual intentions,
we must make as many different constitutions out of this one
instrument, as there were, are, or may be, different individuals
who were, are, or may be, parties to it.

But this is not all. It is probable that, as matter of fact, four
fifths, and, not unlikely, nine tenths, of all those who were legally
parties to the constitution, never even read the instrument, or had
any definite idea or intention at all in regard to the relation it was
to bear, either to slavery, or to any other subject. Every inhab-

itant of the country, man, woman, and child, was legally a party to the constitution, else they would not have been bound by it. Yet how few of them read it, or formed any definite idea of its character, or had any definite intentions about it. Nevertheless, they are all *presumed* to have read it, understood it, agreed to it, and to have intended just what the instrument legally means, as well in regard to slavery as in regard to all other matters. And this *presumed* intention of each individual, *who had no actual intention at all*, is of as much weight in law, as the actual intention of any of those individuals, whose real or pretended intentions have been so much trumpeted to the world. Indeed the former is of altogether more importance than the latter, if the latter were contrary to the legal meaning of the instrument itself.

The whole matter of the adoption of the constitution is mainly a matter of assumption and theory, rather than of actual fact. Those who voted against it, are just as much presumed to have agreed to it, as those who voted for it. And those who were not allowed to vote at all, are presumed to have agreed to it equally with the others. So that the whole matter of the assent and intention of the people, is, in reality, a thing of assumption, rather than of reality. Nevertheless, this assumption must be taken for fact, as long as the constitution is acknowledged to be law; because the constitution asserts it as a fact, that the people ordained and established it; and if that assertion be denied, the constitution itself is denied, and its authority consequently invalidated, and the government itself abolished.

Probably not one half, even, of the male adults ever so much as read the constitution, before it was adopted. Yet they are all *presumed* to have read it, to have understood the legal rules of interpreting it, to have understood the true meaning of the instrument, legally interpreted, and to have agreed to it in that sense, and that only. And this *presumed* intention of persons who never actually read the instrument, is just as good as the actual intention of those who studied it the most profoundly; and better, if the latter were erroneous.

The sailor, who started on a voyage before the constitution was framed, and did not return until after it was adopted, and knew nothing of the matter until it was all over, is, in law, as much a party to the constitution as any other person. He is presumed to have read it, to have understood its legal meaning, and to have agreed to that meaning, and that alone; and his *presumed* intention

is of as much importance as the actual intention of George Washington, who presided over the convention that framed it, and took
the first presidential oath to support it. It is of altogether more
consequence than the intention of Washington, if Washington
intended anything different from what the instrument, legally
interpreted, expresses; for, in that case, his intention would be of
no legal consequence at all.

Men's *presumed* intentions were all uniform, all certainly right,
and all valid, because they corresponded precisely with what they
said by the instrument itself; whereas their actual intentions were
almost infinitely various, conflicting with each other, conflicting
with what they said by the instrument, and therefore of no legal
consequence or validity whatever.

It is not the intentions men actually had, but the intentions they
constitutionally expressed, that make up the constitution. And
the instrument must stand, as expressing the intentions of the people, (whether it express them truly or not,) until the people either
alter its language, or abolish the instrument. If "the people of
the United States" do not like the constitution, they must alter, or
abolish, instead of asking their courts to pervert it, else the constitution itself is no law.

Finally. If we are bound to interpret the constitution by any
rules whatever, it is manifest that we are bound to do it by such
rules as have now been laid down. If we are *not* bound to interpret it by any rules whatever, we are wholly without excuse for
interpreting it in a manner to legalize slavery. Nothing can justify such an interpretation but rules of too imperative a character
to be evaded.*

---

* *Story* says, "In construing the constitution of the United States, we are, in the
first instance, to consider what are its nature and objects, its scope and design, as
apparent from the structure of the instrument, viewed as a whole, and also viewed
in its component parts. Where its words are plain, clear, and determinate, they
require no interpretation; and it should, therefore, be admitted, if at all, with great
caution, and only from necessity, either to escape some absurd consequence, or to
guard against some fatal evil. *Where the words admit of two senses, each of
which is conformable to common usage, that sense is to be adopted, which, without
departing from the literal import of the words, best harmonizes with the nature
and objects, the scope and designs, of the instrument.* Where the words are unambiguous, but the provision may cover more or less ground, according to the intention, which is subject to conjecture; or where it may include in its general terms more
or less than might seem dictated by the general design, as that may be gathered
from other parts of the instrument, there is much more room for controversy; and,
the argument from inconvenience will probably have different influences upon different minds. Whenever such questions arise, they will probably be settled, each
upon its own peculiar grounds; and whenever it is a question of power, it should

be approached with infinite caution, and affirmed only upon the most persuasive reasons. In examining the constitution, the antecedent situation of the country, and its institutions, the existence and operations of the state governments, the powers and operations of the confederation, in short, all the circumstances which had a tendency to produce or to obstruct its formation and ratification, deserve a careful attention. Much, also, may be gathered from contemporary history, and contemporary interpretation, to aid us in just conclusions.

" *It is obvious, however, that contemporary interpretation must be resorted to with much qualification and reserve.* In the first place, the private interpretation of any particular man, or body of men, must manifestly be open to much observation. The constitution was adopted by the people of the United States; and it was submitted to the whole, upon a just survey of its provisions, as they stood in the text itself. In different states, and in different conventions, different and very opposite objections are known to have prevailed; and might well be presumed to prevail. Opposite interpretations, and different explanations of different provisions, may well be presumed to have been presented in different bodies, to remove local objections, or to win local favor. And there can be no certainty, either that the different State conventions, in ratifying the constitution, gave the same uniform interpretation to its language, or that, even in a single state convention, the same reasoning prevailed, with a majority, much less with the whole, of the supporters of it. In the interpretation of a state statute, no man is insensible of the extreme danger of resorting to the opinions of those who framed it, or those who passed it. Its terms may have differently impressed different minds. Some may have implied limitations and objects, which others would have rejected. Some may have taken a cursory view of its enactments, and others have studied them with profound attention. Some may have been governed by a temporary interest or excitement, and have acted upon that exposition which most favored their present views. Others may have seen, lurking beneath its text, what commended it to their judgment, against even present interests. Some may have interpreted its language strictly and closely; others, from a different habit of thinking, may have given it a large and liberal meaning. It is not to be presumed, that, even in the convention which framed the constitution, from the causes above mentioned, and other causes, the clauses were always understood in the same sense, or had precisely the same extent of operation. *Every member necessarily judged for himself; and the judgment of no one could, or ought to be, conclusive upon that of others.* The known diversity of construction of different parts of it, as well as the mass of its powers, in the different state conventions; the total silence upon many objections, which have since been started; and the strong reliance upon others, which have since been universally abandoned, add weight to these suggestions. *Nothing but the text itself was adopted by the people.* And it would certainly be a most extravagant doctrine to give to any commentary then made, and, *a fortiori*, to any commentary since made under a very different posture of feeling and opinion, an authority which should operate an absolute limit upon the text, or should supersede its natural and just construction.

" Contemporary construction is properly resorted to, to illustrate and confirm the text, to explain a doubtful phrase, or to expound an obscure clause; and in proportion to the uniformity and universality of that construction, and the known ability and talents of those by whom it was given, is the credit to which it is entitled. *It can never abrogate the text; it can never fritter away its obvious sense; it can never narrow down its true limitations; it can never enlarge its natural boundaries.* We shall have abundant reason hereafter to observe, when we enter upon the analysis of the particular clauses of the constitution, how many loose interpretations and plausible conjectures were hazarded at an early period, which have since silently died away, and are now retained in no living memory, as a topic either of praise or blame, of alarm or of congratulation. — 1 *Story's Com. on the Const.* pp. 387 *to* 392.

Story makes the following caustic comments upon Mr. Jefferson's rules of interpretation. They are particularly worthy the attention of those modern commentators, who construe the constitution to make it sanction slavery. He says, —

"Mr. Jefferson has laid down two rules, which he deems perfect canons for the interpretation of the constitution.* The first is, 'The capital and leading object of the constitution was, to leave with the states all authorities which respected their own citizens only, and to transfer to the United States those which respected citizens of foreign or other states ; to make us several as to ourselves, but one as to all others. In the latter case, then, constructions should lean to the general jurisdiction, if the words will bear it ; and in favor of the states in the former, *if possible* to be so construed.' Now, the very theory on which this canon is founded, is contradicted by the provisions of the constitution itself. In many instances, authorities and powers are given, which respect citizens of the respective states, without reference to foreigners, or the citizens of other states.† But if this general theory were true, it would furnish no just rule of interpretation, since a particular clause might form an exception to it ; and, indeed, every clause ought, at all events, to be construed according to its fair intent and objects, as disclosed in its language. What sort of rule is that, which, without regard to the intent or objects of a particular clause, insists that it shall, *if possible,* (not if *reasonable,*) be construed in favor of the states, simply because it respects their citizens ? The second canon is : 'On every question of construction (we should) carry ourselves back to the time when the constitution was adopted ; recollect the spirit manifested in the debates ; and instead of trying what meaning may be squeezed out of the text, or invented against it, conform to the probable one in which it was passed.' Now, who does not see the utter looseness and incoherence of this canon ? How are we to know what was thought of particular clauses of the constitution at the time of its adoption ? In many cases, no printed debates give any account of any construction ; and where any is given, different persons held different doctrines. Whose is to prevail ? Besides, of all the state conventions, the debates of five only are preserved, and these very imperfectly. What is to be done as to the other eight states ? What is to be done as to the eleven new states, which have come into the Union under constructions, which have been established against what some persons may deem the meaning of the framers of it ? How are we to arrive at what is the most probable meaning ? Are Mr. Hamilton, and Mr. Madison, and Mr. Jay, the expounders in the Federalist, to be followed ? Or are others of a different opinion to guide us ? Are we to be governed by the opinions of a few, now dead, who have left them on record ? Or by those of a few, now living, simply because they were actors in those days, (constituting not one in a thousand of those who were called to deliberate upon the constitution, and not one in ten thousand of those who were in favor or against it, among the people) ? Or are we to be governed by the opinions of those who constituted a majority of those who were called to act on that occasion, either as framers of, or voters upon, the constitution ? If by the latter, in what manner can we know those opinions ? Are we to be governed by the sense of a majority of a particular state, or of all of the United States ? If so, how are we to ascertain what that sense was ? *Is the sense of the constitution to be ascertained, not by its own text, but by the ' probable meaning,' to be gathered by conjectures from scattered documents, from private papers, from the table-talk of some statesmen, or the jealous exaggerations of others ? Is the constitution of the United States to be the only instrument, which is not to be interpreted by what is written, but by probable guesses, aside from the text? What*

---

* 4 Jefferson's Correspondence, 373, 391, 392, 396.

† 4 Jefferson's Correspondence, 391, 392, 396.

would be said of interpreting a statute of a state legislature, by endeavoring to find out, from private sources, the objects and opinions of every member; how every one thought; what he wished; how he interpreted it? Suppose different persons had different opinions, what is to be done? Suppose different persons are not agreed as to 'the probable meaning' of the framers or of the people, what interpretation is to followed? These, and many questions of the same sort, might be asked. *It is obvious, that there can be no security to the people in any constitution of government, if they are not to judge of it by the fair meaning of the words of the text; but the words are to be bent and broken by the 'probable meaning' of persons, whom they never knew, and whose opinions, and means of information, may be no better than their own? The people adopted the constitution, according to the words of the text in their reasonable interpretation, and not according to the private interpretation of any particular men.* The opinions of the latter may sometimes aid us in arriving at just results, but they can never be conclusive. The Federalist denied that the president could remove a public officer without the consent of the senate. The first congress affirmed his right by a mere majority. Which is to be followed?" — 1 *Story's Com. on Const.*, 390, 392, *note*.

Story says, also, " Words, from the necessary imperfection of all human language, acquire different shades of meaning, each of which is equally appropriate, and equally legitimate; and each of which recedes in a wider or narrower degree from the others, according to circumstances; and each of which receives from its general use some indefiniteness and obscurity, as to its exact boundary and extent. We are, indeed, often driven to multiply commentaries from the vagueness of words in themselves; and, perhaps, still more often from the different manner in which different minds are accustomed to employ them. They expand or contract, not only from the conventional modifications introduced by the changes of society, but also from the more loose or more exact uses, to which men of different talents, acquirements, and tastes, from choice or necessity, apply them. No person can fail to remark the gradual deflections in the meaning of words, from one age to another, and so constantly is this process going on, that the daily language of life, in one generation, sometimes requires the aid of a glossary in another. It has been justly remarked, that no language is so copious, as to supply words and phrases for every complex idea; or so correct, as not to include many equivocally denoting different ideas. Hence it must happen, that, however accurately objects may be discriminated in themselves, and however accurately the discrimination may be considered, the definition of them may be rendered inaccurate by the inaccuracy of the terms in which it is delivered. *We must resort, then, to the context, and shape the particular meaning so as to make it fit that of the connecting words, and agree with the subject matter.*" — 1 *Story's Com.*, 437.

Ch. J. Marshall, speaking for the Sup. Court United States, says, " The spirit of an instrument, especially of a constitution, is to be respected not less than its letter, yet the spirit is to be collected chiefly from its words. It would be dangerous in the extreme to infer from *extrinsic* circumstances, that a case for which the words of an instrument expressly provide, shall be exempted from its operation. Where words conflict with each other, where the different clauses of an instrument bear upon each other, and would be inconsistent unless the natural and common import of words be varied, construction becomes necessary, and a departure from the obvious meaning of words is justifiable." — 4 *Wheaton*, 202.

Ch. J. Taney, giving the opinion of the Supreme Court of the United States, says, " In expounding this law, the judgment of the court cannot, in any degree, be influenced by the construction placed upon it by individual members of congress in the debate which took place on its passage, nor by the motives or reasons assigned by them for supporting or opposing amendments that were offered. The law, as it is passed, is the will of the majority of both houses, and the only mode in which that will is spoken, is in the act itself; and we must gather their intention from the language there used, comparing it, when any ambiguity exists, with the laws upon the same subject, and looking, if necessary, to the public history of the times in which it was passed."—3 *Howard*, 24.

Coke says, "The words of an act of parliament must be taken in a lawful and rightful sense."—*Coke Lit.*, 381, *b.*

Also, "The surest construction of a statute is by the rule and reason of the common law."—*Same*, 272, *b.*

"Acts of parliament are to be so construed as no man that is innocent, or free from injury or wrong, be by a literal construction punished or endamaged."—*Same*, 360, *a.*

"When the construction of any act is left to the law, the law, which abhorreth injury and wrong, will never so construe it, as it shall work a wrong."—*Same*, 42, *a.*

"It is a maxim in law, that the construction of a law shall not work an injury." *Same*, 183, *a.*

"The rehearsal or preamble of the statute is a good mean to find out the meaning of the statute, and as it were a key to open the understanding thereof."—*Same*, 79, *a.*

"It is the most natural and genuine exposition of a statute to construe one part of the statute by another part of the same statute, for that best expresseth the meaning of the makers."—*Same*, 381, *b.*

"If the words of a statute are obscure, they shall be expounded most strongly for the public good."—*Plowden*, 82.

"It is most reasonable to expound the words which seem contrary to reason, according to good reason and equity."—*Same*, 109.

"Such construction ought to be made of acts of parliament as may best stand with equity and reason, and mostly avoid rigor and mischief."—*Same*, 364.

"The judges took the common law for their guide, which is a master in exposition, the reason whereof they pursued as near as they could."—*Same*, 364.

"Words of a statute ought not to be interpreted to destroy natural justice."—*Viner's Abridg. Constr. of Stat.*, sec. 156.

Blackstone's rules of interpretation are as follows:

"The fairest and most rational method to interpret the will of the legislator, is by exploring his intentions at the time when the law was made, by *signs* the most natural and probable. And these signs are either the words, the context, the subject matter, the effects and consequence, or the spirit or reason of the law. Let us take a view of them all.

"1. Words are *generally* to be understood in their usual and most known significations; not so much regarding the propriety of grammar as their general and popular use." * * *

"Terms of art, or technical terms, must be taken according to the acceptation of the learned in each art, trade, or science." * * *

"2. If words happen to be still dubious, we may establish their meaning by the *context;* with which it may be of singular use to compare a word or sentence, whenever they are ambiguous, equivocal, or intricate. Thus the proem, or preamble, is often called in to help the construction of an act of parliament." * * *

"3. As to the *subject matter*, words are always to be understood as having regard thereto; for that is always supposed to be in the eye of the legislator, and all his expressions directed to that end." * * *

"4. As to the *effects and consequence*, the rule is, that where words bear either none, or a very absurd signification, if literally understood, we must a little deviate from the received sense of them." * * *

"5. But lastly, the most universal and effectual way of discerning the true mean ir g of a law, where the words are dubious, is by considering the reason and spirit of it; or the cause which moved the legislator to enact it. For when this reason ceases, the law itself ought likewise to cease with it." * * * — 1 *Blackstone*, 59, 60.

Blackstone (1, 59) also lays it down as being "*Contrary to all true forms of reasoning, to argue from particulars to generals.*" Yet this is the *universal* mode of reasoning among those who hold slavery to be constitutional. Instead of reasoning from generals to particulars, they reason from particulars to generals. For example. Instead of judging of the word " free " by reference to the rest of the instrument, they judge of the whole instrument by reference to the word " free." They first fix the meaning of the word " free," by *assuming* for it, in defiance of the rest of the instrument, and of all legal rules, the worst possible meaning of which it is capable, simply on the illegal grounds that the slaveholders cannot be presumed to have been willing to do justice, but that all the rest of the country can be presumed willing to do injustice ; and they then limit, bend, and break all the rest of the instrument to make it conform to that meaning. It is only by such process as this that the constitution is ever made to sanction slavery.

" The constitution is law, *the people having been the legislators*. And the several statutes of the commonwealth, enacted pursuant to the constitution, are law, the senators and representatives being the legislators. But the provisions of the constitution, and of any statute, are the intentions of the legislature thereby manifested. *These intentions are to be ascertained by a reasonable construction, resulting from the application of correct maxims, generally acknowledged and received.*

" Two of these maxims we will mention. That the natural import of the words of any legislative act, according to the common use of them, when applied to the subject matter of the act, is to be considered as expressing the intention of the legislature, unless the intention, so resulting from the ordinary import of the words, be repugnant to sound, acknowledged principles of national policy. And if that intention be repugnant to such principles of national policy, then the import of the words ought to be enlarged or restrained, so that it may comport with those principles ; unless the intention of the legislature be clearly and manifestly repugnant to them." — *Opinion of the justices, Parsons, Sewall, and Parker,* 7 *Mass.*, 524.

Chief Justice Parker says, " I have always understood that it was right and proper to consider the whole of a statute, and the preamble, and the probable intention of the legislature, in order to ascertain the meaning of any particular section ; and that this mode of interpretation is justifiable, even where the words of the section itself may be unambiguous. *Certainly if one section, however explicit its terms, if taken literally, would contravene the general object of the statute, it should be restrained so as to conform to that object.*" — 1 *Pickering,* 258.

" It is unquestionably a well-settled rule of construction, that when words are not precise and clear, such construction will be adopted as shall appear most reasonable, and best suited to accomplish the objects of the statute ; and where any particular construction would lead to an absurd consequence, it will be presumed that some exception or qualification was intended by the legislature, to avoid such a conclusion." — 24 *Pickering,* 370.

" When the meaning of any particular section or clause of a statute is questioned, it is proper, no doubt, to look into the other parts of the statute ; otherwise the different sections of the same statute might be so construed as to be repugnant, and the intention of the legislature might be defeated. And if, upon examination, the general meaning and object of the statute should be found inconsistent with the literal import of any particular clause or section, such clause or section must, if possible, be construed according to the spirit of the act." — 1 *Pickering,* 250.

The Supreme Court of the United States say, " It is undoubtedly a well-established principle in the exposition of statutes, that every part is to be considered, and the intention of the legislature to be extracted from the whole. It is also true that where great inconvenience will result from a particular construction, that construction is to be avoided ; unless the meaning of the legislature be plain, in which case it must be obeyed." — 2 *Cranch*, 358.

"When the words are not explicit, the intention is to be collected from the context, from the occasion and necessity of the law, from the mischief felt, and the remedy in view ; and the intention is to be taken or presumed, according to what is consonant to reason and good discretion. These rules, by which the sages of the law, according to Plowden, have ever been guided in seeking for the intention of the legislature, are maxims of sound interpretation, which have been accumulated by the experience, and ratified by the wisdom of ages." — 1 *Kent*, 61.

Kent declares the rule of the English courts to be this : "They will not readily presume, out of respect and duty to the lawgiver, that any very *unjust* or absurd consequence was within the contemplation of the law. But if it should be too palpable in its direction *to admit of but one construction*, there is no doubt, in the English law, as to the binding efficacy of the statute." — 1 *Kent*, 447.

This rule implies that if a statute be susceptible of more than "*one* construction," the just or reasonable one must be preferred to "any very unjust or absurd one."

Kent also says, "Statutes are likewise to be construed in reference to the principles of the *common law ;*" (which, in vol. 1, p. 470, he describes as being, in great part, but "*the dictates of natural justice and cultivated reason ;*") "for it is not to be presumed the legislature intended to make any innovation upon the common law, further than the case absolutely required. *This has been the language of the courts in every age*, and when we consider the constant, vehement, and exalted eulogy which the ancient sages bestowed upon the common law, as the perfection of reason, and the best birthright and noblest inheritance of the subject, we cannot be surprised at the great sanction given to this rule of construction." — 1 *Kent*, 463.

Rutherforth says, "All civil laws, and all contracts in general, are to be so construed, where the words are of doubtful meaning, as to make them produce no other effect but what is consistent with reason, or with the law of nature." — *B.* 2, *ch.* 7, *p.* 327.

"Lord Coke has laid it down as a general rule, that where words may have a double intendment, and the one standeth with law and right, and the other is wrongful and against law, the intendment which standeth with law shall be taken." — *Co. Lit.*, 42, *a.* 6, 183, *a.* Cited also in *Pothier*.

"When the terms of a contract are capable of two significations, we ought to understand them in the sense which is most agreeable to the nature of the contract." — *Pothier on Contracts, part* 1, *ch.* 1, *art.* 7, *rule* 3.

The Supreme Court of the United States say, "An act of congress ought never to be construed to violate the law of nations," (or the law of nature, they might have said, for the same reason, for the two are substantially synonymous in principle,) "if any other *possible* construction remains." — 2 *Cranch*, 64.

Parsons, Chief Justice, says, "It is always to be presumed that the legislature intend the most beneficial construction of their acts, when the design of them is not apparent." — 4 *Mass.*, 537.

"Statutes are not to be construed as taking away a common law right, unless the intention is manifest." — 4 *Mass.*, 473.

"It is an established rule, that a statute is not to be construed so as to repeal the common law, unless the intent to alter it is clearly expressed." — 9 *Pickering*, 514.

"Laws are construed strictly to save a right, or avoid a penalty ; and liberally to give a remedy, or effect an object declared in the law." — 1 *Baldwin*, 316.

"Statutes are expounded by the rules and reasons of the common law ; and though the words of a statute be general, yet they shall be specially construed to avoid an apparent injury." — 6 *Dane*, 533.

"This policy, founded in manifest justice, ought to be enforced in this case, if the several laws in the statute-book, or any one of them, will admit of a reasonable construction to this effect."— 14 *Mass.*, 92.

"No statute ought to be so construed as to defeat its own end ; nor so as to operate against reason ; nor so as to punish or damnify the innocent ; nor so as to delay justice."— 6 *Dane*, 596.

"The best construction of a statute is to construe it as near to the rule and reason of the common law as may be, and by the course which that observes in other cases." — *Bacon's Abr. Stat.*, I. 32.

Lord Coke, cited by Chief Justice Abbott, says, "Acts of parliament are to be so construed, as no man that is innocent, or free from injury, or wrong, be by a literal construction punished or endamaged."— 3 *Barnwell & A.* 271.

"When any words or expressions in a writing are of doubtful meaning, the first rule in mixed interpretation is to give them such a sense as is agreeable to the subject matter of which the writer is treating. For we are sure on the one hand that this subject matter was in his mind, and can on the other hand have no reason for thinking that he intended anything which is different from it, and much less that he intended anything which is inconsistent with it."— *Rutherforth, b.* 2, *ch.* 7, *p.* 323.

"The interpretation or construction of the constitution is as much a judicial act, and requires the exercise of the same legal discretion, as the interpretation of a law." — 1 *Kent*, 449.

"But we should particularly regard the famous distinction of things *favorable*, and things *odious*." — *Vattel, B.* 2, *ch.* 17, sec. 300.

"The precise point of the will of the legislature, or of the contracting powers, is what ought to be followed ; but if their expressions are indeterminate, vague, or susceptible of a more or less extensive sense, — if this precise point of their intention in the particular case in question cannot be discovered and fixed, by other rules of interpretation, it should be presumed, according to the laws of reason and equity." — *Same*.

"*All the things which, without too much burthening any one person in particular, are useful and salutary to human society, ought to be reckoned among the favorable things.* For a nation is already under a natural obligation with respect to things of this nature ; so if it has in this respect entered into any particular engagements, we run no risk in giving these engagements the most extensive sense they are capable of receiving. Can we be afraid of doing violence to equity by following the law of nature, and in giving the utmost extent to obligations that are for the common advantage of mankind ? Besides, things useful to human society, on this account, tend to the common advantage of the contracting powers, and are consequently favorable. Let us, on the contrary, *consider as odious everything that, in its own nature, is rather hurtful than of use to the human race.*" — *Same, sec.* 302.

"When the legislature, or the contracting powers, have not expressed their will in terms that are precise and perfectly determinate, it is to be presumed that they desire what is most equitable."— *Same, sec.* 307.

"We favor equity, and fly from what is odious, so far as that may be done without going directly contrary to the tenor of the writing, and without doing violence to terms."— *Same, sec.* 308.

Assuming that the preceding principles of interpretation are correct, it may be allowable, on account of the importance of the subject, and the contrary opinions which appear to prevail, to apply them to another clause of the constitution than those claimed for slavery.

The constitution declares that "*the congress shall have power to declare war.*"

This power, unqualified in its terms, would, if taken literally, and independently of the declared objects of this and all the other powers granted to the government, give congress authority to declare war for any cause whatever, just or unjust, for reasons the most frivolous and wicked, as well as for the most important and necessary purposes of self-preservation. Yet such is not the power that is actually granted. All the principles of interpretation before laid down, requiring a construction consistent with justice, and prohibiting the contrary, limit this power to cases of just war ; war that is necessary for the defence and enforcement of rights.

The objects of the powers granted to congress are " to establish justice," " secure liberty," "*provide for the common defence,*" *&c. ;* and the powers are to be construed with reference to the accomplishment of these objects, and are limited by them. Congress, therefore, have no constitutional authority to make wars of aggression and conquest. And all acts of congress, of that nature, are unconstitutional.

Law-books abound with cases in which general words are restrained to such particular meanings as are consistent with justice and reason. And the rule is well established that general words are always to be thus restrained, unless there be something in the context to forbid it.

" A thing which is within the letter of the statute is not within the statute, unless it be within the intention of the makers." — 15 *Johnson,* 381 ; 3 *Cowen,* 92 ; 1 *Blackstone,* 60-61 ; 3 *Mass.,* 510 ; 5 *Mass.,* 382 ; 15 *Mass.,* 206 ; *Bac. Abr. Stat., I.,* 45.

Was it the intent of " the people of the United States " to authorize their government to make wars of aggression and conquest ? Their intention must be collected from their words, but their words must always be taken in a sense consistent with justice, and in no other, if the words are capable of a just meaning. " War " may be made for just, and for unjust purposes. But as two conflicting intentions cannot be attributed to the same provision, the just intention must be preferred to the unjust one. The preamble, also, as we have seen, shows the object of this power to be " to secure liberty," and " provide for the common defence." A good object, and a sufficient object, being thus apparent, and being also specially declared in the preamble, no other can be attributed, and the power is consequently limited to that object.*

Plowden says, " And the judges of the law in all times past have so far pursued the intent of the makers of statutes, that they have expounded acts, which were general in words, to be but particular, when the intent was particular." — *Plowden,* 204.

Vattel says, " We limit a law or a promise contrary to the literal signification of the terms, by regulating our judgment by the reason of that law, or that promise." — *Vattel, B.* 2, *ch.* 17, *sec.* 292.

Also, " The restrictive interpretation takes place, when a case is presented in which the law or the treaty, according to the rigor of the terms, lead to something unlawful. This exception must then be made, since nobody can promise or ordain what is unlawful. For this reason, though assistance has been promised to an ally in all his wars, no assistance ought to be given him when he undertakes one that is manifestly unjust." — *Same, sec.* 293.

Also, " We should, in relation to things odious," (that is, " everything that in its own nature is rather hurtful than of use to the human race,") " take the terms in the most confined sense." — *Same, sec.* 308.

The Supreme Court of the United States, also, say, " An act of congress," (and

---

* Story says, " The true office of the preamble is to expound the nature, *and extent,* and application of the powers actually conferred by the constitution." — 1 *Story's Com. on Const.,* 445.

the same reason applies to the constitution,) " ought never to be construed to violate the law of nations, if any other *possible* construction remains."—2 *Cranch*, 64.

To understand the force of this last rule, some definition of the law of nations is necessary. The best *general* definition of it is, that which considers nations as individuals, and then applies the same principles of natural law to them, that are applicable to individuals. This rule, however, requires to be modified by being made more lenient to nations, in certain cases, than to individuals. For example; the whole people of a nation are not to have war made upon them, for wrongs done by their government, any sooner or further than is necessary to compel them to redress those wrongs as soon as, in the nature of things, they (the people) can do it, by changing, or operating upon their government. The reasons are these: The people, by instituting government, or appointing certain individuals to administer it, do not authorize those individuals to commit any wrongs against foreign nations. They are not, therefore, themselves culpable for those wrongs. When, then, such wrongs are committed, all that the people can be required to do, is that they dismiss the wrong doers from power, and appoint others who will redress the injuries committed. And to do this, the people must be allowed such time as is reasonable and necessary, which will be more or less, according to circumstances. But ample time must be sure to be allowed in all cases, before war against them can be lawful.

2. In controversies as to their respective rights and wrongs, nations are each entitled to longer time for investigating and determining their rights than individuals, because it is not in the nature of things possible that a whole people can investigate such questions with the same promptness that individuals can investigate their respective rights in their private controversies ; and a whole people are not to be held liable, by having war made upon them, until they have had ample, or, at least, reasonable, time to investigate the matters in controversy.

3. Nations are entitled to longer delays for fulfilling their contracts, paying their debts, &c., than individuals, because governments, no more than individuals, can be required to perform impossibilities, and a government's means of paying its debts must be obtained by systematic processes of taxation, which require a longer or shorter time, according to the wealth and resources of the country.

4. But another reason why greater forbearance is due to nations than to individuals, is, that it generally happens that a part only of a nation are disposed to withhold justice, while the rest are willing to do it. Yet if the nation, as a whole, were held responsible to the same rigid rules as an individual, by having war declared on the first want of promptitude in fulfilling their duty, the innocent would be involved in the same punishment with the guilty.

For all these reasons, and some others, great lenity and forbearance in the enforcement of rights is demanded by the law of nations, or by the natural law applicable to nations.

To apply the foregoing principles : If the war in which the United States are now engaged with Mexico, be one, not of defence, but of aggression, on their part, or be made in violation of natural law, it is unconstitutional, and all proceedings had in the prosecution of it are illegal. The enlistments of soldiers for that service are illegal ; and the soldiers are not bound by their enlistments. The soldiers legally owe no obedience to their officers. The officers have no legal authority over their soldiers. The oaths of the officers to obey the laws of the United States, while they are in the territory of Mexico, are of no legal obligation. And the officers and soldiers, while in Mexico, are in no way legally amenable to the government or laws of the United States for their conduct. They owe no legal obedience to the orders of the president. They are, in the eye of our own law, mere banditti. They may throw off all allegiance to the government of the United States, turn conquerors on their own account, and it will be no offence against the laws of the

United States.   The appropriations for carrying on the war in Mexico are illegal, and might, with as much constitutional authority, be made to Mexican brigands, as to our own soldiers.   Finally, our soldiers are bound to know our own constitutional law on this point, and to know that they are acting without legal authority.   They are, therefore, not entitled to the rights of prisoners of war, in case they should fall into the hands of the Mexican government, but are liable to be treated as robbers and murderers ; and our government, in such an event, would have no constitutional right to protect them, by force, from their liability to Mexican laws, for all the crimes they are now committing.

CHAPTER XVIII.

SERVANTS COUNTED AS UNITS.

THE constitution (Art. 1, Sec. 2) requires that the popular basis of representation and taxation be made up as follows, to wit:

" By adding to the whole number of *free* persons, *including those bound to service for a term of years*, and excluding Indians not taxed, three fifths of all other persons."

If the word *free*, in this clause, be used as the correlative of slaves, and the words " all other persons" mean slaves, the words " *including those bound to service for a term of years*" are sheer surplusage, having no legal force or effect whatever ; for the persons described by them would of course have been counted with the free persons, *without the provision*. If the word *free* were used as the correlative of slaves at all, it was used as the correlative of slaves alone, and not also of servants for a term of years, nor of prisoners, nor of minors under the control of their parents, nor of persons under any other kind of restraint whatever, than the simple one of chattel slavery.*

It was, therefore, wholly needless to say that " persons bound to service for a term of years" should not be counted in the class with slaves, for nobody, who understood the word *free* as the correlative of slaves, would have imagined that servants for a term of years were to be included in the class with slaves. There would have been nearly or quite as much reason in saying that minors under the control of their parents, persons under guardianship, prisoners for debt, prisoners for crime, &c., should not be counted in the class with slaves, as there was in saying that servants for a term of years should not be counted in that class. In fact, the whole effect of the provision, if it have any, on the slave hypothesis, is to *imply* that all other persons under restraint, except

---

* If the word *free* were used as the correlative of any *other* kinds of restraint than slavery, it would not have implied slavery as its correlative, and there would have been no ground for the argument for slavery. On the other hand, if it *were* used as the correlative of slavery, there was no need of specially excepting from the implication of slavery " those bound to service for a term of years," for they were known by everybody not to be slaves.

" those bound to service for a term of years," shall be counted in the class with slaves : because an exception of particular persons strengthens the rule against all persons not excepted.   So that, on the slave hypothesis, the provision would not only be unnecessary in favor of the persons it describes, but it would even be dangerous in its implications against persons not included in it.

But we are not allowed to consider these words even as surplusage, if any reasonable and legal effect can be given them. And under the alien hypothesis they have such an effect.

Of the " persons bound to service for a term of years " in those days, large numbers were aliens, who, but for this provision, would be counted in the three fifths class.   There was, nevertheless, a sound reason why they should be distinguished from other aliens, and be counted as units, and that was, that they were bound to the country for a term of years as laborers, and could not, like other aliens, be considered either a transient, unproductive, or uncertain population.   Their being bound to the country for a term of years as laborers, was, to all practical purposes, equivalent to naturalization ; for there was little or no prospect that such persons would ever leave the country afterwards, or that, during their service, they would recognize the obligations of any foreign allegiance.

On the alien hypothesis, then, the words have an effect, and a reasonable one.   On the slave hypothesis, they either have no effect at all, or one adverse to all persons whatsoever that are under any kind of restraint, except servants for a term of years.

CHAPTER XIX.

SLAVE REPRESENTATION.

The injustice to the *North* that is involved in allowing slaves, who can have no rights in the government, who can owe it no allegiance, *who are necessarily its enemies*, and who therefore weaken, instead of supporting it — the injustice and inequality of allowing such persons to be represented at all in competition with those who alone have rights in the government, and who alone support it, is so palpable and monstrous, as utterly to forbid any such construction being put upon language that does not necessarily mean it.   The absurdity, also, of such a representation, is, if possible, equal to its injustice.   We have no right — legal rules, that are universally acknowledged, imperatively forbid us — unnecessarily to place upon the language of an instrument a construction, that either stultifies the parties to it to such a degree as the slave construction does the people of the North, or that makes them consent to having such glaring and outrageous injustice practised upon them.

But it will be said in reply to these arguments, that, as a compensation to the North for the injustice of slave representation, all *direct* taxes are to be based on population; that slaves are to be counted as three fifths citizens, in the apportionment of those taxes; and that the injustice of the representation being thus compensated for, by a corresponding taxation, its absurdity is removed.

But this reply is a mere *assumption* of the fact that the constitution authorizes slave *taxation;* a fact, that, instead of being assumed, stands only on the same evidence as does the slave representation, and therefore as much requires to be proved by additional evidence, as does the representation itself. The reply admits that the slave representation is so groundless, absurd, unequal, and unjust, that it would not be allowable to put that construction upon the clause, if it had provided only for *representation.* Yet it attempts to support the construction by alleging, without any additional evidence, that the direct taxation, (if there should ever be any direct taxation,) was to be on the same absurd principle. But this is no answer to the objection. It only fortifies it; for it accuses the constitution of two absurdities, instead of one, and does it upon evidence that is admitted to be insufficient to sustain even one. And the argument for slavery does, in reality, accuse the constitution of these two absurdities, without bringing sufficient evidence to prove either of them. Not having sufficient evidence to prove either of these absurdities, independently of the other, it next attempts to make each absurdity prove the other. But two legal absurdities, that are proved only by each other, are not proved at all. And thus this whole fabric of slave representation and slave taxation falls to the ground.

Undoubtedly, if the clause authorizes slave representation, it also authorizes slave taxation; or if it authorizes slave taxation, it undoubtedly authorizes slave representation. But the first question to be settled is, whether it authorizes either? And this certainly is not to be answered in the affirmative, by simply saying that, *if* it authorizes one, it authorizes the other.

If any one wishes to prove that the clause authorizes slave representation, he must first prove that point independently of the taxation, and then he may use the representation to prove the taxation ; or else he must first prove the slave taxation, and then he may use the taxation to prove the representation.   But he cannot use either to prove the other, until he has first proved one independently of the other ; a thing which probably nobody will ever undertake to do.   No one certainly will ever undertake to prove the representation independently of the taxation ; and it is doubtful whether any one will ever undertake to prove the taxation, independently of the representation.   The absurdity and incongruity of reckoning one single kind of property as persons, in a government and system of taxation founded on persons, are as great as would be that of valuing one single class of persons as property, in a government and system of taxation founded on property.   The absurdity and incongruity in each case would be too great to be allowable, if the language would admit, (as in this case it does admit,) of another and reasonable construction.

Nevertheless, if any one should think that this slave *taxation* is not a thing so absurd or unjust as to forbid that construction, still, the fact that, if that construction be established, the absurd and unjust *representation will follow* as a consequence from it, is a sufficient reason why it cannot be adopted.   For we are bound to make the entire clause harmonious with itself, if possible ; and, in doing so, we are bound to make it *reasonable* throughout, if that be possible, rather than absurd throughout.

I have thus far admitted, for the sake of the argument, the common idea, that the taxation, which the slave construction of this clause would provide for, would be some compensation to the North, for the slave representation.   But, in point of fact, it would not *necessarily* be any compensation at all ; for it is only *direct* taxes that are to be apportioned in this manner, and the government is not required to lay direct taxes at all.   Indeed, this same unjust representation, which it is claimed that the clause authorizes, may be used to defeat the very taxation which it is said was allowed as an equivalent for it.   So that, according to the slave argument, the unjust representation is made certain, while the compensating taxation is made contingent ; and not only contingent, but very likely contingent upon the will of the unjust representation itself. Here, then, are another manifest and gross absurdity and injustice, which the slave construction is bound to overcome, before it can be adopted.

But suppose tne taxation had been made certain, so as to correspond with, and compensate for, the representation — what then? The purport of the clause would then have been, that the North said to the South, " *We will suffer you to govern us,* (by means of an unequal representation,) if you will pay such a portion, (about one sixth,) of our taxes." Certainly no construction, unless an unavoidable one, is allowable, that would fasten upon the people of the north the baseness and the infamy of having thus bargained away their equal political power for money ; of having sold their freedom for a price. But when it is considered how paltry this price was, and that its payment was not even guarantied, or likely ever to be made, such a construction of the contract would make the people of the North as weak and foolish, as infamous and despicable. Is there a man in the whole northern states, that would now consent to such a contract for himself and his children ? No. What right, then, have we to accuse *all* our fathers, (fathers too who had proved their appreciation of liberty by risking life and fortune in its defence,) of doing what *none* of us would do ? No legal rules of interpretation, that were ever known to any decent tribunal, authorize us to put such a construction upon their instrument as no reasonable and honorable man would ever have agreed to. There never lived a man in the northern states, who would have consented to such a contract, unless bribed or moved to it by some motive beyond his proportionate share in such a price. Yet this price is all the motive that can be *legally* assigned for such a contract ; for the general benefits of the Union must be presumed to have been equal to each party. If any difference were allowable in this respect, it must have been in favor of the North, for the South were the weaker party, and needed union much more than the north.

This question has thus far been treated as if the South had really made some pretence, at least, of paying more than her share of taxation. But this is by no means the true mode of presenting the question ; because these persons, it must be remembered, whom it is claimed were to be represented and taxed only as three fifths of a person each, were legally free by the then existing State constitutions ; and, therefore, instead of being slaves, not entitled to be represented or taxed at all as persons, were really entitled to be represented, and liable to be taxed, as units, equally with the other people of the United States. *All this the North must be presumed to have known.* The true mode of presenting the ques-

21

tion, therefore, is this, viz., 1. Whether the South, for the privilege of enslaving a portion of her people, of holding them in slavery under the protection of the North, and of saving two fifths of her direct taxation upon them, agreed to surrender two fifths of her representation on all she should enslave ? and, 2. Whether the *North*, in order to secure to herself a superiority of representation, consented to the enslavement of a portion of the Southern people, guarantied their subjection, and agreed to abate two fifths of the direct taxation on every individual enslaved ? This is the true mode of presenting the subject; and the slave construction of the clause answers these questions in the affirmative. It makes the North to have purchased for herself a superior representation, and to have paid a bounty on slavery, by remitting taxes to which the South would have been otherwise liable ; and it makes the South to have bartered away her equal representation, her equal political power — makes her, in fact, to have sold her own liberties to the North, for a pitiful amount of taxation, and the privilege of enslaving a part of her own people.

Such is the contract — infamous on the part of both North and South, and base, suicidal, and servile on the part of the South — which the slave construction would make out of this provision of the constitution. Such a contract cannot be charged upon political communities, unless it be " expressed with irresistible clearness." Much less can it be done on the evidence of language, which equally well admits of a construction that is rational, honorable, and innocent, on the part of both.

The construction which legal rules require, to wit, that " free persons" mean the citizens, and " all other persons" the aliens, avoids all these obstacles in the way of making this clause an honorable, equal, and reasonable contract.

CHAPTER XX.

WHY ALIENS ARE COUNTED AS "THREE FIFTHS."

THERE are both justice and reason in a partial representation, and a partial taxation, of aliens. They are protected by our laws, and should pay for that protection. But as they are not allowed the full privileges of citizens, they should not pay an equal tax with the citizens. They contribute to the strength and resources of the government, and therefore they should be represented. But as they are not sufficiently acquainted with our system of government, and as their allegiance is not made sufficiently sure, they are not entitled to an equal voice with the citizens, especially if they are not equally taxed.

But it has been argued* that aliens were likely to be in about equal numbers in all the States, in proportion to the citizens; and that therefore no great inequality would have occurred, if no separate account had been taken of them. But it is not true that aliens were likely to be in equal numbers in the several States in proportion to the citizens. Those States whose lands were already occupied, like Connecticut, Rhode Island, and Massachusetts, (exclusive of Maine,) and who could not expect to retain even so much as their natural increase of population, could not expect to receive the same additions to it by the immigration of foreigners as New York, Pennsylvania, and other States, that still had immense bodies of unoccupied lands. And none of the old thirteen States could expect long to have the same proportion of aliens as the new States that were to be opened in the west. And even those new States, that were then about to be opened, would soon become old, and filled with citizens, compared with other States that were to be successively opened still further west.

This inequality in the proportion of aliens in the respective States, was *then*, and still is, likely to be for centuries an important political element; and it would have been weak, imprudent, short-sighted, and inconsistent with the prevailing notions of that time, of all previous time, and of the present time, for the constitution to have made no provision in regard to it. And yet, on the slave hypothesis, the constitution is to be accused of all this weakness, imprudence, short-sightedness, and inconsistency; and, what is equally inadmissible, is to be denied all the credit of the intentions, which, on the alien hypothesis, the clause expresses; intentions, the wisdom, justice, and liberality of which are probably more conspicuous, and more harmoniously blended, than in any other provision in regard to aliens, that any nation on earth ever established, before or since.

It is as unnatural and absurd, in the interpretation of an instrument, to withhold the credit of wise and good intentions, where the language indicates them, as it is to attribute bad or foolish ones,

---

* By Wendell Phillips.

where the language does not indicate them. And hence the positive merits of this clause, on the alien hypothesis, are entitled to the highest consideration; and are moreover to be contrasted with its infamous demerits, on the slave hypothesis.

The preceding view of this clause is strongly confirmed by other parts of the constitution. For example: The constitution allows aliens, equally with the citizens, to vote directly in the choice of representatives to congress, and indirectly for senators and president, *if such be the pleasure of the State governments.** Yet they are not themselves eligible to these three offices, although they are eligible to all other offices whatsoever under the constitution.† All that is required of them is simply the official oath to support the constitution; the same oath that is required of citizens.

Again. The constitution of the United States lays no restraint upon their holding, devising, and inheriting real estate, if such should be the pleasure of the State governments. And in many, if not all, the States, they are allowed to hold, devise, and inherit it.

Now the facts, that they are not restrained by the constitution from holding, devising, and inheriting real estate; that they have the *permission* of the constitution to vote, (if the State governments shall please to allow them to do so;) and that they are eligible to a part of the offices, *but not to all*, show that the constitution regards them *not as aliens*, in the technical sense of that term,‡ *but as partial citizens.* They indicate that the constitution intended to be consistent with itself throughout, and to consider them, *in reality*, what this argument claims that it considers them in respect of representation and taxation, viz., as *three fifths citizens.*

The same reason that would induce the constitution to make aliens eligible to all offices, *except the three named*, (to wit, those

---

* And in some of the States, as Illinois and Michigan, for example, they are allowed to vote.

The provision in the constitution of the United States, in regard to electors, is this: (art. 1, sec. 2.)

"The House of Representatives shall be composed of members chosen every second year, by *the people* of the several States," (not by the citizens of the United States in each State, but by "*the people* of the several States,") "and the electors in each State shall have the qualifications requisite for electors of the most numerous branch of the State legislature."

† They may be judges, ambassadors, secretaries of the departments, commanders in the army and navy, collectors of revenue, postmasters, &c., equally with the citizens.

‡ For the term *alien* technically implies exclusion from office, exclusion from the right of suffrage and inability to hold real estate.

of representative, senator, and president,) and to allow them the right of voting, would also induce it to allow them *some* right of being counted in making up the basis of representation. On the other hand, the same reasons which *would forbid their eligibility, as representatives, senators, and presidents,* would forbid their being reckoned equal to citizens, in making up the basis of representation; and would also forbid their votes for those officers being counted as equal to the votes of citizens. Yet a single vote could not be divided so as to enable each alien to give three fifths, or any other fraction, of a vote. Here then was a difficulty. To have allowed the separate *States* full representation for their aliens, as citizens, while it denied the aliens themselves the full rights of citizenship, (as, for instance, eligibility to the legislative and highest executive offices of the government,) would have been inconsistent and unreasonable. How, then, was this matter to be arranged? The answer is, just as this argument claims that it was arranged, viz., by allowing the aliens full liberty of voting, at the discretion of the State governments, yet at the same time so apportioning the representation among the States, that each State would acquire no more weight in the national government, than if her aliens had each given but three fifths of a vote, instead of a full vote.

In this manner all the inconsistency of principle, which, it has been shown, would have otherwise existed between the different provisions of the constitution, relative to aliens, as compared with citizens, was obviated. At the same time justice was done to the States, as States; also to the citizens, as citizens; while justice, liberality, and consistency were displayed towards the aliens themselves. The device was as ingenious, almost, as the policy was wise, liberal, and just.

Compare now the consistency and reason of this arrangement with the inconsistency and absurdity of the one resulting from the slave hypothesis. According to the latter, the *States* are allowed the *full* weight of their aliens, as citizens, in filling those departments of the government, (the legislative and highest executive,) which aliens themselves are not allowed to fill. 2. Aliens are allowed full votes with the citizens in filling offices, to which, (solely by reason of not being citizens,) they are not eligible. 3. And what is still more inconsistent, absurd, and atrocious even, half the States are allowed a three fifths representation for a class of persons, whom such States have made enemies to the nation,

21*

and who are allowed to fill no office, are allowed no vote, enjoy no protection, and have no rights in, or responsibility to, the government.

If legal rules require us to make an instrument consistent, rather than inconsistent, with itself, and to give it all a meaning that is reasonable and just, rather than one that is unjust and absurd, what meaning do they require us to give to the constitution, on the point under consideration ?

The only imperfection in the constitution on this point seems to be, that it does not *secure* the elective franchise to aliens. But this omission implies no disfavor of aliens, and no inconsistency with the actual provisions of the constitution ; nor is it any argument against the theory here maintained ; for neither does the constitution *secure* this franchise to the *citizens, individually,* as it really ought to have done. It leaves the franchise of both citizens and aliens at the disposal of the State governments separately, as being the best arrangement that could then be agreed upon, trusting, doubtless, that the large number of aliens in each State would compel a liberal policy towards them.

From this whole view of the subject, it will be seen that the constitution does not, in reality, consider unnaturalized persons as *aliens,* in the technical sense of that term.* It considers them *as partial citizens,* that is, *as three fifths citizens, and two fifths aliens.* The constitution could find no single term by which to describe them, and was therefore obliged to use the phrase, " all other persons " than " the free," that is, " all other persons " than those entitled to *full* representation, *full* rights of eligibility to office, and full rights of citizenship generally. The term " alien " would have been a repulsive, unfriendly, and wholly inappropriate one, by which to designate persons who were in fact members of the government, and allowed to participate in its administration on a footing so near to an equality with the citizens. As the word had acquired a technical meaning, indicative of exclusion from office, from suffrage, from the basis of representation, and from the right of holding real estate, its use in the constitution would have served to keep alive prejudices against them, and would have been made a pretext for great illiberality and injustice towards them. Hence the constitution nowhere uses the word.

How much more reasonable in itself, and how much more cred-

---

* They are called aliens in this argument, for the want of any other word that will describe them.

itable to the constitution and the people, is this mode of accounting for the use of the words "all other persons," than the one given by the advocates of slavery, viz., that the people had not yet become sufficiently shameless to avow their treason to all the principles of liberty for which they had been distinguished, and, therefore, instead of daring to use the word "slaves," they attempted to hide their crime and infamy under such a fig-leaf covering as that of the words "all other persons." But the law knows nothing of any such motives for using unnatural and inappropriate terms. It presumes that the term appropriate for describing the thing is used when that term is known — as in this case it was known, if tho things intended to be described were slaves.

CHAPTER XXI.

WHY THE WORDS "FREE PERSONS" WERE USED.

THE words "free persons" were, I think, *of themselves* — that is, independently of any desire that we may suppose a part of the people to have had to pervert their true meaning — the most appropriate words that could have been used to describe the native and naturalized citizens — that is, the *full* citizens, as distinguished from those partial citizens, (not *technically* aliens, though commonly called aliens,) — whom I have supposed the words "all other persons" were intended to describe.

The real distinction between these two classes was, that the first class were *free of the government* — that is, they were *full* members of the State, and could claim the *full* liberty, enjoyment and protection of the laws, *as a matter of right, as being parties to the compact;* while the latter class were not thus free; they could claim hardly anything *as a right*, (perhaps nothing, unless it were the privilege of the writ of *habeas corpus*,) and were only allowed, *as a matter of favor and discretion*, such protection and privileges as the general and State governments should see fit to accord to them.

It was important that the first of these classes should bo described by some *technical* term; because technical terms are more definite, precise, and certain, in their meaning, than others. And in this case, where representation and taxation were concerned, the greatest precision that language admitted of was requisite. Now, I think, there was no other word in the language that would have described so accurately, as does the word " free," (when used in its technical sense,) the class which I have supposed it was intended to describe.

The technical term, in the English law, for describing *a member of the state,* is " free subject."* " Free subjects" are the whole body of the people, men, women, and children, who were either born within the dominions and allegiance of the crown,† or have been naturalized by act of parliament. Individually, they *are members of the state;* collectively, they *constitute the state.* As members of the state, they are individually entitled, *of right,* to all the essential liberties and rights which the laws secure to the people at large.

" Free subjects" are distinguishable from aliens, or persons born out of the country, but residing in the country, and allowed, *as a matter of privilege,* such protection as the government sees fit to accord to them.

" Free subjects" are also distinguishable from *denizens,* who, in the English law, are persons born out of the country, and not naturalized by act of parliament, but have certain privileges conferred upon them by the king's letters patent.‡

This term, " free subject," had been universally used in this country, up to the time of the revolution, to describe members of the state, as distinguished from aliens. The colonial charters guarantied to the subjects of the British crown, settling in the colonies, that they and their children should " have and enjoy all the liberties and immunities of *free and natural subjects,* to all intents, constructions, and purposes whatsoever, as if they and every of them were born within the realm of England." And up to the revolution, the colonists, as everybody knows, all claimed the rights and the title of "*free* British subjects." They did not call themselves *citizens* of Massachusetts, and *citizens* of Virginia. They did not call themselves *citizens* at all. The word *citizen* was never, I think, used in the English law, except to describe persons residing, or having franchises, in a *city;* as, for example,

---

* " Subjects are *members of the commonwealth,* under the king their head." — *Jacob's, Williams', and Cunningham's Law Dictionaries.*

† " All those are natural-born subjects, whose parents, at the time of their birth, were under the actual obedience of our king, and whose place of birth was within his dominions." — 7 *Coke's Rep., p.* 18. *Bacon's Abridg., title Alien. Cunningham's Law Dictionary, title Alien.*

‡ " A denizen is in a kind of middle state, between an alien and a natural-born subject, and partakes of both of them." — 1 *Blackstone,* 373. *Jacob's Law Dict.*

citizens of London. But as members of the state, they were all called " free subjects," or " free British subjects."

Up to the time of the revolution, then, the term " free subject" was the *only* term in *common* use to describe members of the state, as distinguished from aliens. As such it was universally known in the country, and universally used.*

The term " free" was also *naturally* an appropriate one by which to describe a member of a *free* state; one who was *politically free*, and entitled, of right, to the full and free enjoyment of all the liberties and rights that are secured to the members of a government established for the security of men's personal freedom. What but a " free subject," or " free person," could such a member of a free state be appropriately called ?

And when it is considered in what estimation " the liberties of England," " of Englishmen," and of English subjects everywhere, were held ; that they were the peculiar pride and boast of the nation ; the title of " free " is seen to be a perfectly natural and appropriate one, by which to designate the political rank of those who were entitled, of right, to the possession and enjoyment of all those liberties, as distinguished from those not entitled to the same liberties.

After the Declaration of Independence, the word ' subject" was no longer an appropriate name for the people composing our republican States ; for " subject" implied a sovereign ; but here the people had themselves become the sovereigns. The term " subject" was, therefore, generally dropped. It seldom appears in the State constitutions formed after the Declaration of Independence.

But although the term " subject" had been generally dropped, yet, up to the adoption of the United States constitution, no other single term had been generally adopted in the several State constitutions, as a substitute for " free subject," to describe the members of the state, as distinguished from aliens.

The terms people, inhabitants, residents, which were used in most of the State constitutions, did not mark the difference between native and naturalized members of the state, and aliens.

The term " freeman" was used in some of the State constitu-

* The only other term, I think, that was *ever* used in the English law, in a similar sense, was " freeman ;" as, for instance, " freeman of the realm." But " free subject " was the common term. " Freeman " was more generally used to denote members of incorporated trading companies, and persons possessing franchises in a *city*. Besides, it did not, I think, so generally, if ever, include women and children, as did " free subjects."

tions; but its meaning is sometimes indefinite, and sometimes different from what it appears to be in others. For example. In the then existing Declaration of Rights of the State of Delaware, (Sec. 6,) it would seem to be applied only to male adults. In the then existing "constitution and form of government" of Maryland, (Sec. 42,) it would seem to include only males, but males under as well as over twenty-one years of age. Again, in the "Declaration of Rights" of the same State, (Secs. 17 and 21,) it would seem to include men, women, and children. In the "Declaration of Rights" of North Carolina, (Secs. 8, 9, 12, and 13,) it would seem to include men, women, and children. Again, in the "constitution or form of government" of the same State, (Secs. 7 and 8,) it would seem to mean only male persons.

The result was, that the precise legal meaning of the word was not sufficiently settled by usage *in this country*, nor had the word itself been so generally adopted in the State constitutions, as to make it either a safe or proper one to be introduced into the representative clause in the United States constitution. It would also have been equally objectionable with the words "*free* persons," in its liability to be interpreted as the correlative of slavery.

What term, then, should the United States constitution have adopted to distinguish the full members of the state from unnaturalized persons? "Free subjects" was the only term, whose meaning was well settled, and with which the whole people of the United States had ever been acquainted, as expressing that idea, and no other. But the word "subject," we have already mentioned, was no longer appropriate. By retaining the word "free," which was the significant word, and substituting the word "persons" for "subjects," the same body of people would be described as had before been described by the term "free subjects," to wit, all the full members of the state, the native and naturalized persons, men, women, and children, as distinguished from persons of foreign birth, not naturalized. What term, then, other than "free persons," was there more appropriate to the description of this body of the people?

The word "free," it must be constantly borne in mind, if introduced into the constitution, would have to be construed with reference to the rest of the instrument, in which it was found, and of course with reference to the government established by that instrument. In that connection, it could legally mean nothing else than the members of the state, as distinguished from others, unless, (as

was not the case,) other things should be introduced into the
instrument to give the word a different meaning.

The word " free," then, was an appropriate word, *in itself*, and,
in its *technical* sense, (which was its presumptive sense,) it was precisely *the* word, to be used in the constitution, to describe with
perfect accuracy all that body of the people, native and naturalized,
who were *full* members of the state, and entitled, *of right*, to the
full liberty, or political freedom, secured by the laws, as distinguished from aliens and persons partially enfranchised. In short,
it described, with perfect accuracy, those who were *free of the
government established by the constitution*. This was its precise
legal meaning, when construed, as it was bound to be, with reference to the rest of the instrument ; and it was the *only* meaning
that it *could* have, *when thus construed*.

A word of this kind was wanted — that is, a word of precisely
the same meaning, which the word *free*, in its technical sense,
bears, with reference to the rest of the instrument and the government established by it, was wanted — because representation and
taxation were to be based upon the persons described, and perfect
accuracy of description was therefore all important.

Now, those who object to the term " free persons " being taken
in that sense, are bound to show a better term that might have
been used to describe the same class of persons. I think there is
not another word in the language, technical, or otherwise, that
would have described them so accurately, or so appropriately.

The term " freemen," we have seen, would not have been so
appropriate, for it was liable to be taken in a narrower signification, so as to include only male adults, or persons entitled to the
elective franchise. But " free persons " included men, women, and
children, voters and non-voters, who were entitled to protection
under the laws as of right.

" People," " residents," and " inhabitants " would not do, because
they included all persons living in the country, native, naturalized,
and aliens.

The only other word, that could have been used, was " *citizens*.'
Perhaps if that word had been used, the courts, construing it with
reference to the rest of the instrument, would have been bound to
put the same construction upon it that they were bound to put
upon the words " free persons." Nevertheless, there were decisive objections against the adoption of it in the representative clause.
The word " citizens " was not, *at that time certainly*, (even if it be

now,) a word that had acquired any such definite meaning, either in England, or in this country, as describing the great body of free and equal members of the state, men, women, and children, as had the word "free." In fact, it had probably never been used in that sense at all in England; *nor in this country up to the time of the revolution.* And it is probable, (as will hereafter be seen,) that it had never been used in that sense in this country, up to the adoption of the constitution of the United States, unless in the single constitution of Massachusetts. Its meaning, in this country, is, *to this day*, a matter of dispute. Lawyers, as well as others, differ about it, as will presently be seen.

The word "citizen" is derived from the Latin *civis;* and its true signification is to describe one's relations to a *city*, rather than to a state. It properly describes either a freeman of a city, or a mere resident, as will be seen by the definitions given in the note.*

---

* "Civis, a citizen; a freeman or woman; a denizen." — *Ainsworth.*

"Citizen, a freeman of a *city;* not a foreigner; not a slave." — *Johnson.*

"Citizen, a freeman of a *city*." — *Bailey.*

"Citizens (*cives*) are either freemen, *or such as reside and keep a family in the city, &c.*, and some are citizens and freemen, and some are not, who have not so great privileges as the others." — *Williams' Law Dictionary; Cunningham's do.*

"Citizen, a native or inhabitant of a *city*, vested with the freedom and rights thereof." — *Rees' Cyclopedia.*

"The civil government of the city of London is vested by charters and grants from the kings of England, in its own corporation, or body of citizens." — *Rees' Cyclopedia.*

"Citoyen, (Fr.) citizen, an inhabitant, or freeman of a city." — *Boyer.*

"Citizen, an inhabitant of a *city;* one who dwells or inhabits in a *city;* one who possesses or enjoys certain privileges of a *city;* a freeman of a *city;* one who follows, pursues, or practises the trades or businesses of a *city*, as opposed to those who do not." — *Richardson.*

"Though they are in the world, they are not of it, as a *citizen* of one city may live in another, and yet not be *free of it*, nor properly of it, but a mere stranger and a foreigner." — *Bishop Beveridge, cited by Richardson.*

"Citizen. 1. The native of a *city*, or an inhabitant who enjoys the freedom and privileges of the *city* in which he resides; the freeman of a *city*, as distinguished from a foreigner, or one not entitled to its franchises. * * *

5. In the United States, a person, native or naturalized, who has the privilege of *exercising the elective franchise*, or the qualifications which enable him to vote for rulers, and to purchase and hold real estate." — *Webster.*

"Citizens, persons. One who, under the constitution and laws of the United States, *has a right to vote for representatives in congress, and other public officers, and who is qualified to fill offices in the gift of the people.*" — *Bouvier's (American) Law Dict.*

Kent denies that citizenship depends on one's right of suffrage, and says that women and children are citizens. — *2 Kent*, 253, *note in third edition.*

I am not aware that Story anywhere gives a definition of the word *citizen*, as it

It will be seen also, by these definitions, that, taking the word in its *best* sense, and also with reference to the *state*, it could, *at most*, only have been held synonymous with the "free persons" or "freemen" of the state; and that we should then have been obliged to employ these. latter terms, *in their technical senses*, in order to define it.

It would also have been even more liable than the term "free" to the objection of impliedly excluding slaves; for in Rome, where the term was used, and whence it has come down to us, they had slaves, who of course were not regarded as citizens; while in England, whence the term "free" was borrowed, they had no slaves.

The term "free citizen" was also used in the then existing State constitutions of Georgia and North Carolina, where they held slaves, (though not legally.) If, then, the word had been employed in the United States constitution, there would have been at least as much reason to say that it excluded slaves, as there would be for saying that the word "free" excluded them.

The term "citizen" was objectionable in still another respect, viz., that it seems to have been previously, as it has been since, employed *to define those who enjoyed the elective franchise.* But it would be unreasonable that the constitution should base representation and taxation upon a distinction between those enjoying the elective franchise, and "all other persons" — it being left with the States to say who should enjoy that franchise. Yet, if the constitution had used the word "citizen" in connection with representation and taxation, it might have given some color to that idea.

But to prove how inappropriate would have been the use of the word "citizens," in the representative clause — where a word of a

---

is used in the constitution. He says, that "every citizen of a State is *ipso facto* a citizen of the United States;" and that "a person who is a *naturalized* citizen of the United States, by a like residence in any State in the Union, becomes *ipso facto* a citizen of that State." — (3 *Com. on Const., p.* 565-6.) But this saying that a citizen of a State is a citizen of the United States, and *vice versa,* gives us no information as to who is either a citizen of a State, or of the United States, other than those "*naturalized*" by act of Congress.

These authorities show that the word *citizen* has had different meanings, and that its meaning was not, at the adoption of the constitution, and even now is not, well settled, and therefore that it was not a proper word to be used in a clause where certainty was so important.

It is especially uncertain whether the word citizens would have included women and children, as do the words "free persons."

22

precise and universally known meaning was required — the follow-ing facts are sufficient; for we are to look at the word as people looked at it at that day, and not as we look at it now, when it has grown into use, and we have become familiar with it.

Of all the State constitutions in existence in 1789, the word *citizen* was used in but *three*, to wit, those of Massachusetts, North Carolina, and Georgia; and in those, only in the following man-ner:

In the constitution of Massachusetts it was used some half dozen times, and in such connections as would indicate that it was used synonymously with the members of the state.

In the constitution of North Carolina it was used but *once*, (Sec. 40,) and then the term "*free* citizen," was used; thus indicating, either that they had more than one kind of citizens, or that the word citizen itself was so indefinite that its meaning would be liable to be unknown to the people, unless the word *free* were used to define it.

In the constitution of Georgia it was used but *once*, (Art. 11,) and then in the same manner as in the constitution of North Car-olina, that is, with the word *free* prefixed to it for the purpose of definition.

In the constitutions of the other ten States, (including the char-ters of Rhode Island and Connecticut,) the word *citizen* was not used at all.

In the Articles of Confederation it was used but *once*, (Art. 4, Sec. 1,) and then the term was, as in the constitutions of Georgia and North Carolina, "*free* citizens."

So that there was but one constitution, (that of Massachusetts,) out of the whole fourteen then in the country, in which the word *citizen* could be said to be used with any definite meaning attached to it. In the three other cases in which it was used, its own indefi-niteness was confessed by the addition of the word *free*, to define it.

A word so indefinite, and so little known to the people, as was the word *citizen*, was of course entirely unsuitable to be used in the representative clause for the purpose of describing the native and naturalized members of the state, men, women and children, as distinguished from persons not naturalized.

For all these reasons the word *citizens* was objectionable; while in reference to slavery, it would seem to have been not one whit better than the words "free persons."

Finally, the term "free persons" was much more appropriate,

in itself, to designate the members of a *free state*, of a republican government, than was the word *citizen*, which, *of itself*, implies no necessary relationship to a free state, any more than to an aristocracy.

What objection was there, then, to the use of the words " free persons," in the constitution, for describing the members of the state ? None whatever, save this, viz., the liability of the words to be perverted from that meaning, if those who should administer the government should be corrupt enough to pervert them. This was the only objection. In every other view, the words chosen, (as well the words " free persons" as the words " all other persons,"*) were the best the English language afforded. They were the most accurate, the most simple, the most appropriate, to express the true idea on which a classification for purposes of representation and taxation should be founded.

These words, then, being, *in themselves*, the best that could be used, *could the North have reasonably objected to their use?* No. They could not say to the South, " We fear you do not understand the legal meaning which the word *free* will bear in this instrument." For everybody knew that such was the meaning of that word when used to describe men's relation to the state ; and everybody was bound to know, and every lawyer and judge did actually know, that the word, if used in the manner it is in the constitution, could legally be construed only with reference to the rest of the instrument, and consequently could describe only one's relation to the government established by the instrument ; that it was only by violating all legal principles of interpretation that it could be made to describe any merely personal relation between man and man, illegal and criminal in itself, and nowhere else recognized by the instrument, but really denied by its whole purport.

The *legal* meaning of the word, then, was undoubted ; and that was all the North could require. They could not require that other language should be introduced for the special purpose of preventing a fraudulent construction of this word. If it had been intended to form the constitution on the principle of making everything so plain that no fraudulent construction could possibly be put upon it, a new language must have been invented for the purpose ; the English is wholly inadequate. Had that object been attempted, the instrument must have been interminable in length, and vastly

---

* See Chap. 20 and 22.

more confused in meaning than it now is. The only practicable way was for the instrument to declare its object in plain terms in the preamble, as it has done, viz., the establishment of justice, and the security of liberty, for " the people of the United States, and their posterity," and then to use the most concise, simple, and appropriate language in all the specific provisions of the instrument, trusting that it would all be honestly and legally interpreted, with reference to the ends declared to be in view. And this rule could no more be departed from in reference to slavery, than in reference to any other of the many crimes then prevalent.

It would have been only a mean and useless insult *to the honest portion of the South,* (if there were any honest ones amongst them,) to have said to the whole South, (as we virtually should have done if any specific reference to slavery had been made,) " We fear you do not intend to live up to the legal meaning of this instrument. We see that you do not even enforce the State constitutions, which you yourselves establish ; and we have suspicions that you will be equally false to this. We will, therefore, insert a special provision in relation to slavery, which you cannot misconstrue, if you should desire to do so."

The South would have answered, " Whatever may be your suspicions of us, you must treat with us, if at all, on the presumption that we are honorable men. It is an insult to us for you to propose to treat with us on any other ground. If you dare not trust us, why offer to unite with us on any terms ? If you *dare* trust us, why ask the insertion of specifications implying your distrust ? We certainly can agree to no instrument that contains any imputations upon our own integrity. We cannot reasonably be asked to defame ourselves."

Such would have been the short and decisive answer of the South, as of any other community. And the answer would have been as just, as it would be decisive.

All, then, that the North could ask of the South was to agree to an honest instrument, that should " be the supreme law of the land, anything in the constitution or laws of any State to the contrary notwithstanding," and that all State, as well as national officers, executive, legislative, and judicial, should swear to support it. This the South were ready to do, some probably in good faith, others in bad faith. But no compact could be formed except upon the presumption that all were acting in good faith, whatever reason they may have had to suspect the contrary on the part of particular portions of the country, or with reference to particular portions of the instrument. And it would have been as foolish as useless to have suggested the idea of especial guards against fraudulent constructions in particular cases.

It was a great point gained for liberty, to get the consent of the whole country to a constitution *that was honest in itself*, however little prospect there might be that it would be speedily enforced in every particular. An instrument, honest in itself, saved the character and conscience of the nation. It also gave into the hands of the true friends of liberty a weapon sure to be sufficient for their purposes, whenever they should acquire the numbers necessary to wield it to that end.

CHAPTER XXII.

"ALL OTHER PERSONS."

It has been already shown, (in chapter 20,) that there was a sufficient, and even a necessary reason for the use of the words "all other persons," in preference to the word "aliens."

That reason was, that the word "alien" had a technical meaning, implying exclusion from office, exclusion from suffrage, and exclusion from the right to hold real estate; whereas, the constitution intended no exclusion whatever, except simply from the three offices of president, senator, and representative. The word "aliens," then, would have been a false word of itself, and would also have furnished ground for many mischievous and unfriendly implications and prejudices against the parties concerned.

If, then, only this single class of persons had been intended, there was ample reason for the use of the words, "all other persons;" while, on the slave hypothesis—that is, on the hypothesis that the words include *only* slaves, as they are generally supposed to do—no reason at all can be assigned for the use of these words, instead of the word *slave*, except such a reason as we are not at liberty to attribute to a law or constitution, if by any other reasonable construction it can be avoided.

But whether the words "all other persons" include slaves, or unnaturalized persons, there was still another reason for the use of the words, "all other persons," in preference either to the

word *slaves*, or the word *aliens*.   That reason was, that the three
fifths class was to include more than one kind of persons, whether
that one kind were slaves or unnaturalized persons.   " *Indians
not taxed*" *were to be included in the same count*, and, therefore,
neither the word *slaves*, nor the word *aliens*, would have correctly
described *all* the persons intended.

So far as I am aware, all those who hold slavery to be constitutional, have believed that " Indians not taxed" were excluded both
from the count of units, and the three fifths count; that the words
"all other persons " refer solely to slaves; and that those words
were used solely to avoid the mention of slaves, of which the people were ashamed.   *They have believed these facts just as firmly
as they have believed that slavery was constitutional.*

I shall attempt to prove that " Indians not taxed," instead of
being excluded from both counts, were included in the three fifths
class, and, consequently, that the words " all other persons " were
perfectly legitimate to express the two kinds of persons, of which
that class were to be composed.   If this proof be made, it will
furnish another instance in which those who hold slavery to be
constitutional, have made false law, by reason of their abandoning
legal rules of interpretation, and construing everything in the
light of their assumed insight into certain knavish intentions that
are nowhere expressed.

The clause reads as follows : —

" Representatives and direct taxes shall be apportioned among
the several States which may be included within this union, according to their respective numbers, which shall be determined by
adding to the whole number of free persons, (including those
bound to service for a term of years, and excluding Indians not
taxed,) three fifths of all other persons."

The question arising on this clause is, whether there be any
class made by it, except the class of *units*, and the *three fifths*
class ?   Or whether there be three classes, to wit, the class of units,
the three fifths class, and another class, " Indians not taxed," *who
are not to be counted at all?*

To state the question is nearly enough to answer it, for it is
absurd to suppose there is any class of " the people of the United
States " who are not to be counted at all.   " Indians not taxed,"
(that is, not taxed *directly*, for all Indians are taxed *indirectly*,)
are as much citizens of the United States as any other persons,

and they certainly are not to be unnecessarily excluded from the basis of representation and taxation.*

It would seem to be grammatically plain that the words "*all other persons*" include all except those counted as *units*. And it would probably have always been plain that such was their meaning, but for the desire of some persons to make them include slaves, and their belief that, in order to make them include slaves, they must make them include nobody but slaves.

The words "*including those bound to service for a term of years, and excluding Indians not taxed,*" are parenthetical,† and might have been left out, without altering the sense of the main sentence, *or diminishing the number of classes.* They are thrown in, not to increase the number of classes, but simply to define who may, and who may *not*, be included in the *first* class, the class of units.

This is proved, not only by the fact, that the words are parenthetical, (which would alone be ample proof,) but also by the fact that the two participles, "*including*" and "*excluding*," are connected with each other by the conjunction "and," and are both parsed in the same manner, both having relation to the "number" counted as units, *and to that alone.*

The words, "*excluding Indians not taxed,*" exclude the Indians mentioned simply from the count of the *preceding* "number," the

---

* In saying that Indians were "citizens of the United States," I of course mean those living under the actual jurisdiction of the United States, and not those who, though living within the chartered limits of the States, had never had the State or United States jurisdiction extended over them ; but by treaty, as well as of right, retained their independence, and were governed by their own usages and laws.

It may be necessary for the information of some persons to state that the jurisdictions of the several States have not always been coëxtensive with their chartered limits. The latter were fixed by the charters granted by the crown, and had reference only to the boundaries of the respective colonies. *as against each other.* But the rights of the colonies, (and subsequently of the States,) within their chartered limits, were subject to the Indian right of soil, or occupancy, except so far as that right should be extinguished by the consent of the Indians. So long as the Indians should choose to retain their right of soil, or occupancy, and their independence, and separate government, our governments had no jurisdiction over them, and they were not citizens of the United States. But when they surrendered their right of soil, or occupancy, abandoned their separate government, and came within our jurisdiction, or the States and the United States extended their jurisdiction over them, they became citizens of the United States, equally with any other persons. At the adoption of the constitution, there were several independent tribes within the chartered limits of the States. Others had surrendered their independent existence, and intermingled with the whites.

† I have inclosed them in parenthesis to show the sense more distinctly.

number to which the word "excluding" relates; that is, the count of units. They do nothing more. They do not exclude them from any other count; they do not create, or at all purport to create, out of them a distinct class. They do not at all imply that they are not to be counted at all. They do not, *of themselves,* indicate whether these Indians, that are excluded from the count of units, are, *or are not,* to be included in, or excluded from, any other count. *They simply exclude them from the first count,* leaving them to be disposed of as they may be, by the rest of the clause.

To make this point more evident, let us write the clause again, supplying two words that are necessary to make the sense more clear.

"Representatives and direct taxes shall be apportioned among the several States which may be included within this union, according to their respective numbers, which shall be determined by adding to the whole number of free persons, (including *therein* those bound to service for a term of years, and excluding *therefrom* Indians not taxed,) three fifths of all other persons."

Such is plainly the true grammatical construction of the sentence; and the phrases, "including *therein,*" and "excluding *therefrom,*" both plainly relate to one and the same number or count, to wit, the number counted as units, *and to that only.* Grammatically, one of these phrases has no more to do with the class of "all other persons," than the other.

On grammatical grounds there would be just as much reason in saying that the word "including" *includes servants* in the class of 'all other persons,' as there is in saying that the word "excluding" *excludes* Indians from that class; for it is perfectly apparent, that the words *including* and *excluding* refer only to one and the same number, and that number is the number counted as units.

To illustrate this point further, let us suppose these parenthetical sentences to have been transposed, and the clause to have read thus:

"By adding to the whole number of free persons, (*excluding therefrom* Indians not taxed, and *including therein* those bound to service for a term of years,) three fifths of all other persons."

It is plain that the sense of the clause would not have been in the least altered by this transposition. Yet would anybody then have supposed that Indians were *excluded* from the class of "*all other persons?*" Or that "those bound to service for a term of years" were *included* in the class of "*all other persons?*" Certainly not. Everybody would then have seen that the words *including* and *excluding* both related only to the *preceding* number —the number counted as units. Yet it is evident that this transposition has not at all altered the grammatical construction or the legal sense of the clause.

The argument for slavery, while it claims that the word *including* includes servants in the number of *units* only, claims that the word *excluding* excludes Indians both from the number of units, and *also* from the number of " *all other persons ;*" that the word *including* includes servants in only *one* count, but that the word *excluding* excludes Indians from *both* counts ; whereas it is perfectly manifest that the two words, *including* and *excluding*, relate to one and the same count, to wit, the count of units, and to that alone.

There would be just as much reason, on grammatical grounds, in saying that the word *including includes* servants in *both* counts, as there is in saying that the word *excluding excludes* Indians from both counts.

Inasmuch, then, as the words of the parenthesis, viz., the words " *including those bound to service for a term of years, and excluding Indians not taxed,*" refer only to the count of units, and serve only to define those who may, and those who may not, be included in that count, they do not, and cannot, create any new class, additional to the two named exteriorly to the parenthesis, to wit, the class of units, and the three fifths class.

There being, then, but two classes made, and " Indians not taxed," being specially excluded from the first, *are necessarily included in the last.*

Both the grammar and the law of the clause, (though perhaps not its rhetoric,) would therefore be adequately provided for, even if there were no other persons than " Indians not taxed " to be reckoned in the class of " *all other persons ;*" for " Indians not taxed " are " *other* persons " than those counted as units. And we cannot, I think, make these words, " all other persons," imply the existence of slaves, if we can find any other persons than slaves for them to refer to.

Further. There being but two classes made, to wit, the class of units and the three fifths class, and " Indians not taxed " being excluded from the first, and therefore necessarily included in the last, it would follow, if the constitution uses the word " free " as the correlative of slaves, that it either considers these Indians as *slaves,* or that, for purposes of representation and taxation, it counts them in the same class with slaves — a thing that, so far as I know has never been done.

But perhaps it will still be said by the advocates of slavery, (for this is all they *can* say,) that "Indians not taxed" *are not to be counted at all ;* that they are to be excluded from both classes.

But this is, if possible, making their case still worse. It shows how, in order to extricate themselves from one dilemma, they are obliged to involve themselves in another — that of excluding entirely from the popular basis of representation and taxation, a part of those who are not only not slaves, but are confessedly actual citizens.

To say that "Indians not taxed" are not to be counted at all ; that they are to be excluded both from the class of units and the three fifths class, is not only violating the grammar of the clause, (as has already been shown,) but it is violating all common sense. Indians living under the governments of the States and the United States — that is, within the territory over which the United States and one of the several States have actually extended their civil jurisdiction — are as much citizens of the United States as anybody else ; and there is no more authority given in the constitution for excluding them from the basis of representation and taxation, than there is for excluding any other persons whatever. In fact, the language of the constitution is express, that all persons shall be counted either in the class of units or in the three fifths class ; and there is no escape from the mandate. The only exclusion that the constitution authorizes, is the exclusion of "Indians not taxed" from the count of *units.*

But perhaps it will be claimed that Indians are not citizens, and therefore they are excluded of course. But there is not the least authority for this assertion, unless it be in regard to those tribes, or nations, who, living within the chartered limits of the States, have, nevertheless, retained their separate independence, usages, and laws, and over whom the States have not extended their civil jurisdiction. The assertion is wholly groundless as to all those Indians who have abandoned their nationality, intermingled with the whites, and over whom the States have extended their jurisdiction. Such persons were as much a part of the people of the United States, and were as much made citizens by the constitution, as any other portion of the people of the country.

This exception of "Indians not taxed" from the count of units, of itself implies that Indians are citizens ; for it implies that, but for this express exception, they would *all* have been counted as *units*.

Again. This exception cannot be extended beyond the letter of it. It therefore applies only to those " *not taxed;*" and it excludes even those only from the count of *units ;* thus leaving all that *are taxed* to be counted as units ; which of course implies that *they* are citizens. And if those Indians, *who are taxed*, are citizens, those who are " *not taxed*" are equally citizens. Citizenship does not depend at all upon taxation, in the case of the Indian, any more than in the case of the white man ; if it did, a man would be a citizen this year, if he happened to be taxed this year, and yet lose his citizenship next year, if he should happen not to be taxed next year.

But it will be asked, If Indians are citizens, why are they not all counted as units ? The reason is obvious. The numbers of Indians in the different States were so unequal, and they contributed so little to the resources of the States in which they lived, that justice required that, in apportioning representation and taxation among the separate States, some discrimination should be made on account of this class of population. Being citizens, they must be represented ; and being represented, their State must be taxed for them. And no better arrangement could be agreed on, without making too many classes, than that of ranking them, (so far as representation and taxation were concerned,) on an equality with unnaturalized persons.

It being established that Indians are citizens, it follows that those " not taxed " must be included in the basis of representation and taxation, *unless expressly excluded.* But the express exclusion does no more than exclude them from the count of *units,* and the exclusion cannot go beyond the letter. They are therefore necessarily included in the three fifths class, the class which embraces " all other persons" than those counted as units.

If " Indians not taxed " were also to be excluded from the three fifths class, the constitution would have said so ; and would also have told us expressly how they should be counted, or that they should not be counted at all.

The clause has thus been explained on the ground of there being but two classes made by it, to wit, the class counted as units, and the three fifths class ; which are all the classes that the grammar of the clause will allow to be made. It is to be remarked, however, that if the grammar of the clause be disregarded, and

three classes be made, the clause will still be consistent with the
alien hypothesis. Indeed, it is immaterial, on the alien hypothesis,
whether two or three classes be made. Whether the slave hypothesis can be sustained without making more than two classes, I
leave for the advocates of slavery to determine.* They will, at
any rate, be obliged to admit that " Indians not taxed" are included
in the class described as " all other persons," and thus lose the
benefit of their stereotyped argument, that those words must mean
slaves, because they could mean nothing else. They will also be
obliged to give up their old surmise about the motive for using the
words " all other persons " — a surmise which has always, (in their
opinion,) wonderfully strengthened their law, although it seems to
have contained not a particle of fact. †

* I think it cannot be sustained without making three classes, for the reason
before given, viz., that the words "all other persons " must not be held to mean
slaves, if there be any other persons that they can apply to.

† The following illustration will make it perfectly apparent that the representative clause of the constitution requires *all* the people of the country, ("Indians
not taxed," as well as others), to be counted in making up the basis of representation and taxation; that it requires and permits them to be divided into *two
classes only*, viz., the class of units, and the three-fifths class ; and, finally, that it
imperatively requires that "Indians not taxed " be included in the three-fifths
class, or class described as "all other persons."

The illustration is this. Suppose Congress were to order a census of the people,
for the purpose of making a constitutional apportionment of representation and
taxation, and should require that the several classes of persons be arranged in
separate columns, each under its appropriate head, *according to the terms used in the
constitution.* The table would stand thus :

CLASS OF UNITS.	THREE-FIFTHS CLASS.
" The whole number of free persons, including those bound to service for a term of years, and excluding Indians not taxed."	" All other persons."

This table follows the directions of the constitution, *to the letter*. And yet, it
clearly makes but two classes ; and the two classes clearly include *all* the people
of the United States. The word " *excluding* " clearly excludes " Indians not

CHAPTER XXIII.

ADDITIONAL ARGUMENTS ON THE WORD "FREE."

ARGUMENT I.

THE constitutional argument for slavery rests mainly, if not wholly, upon the word *free*, in the representative clause; (Art. 1, Sec. 2.)

Yet this clause does not, *of itself*, at all purport to fix, change, *or in any way affect*, the civil rights or relations of any single individual. *It takes it for granted that those rights and relations are fixed, as they really are, by other parts of the instrument.* It purports only to prescribe the *manner* in which the population shall be *counted*, in making up the basis of representation and taxation; and to prescribe that representation and taxation shall be apportioned among the several States, according to the basis so made up. This is the whole purport of the language of the clause, and the whole of its *apparent* object; and it is a palpable violation of all legal rules to strain its legal operation beyond this purpose. To use the clause for a purpose nowhere avowed,

---

taxed" only from the first class. The second class also clearly *includes* all that *are excluded* from the first. It, therefore, clearly includes "Indians not taxed."

These facts entirely overthrow the argument that "all other persons" must mean slaves, because there were no other persons whom they could mean.

It is of no importance to say that "Indians not taxed" *have never been included* in the three-fifths count. The answer is, *There is the plain letter of the constitution;* and if Congress have not complied with it, it has been owing either to their ignorance, or their corruption.

23

either in itself or the rest of the instrument, viz., that of destroying rights with which it does not at all purport to intermeddle, is
carrying fraudulent and illegal interpretation to its last extent.

Yet this provision for simply *counting* the population of the
country, and apportioning representation and taxation according to
that count, has been transmuted, by unnecessary interpretation,
into a provision denying all civil rights under the constitution to a
part of the very " people" who are declared by the constitution
itself to have " ordained and established " the instrument, and
who, of course, are equal parties to it with others, and have equal
rights in it, and in all the privileges and immunities it secures.

If parties, answering to the several descriptions given of them
in this clause, can be *found,* (so as simply to be *counted,*) without
supposing any change or destruction of individual rights, as established by other parts of the instrument, we are bound thus to find
and count them, without prejudice to any of their rights.   This is
a self-evident proposition.   That parties, answering to the several
descriptions, *can* be found, without supposing any change or destruction of individual rights, as contemplated by the other parts of
the instrument to exist, has already been shown.   And this fact is
enough to settle the question as to the legal effect of the clause.

The whole declared and apparent object of the clause, viz., the
counting of the population, and the apportionment of the representation and taxation according to that count, can be effected without prejudice to the rights of a single individual, as established by
the rest of the instrument.   This being the case, there is no
epithet strong enough to describe the true character of that fraud
which would pervert the clause to a purpose so entirely foreign to
its declared and apparent object, as that of licensing the denial
and destruction of men's rights; rights everywhere implied
throughout the entire instrument.

ARGUMENT II.

It would have been absurd to have used the word *"free"* in a
sense correlative with slaves, because it is a self-evident truth that,
taking the word in that sense, *all* men are *naturally* and rightfully
free.   This truth, like all other natural truths, must be presumed
to be taken for granted by all people, in forming their constitutions, unless they plainly deny it.   Written constitutions of government could not be established at all, unless they took for

granted all natural truths that were not plainly denied; because, the natural truths that must be acted upon in the administration of government are so numerous, that it would be impossible to enumerate them. They must, therefore, *all* be taken for granted unless particular ones be plainly denied. Furthermore, this particular truth, that all men are naturally free, had but recently been acknowledged, and proclaimed even, by the same people who now established the constitution. For this people, under such circumstances, to describe themselves, in their constitution, as "the whole number of free persons, and three fifths of all other persons," (taking the word "free" in the sense correlative with slaves,) would have been as absurd, *in itself,* (independently of things exterior to the constitution, and which the constitution certainly cannot be *presumed* to sanction,) as it would have been to have described themselves as "the whole number of males and females, and three fifths of all other persons."

Such an absurdity is not to be charged upon a people, upon the strength of a single word, which admits of a rational and appropriate construction.

ARGUMENT III.

The constitution is to be construed in consistency with the Declaration of Independence, if possible, because the two instruments are the two great enactments of the same legislators — the people. They purport to have the same objects in view, viz., the security of their liberties. The Declaration had never been repealed, and legal rules require that an enactment later in time than another, more especially if the former one be not repealed, should be construed in consistency with the earlier one, if it reasonably can be, unless the earlier one be opposed to reason or justice.*

---

* Lord Mansfield says, "Where there are different statutes *in pari materia,* (upon the same subject,) though made at different times, or even expired, and not referring to each other, they shall be taken and *construed together,* as one system, and explanatory of each other." — 1 *Burrows,* 447.

"It is an established rule of construction, that statutes *in pari materia,* or upon the same subject, must be construed with reference to each other; that is, that what is clear in one statute, shall be called in aid to explain what is obscure and ambiguous in another." — 1 *Blackstone,* 60, *note;* 1 *Kent,* 462.

Rutherforth says, "In doubtful matters it is reasonable to presume that the same person is always in the same mind, when nothing appears to the contrary; that whatever was his design at one time, the same is likewise his design at another time, where no sufficient reason can be produced to prove an alteration of

ARGUMENT IV.

It is perfectly manifest, from all the evidence given in the preceding pages, (including Part First of the argument,) that the word "free," when used in laws and constitutions, to describe one class of persons, as distinguished from another living under the same laws or constitutions, is not sufficient, *of itself*, to imply slavery as its correlative. The word itself is wholly indefinite, as to the kind of restraint implied as its correlative.* And as slavery is the worst, it is necessarily the last, kind of restraint which the law will imply. There must be some other word, or provision, *in the instrument itself*, to warrant such an implication against the other class. But the constitution contains no such other word or provision. It contains nothing but the simple word "free." While, on the other hand, it is full of words and provisions, perfectly explicit, that imply the opposite of slavery.

Under such circumstances, there can be no question which construction we are legally bound to put upon the word in the constitution.†

---

it. If the words, therefore, of any writing, will admit of two or more different senses, when they are considered separately, but must necessarily be understood in one of these senses rather than the other, in order to make the writer's meaning agree with what he has spoken or written upon some other occasion, the reasonable presumption is, that this must be the sense in which he used them." — *Rutherforth, B.* 2, *ch.* 7, *p.* 331-2.

* See page 179.

† I doubt if a single instance can be found, even in the statutes of the slaveholding States themselves, *in force in* 1789, where the word *free* was used, (as the slave argument claims that it was used in the constitution,) to describe either white persons, or the mass of the people *other than slaves*, (that is, the white and free colored,) *as distinguished from the slaves*, unless the statute also contained the word *slave*, or some other evidence, beside the word *free* itself, that that was the sense in which the word *free* was used. If there were no such statute, it proves that, by the usage of legislation, in 1789, even in the slaveholding States themselves, the word *free* was insufficient, *of itself*, to imply slavery as its correlative.

I have not thought it necessary to verify this supposition, by an examination of the statute books of the States, because the labor would be considerable, and the fact is not necessary to my case. But if the fact be as I have supposed, it takes away the last shadow of pretence, founded on the usage of legislation at that day, that such was the sense in which the word *free* was used in the constitution. I commend to the advocates of slavery, (on whom rests the burthen of proving the meaning of the word,) the task of verifying or disproving the supposition.

ARGUMENT V.

Even if the word "free" were taken in the sense correlative with slaves, and if the words "importation of persons" were taken to authorize the importation of slaves, slavery would, nevertheless, *for the most part*, be now unconstitutional. The constitution would then sanction the slavery of only those individuals who were slaves at the adoption of the constitution, and those who were imported as slaves. It would give no authority whatever for the enslavement of any born in the country, after the adoption of the constitution.

The constitution is the supreme law of the land, and it operates "*directly on the people and for their benefit.*"* No State laws or constitutions can stand between it and the people, to ward off its benefits from them. Of course, it operates upon *all* the people, except those, if any, whom it has *itself* specially excepted from its operation. If it have excepted any from its operation, it has, *at most*, excepted only those particular individuals who were slaves at the adoption of the constitution, and those who should subsequently be imported as slaves. It has nowhere excepted any that should thereafter be born in the country. It has nowhere authorized Congress to pass laws excepting any who should be born in the country. It has nowhere authorized the States, or recognized the right of the States, to except from its operation any persons born in the country after its adoption. It has expressly *prohibited* the States from making any such exception; for it has said that *itself* "shall be the supreme law of the land," (operating "directly on the people, and for their benefit," the Supreme Court say,) "anything in the constitution or laws of any State to the contrary notwithstanding." If the States can say, previous to any one person's being born under the constitution, that, when born, the constitution shall not operate upon that person, or for his benefit, they may say in advance that it shall not operate upon, or for the benefit of, any person whatever who may be born under the constitution, and thus compel the United States government to die out, or fall into the hands of the naturalized citizens alone, for the want of any recruits from those born in the country.

---

* The Sup. Court United States say, of "the government of the Union," that 'its powers are granted by the people, *and are to be exercised directly on them*," (that is, upon them as individuals,) "*and for their benefit.*" — 4 *Wheaton*, 404, 405.

23*

If, then, the slavery of those who were slaves at the adoption of the constitution, and of those who have since been imported as slaves, were constitutional, the slavery of all born in the country since the adoption of the constitution, is, nevertheless, unconstitutional.*

CHAPTER XXIV.

POWER OF THE GENERAL GOVERNMENT OVER SLAVERY.

It is a common assertion that the general government has no power over slavery in the States. If by this be meant that the States may reduce to slavery the citizens of the United States within their limits, and the general government cannot liberate them, the doctrine is nullification, and goes to the destruction of the United States government within the limits of each State, whenever such State shall choose to destroy it.

The pith of the doctrine of nullification is this, viz., that a State has a right to interpose between her people and the United States government, deprive them of its benefits, protection, and laws, and annul their allegiance to it.

If a State have this power, she can of course abolish the government of the United States at pleasure, so far as its operation within her own territory is concerned; for the government of the United States is nothing, any further than it operates upon the persons, property, and rights of the people.† If the States can arbitrarily intercept this operation, can interpose between the people and the government and laws of the United States, they can of course abolish that government. And the United States constitution, and the laws made in pursuance thereof, instead of being "the supreme law of the land," "anything in the constitution or laws of any State to the contrary notwithstanding," are dependent entirely upon the will of the State governments for permission to be laws at all.

A State law reducing a man to slavery, would, if valid, interpose

* See *Chap.* 13.

† The Supreme Court of the United States say, the "powers" of the general government "*are to be exercised directly on the people, and for their benefit.*"—4 *Wheaton*, 205.

between him and the constitution and laws of the United States annul their operation, (so far as he is concerned,) and deprive him of their benefits. It would annul his allegiance to the United States; for a slave can owe no allegiance to a government that either will not, or cannot protect him.

If a State can do this in the case of one man, she can do it in the case of any number of men, and thus completely abolish the general government within her limits.

But perhaps it will be said that a State has no right to reduce to slavery the people *generally* within her limits, but only to hold in slavery those who were slaves at the adoption of the constitution, and their posterity.

One answer to this argument is, that, at the adoption of the constitution of the United States, there was no legal or constitutional slavery in the States. Not a single State constitution then in existence, recognized, authorized, or sanctioned slavery. All the slaveholding then practised was merely a private crime committed by one person against another, like theft, robbery, or murder. All the statutes which the slaveholders, through their wealth and influence, procured to be passed, were unconstitutional and void, for the want of any constitutional authority in the legislatures to enact them.

But perhaps it will be said, as is often said of them now, that the State governments *had all power that was not forbidden to them.* But this is only one of those bald and glaring falsehoods, under cover of which, even to this day, corrupt and tyrannical legislators enact, and the servile and corrupt courts, who are made dependent upon them, sustain, a vast mass of unconstitutional legislation, destructive of men's natural rights. Probably half the State legislation under which we live is of this character, and has no other authority than the pretence that the government has all power except what is prohibited to it. The falsehood of the doctrine is apparent the moment it is considered that our governments derive all their authority from the grants of the people. Of necessity, therefore, instead of their having all authority except what is forbidden, they can have none except what is granted.

Everybody admits that this is the true doctrine in regard to the United States government; and it is equally true of the State governments, and for the same reason. The United States constitution, (amendment 10,) does indeed specially provide that the U. S. government shall have no powers except what are delegated

to it.   But this amendment was inserted only as a special guard
against usurpation.   The government would have had no additional powers if this amendment had been omitted.   The simple
fact that all a government's powers are delegated to it by the people, proves that it can have no powers except what are delegated.
And this principle is as true of the State governments, as it is of
the national one; although it is one that is almost wholly disregarded in practice.*

The State governments in existence in 1789 purported to be
established by the people, and are either declared, or must be presumed, to have been established for the maintenance of justice, the
preservation of liberty, and the protection of their natural rights.
And those governments consequently had no constitutional authority whatever inconsistent with these ends, unless some *particular*
powers of that kind were *explicitly* granted to them.   No power
to establish or sustain slavery was granted to any of them.   All
the slave statutes, therefore, that were in existence in the States,
at the adoption of the United States constitution, were unconstitutional and void ; *and the people who adopted the constitution of the
United States must be presumed to have known this fact, and acted
upon it, because everybody is presumed to know the law.*   The
constitution of the United States, therefore, can be presumed to
have made no exceptions in favor of the slavery then existing in
the States.†

But suppose, for the sake of the argument, that slavery had been
authorized by the State constitutions at the time the United States
constitution was adopted, the constitution of the United States
would nevertheless have made it illegal ; because the United States
constitution was made " the supreme law of the land," "anything

---

* The doctrine that the government has all power except what is prohibited to it,
is of despotic origin.   Despotic government is supposed to originate, and does in
fact originate, with the despot, instead of the people ; and he claims all power over
them except what they have from time to time wrested from him.   It is a consistent doctrine that such governments have all power except what is prohibited to
them.   But where the government originates with the people, precisely the opposite doctrine is true, viz., that the government has no power except what is granted
to it.

† If, however, they had *not* known that the existing slavery was unconstitutional,
and had proceeded upon the mistaken belief that it was constitutional, and had
intended to recognize it as being so, such intended recognition would have availed
nothing ; for it is an established principle, recognized by the Supreme Court of
the United States, that "a legislative act, founded upon a mistaken opinion of
what was law, does not change the actual state of the law, as to pre-existing
cases."— 1 *Cranch*, 1 ; *Peter's Digest*, 573.

in the constitution or laws of any State to the contrary notwith-standing." It therefore annulled everything inconsistent with it, *then existing* in the State constitutions, as well as everything that should ever after be added to them, inconsistent with it. It of course abolished slavery as a legal institution, (supposing slavery to have had any legal existence to be abolished,) if slavery were inconsistent with anything expressed, or legally implied, in the constitution.

Slavery is inconsistent with nearly everything that is either expressed or legally implied in the constitution. All its express provisions are general, making no exception whatever for slavery. All its legal *implications* are that the constitution and laws of the United States are for the benefit of the *whole* "people of the United States," and their posterity.

The preamble expressly declares that " We the people of the United States" establish the constitution for the purpose of secur-ing justice, tranquillity, defence, welfare, and liberty, to " ourselves and our posterity." This language certainly implies that all " the people" who are parties to the constitution, or join in establishing it, are to have the benefit of it, and of the laws made in pursuance of it. The only question, then, is, who were " the people of the United States ?"

We cannot go out of the constitution to find who are the parties to it. And there is nothing in the constitution that can limit this word " people," so as to make it include a part, only, of " the peo-ple of the United States." The word, like all others, must be taken in the sense most beneficial for liberty and justice. Be-sides, if it did not include *all* the then " people of the United States," we have no *legal* evidence whatever of a single individual whom it did include. There is no legal evidence whatever in the constitution, by which it can be proved that any one man was one of " the people," which will not also equally prove that the slaves were a part of the people. There is nothing in the constitution that can prove the slaveholders to have been a part of " the peo-ple," which will not equally prove the slaves to have been also a part of them. And there is as much authority in the constitution for excluding slaveholders from the description, " the people of the United States," as there is for excluding the slaves. The term " the people of the United States " must therefore be held to have included *all* " the people of the United States," or it can legally be held to have included none.

But this point has been so fully argued already, that it need not be dwelt upon here.*

The United States government, then, being in theory formed by, and for the benefit of, the whole " people of the United States," the question arises, whether it have the power of securing to " the people " the benefits it intended for them? Or whether it is dependent on the State governments *for permission* to confer these benefits on " the people?" This is the whole question. And if it shall prove that the general government has no power of securing to the people its intended benefits, it is, in no legal or reasonable sense, a government.

But *how* is it to secure its benefits to the people? That is the question.

The first step, and an indispensable step, towards doing it, is to secure to the people their personal liberty. Without personal liberty, none of the other benefits intended by the constitution can be secured to an individual, because, without liberty, no one can prosecute his other rights in the tribunals appointed to secure them to him. If, therefore, the constitution had failed to secure the personal liberty of individuals, all the rest of its provisions might have been defeated at the pleasure of the subordinate governments. But liberty being secured, all the other benefits of the constitution are secured, because the individual can then carry the question of his rights into the courts of the United States, in all cases where the laws or constitution of the United States are involved.

This right of personal liberty, this *sine qua non* to the enjoyment of all other rights, is secured by the writ of *habeas corpus*. This writ, as has before been shown, necessarily denies the right of property in man, and therefore liberates all who are restrained of their liberty on that pretence, as it does all others that are restrained on grounds inconsistent with the intended operation of the constitution and laws of the United States.

Next after providing for the " public safety, in cases of rebellion and invasion," the maintenance of courts for dispensing the privileges of this writ is the duty first in order, and first in importance, of all the duties devolved upon the general government; because, next after life, liberty is the right most important in itself; it is also indispensable to the enjoyment of all the other rights which

---

* See Part First, pages 90 to 94, sec. edition. Also the argument under the " Sixth Rule of Interpretation," p. 182 to 189 of this part, and under the " Second Rule cited for Slavery," p. 214 to 216.

the general government is established to secure to the people.   All the other operations of government, then, are works of mere supererogation until liberty be first secured; they are nothing but a useless provision of good things for those who cannot partake of them.

As the government is bound to dispense its benefits impartially to all, it is bound, first of all, after securing "the public safety, in cases of rebellion and invasion," to secure liberty to all.   And the whole power of the government is bound to be exerted for this purpose, *to the postponement, if need be,* of everything else save "the public safety, in cases of rebellion and invasion." And it is the constitutional duty of the government to establish as many courts as may be necessary, (no matter how great the number,) and to adopt all other measures necessary and proper, for bringing the means of liberation within the reach of every person who is restrained of his liberty in violation of the principles of the constitution.*

We have thus far, (in this chapter,) placed this question upon the ground that those held in slavery are constitutionally a part of " the people of the United States," and parties to the constitution. But, although this ground cannot be shaken, it is not necessary to be maintained, in order to maintain the duty of Congress to provide courts, and all other means necessary, for their liberation.

The constitution, by providing for the writ of *habeas corpus,* without making any discrimination as to the persons entitled to it, has virtually declared, and thus established it as a constitutional principle, that, in this country, there can be no property in man; for the writ of *habeas corpus,* as has before been shown,† necessarily involves a denial of the right of property in man.   By declaring that the privilege of this writ " shall not be suspended, unless when, in cases of rebellion or invasion the public safety may require it," the constitution has imposed upon Congress the duty of providing courts, and if need be, other aids, for the issuing of this writ in behalf of all human beings within the United States, who may be restrained on claim of being property.   Congress are

---

* It is not necessary, as some imagine, for Congress to enact a law *making* slavery illegal.   Congress have no such power.   Such a power would imply that slavery was now legal.   Whereas it is now as much illegal as it is possible to be made by all the legislation in the world.   Congress, *assuming* that slavery is illegal, are constitutionally bound to provide all necessary means for having that principle maintained in practice.

† *Part First, ch. 8, p.* 101, 2d ed.

bound by the constitution to aid, if need be, a foreigner, an alien, an enemy even, who may be restrained as property. And if the people of any of the civilized nations were now to be seized as slaves, on their arrival in this country, we can all imagine what an abundance of constitutional power would be found, and put forth, too, for their liberation.

Without this power, the nation could not sustain its position as one of the family of civilized nations; it could not fulfil the law of nations, and would therefore be liable to be outlawed in consequence of the conduct of the States. For example. If the States can make slaves of anybody, they can certainly make slaves of foreigners. And if they can make slaves of foreigners, they can violate the law of nations; because to make slaves of foreigners, is to violate the law of nations. Now the general government is the only government known to other nations; and if the States can make slaves of foreigners, and there were no power in the general government to liberate them, any one of the States could involve the whole nation in the responsibility of having violated the law of nations, and the nation would have no means of relieving itself from that responsibility by liberating the persons enslaved; but would have to meet, and conquer or die in, a war brought upon it by the criminality of the State.

This illustration is sufficient to prove that the power of the general government to liberate men from slavery, by the use of the writ of *habeas corpus*, is of the amplest character; that it is not confined to the cases of those who are a part of " the people of the United States," and so parties to the constitution; that it is limited only by the territory of the country; and that it exists utterly irrespective of " anything in the constitution or laws of any State."

This power, which is bound to be exerted for the liberation of foreigners, is bound to be exerted also for the liberation of persons born on the soil, even though it could be proved, (which it cannot.) that they are *not* legally parties to the constitution. The simple fact of their not being parties to the constitution, (if that fact were proved,) would no more alter the power or duty of Congress in relation to securing them the privilege of the writ of *habeas corpus*, than the same fact does in the case of foreigners, who confessedly are not parties to the constitution; unless, indeed, their coming into the country under the guaranty afforded by the *habeas corpus* clause of the constitution makes them, *so far*, parties to it. Bu this clause could operate as no guaranty of liberty to foreigners, unless it guarantied liberty to *all* born on the soil : for, there being no distinction of persons made, it certainly could not be claimed that it guarantied greater privileges to foreigners than to the *least favored* of those born on the soil. So that it will still result that, unless the constitution, (as it may be executed by the general government alone,) guaranties personal liberty to all born in the country, it does not guaranty it to foreigners coming into the country ; and if it do not guaranty it to foreigners coming into the country, any single State, by enslaving foreigners, can involve the whole nation in a death struggle in support of such slavery.

If these opinions are correct, it is the constitutional duty of Congress to establish courts, if need be, in every county and township even, where there are slaves to be liberated ; to provide attorneys to bring the cases before the courts ; and to keep a standing military force, if need be, to sustain the proceedings.

In addition to the use of the *habeas corpus*, Congress have power to prohibit the slave trade between the States, which, of itself, would do much towards abolishing slavery in the northern slaveholding States. They have power also to organize, arm, and discipline the slaves as militia, thus enabling them to aid in obtaining and securing their own liberty.

24

APPENDIX A.

FUGITIVE SLAVES.

[THE following article was first published in 1850, as an appendix to an argument, entitled "A DEFENCE FOR FUGITIVE SLAVES, *against the Acts of Congress of February,* 12, 1793 *and September* 18, 1850. *By* LYSANDER SPOONER." It repeats some ideas already advanced in the preceding pages; but, as it is mostly new, it has been thought worthy of preservation by being included in this volume.]

NEITHER THE CONSTITUTION, NOR EITHER OF THE ACTS OF CONGRESS OF 1793 OR 1850, REQUIRES THE SURRENDER OF FUGITIVE SLAVES.

IN the preceding chapters it has been admitted, for the sake of the argument, that the constitution, and acts of Congress of 1793 and 1850, require the delivery of Fugitive Slaves. But such really is not the fact. Neither the constitutional provision, nor either of said acts of Congress, uses the word slave, nor slavery, nor any language that can *legally* be made to apply to slaves. The only "person" required by the constitution to be delivered up is described in the constitution as a "person *held* to service or labor in one state, under the laws thereof." This language is no legal description of a slave, and can be made to apply to a slave only by a violation of all the most imperative rules of interpretation by which the meaning of all legal instruments is to be ascertained.

The word "held" is a material word, in this description. Its legal meaning is synonymous with that of the words "bound," and "obliged." It is used in bonds, as synonymous with those words, and in no other sense. It is also used in laws, and other legal instruments. *And its legal meaning is to describe persons held by some legal contract, obligation, duty, or authority, which the law will enforce.* Thus, in a bond, a man acknowledges himself "*held,* and firmly bound and obliged" to do certain things mentioned in the bond, — and the law will compel a fulfilment of the obligation. The laws "hold" men to do various things; and by holding them to do those things is meant that the laws will compel them to do them. Wherever a person is described in the laws as being "*held*" to do anything, — as to render "service or labor," for example, — the legal meaning *invariably* is that he is held by some *legal* contract, obligation, duty, or authority, which the laws will enforce, — (either specifically, or by compelling payment of damages for non-performance.) I presume no single instance can be found, in any of the laws of this country, since its first settlement, in which the word "held" is used in any other than this legal sense, when used to describe a person who is "*held*" *to do anything* "under the laws." And such is its meaning, *and its only meaning,* in this clause of the constitution. If there could be a doubt on this point, that doubt would be removed by the additional words, "under the laws," and the word "due," as applied to the "service or labor," to which the person is "held."

Now, a slave is not "held" by any legal contract, obligation, duty, or authority, which the laws will enforce. He is "held" only by brute force. One person boats another until the latter will obey him, work for him if he require it, or do nothing if he require it. This is slavery, and the whole of it. This is the only manner in which a slave is "*held* to service or labor."

The laws recognize no obligation on the part of the slave to labor for or serve his master If he refuse to labor, the law will not interfere to compel him. The master must do his own flogging, as in the case of an ox or a horse. The laws take no more cognizance of the fact whether a slave labors or not, than they do of the fact whether an ox or a horse labors

A slave, then, is no more "held" to labor, in any *legal* sense, than a man would be in Massachusetts, whom another person should seize and beat until he reduced him to subjection and obedience. If such a man should escape from his oppressor, and take refuge in Carolina, he could not be claimed under this clause of the constitution, because he would not be "held" in any *legal* sense, (that is, by any legal contract, obligation, duty, or authority,) but only by brute force. And the same is the case in regard to slaves.*

It is an established rule of legal interpretation, that a word used in laws, to describe *legal* rights, must be taken in a *legal* sense. This rule is as imperative in the interpretation of the constitution as of any other legal instrument. To prove this, let us take another example. The constitution (Art. I. Sec. 6) provides that "for any speech or debate in either house, they (the senators and representatives) *shall not be questioned* in any other place." Now, this provision imposes no restriction whatever upon the senators and representatives being "questioned for any speech or debate," by anybody and everybody, who may please to question them, or in any and every place, with this single exception, that they must not "be questioned" *legally*, — that is, they must not be held to any *legal* accountability.

It would be no more absurd to construe this provision about *questioning* senators and representatives, so as to make it forbid the people, in their private capacity, to ask any questions of their senators and representatives, on their return from Congress, as to their doings there, instead of making it apply to a *legal* responsibility, than it is to construe the words "held to service or labor" as applied to a

---

* In a speech, in the Senate of the United States, upon the Fugitive Slave bill, so called, on the 19th day of August, 1850, (as reported in the Washington Union and National Intelligencer,) senator Mason, of Virginia, the chairman of the committee that reported the bill, and the principal champion of the bill in the Senate, in describing "the actual evils under which the slave States labor in reference to the reclamation of these fugitives," said :

"Then, again, it is proposed [by one of the opponents of the bill], as a part of the proof to be adduced at the hearing, after the fugitive has been recaptured, that evidence shall be brought by the claimant to show that slavery is established in the state from which the fugitive has absconded. Now, this very thing, in a recent case in the city of New York, was required by one of the judges of that state, which case attracted the attention of the authorities of Maryland, and against which they protested, because of the indignities heaped upon their citizens, and the losses which they sustained in that city. In that case, the judge of the state court required proof that slavery was established in Maryland, and went so far as to say that the only mode of proving it was by reference to the statute-book. Such proof is required in the senator's amendment ; and, if he means by this that proof shall be brought that slavery is established by existing laws, *it is impossible to comply with the requisition, for no such proof can be produced, I apprehend, in any of the slave states. I am not aware that there is a single state in which the institution is established by positive law.* On a former occasion, and on a different topic, it was my duty to endeavor to show to the senate that no such law was necessary for its establishment ; *certainly none could be found, and none was required, in any of the states of the Union.*"

I am confident that Mr Calhoun made the same admission within two or three years last past, but I have not the paper containing it at hand.

It was only by such a naked and daring fraud as this that the court could make the constitution authorize the recovery of fugitive slaves.

And what were the rules of interpretation which they thus discarded, "in order to clear the case of difficulty," and make the constitution subserve the purposes of slavery? One of them is this, laid down by the Supreme Court of the United States:

"The intention of the instrument must prevail; *this intention must be collected from its words.*" — 12 *Wheaton*, 332.

Without an adherence to this rule, it is plain we could never know what was, and what was not, the constitution.

Another rule is that universal one, acknowledged by all courts to be imperative, *that language must be construed strictly in favor of liberty and justice.*

The Supreme Court of the United States have laid down this rule in these strong terms:

"Where rights are infringed, where fundamental principles are overthrown, where the general system of the laws is departed from, the legislative intention must be expressed with *irresistible clearness*, to induce a court of justice to suppose a design to effect such objects." — *United States* vs. *Fisher*, 2 *Cranch*, 390.

Story delivered this opinion of the court, (in the Prigg case,) discarding all other rules of interpretation, and resorting to history to make the clause apply to slaves. And yet no judge has ever scouted more contemptuously than Story the idea of going out of the words of a law, or the constitution, and being governed by what history may say were the intentions of the authors. He says:

"Such a doctrine would be novel and absurd. It would confuse and destroy all the tests of constitutional rights and authorities. Congress could never pass any law without an inquisition into the motives of every member; and even then they might be reexaminable. Besides, what possible means can there be of making such investigations? The motives of many of the members may be, nay, must be, utterly unknown, and incapable of ascertainment by any judicial or other inquiry; they may be mixed up in various manners and degrees; they may be opposite to, or wholly independent of, each other. The constitution would thus depend upon processes utterly vague and incomprehensible; and the written intent of the legislature upon its words and acts, the *lex scripta*, would be contradicted or obliterated by conjecture, and parole declarations, and fleeting reveries, and heated imaginations. No government on earth could rest for a moment on such a foundation. It would be a constitution of sand, heaped up and dissolved by the flux and reflux of every tide of opinion. Every act of the legislature [and, for the same reason also, every clause of the constitution] must, therefore, be judged of from its objects and intent, as they are embodied in its provisions." — 2 *Story's Comm.*, 531.

Also, he says.

"The constitution was adopted by the people of the United States; and it was submitted to the whole, upon a just survey of its provisions, as they stood in the text itself. * * Opposite interpretations, and different explanations of different provisions, may well be presumed to have been presented in different bodies, to remove local objections, or to win local favor. And there can be no certainty either that the different state conventions, in ratifying the constitution, gave the same uniform interpretation to its language, or that, even in a single state convention, the same reasoning prevailed with a majority, much less with the whole, of the supporters of it. * * It is not to be presumed that even in the convention which framed the constitution, from the causes above mentioned, and other causes, the clauses were always understood in the same sense, or had precisely the same extent of operation. Every member necessarily judged for himself; and the judgment of no one could, or ought to be, conclusive upon that of others. * * * *Nothing but the text itself was adopted by the people.* * * *Is the sense of the constitution to be ascertained, not by its own text, but by the 'probable meaning' to be* gathered by conjectures from scattered documents, from private papers, from the table-talk of some statesmen, or the jealous exaggerations of others ? Is the constitution of the United States to be the only instrument which is not to be interpreted by what is written, but by probable guesses, aside from the text ? What would be said of interpreting a statute of a state legislature by endeavoring to find out, from private sources, the objects and opinions of every member ; how every one thought ; what he wished ; how he interpreted it ? Suppose different persons had different opinions, — what is to be done ? Suppose different persons are not agreed as to the ' probable meaning' of the framers, or of the people, — what interpretation is to be followed ? These, and many questions of the same sort, might be asked. *It is obvious that there can be no security to the people in any constitution of government, if they are not to judge of it by the fair meaning of the words of the text, but the words are to be bent and broken by the 'probable meaning' of persons whom they never knew, and whose opinions, and means of information, may be no better than their own ? The people adopted the constitution according to the words of the text in their reasonable interpretation, and not according to the private interpretation of any particular men.*" — 1 *Story's Comm. on Const.*, 287 *to* 392.

And Story has said much more of the same sort, as to the absurdity of relying upon " history " for the meaning of the constitution.

It is manifest that, if the meaning of the constitution is to be warped in the least, it may be warped to any extent, on the authority of history ; and thus it would follow that the constitution would, in reality, be *made* by the historians, and not by the people. It would be impossible for the people to make a constitution which the historians might not change at pleasure, by simply asserting that the people intended thus or so.

But, in truth, Story and the court, in saying that history tells us that the clause of the constitution in question was intended to apply to fugitive slaves, are nearly as false to the history of the clause as they are to its law.

There is not, I presume, a word on record (for I have no recollection of having ever seen or heard of one) that was uttered, either in the national convention that framed the constitution, or in any *northern* state convention that ratified it, that shows that, *at the time the constitution was adopted,* any *northern* man had the least suspicion that the clause of the constitution in regard to " persons held to service or labor " was ever to be applied to slaves.

In the national convention, " Mr. Butler and Mr. Pinckney moved to require ' fugitive *slaves* and *servants* to be delivered up like criminals.' " " Mr. Sherman saw no more propriety in the public seizing and surrendering a *slave or servant* than a horse." — *Madison papers*, 1447—8.

In consequence of this objection, the provision was changed, and its language, as it now stands, shows that the claim to the surrender of *slaves* was abandoned, and only the one for *servants* retained.*

It does not appear that a word was ever uttered, *in the National Convention,* to show that any member of it imagined that the provision, *as finally agreed upon,* would apply to slaves.

But, after the national convention had adjourned, Mr. Madison and Mr. Randolph went home to Virginia, and Mr. Pinckney to South Carolina, and, in the *state* conventions of those states, set up the pretence that the clause was intended to apply to slaves. I think there is no evidence that any other southern member of the national convention followed their example. In North Carolina, Mr. Iredell (not

---

* *Servants* were, at that time, a very numerous class in all the states ; and there were many laws respecting them, all treating them as a distinct class from slaves.

segment281APPENDIX A.

person held simply by brute force, (as in the case supposed in Massachusetts,) instead of persons held by some legal contract, obligation, or duty, which the law will enforce.

As the slave, then, is " held to service or labor " by no contract, obligation, or duty, which the law will enforce, but only by the brute force of the master, the provision of the constitution in regard to " persons held to service or labor " can have no more legal application to him than to the person supposed in Massachusetts, who should at one time be beaten into obedience, and afterwards escape into Carolina.

The word " *held* " being, in law, synonymous with the word " *bound*," the description, " person *held* to service or labor," is synonymous with the description in another section, (Art. 1, Sec. 2,) to wit, " those *bound* to service for a term of years." The addition, in the one case, of the words " for a term of years," does not alter the meaning ; for it does not appear that, in the other case, they are " held " beyond a fixed term.

In fact, everybody, courts and people, admit that " persons *bound* to service for a term of years," as apprentices, and other indented servants, are to be delivered up under the provision relative to " persons *held* to service or labor." The word " *held*," then, is regarded as synonymous with " *bound*," whenever it is wished to deliver up " persons *bound* to service." If, then, it be synonymous with the word " *bound*," it applies only to persons who are " *bound* " in a *legal* sense, — that is, by some *legal* contract, obligation, or duty, which the law will enforce. The words cannot be stretched beyond their *necessary* and proper *legal* meaning ; because all legal provisions in derogation of liberty must be construed strictly. The same words that are used to describe a " person held to service or labor " by a *legal* contract, or obligation, certainly cannot be legally construed to include also one who is " held " only by private violence, and brute force.

Mr. Webster, in his speech of March 7th, 1850, admits that the word " held " is synonymous with the word " bound," and that the language of the constitution itself contains no requirement for the surrender of fugitive slaves. He says :

" It may not be improper here to allude to that — I had almost said celebrated — opinion of Mr. Madison. *You observe, sir, that the term slavery is not used in the constitution. The constitution does not require that fugitive slaves shall be delivered up; it requires that persons bound to service in one state, and escaping into another, shall be delivered up.* Mr. Madison opposed the introduction of the term slave or slavery into the constitution ; for he said he did not wish to see it recognized by the constitution of the United States of America that there could be property in men."

Had the constitution required only that " persons *bound* to service or labor " should be delivered up, it is evident that no one would claim that the provision applied to slaves. Yet it is perfectly evident, also, that the word " held " is simply synonymous with the word " bound."

One can hardly fail to be astonished at the ignorance, fatuity, cowardice, or corruption, that has ever induced the North to acknowledge, for an instant, any constitutional obligation to surrender fugitive slaves.

The Supreme Court of the United States, in the Prigg case, (the first case in which this clause of the constitution ever came under the adjudication of that court,) made no pretence that the *language itself* of the constitution afforded any justification for a claim to a fugitive slave. On the contrary, they made the audacious and atrocious avowal, that, for the sole purpose of *making* the clause apply to slaves, they would disregard — as they acknowledged themselves *obliged* to disre-

24*

gard — all the primary, established and imperative rules of legal interpretation.
and be governed solely by the history of men's intentions, outside of the constitution.
Thus they say :

" Before, however, we proceed to the points more immediately before us, it may
be well — *in order to clear the case of difficulty* — to say that, in the exposition of
this part of the constitution, we shall limit ourselves to those considerations which
appropriately and exclusively belong to it, without laying down any rules of interpretation of a more general nature. It will, indeed, probably, be found, when we
look to the character of the constitution itself, the objects which it seeks to attain,
the powers which it confers, the duties which it enjoins, and the rights which it
secures, as well as the known *historical* fact that many of its provisions were matters of compromise of opposing interests and opinions, *that no uniform rule of interpretation can be applied to it, which may not allow, even if it does not positively demand,
many modifications in its actual application to particular clauses.* And perhaps the
safest rule of interpretation, after all, will be found to be to look to the nature and
objects of the particular powers, duties, and rights, with all the lights and aids of
contemporary history; and to give to the words of each just such operation and force,
consistent with their legitimate meaning, as may fairly secure and attain the ends
proposed. * * * *Historically,* it is well known that the object of this clause
was to secure to the citizens of the slaveholding states the complete right and title
of ownership in their slaves, as property, in every state in the Union into which
they might escape from the state where they were held in servitude." — 16
Peters, 610—11.

Thus it will be seen that, on the strength of *history alone,* they *assume* that
" *many of the provisions of the constitution were matters of compromise* " (that is, in
regard to slavery); but they admit that the words of those provisions cannot be
made to express any such compromise, if they are interpreted according to any
" *uniform rule of interpretation,*" or " *any rules of interpretation of a more general
nature* " than the mere history of those particular clauses. Hence, " *in order to
clear the case of (that) difficulty,*" they conclude that "*perhaps the safest rule of interpretation, after all, will be found to be to look to the nature and objects of the particular
powers, duties, and rights, with all the lights and aids of contemporary history; and to
give to the words of each just such operation and force,* consistent with their legitimate
meaning, *as may fairly secure and attain the ends proposed.*"

The words " *consistent with their legitimate meaning* " contain a deliberate falsehood, thrown in by the court from no other motive than the hope to hide, in some
measure, the fraud they were perpetrating. If it had been "*consistent with the
legitimate meaning of the words* " of the clause to apply them to slaves, there would
have been no necessity for discarding, as they did, all the authoritative and inflexible rules of legal interpretation, and resorting to *history* to find their meaning.
They discarded those rules, and resorted to history, to make the clause apply to
slaves, for no other reason whatever than that such meaning was *not* " consistent
with the legitimate meaning of the words." It is perfectly apparent that the
moment their eyes fell upon the " words " of the clause, they all saw that they
contained no legal description of slaves.

Stripped, then, of the covering which that falsehood was intended to throw over
their conduct, the plain English of the language of the court is this : that *history*
tells us that certain clauses of the constitution were intended to recognize and
support slavery ; but, inasmuch as such is not the legal meaning of the words of
those clauses, if interpreted by the established rules of interpretation, we will, " *in
order to clear the case of (that) difficulty,*" just discard those rules, and pervert the
words so as to *make* them accomplish whatever ends *history* tells us were intended
to be accomplished by them.

a member of the national convention) said the provision was intended to refer to slaves ; but that " the northern delegates, owing to their particular scruples on the subject of slavery, did not choose the word *slave* to be mentioned."

I think the declarations of these four men — Madison, Randolph, Pinckney, and Iredell — are all the "*history*" we have, that even *southern* men, *at that time*, understood the clause as applying to slaves.

In the *northern* conventions no word was ever uttered, so far as we have any evidence, that any man dreamed that this language would ever be understood as authorizing a claim for fugitive slaves. It is incredible that it could have passed the northern conventions without objection, (indeed, it could not have passed them at all,) if it had been understood as requiring them to surrender fugitive slaves ; for, in several of them, it was with great difficulty that the adoption of the constitution was secured when no such objection was started.

The construction placed upon the provision at the present day is one of the many frauds which the slaveholders, aided by their corrupt northern accomplices, have succeeded in palming off upon the north. In fact, the south, in the convention, as it has ever done since, acted upon the principle of getting by fraud what it could not openly obtain. It was upon this principle that Mr. Madison acted when he said that they ought not to admit, *in the constitution*, the idea that there could be property in man. He would not admit that idea *in the constitution itself* ; but he immediately went home, and virtually told the state convention that that was the meaning which he intended to have given to it in practice. He knew well that if that idea were admitted in the instrument itself, the north would never adopt it. He therefore conceived and adhered to the plan of having the instrument an honest and free one in its terms, to secure its adoption by the north, and of then trusting to the fraudulent interpretations that could be accomplished afterward, to make it serve the purposes of slavery.

Further proof of his fraudulent purpose, in this particular, is found in the fact that he wrote the forty-second number of the Federalist, in which he treats of " the powers which provide for the harmony and proper intercourse among the states." But he makes no mention of the surrender of fugitives from " service or labor," as one of the means of promoting that " harmony and proper intercourse." He did not then dare say to the *north* that the south intended ever to apply that clause to slaves.

But it is said that the passage of the act of 1793 shows that the north understood the constitution as requiring the surrender of fugitive slaves. That act is supposed to have passed without opposition from the north ; and the reason was that it contained no authority for, or allusion to, the surrender of fugitive *slaves ;* but only to fugitives from *justice,* and " persons held to service or labor." The south had not at that time become sufficiently audacious to make such a demand. And it was twenty-three years, so far as I have discovered, (and I have made reasonable search in the matter,) after the passage of that act, before a slave was given up, *under it,* in any *free* state, or the act was acknowledged, by the Supreme Court of any *free* state, to apply to slaves.

In 1795, two years after the passage of the act of Congress, and after the constitution had been in force six years, a man was tried in the Supreme Court of Pennsylvania, on an indictment, under a statute of the state, against seducing or carrying negroes or mulattoes out of the state, with the intention to sell them, or keep them, as slaves.

" Upon the evidence in support of the prosecution, it appeared that negro Toby had been brought upon a temporary visit to Philadelphia, as a servant in the family of General Sevier, of the State of Virginia ; that, when General Sevier proposed returning to Virginia, the negro refused to accompany him ;" but was afterwards *forcibly* carried out of the state. It appeared also, in evidence, that it was *proposed* by Richards, the defendant, that the negro be *enticed* into New Jersey, (a slave state,) and there seized and carried back to Virginia.

"The evidence on behalf of the defendant proved that Toby was a slave, belonging to the father of General Sevier, who had lent him to his son merely for the journey to Philadelphia."

The defendant was found *not guilty*, agreeably to the charge of the Chief Justice; and what is material is, that the case was tried wholly under the laws of Pennsylvania, which permitted any traveller who came into Pennsylvania, upon a temporary excursion for business or amusement, to detain his slave *for six months*, and entitled him to the aid of the civil police to secure and carry him away. — *Respublica* vs. *Richards*, 2 *Dallas*, 224.

Not one word was said, by either court or counsel, of the provision of the United States constitution in regard to "persons held to service or labor," or the act of 1793, as having any application to slaves, or as giving any authority for the recovery of fugitive slaves. Neither the constitution nor the act of Congress was mentioned in connection with the subject.

Is it not incredible that this should have been the case, if it had been understood, at that day, that either the constitution or the act of 1793 applied to slaves ? Would a man have used force in the case, and thus subjected himself to the risk of an indictment under the state laws ? or would there have been any proposition to entice the slave into a slave state, for the purpose of seizing him, if it had been understood that the laws of the United States were open to him, and that every justice of the peace (as provided by the act of 1793) was authorized to deliver up the slave ?

It cannot reasonably be argued that it was necessary to use force or fraud to take the slave back, for the reason that he had been *brought*, instead of having *escaped*, into Pennsylvania ; for that distinction seems not to have been thought of until years after. The first mention I have found of it was in 1806. — *Butler* vs. *Hopper*, 1 *Washington*, C. C. R. 499.

In 1812 it was first acknowledged by the Supreme Court of New York that the act of 1793 applied to slaves, although no slave was given up at the time. But New York then had slaves of her own. — *Glen* vs. *Hodges*, 9 *Johnson*, 67.

In 1817 the Supreme Court of Pennsylvania first acknowledged that the constitution and the act of 1793 applied to slaves. But no slave was then given up. — *Commonwealth* vs. *Holloway*, 2 *Sargent and Rawle*, 305.

In 1823 the Supreme Court of Massachusetts first acknowledged that the constitutional provision in regard to "persons held to service or labor" applied to slaves. — *Commonwealth* vs. *Griffith*, 2 *Pickering*, 11.

Few, if any, slaves have ever been given up under the act of 1793, in the free states, until within the last twenty or thirty years. And the fact furnishes ground for a strong presumption that, during the first thirty years after the constitution went into operation, it was not generally understood, in the free states, that the constitution required the surrender of fugitive slaves.

But, it is said that the ordinance of 1787, passed contemporaneously with the formation of the constitution, requires the delivery of fugitive slaves, and that tho constitution ought to be taken in tho same sense. The answer to this allegation is, that the ordinance does *not* require the delivery of fugitive slaves, but only of persons " from whom service or labor is lawfully claimed." This language, certainly, is no legal description of a slave.

But beyond, and additional to, all this evidence, that the constitution does not require the surrender of fugitive slaves, is the conclusive and insuperable fact, that there is not now, nor ever has been, any legal or constitutional slavery in this country, from its first settlement. All the slavery that has ever existed, in any of the colonies or states, has existed by mere toleration, in defiance of the fundamental constitutional law.

Even the statutes on the subject have either wholly failed to declare who might and who might not be made slaves, or have designated them in so loose and imperfect a manner, that it would probably be utterly impossible, at this day, to prove, under those statutes, the slavery of a single person now living. Mr. Mason admits as much, in the extracts already given from his speech.

But all the statutes on that subject, whatever the terms, have been unconstitutional, whether passed under the colonial charters, or since under the state governments. They were unconstitutional under the colonial charters, because those charters required the legislation of the colonies to " be conformable, as nearly as circumstances would allow, to the laws, customs and rights, of the realm of England." Those charters were the fundamental constitutions of the colonies, and, of course, made slavery illegal in the colonies, — inasmuch as slavery was inconsistent with the "laws, customs, and rights, of the realm of England.*

There was, therefore, no legal slavery in this country so long as we were colonies, — that is, up to the time of the Revolution.

After the Declaration of Independence, new constitutions were established in eleven of the states. Two went on under their old charters. Of all the new constitutions that were in force at the adoption of the constitution of the United States in 1789, not one authorized, recognized or sanctioned, slavery.† *All the recog-*

---

* Washburn, in his " Judicial History of Massachusetts," (p. 202,) says :

" As early as 1770, and two years previous to the decision of Somersett's case, so famous in England, the right of a master to hold a slave had been denied, by the Superior Court of Massachusetts, and upon the same grounds, substantially, as those upon which Lord Mansfield discharged Somersett, when his case came before him. The case here alluded to was James *vs.* Lechmere, brought by the plaintiff, a negro, against his master, to recover his freedom."

† Perhaps it may be claimed by some that the constitution of South Carolina was an exception to this rule. By that constitution it was provided that the qualifications of members of the Senate and House of Representatives " *shall be the same as mentioned in the election act.*"

"The election act " was an act of the Provincial Assembly, passed in 1759, which provided that members of the Assembly "shall have in this province a settled plantation, or freehold estate, of at least five hundred acres of land, *and twenty slaves.*"

But this act was necessarily void, so far as the requirement in regard to slaves was concerned ; because, slavery being repugnant to the laws of England, it could have no legal existence in the colony, which was restricted from making any laws, except such as were conformable, as nearly as circumstances would allow, to the laws, statutes, and rights, of the realm of England.

This part of the act, then, being void at the time it was passed, and up to the time of the adoption of the constitution of the state, the provision in that constitution could not legally be held to give force *to this part of the act.* Besides, there could be no slaves, *legally speaking,* in 1778, for the act to refer to.

nitions of slavery that are now to be found in any of the state constitutions, have been inserted since the adoption of the constitution of the United States.

There was, therefore, no legal or constitutional slavery, in any of the states, up to the time of the formation and adoption of the constitution of the United States, in 1787 and 1789.

There being no legal slavery in the country at the adoption of the constitution of the United States, all " the people of the United States " became legally parties to that instrument, and, of course, members of the United States government, by its adoption. The constitution itself declares, that " We, the people of the United States, * * do ordain and establish this constitution." The term " people," of necessity, includes the whole people ; no exception being made, none can be presumed ; for such a presumption would be a presumption against liberty.

After " the people " of the whole country had become parties to the constitution of the United States, their rights, as members of the United States government, were secured by it, and they could not afterwards be enslaved by the state governments ; for the constitution of the United States is " the supreme law," (operating " directly on the people, and for their benefit," says the Supreme Court, 4 *Wheaton*, 404—5,) and necessarily secures to *all* the people individually all the rights it intended to secure to any ; and these rights are such as are incompatible with their being enslaved by subordinate governments.

But it will be said that the constitution of the United States itself recognizes slavery, to wit, in the provision requiring " the whole number of *free* persons," and " three-fifths of all other persons," to be counted, in making up the basis of representation and taxation. But this interpretation of the word " free " is only another of the fraudulent interpretations which the slaveholders and their northern accomplices have succeeded in placing upon the constitution.

The legal and technical meaning of the word " free," as used in England for centuries, has been to designate a native or naturalized member of the state, as distinguished from an alien, or foreigner not naturalized. Thus the term "*free* British subject " means, not a person who is not a slave, but a native born or naturalized subject, who is a member of the state, and entitled to all the rights of a member of the state, in contradistinction to aliens, and persons not thus entitled.

The word " free " was used in this sense in nearly or quite all the colonial charters, the fundamental constitutions of this country, up to the time of the revolution. *In 1787 and 1789, when the United States constitution was adopted, the word "free" was used in this political sense in the constitutions of the three slaveholding states, Georgia, South Carolina, and North Carolina. It was also used in this sense in the articles of Confederation.*

The word "*free*" was also used in this political sense in the ordinance of 1787, in four different instances, to wit, three times in the provision fixing the basis of representation, and once in the article of compact, which provides that when the states to be formed out of the territory should have sixty thousand *free* inhabitants they should be entitled to admission into the confederacy.

That the word " free " was here used in its political sense, and not as the correlative of slaves, is proved by the fact that the ordinance itself prohibited slavery in the territory. It would have been absurd to use the word " free " as the correlative of slaves, when slaves were to have no existence under the ordinance.

This political meaning which the word " free " had borne in the English law, and in all the constitutional law of this country, up to the adoption of the constitution of the United States, was the meaning which all legal rules of interpretation required that Congress and the courts should give to the word in that instrument.

But we are told again that the constitution recognizes the legality of the slave trade, and, by consequence, the legality of slavery, in the clause respecting the "importation of persons." But the word "importation," when applied to "persons," no more implies that the persons are slaves than does the word "transportation." It was perfectly understood, in the convention that framed the constitution, — and the language was chosen with special care to that end, — that there was nothing in the language itself that legally recognized the slavery of the persons to be imported ; although some of the members, (how many we do not know,) while choosing language with an avowed caution against "admitting, *in the constitution*, the idea that there could be property in man," intended, if they could induce the people to adopt the constitution, and could then get the control of the government, to pervert this language into a license to the slave-trade.

This fraudulent perversion of the legal meaning of the language of the constitution is all the license the constitution ever gave to the slave-trade.

Chief Justice Marshall, in the case of the brig Wilson, (1 *Brockenbrough*, 433—5,) held that the words "import" and "imported," in an act of Congress, applied to free persons as well as to slaves. If, then, the word "importation," in the constitution, applies properly to free persons, it certainly cannot imply that any of the persons imported are slaves.

If the constitution, truly interpreted, contain no sanction of slavery, the slaves of this country are as much entitled to the writ of *habeas corpus*, at the hands of the United States government, as are the whites.

25

APPENDIX B.

SUGGESTIONS TO ABOLITIONISTS.

THOSE who believe that slavery is unconstitutional, are the only persons who propose to abolish it. They are the only ones who claim to have the power to abolish it. Were the entire North to become abolitionists, they would still be unable to touch the chain of a single slave, so long as they should concede that slavery was constitutional. To say, as many abolitionists do, that they will do all they constitutionally can towards abolishing slavery, is virtually saying that they will do nothing, if they grant, at the same time, that the constitution supports slavery. To suppress the slave trade between the States, as some propose, is certainly violating the spirit, and probably the law, of the constitution, if slavery be constitutional. To talk of amending the constitution, by the action of three fourths of the States, so as to abolish slavery, is to put off the matter to some remote and unknown period. While abolitionists are amusing themselves with these idle schemes for abolishing slavery without the agency of any adequate means, slaves are doubling in numbers every twenty-five years, and the slave power is rapidly increasing in numbers, wealth, and territory. To concede that this power is entrenched behind the constitution, is, in the minds of practical men, to concede the futility of all efforts to destroy it. And its effect is to dissuade the great body of the North from joining in any efforts to that end. The mass of men will insist upon seeing that a thing *can* be done, before they will leave the care of their other interests to assist in doing it. Hence the slow progress of all political movements based on the admission that slavery is constitutional. What sense would there be in placing the political power of the country in the hands of men, who can show nothing that they can do with it towards accomplishing the end for which they ask it? Abolitionists, therefore, who ask political power, and yet concede slavery to be constitutional, stand in the attitude of men asking for power for their own gratification, and not for any great practical good that they can do with it.* Let them but show that they can abolish slavery, and they can then consistently ask that the government be intrusted to their hands.†

The North, with no very important exceptions, although not enthusiastic in the matter, are abolitionists at heart. It is a slander on human nature to assert that they are not. To suppose that a people, themselves the freest in the world, having no pecuniary interests that bind them to slavery, inheriting all the principles of English liberty, and living for the last seventy years under the incessant teachings of the truth that all men are born free and equal — to suppose that such a people, *as a people*, are not opposed to slavery, is equivalent to supposing that they are naturally incapable of such a sentiment as the love of liberty, or the hatred of oppres-

---

* No one, I trust, will suppose I am actually accusing abolitionists of seeking power for their own gratification. I am only showing their political position, so long as they concede that slavery is constitutional.

† If abolitionists think that the constitution supports slavery, they ought not to ask for power under it, nor to vote for any one who will support it. Revolution should be their principle. And they should vote against all constitutional parties, block the wheels of government and thus compel revolution.

sion. If the supposition were correct, it would furnish an argument against all further effort of any kind ; for the task of radically changing human nature, for the purpose of abolishing slavery, is one quite too chimerical for rational men to engage in.

If the North love slavery, why did they unite to abolish the slave trade ? or to exclude slavery from the north-western States ? And why do they not have slaves themselves ?

The people of the North want simply to know if they can do anything for the abolition of slavery, without violating their constitutional faith. For this alternative they are not prepared, (as I admit they ought to be, if they had ever pledged themselves to the support of slavery;) but they are prepared for almost anything short of that. At any rate, they are prepared to stand by the constitution, if it supports liberty. If it be said that they are not, the speediest process by which to bring them to that state of preparation, is to prove to them that slavery is unconstitutional, and thus present to them the alternative of overthrowing the constitution for the support of slavery, or of standing by it in support of freedom.

In a speech at Charleston, on the 9th of March last, (1847,) Mr. Calhoun gave he following estimate of popular feeling at the North, on the subject of slavery : —

He said, " They, (the people of the North,) may, in reference to the subject under consideration, be divided into four classes. Of these, the abolitionists proper – the rabid fanatics, who regard slavery as a sin, and thus regarding it, deem it their highest duty to destroy it, even should it involve the destruction of the constitution and the Union — constitute one class. It is a small one, not probably exceeding *five per cent.* of the population of those States. They voted, if I recollect correctly, about fifteen thousand, or, at most, twenty thousand votes in the last test of their strength, in the State of New York, out of about four hundred thousand votes, which would give about five per cent. Their strength in that State, I would suppose, was fully equal to their average strength in the non-slaveholding States generally.

" Another class consists of the great body of the citizens of those States, constituting at least *seven tenths* of the whole, who, while they regard slavery as an evil, and as such, are disposed to aid in restricting and extirpating it, when it can be done consistently with the constitution, and without endangering the peace and prosperity of the country, do not regard it as a sin to be put down by all and every means.

" Of the two others, one is a small class, perhaps, not exceeding five per cent. of the whole, who view slavery as we do, more as an institution, and the only one, by which two races, so dissimilar as those inhabiting the slaveholding States, can live together in equal numbers, in peace and prosperity, and that its abolition would end in the expatriation of one or the other race. If they regard it as an evil, it is in the abstract, just as government and all its burdens, labor with all its toils, punishment with all its inflictions, and thousands of other things, are evils, when viewed in the abstract, but far otherwise when viewed in the concrete, because they prevent a greater amount of evil than what they inflict, as is the case with slavery as it exists with us.

" The remaining class is much larger, but still relatively a small one, less, perhaps, than twenty per cent. of the whole, but possessing great activity and political influence in proportion to its numbers. It consists of the political leaders of the respective parties, and their partisans and followers. They, for the most part, are perfectly indifferent about abolition, and are ready to take either side, for or against, according to the calculation of the political chances, their great and leading object being to carry the elections, especially the presidential, and thereby receive the honors and emolument, incident to power, both in the Federal and State governments."

This estimate is probably sufficiently accurate for all practical purposes. Adopting it as correct, it shows that *five per cent.* only of the North sympathize with the South; that the other *ninety-five per cent.*, (seventy-five per cent. acting from principle, and twenty per cent. for spoils,) "are disposed to aid in restricting and extirpating slavery, when it can be done consistently with the constitution, and without endangering the peace and prosperity of the country."

The South has long been teaching the North, (and more of late than ever,) how much the maintenance of slavery has to do with promoting "the peace and prosperity of the country." The lesson is learned. The only other point is the constitution. The North have but to have their eyes opened to the great constitutional fraud that has been perpetrated upon the country, to be found, *ninety-five per cent. of them*, on the side of liberty. When the North are united, they will control the national legislation, and the appointment of the national judiciary. Of course they will then abolish slavery. Does not this prove that the only labor the abolitionists really have to perform, is to spread the truth in regard to the constitution? And should they not adopt such measures as will *compel* public attention to, and a speedy decision of, that question?

How shall they do this? Probably, the most speedy and effectual mode of awaking the whole nation to the question is, by stirring up discussions of it in the national and State legislatures, by means of petitions.

The subject admits of petitions of a variety of kinds. To some of them the signatures of a very large portion of the people of the North might now be obtained: while others would be signed only by the more thoroughgoing abolitionists.

Who would not sign a petition praying Congress to inform the people whether slavery had any constitutional existence in the States at the time the United States constitution was adopted?

Who would not sign a petition praying Congress to inform the people what was the meaning of the word "free," in the English law? In the colonial charters? In the State constitutions, existing in 1789, in the States of Georgia, South Carolina, North Carolina, Delaware, and in the Articles of Confederation? And whether Congress and the courts were not bound to give it the same meaning in the representative clause of the constitution of the United States?

Who would not sign a petition praying Congress to inform the people whether any person, born in the country since the adoption of the constitution of the United States, can, consistently with that constitution, be held as a slave?

Who would not sign a petition praying Congress to inform the people whether the Supreme Court of the United States have ever given any, and if any, what, valid reasons for holding slavery to be constitutional?

Other petitions would be signed by smaller numbers of the people, such as the following : —

1. Petitions praying Congress to establish courts throughout the slaveholding States, in such numbers, and aided by such agents and attorneys, as may be necessary to bring the privileges of the writ of *habeas corpus* within the reach of every slave.

2. Petitions for the suppression of the slave trade between the States.

3. Petitions for organizing, arming, and disciplining the slaves as militia.

4. Petitions for having the next census distinguish the respective numbers of citizens and unnaturalized persons, and for basing the next representation upon them, counting the citizens as units, and the unnaturalized persons as three fifths units.

5. Petitions for the abolition of indirect taxation, and the apportionment of direct taxation among the States, counting the citizens as units, and the unnaturalized persons as three fifths.

The *general* question of the unconstitutionality of slavery should also be pressed upon the consideration of the *State* legislatures, by means of petitions. The opinions of these legislatures are important for these reasons:

1. The State legislatures choose the U. S. senators, and thus have a voice in the national legislation, and in the appointment of the national judiciary.

2. The *free* States, so called, are not free. They are liable to the incursions of the slave-hunter. They should be made free.

3. Several of the nominally free States have, on their statute-books, what are called "Black Laws," which are all unconstitutional. *

It is not very infrequent for legislative bodies to ask the opinions of their co-or dinate judiciaries on important questions of law. Let the State legislatures be petitioned to ask the opinions of the State judges, that we may have the opinions of the entire judiciary of the North, on this question of the constitutionality of slavery; each judge being requested to give his opinion separately, *and independently of precedents*.

If only a small number should at first give their opinions in favor of liberty, it would awaken universal interest in the question.

If any considerable number, influential for their talents and integrity, should give their opinions in favor of liberty, it would change the opinions of the North on this question, as it were, instantaneously.

If they should give their opinions in favor of *slavery*, and should give their reasons for their opinions, their reasons will be likely to pass for what they are worth. If sound, they will stand; if false, they will expose the weakness of their position, and will speedily be swept away.

If they should give their opinions in favor of slavery, and should give *no reasons* for their opinions, they will thereby disclose their own characters, and indicate the falsehood of their assumptions for slavery.

In order that these appeals to Congress, the State legislatures, and the courts, may be effectual, all representatives, senators, and judges should be furnished with all the evidence on which abolitionists rely for proving slavery unconstitutional.

Senators, representatives, and judges are but the servants of the people. They all swear to support the constitution of the United States. The people have a right to know how these servants understand that constitution; and to know specifically their reasons, if they have any, for officially conceding that it legalizes slavery. They are especially responsible for the freedom of their own States, and should be held to that responsibility. These agents, then, have no right to complain at having these questions addressed to them. Should they complain of it, or refuse to answer, they will thereby furnish evidence of the necessity there was for asking the questions.

Another reason why these public servants ought not to be embarrassed at having these questions addressed to them, is, that in making their answers, they will have the benefit of all the reasons ever given in support of the constitutionality of slavery, by the Supreme Court of the United States, *if they can find them*.

Some timid persons may imagine that if this question be pressed to a decision, and that decision should be against slavery, the result will be a dissolution of the Union. But this is an ignorant and ridiculous fear. The actual slaveowners are few in number, compared with the slaves and non-slaveholders of the South. The supposed guaranty of the constitution to slavery is the great secret of their influence at home, as well as at the North. It is that that secures their wealth and their political power. The simple agitation of the question of the unconstitutionality of slavery will strike a blow at their influence, wealth, and power, that will be felt throughout the South, and tend to separate the non-slaveholders from them. It is idle to suppose that the non-slaveholders of the South are going to sacrifice the Union for the sake of slavery. Many of them would hail as the highest boon

---

* If slavery be unconstitutional, all the colored persons in the United States are citizens of the United States, and consequently citizens of the respective States. And when they go from one State into another, they are "entitled to all the privileges and immunities of citizens " in the latter State. And all statutes forbidding them to testify against white persons, or requiring them to give bail for good behavior, or not to become chargeable as paupers, are unconstitutional.

a constitutional deliverance from slaveholding oppressions. And when the question shall be finally settled against the constitutionality of slavery, the slaveholders will find themselves deserted of all reliable support ; the pecuniary value of their slaves will have vanished before the prospect of a compulsory emancipation ; and this slave power, that has so long strode the country like a colossus, will sink into that contempt and insignificance, both at home and abroad, into which tyrants, so mean and inhuman, always do sink, when their power is broken.   They will hardly find a driver on their plantations servile enough, or fool enough, to go with them for a dissolution of the Union.

POVERTY,

ITS ILLEGAL CAUSES AND LEGAL CURE.—PART I.

BY LYSANDER SPOONER.

JUST PUBLISHED, and for sale by BELA MARSH, No. 25 Cornhill, Boston. Price 25 cents. Postage on the book for any distance is but seven cents.

☞ A liberal discount will be made to Booksellers and Agents, who buy to sell again.

RECOMMENDATIONS.

"We have read this pamphlet carefully, and are prepared to say we have seen no work for a long time which we think so much deserves the attention of laboring men as this."—*Charter Oak.*

"It abounds in bold and original thoughts. The illegal causes of poverty are stated, and a number of important propositions bearing on the subject laid down; and, on the whole, we consider it a work well worth studying—affording, as it does, many valuable hints to the statesman and political economist."—*Hunt's Merchant's Magazine.*

"An able, and certainly *original* work, from the pen of LYSANDER SPOONER, Esq.,—author of that powerful book which demonstrates the unconstitutionality of American Slavery. There is no writer of the age, of logical acumen more searching than Spooner." "This new work is destined to lead to a re-examination of all former systems of political economy." "At first blush his economical propositions strike us as sustainable—and if they are so, his work will prevail, and produce an important revolution in the present prevailing system." "Every one should read it."—*Bangor Gazette.*

"It is a bold attack upon some of the principles that regulate the Judiciary in their decisions in regard to contracts. In so far as the causes of poverty are to be traced to such sources at all, and to be remedied by legal means, the work is one of great discrimination and power."—*Herald of Freedom.*

"A neat pamphlet of 103 pages—a very remarkable production." "Whether all the anticipations of Mr. Spooner would be realized by the full adoption of his theory, we do not here stop to inquire; but we heartily commend his endeavor to the notice of all who love a transparent, forcible diction—intrepid independence—original thought, and entire freedom from the cant of sect or party. As a judicial writer, he has a depth, a compass, far beyond any one whose productions have met our eye in a long time."—*Albany Patriot.*

"Most men, in discussing this subject, would rear a pile of hypotheses heaven-high, and spin a web of sophisms broad enough to cover it, but all to no practical use. To elucidate, to any purpose, the Causes and Cure of Poverty requires the hair-splitting subtlety of a thorough-bred lawyer, or doctor of divinity, united to profound legal knowledge, and a strong, practical, unhampered intellect; and the very man, of all others, to broach this business is LYSANDER SPOONER, the author of the above-named work. This book is written with wonderful clearness and force. The propositions are squared as exact, and lit as smooth as a set of mathematical blocks; and the whole work will form an enduring monument of legal learning and acumen." "He lays down seven propositions as the basis of his own scheme, each one of which is logically demonstrated and put beyond controversy. Every man is personally interested in the subject of which this work treats, and this fact alone should secure for it an immense circulation."—*Hampshire Herald.*

"The work now under notice fully sustains the reputation of the author as a deep abstract thinker, legal critic, acute reasoner, and benevolent political economist."—*Adin Ballou.*

"Even propositions which appeared to us at first view untenable, are made to appear at least plausible. His views of the causes of many deplorable evils in the existing state of society, under the present system of legislation, are not easily put by. We do not now agree with all the views of Mr. Spooner. But we do say that we have derived instruction from the perusal of his work before us, and that no intelligent man can give it a careful perusal without perceiving that he is following the train of a strong, comprehensive, and cultivated mind,—and that he is coming in contact with principles and arguments which it is well that the community should know."—*Christian Freeman.*

"We would commend it to those who are interested in such speculations, as a clear, dispassionate, well-considered examination. On paper, the conclusions follow beautifully and naturally from the premises."—*Christian Register.*

"MR. SPOONER has a clear head, and a right noble heart." "POVERTY," &c. is a well reasoned and admirably written book. From our soul we thank him for its timely and lucid exhibition of the demands of natural justice, or the requirements of natural law, and we sincerely hope that he may continue his investigations until he has completed a series of political essays, adapted to the wants of the times, such as no other man within our knowledge is capable of preparing." "We warmly recommend it to the perusal of all earnest and thoughtful."—*Correspondence of Voice of Industry.*

www.ingramcontent.com/pod-product-compliance
Lightning Source LLC
Chambersburg PA
CBHW031401270326
41929CB00010BA/1275